HOUSE OF COLLECTIBLES PRICE GUIDE TO

STAR TREK

COLLECTIBLES

HOUSE OF COLLECTIBLES PRICE GUIDE TO

STAR TREK
COLLECTIBLES

SUE CORNWELL AND MIKE KOTT

FOURTH EDITION

HOUSE OF COLLECTIBLES
NEW YORK

Important Notice. All of the information, including valuations, in this book has been compiled from the most reliable sources, and every effort has been made to eliminate errors and questionable data. Nevertheless, the possibility of error, in a work of such immense scope, always exists. The publisher will not be held responsible for losses that may occur in the purchase, sale, or other transaction of items because of information contained herein. Readers who feel they have discovered errors are invited to *write* and inform us, so they may be corrected in subsequent editions. Those seeking further information on the topics covered in this book are advised to refer to the complete line of *Official Price Guides* published by the House of Collectibles.

Published by: House of Collectibles
201 East 50th Street
New York, NY 10022

Distributed by Ballantine Books, a division of Random House, Inc., New York, and simultaneously in Canada by Random House of Canada Limited, Toronto.

http://www.randomhouse.com

Manufactured in the United States of America

ISSN: 1091-5400

ISBN: 0-876-37994-3

Text design by Holly Johnson

Cover design by Michelle T. Gengaro
Cover photo by George Kerrigan

Fourth Edition: December 1996
10 9 8 7 6 5 4 3 2 1

CONTENTS

STAR TREK

COLLECTIBLES

MARKET REPORT

These days the market value of Star Trek collectibles is as accurately reflected in the big business world of Wall Street as it is in any collectible publication. When Paramount Pictures was sold to Viacom for a record-breaking amount, it was as much a reflection of Star Trek as it was of Paramount as a whole. The significance of this public awareness of Star Trek's success takes on added meaning to the Star Trek collectible's market because so many of the really hot collectibles right now are not the oldest items but the newest.

Especially now, in Star Trek's thirtieth year, it seems that every Star Trek item manufactured is being produced with an eye toward future collectibility. At the top of this list have to be the Star Trek action figures from Playmates. Ostensibly, these are playthings for children. In reality they are a marketable commodity, not unlike a share of stock, only one that is virtually ensured to increase in value the moment it leaves the store shelf. And, of course, it's not just action figures. Toys, plates, coins, figurines, pens, stamps, watches, and decorative knickknacks of every description are all being produced strictly for the collector. This is not to say,

however, that every item aimed at the collector is destined to be a valuable collectible. A clever advertising campaign can easily lead the buyer to believe that a company's merchandise is something it's not. The current Star Trek marketplace is full of "contrived collectibles." These are items that a manufacturer implies are rare or limited editions when they either have no limit at all or the "limit" is so high as to be inconsequential. Another common ploy is to take an item of relatively low value and repackage it (put it in a frame, for instance) to appear more impressive than it is in reality. Many companies also make minor changes of this nature in order to be able to tout the merchandise as an "exclusive" item available only from them. But for every one of these overpriced trinkets there are probably being produced two genuinely good collectible investments.

The good news is that you don't need to be a Wall Street tycoon to take advantage of this continuing phenomena. All you need is a little knowledge, a healthy portion of common sense, and a dash of initiative. Then Star Trek collecting is not only as good an investment as any stock, it's a lot more fun!

A BRIEF HISTORY OF STAR TREK AND STAR TREK MERCHANDISE

Star Trek in one form or another has now existed for 30 years. The five television series and seven movies produced as of this writing have generated many millions of dollars. The related merchandise manufactured over the years has produced many millions more. Star Trek is the anchor for a major studio, a fledgling television network, and the careers of uncounted people from actors and producers to book editors and convention promoters. Viewed from this perspective, it seems amazing that the people involved in Star Trek's birth had no idea at the time of the scope of what they were creating. Fortunately, what they did have was the integrity to try and make the best product possible with limited resources.

On September 8, 1966, the first *Star Trek* episode, "Man Trap," was aired on NBC. Its creator was Gene Roddenberry, a moderately successful television writer who had developed the series for Desilu studios. In a way, it was a minor miracle that *Star Trek* even made it as far as that initial debut. A serious science fiction television show was an unknown factor, not the kind of thing eagerly accepted by suspicious, audience-conscious network executives. What was a certainty was that the cost of creating the universe of the future was a definite strain on the studio's budget. Unusual sets had to be built (no starship bridges stored on the back lot), unique costumes made (no Gorn suits hanging on the rack in costuming), and all special effects, primitive as they may seem by today's computer-enhanced standards, had to be created from scratch.

Though *Star Trek* was far from a ratings success, after the first season it had developed a loyal following, undoubtedly due in no small part to the care taken by the writers, cast, and crew to deliver a quality product in spite of production difficulties and financial restrictions. *Star Trek* managed, barely, to be renewed for a second season. When *Star Trek*'s second season did not result in a significant increase in ratings, NBC decided to cancel the series. It is at this point that the first glimpse of what was to become the Star Trek phenomena is seen. NBC received thousands of letters from a fan-organized campaign protesting *Star Trek*'s cancellation.

Though NBC reversed its decision and renewed *Star Trek*, it moved the show to a new time slot on Friday nights. In those days, television ratings did not take demographics into account. So NBC either did not understand or did not care that Friday night was the worst possible time slot logistically for *Star Trek*'s mostly high school and college-age viewership. At any rate, this move, coupled with the departure of several key creative people from the show, guaranteed that the 1968/69 network season would be the last for the original series.

If this had been 10 years earlier or perhaps even five, *Star Trek* might very well have been nothing more than a nostalgic curiosity today. But a new trend in television was to play a key role in *Star Trek*'s future. This trend was a new emphasis on syndication. The right to show the 79 original *Star Trek* episodes was sold by Paramount (which had acquired Desilu in 1967) to local stations which could air the show in the time slots of their choice. Many showed them every day and picked time slots that were amenable to a young adult audience. So *Star Trek*, which had barely squeaked by for its three-year initial run on network TV, was now growing in popularity by leaps and bounds.

By 1972 it had become apparent that *Star Trek* had a large, avid fan following but no one realized exactly how large or how avid until late January of that year when the first true Star Trek convention was held in the 18th-floor function rooms of what was then the Statler Hilton Hotel in New York City. Science fiction and comic book conventions had already existed for many years, and Star Trek fans had been attending these in increasingly larger numbers. It therefore seemed a natural progression to hold a convention devoted primarily to *Star Trek*. The organizers of this first convention were a mixture of fans and professional convention organizers who thought that perhaps 300 people would attend the weekend affair and that a good time would be had by all (for the fan organizers) and a little money made (for the professional organizers). There were 16mm *Star Trek* episodes borrowed from the local TV station for viewing, events, panels, a rather sparse dealer's room by today's standards, and Gene Roddenberry and Majel Barret Roddenberry (Gene's wife and Nurse Chapel from the show) who came as guests of honor and brought with them the now famous (or infamous) *Star Trek* Blooper Reel.

Everything went pretty much as planned except that 3,000 people showed up, not 300, a great time was had by all, more than a little money was made, and last but not least, a whole new industry—organizing Star Trek conventions—was created.

It is at about this point that Star Trek merchandising began to be something more than just an afterthought. When the show was initially aired on NBC, its poor ratings had not generated a lot of interest by traditional manufacturers of licensed products. There had been a couple of books, a few model kits based on the show, a lunch box, a Halloween costume, a board game, a few toys from Remco so rare that they may very well have been prototypes, and very little else. What little did exist at this point fell mostly into the category of what we would today call "fan" merchandise, namely unlicensed items that could be easily and inexpensively made in small quantities. The problem was that it was now obvious to everyone that there were hoards of *Star Trek* fans eager to spend their money and almost no merchandise to spend it on.

The next few years were to be exhilarating (and confusing) ones for *Star Trek*. The fan movement was growing by leaps and bounds. Conventions were growing larger and larger and fans were screaming for more *Star Trek* and more Star Trek merchandise. The merchandise, at least, was forthcoming. Dealers' rooms now sported fan-made pictures, posters, T-shirts, buttons, costume jewelry, and fanzines by the ton, but no licensed toys, games, books, clothing, or other knickknacks from regular manufacturers. The basis for this perplexing lack of licensing in the face of overwhelming demand on the part of Paramount was simply this—they did not hold clear copyright to the show. They had belatedly and improperly filed copyright on *Star Trek* under the copyright laws of the time and were understandably none too anxious to let on that they may not have entirely owned what was rapidly becoming a very hot property.

Though in retrospect this might seem like gross negligence, it really only reflected standard business practices of the time. Before *Star Trek*'s syndication miracle took place, no one in the television industry would have dreamed that a show appearing only as reruns would have any merchandising value. If a program wasn't an immediate hit (which *Star Trek* certainly wasn't), why go to the trouble and expense to copyright it? The actors themselves were securely under contract and certainly no other studio would want to steal an idea which was producing so little money. And who would want to pay good money for the merchandising rights on a show that was doing so poorly, right? In later years this lack of foresight was to become a legal nightmare for everyone in-

volved, but in the early 1970s it was mostly covered by a little bravado and a lot of hemming and hawing on the part of Paramount. Nebulous, inexpensive (and usually temporary) licenses were issued for some fan merchandise, but it was not until the mid '70s, when a second live *Star Trek* TV series was being considered, that Star Trek merchandising began again in earnest.

In the meantime, an attempt to appease fan demand for more *Star Trek* episodes was made in 1973 in the form of the *Star Trek* animated series. Again the best was made of a less than ideal situation. All the original actors, with the exception of Walter Koenig, lent their voices to the new show. Quality writers were hired and the production staff took care to make sure that the scripts stayed true in both detail and spirit to the original series. Even though Filmation, the animation company that produced the show, turned out what could be called, at best, visually mediocre products, they did have the redeeming virtue of being cheap, and the 22 episodes that resulted were, in general, well received by both critics and the fans. But it was clear from the outset that this simply wasn't a very good medium for *Star Trek*. The show was placed in a half-hour Saturday morning time slot, the traditional spot for children's cartoons. Despite this the stories were, wisely—considering the audience that the original show had attracted—much more adult in nature than standard cartoon fair. Unfortunately, the half-hour format was very restrictive on this kind of story development and Saturday morning is certainly not adult prime time. With stories aimed not exactly at children and a time slot aimed not exactly at adults, the animated series was not exactly an overwhelming success.

By the time the animated series ended its first-run airings in 1974, it was becoming more and more apparent that another live-action *Star Trek* in some form or another was the only practical alternative. It was soon agreed, in principle at least, that a low-budget version of "Star Trek II" would be produced. Translating these good intentions into tangible reality proved to be another matter altogether. The next several years were spent waffling over whether the new *Star Trek* would take the form of a theatrical movie, a TV movie, a series of TV movies, or a regular TV series on a "fourth network" that Paramount briefly considered inaugurating in the 1970s—all this against the background of the uproar created by Leonard Nimoy's reluctance to return as Spock to the new show.

The fact that there were at least plans for a new *Star Trek* did, however, cause a modest spurt in the manufacture of licensed merchandise. Outside of a series of books with script adaptations, the animated series had produced almost no merchandise. Now with a new live-action Star Trek on the horizon, it seemed to be a reasonable gamble on the part of manufacturers to make some new products. As a result, some of what were to become the best Star Trek collectibles ever made were produced in the mid 1970s, most notably the toy and action figure line done by Mego.

Then in 1977 something was to happen that would cause dramatic changes in the way Paramount was to view

Star Trek and Star Trek merchandising. This thing was *Star Wars*. *Star Wars* was *very* successful . . . and *Star Wars* and *Star Trek* were both science fiction . . . and the success of *Star Wars* indicated the potential of other science fiction vehicles to be successful . . . and Paramount just happened to have a science fiction vehicle (namely *Star Trek*)—with built-in fan loyalty yet . . . and maybe Paramount could use *Star Trek* to do that thing so dear to any studio executive's heart—make lots of MONEY!

Suddenly the plans to do *Star Trek* as a low-budget production of undecided venue were totally revamped. Now *Star Trek* was to become a multimillion-dollar big-screen extravaganza. Even Leonard Nimoy couldn't say no to a project with the scope of what was to become *Star Trek: The Motion Picture*. And it hadn't been just *Star Wars'* box office receipts that had impressed Paramount. *Star Wars* had also produced a merchandising bonanza that was just as much of a money maker as the film itself.

But there was that copyright problem again. This time around they were not about to make the same mistakes—not with *Star Wars* providing them with an example of what kind of money could really be involved in merchandising. From this time on, Paramount was to register everything copyrightable and a few things that probably weren't, and use their extensive legal department to back it all up to the proverbial hilt. (It was rumored that they once tried to tell the U.S. Navy they couldn't call one of their aircraft carriers "Enterprise" because they owned the name.)

To try and regain their merchandising hold on the original show, they tried a variety of legal arguments that danced around their earlier oversight, and if their opponent was still too stubborn to give in they simply dragged out the legal process (and the legal expenses) till the unfortunate party simply gave up in frustration.

With licensing now firmly under their control, Paramount set out to offer manufacturers the opportunity to get in on the ground floor of *Star Trek: The Motion Picture*. The manufacturers were more than happy to oblige. They, too, had seen how *Star Wars* had affected merchandising and were more than willing to pay for expensive licenses in the hope that *Star Trek: The Motion Picture* would do the same thing.

Unfortunately for the merchandisers as well as the fans, *Star Trek: The Motion Picture* was not the mega hit that they had hoped for. It was not that the movie was not a box-office success (in the long run it has made the most money of any of the Star Trek films), but what success it had could not completely balance out the enormous expense of the film (at the time it was the most expensive movie ever made) and, even worse for the merchandisers, it lacked the fan appeal that had made the series a success in the first place.

It was not that the effort had not been made. The visual effects were done by ILM (after the results from another company were deemed insufficient), the sets were lavish, and a director with the impeccable credentials of Robert Wise (*Day the Earth Stood Still, Sound of Music, West Side Story*) was hired. But the story was lackluster and, much worse, the

chemistry between the characters that the fans had grown to love was almost totally absent.

The result for the merchandisers were piles of nearly unsalable dolls, games, toys, T-shirts, and much more that left holes in their bank accounts and a bitter taste in their mouths they would not soon forget.

It is a credit to the fans that they did not give up the hope that there could still be a Star Trek movie made in the image of the show they remembered and loved. It is a credit to the studio that they still thought a viable Star Trek movie could be made. They had observed the long lines at the theaters on the opening day of *Star Trek: The Motion Picture* so they knew that the potential was there. They just needed to lower the expense and raise the fan appeal of their product. The happy result for the viewing audience was *Star Trek II: The Wrath of Khan*.

Star Trek II was everything that the first movie was not. Where the first movie was slow and ponderous, *Star Trek II* moved crisply from scene to scene. Where the characterizations in the first movie were cold and uninvolved, the second movie played perfectly on the old chemistry from the TV show. Though certainly awe inspiring, the special effects in the first movie dragged for endless minutes where plot development was what was really called for. In the second movie the effects were not only spectacular, but also served to propel the action in the story. And most important of all, *Star Trek II* was a successful movie made for a fraction of the cost of the first one.

This success had come at a high price for someone, however. Seen by the studio as having been the architect of an overpriced boondoggle in the form of *Star Trek: The Motion Picture*, Gene Roddenberry was reduced to the role of "Executive Consultant," a title whose actual function consisted of little more than sending indignant memos about what was being done with his creation. But regardless of whether Roddenberry's reduced position helped or hurt the film, the end result was that *Wrath of Khan*'s unqualified success re-launched Star Trek on a new journey that has yet to end.

The results from *Star Trek II* from a merchandising standpoint were not nearly so happy. Burned by *Star Trek: The Motion Picture*, virtually no licensees opted to produce products for the second movie. The ironic result was that while the first movie churned out piles of merchandise no one wanted, the fans were screaming for merchandise from the second movie and there was none to be had.

Star Trek III: The Search for Spock was quickly developed as a sequel to *Wrath of Khan*. The primary interest from the fans point of view centered around Spock and the man who played the part. When the character died in *Star Trek II* it was rumored to be at the request of Leonard Nimoy. Though he has always denied that this was the case, the fact is that being offered the chance to direct the third movie must have been an enticement to continue in the role. Directing is an ambition of many actors and the opportunity to make your directing debut with a major motion picture is something that's hard to pass up. Whatever doubts the critics may have had, the fans were delighted. Not only was Spock going to be resurrected but a man who surely understood Star Trek was to bring it about.

By this time it had pretty well been decided that *Star Trek III* was to be the middle to a three-part story and as such, though far from being bad, it suffered the weakness that most films that occupy this position in a trilogy do. However, one of its weaknesses did not prove to be its director. Any doubts the critics may have had about Nimoy's abilities were laid firmly to rest. In fact, the film and Nimoy's direction were so well received by the fans that it was decided that he should direct the next film as well—which proved to be somewhat of a problem.

Since the days of the original *Star Trek* television series, Leonard Nimoy and William Shatner had had an equal status contract with the studio. In short, whatever one got the other also got. This agreement applied not only to money and perks but to opportunities as well, and it had not escaped Mr. Shatner's attention that Nimoy had been given an opportunity that he had not—namely the directorship of a film. However, *Star Trek IV* was shaping up to be a very big deal. Not only was it to be the finale of the trilogy started in *Star Trek II*, but it was to premiere in the fall of 1986, *Star Trek*'s 20th anniversary. Additionally, Paramount was gearing up for a new Star Trek television series scheduled to debut in 1987. For all these in addition to the usual reasons, Paramount very much wanted to make a good impression with the fourth movie—not the time to be trying out a new director of unknown potential.

Shatner was placated with a firm promise to have his chance at directing the next movie where he would have a chance to make a fresh start (since *Star Trek IV* ended the current storyline). In addition, he was to co-author the film as Nimoy had done in *The Voyage Home*.

Star Trek IV was everything the studio (and the fans) hoped it would be. Premiering in the Christmas season of 1986, its hopeful message, humor, and impressive special effects were the perfect culmination of the movie series. In many ways, it was original *Star Trek*'s finest hour.

In 1986, *Star Trek*'s 20th anniversary plus the anticipated success of *Star Trek IV* finally produced some serious licensed Star Trek products. What little licensing that had occurred in the early 1980s had mostly been from small companies and was aimed at fans. Despite the fact that what *was* generally available to the public, most notably the paperback novel series from Pocket, did gangbuster sales, large manufacturers still seemed to believe that Star Trek's appeal was limited to hardcore devotees. Now with proof to the contrary steadily mounting, a little more serious merchandise began to trickle onto the market. Hollywood Pins and Hamilton Plates both started producing products at this time. Things were looking hopeful for merchandising and for Star Trek in general.

In the fall of 1987 *Star Trek: The Next Generation* premiered. The show that was to become "Star Trek" to most people today, however, had a more tenuous start than is gen-

erally realized. Anxious to settle a long-standing argument with Gene Roddenberry over the ownership of the original *Star Trek*, Paramount agreed to give him total control over the new series. He wanted the new show to go back to his original ideas about the future. Many of these ideas were radical departures from concepts established in the first TV series and the movies. And much of what they initially saw made both the fans and the executives at Paramount alike nervous. In *The Next Generation* the Federation was at peace with everybody, families lived on board the new ship, there was a Klingon in the crew, the phasers looked like Dustbusters, and the captain was bald! The new *Enterprise* had more resemblance to a floating YMCA than the battlecruiser the fans were familiar with.

There were, however, some serious problems with the show. Initially many of the creative people who had made the original series "work" had returned to the new *Star Trek*. But Roddenberry's strict guidelines about what was and wasn't allowed in his new universe made creating workable, interesting storylines almost impossible. How could you create drama when you absolutely *had* to get along with everyone? Given what they perceived as an impossible task, many of the original creative team left the show.

Despite the difficulties the new show was experiencing, there were two areas where it definitely shone. The first was in the quality of the special effects. Though ILM received much of the credit for the show in the first year, outside of a few scenes used primarily in the title sequences, the company actually had very little input. ILM was and is concerned primarily with theatrical effects and weekly television is simply not their cup of tea. The use of their name in association with *Star Trek* and *Star Trek* with theirs was really sort of a mutual promotional gimmick. The real genius of *The Next Generation*'s special effects lay with the people who performed the computer wizardry which allowed the show to have spectacular special effects on time, on a weekly basis. As a measure of exactly how impressive this feat was, most experts at the time did not believe it could be done.

The other area where it was apparent from the outset that *The Next Generation* was at least the equal of the original *Star Trek* was in the competence of the cast in general and, in particular, of Patrick Stewart. This may have been a reflection of Gene Roddenberry's true genius—the ability to pick just the right person for the part. Though he had spent his life in acting and by some accounts was one of the five best actors in the world, Stewart had generally been overlooked in the film community. That this lack of notoriety landed him in the lead role on *The Next Generation* was an extremely lucky break for *Star Trek*.

There was one other initial element of *The Next Generation* that definitely led to the series' long-term success. Remembering that the original *Star Trek* had its first real success in syndicated TV, Roddenberry took the unprecedented step of choosing syndication over network affiliation for first-run episodes. It proved to be as beneficial to the new show as it had been to the old one.

The first two seasons were moderately successful for *The Next Generation*, though there were still problems obtaining good scripts. By the third season, though, things began to turn around. This was due in part to another unprecedented first in TV history. TV shows had always had an iron-clad rule about obtaining scripts only from professional sources. Desperate for good material, the show's producers began to look at some of the multitude of unsolicited scripts they received from hopeful fan writers and found that, amazingly, some of them were really good! The restrictions on the writing were easing up for other, less happy reasons also. Roddenberry, in failing health, was taking less and less of an active role in the production of the show. With him went a more harmonious but less dramatically interesting 24th century.

The new show had even attracted some major merchandisers. Galoob, with their line of action figures and ships, made the first real toys from *The Next Generation*. But just as *Star Trek* was hitting its stride again it also hit a glitch. In 1988 *Star Trek V: The Final Frontier* premiered.

Star Trek V, with William Shatner at the helm this time, was by far the weakest of the *Trek* films. Its faults, some of which must be laid squarely at Mr. Shatner's feet and some of which were merely unhappy circumstance, are numerous and obvious. Suffice it to say that it was not well received by the critics, the fans, or the merchandisers. One of the few pieces of *Star Trek V* merchandise to be made were the five Galoob character figurines. So poorly was the movie received, however, that they were never actually marketed and ironically have become collectible simply by their scarcity. The failure of *Star Trek V* also ended Galoob's involvement with Star Trek merchandise for seven years. It seemed that just as *Star Trek: The Motion Picture* had done, one weak movie was going to again eclipse all of Star Trek's other successes.

Fortunately, though, this was not to be the case. By the end of the 1989–90 TV season, it was apparent that *Star Trek: The Next Generation* was on a roll. The script material had improved, the look of the show had maintained its high quality, the actors felt comfortable in their roles, and more and more the fans began to accept the show as true Star Trek. What's more, it was about to go where the original series had never gone before—into a fourth season. From this point on, *Star Trek: The Next Generation* would never look back.

The year 1991 would be an exciting one for more reason than it being a new television season. This year would be *Star Trek*'s 25th anniversary. Big plans were underway—commemorative conventions, the sixth feature film (the last entirely involving the original crew), and the production of some commemorative merchandise. Though there were a few significant 25th anniversary items—coins and a new line of plates in particular—most of the commemorative products were simple novelties, hats, T-shirts, posters, etc. Something else happened in 1991, however, that was to profoundly change the face of Star Trek merchandising in the '90s. In October of 1991 Gene Roddenberry died.

Though Roddenberry was gone, Star Trek had been left in good hands and their expertise, along with 25 years of mo-

mentum, guaranteed that the "franchise," as it was to come to be known at Paramount, would sail along smoothly without him. But if hardly a ripple was felt in the show itself, merchandising was another matter entirely. While Roddenberry was alive, he, or more accurately people in his employ, kept a tight rein, for better or worse, on licensed Star Trek products. The intentions were probably good. They didn't want frivolous or inferior quality products to demean their show. The result, however, was that practically no product was deemed good enough to be acceptable. The new wave of people in charge of licensing at Paramount were not nearly so cautious. The splash of new products that had started in the 25th anniversary year turned into a tidal wave over the next few years. Now virtually anyone with a fat enough bank account could have a Star Trek license. Many of these new wares would indeed have made the old guard cringe. But many of the new items were first-class products, among them crystal and pewter pieces, watches, new plate series, new reference books, numerous decorative items, and an extensive line of toys and action figures. Even Galoob, which had washed its hands of Star Trek, figuratively speaking, finally jumped on the bandwagon and began producing a very popular line of Star Trek Micro Machines. This merchandise boom has continued on until today.

Meanwhile, what of Star Trek itself? *Star Trek VI: The Undiscovered Country* was and was always intended to be the last movie featuring the original crew. But by the time it was being produced it was becoming apparent that their day was done and the future of Star Trek rested with "The Next Generation." The movie was well done and was well received by critics and audiences alike, but already fans were looking ahead to the first feature film to star the *Next Generation* cast. Before that could happen, however, they had to do a little more work to solidify Star Trek's TV future. It was decided that the 1993–94 season, the show's seventh, would be the last TV year for *The Next Generation*. In 1993 a new show, *Star Trek: Deep Space Nine*, would premiere and run in tandem with *Next Generation* for *Next Generation*'s final year. It was hoped that in this way the new show could get a boost from its (by this time) incredibly successful progenitor. True to plan, *Star Trek: The Next Generation* ended its run in the spring of '94 at the absolute height of its popularity. The last episode, the two-hour "All Good Things," is thought by many to be one of its best. Not that the cast got much of a chance to rest on their laurels. As soon as production closed down on the TV show, they began gearing up for the first *Next Generation* movie, scheduled for release later that year.

Star Trek: Generations was the result of those hectic preparations. In hindsight perhaps the movie was rushed into production a little too quickly. Trying to write for *The Next Generation* TV show, the new *Deep Space Nine*, and the movie all at once seemed to be too much of a strain. Star Trek presents plot restrictions that ordinary movies don't have to deal with. You must see that the details of the film adhere to nearly 30 years of previously established details before you can begin to worry about writing an entertaining plot that fits within a workable budget and is of reasonable length. This applies to all Star Trek, but with a movie you also have the added concern of needing your product to appeal to a wider audience. Though the movie manages, just barely, to fall within these criteria, you get the feeling while watching it that the plot is pushing, shoving, and squirming to make all the pieces fit.

While a financial success, and deemed at least acceptable by most fans, almost everyone involved (including the actors) have expressed a desire to see it done better next time. And as of this writing they will very soon have the chance in the form of the eighth Star Trek feature film, *Star Trek: First Contact*.

Deep Space Nine, meanwhile, while up and running according to plan, was not the runaway success its predecessor had been. Some of the elements that had deliberately been built into the show to solve production problems (i.e., let's put our new crew on a space station so we won't have to do all that expensive gallavanting around the galaxy stuff), had proved to be less of a hit with fans. Part of Star Trek had always been "exploring strange new worlds." Many fans thought the crew spent far too little time traveling through the wormhole and far too much on station security and Bajoran politics. Not that the show was doing badly, or that it didn't have its own cadre of loyal fans, but it just wasn't doing what *The Next Generation* had.

Paramount went about solving this problem in what was, by now, the time-honored Star Trek way. They set about creating still another Star Trek. It was announced that a new series with a brand new ship, the *Voyager*, was to premiere in 1995. The *Voyager* was to do what all good Star Trek ships do—namely plunge around in unexplored space seeing what new dilemmas they can get themselves into in order to delight the fans. Their reasons for the creation of *Star Trek: Voyager* had more of an ulterior motive than simply pleasing the fans, however. Paramount had in recent

years looked with envy at the ever-increasing success of the Fox Television Network. Perhaps they now viewed their scrapped 1970s plans for a fourth network as a missed opportunity. They could also hardly have failed to notice that many of the stations that had carried *The Next Generation* in syndication and were now similarly carrying *Deep Space Nine* were Fox affiliates. If their products could do that for someone else, why not let them do the same thing for their own network? And how better to entice viewers to tune in than a new Star Trek series?

And that's the way it worked. Sort of. The problem with starting up a network is that you have to do some initial scrounging to get affiliate stations. In some cities, like Los Angeles, the stations that signed on were already well-established entertainment stations—the kind of station a network wants for an affiliate. But in many others, the new UPN affiliate used to be the tele-shopping station or the local religious channel, and outside of the few hours of programming per week sent to them by Paramount, didn't have much of interest to offer. In still other areas, Paramount had no affiliate at all. It's hard to get good ratings in a place where no one can see your show.

In its first season, *Voyager* was a modest success. But it was the Paramount networks *only* success. *Voyager* is now entering its third season. It is popular with the fans, and if it had been released into syndication, the way its predecessors were, it might well have been as big a hit as *Next Generation*. Now only time will tell.

The only sure thing about Star Trek's future is that its hold there is secure. Star Trek has gone beyond simple entertainment to become one of the icons of our culture. At this point in time, it is as unimaginable to not have some form of Star Trek around as it would be for Americans to suddenly give up eating pizza en masse. Whatever happens to Star Trek in the future, it has already secured its place in history.

BUYING AND SELLING STAR TREK COLLECTIBLES

BUYING

Few people get into Star Trek collecting simply by waking up one morning and deciding they are going to become a collector. Usually it is a much subtler process. Typically, they have always enjoyed one or more of the shows or movies and have gotten involved from this starting point. Perhaps they decided to attend a Star Trek convention and were fascinated by the various goods offered in the dealers' room. Maybe a particular line of merchandise caught their eye in a local store and they decided starting a collection would be fun. Often, especially now that many Trek fans are in their 40s and 50s, there is an element of nostalgia involved. However you got into collecting, now that you are here it would be wise to familiarize yourself with a few basic concepts of the hobby.

1. WHAT SHOULD I COLLECT?

If your answer to this question is "Star Trek stuff" you had better have a big house and a bigger bank account. These days, when Star Trek merchandise is so abundant, it is wise to limit your collection to your true areas of interest. Many people already have a starting point—toys left over from their childhood (or maybe even their children's childhood) or a library of books they have enjoyed. If you are not really sure, start off with a few different kinds of pieces and soon a direction will probably emerge, either because your own interests will become more focused or because certain collecting opportunities will present themselves. If you wish your acquisitions to also serve as an investment, then you probably need to do a little more research into which areas have the best potential, as well as be a little more discriminating in your buying habits. Whatever direction you choose, you will get the most enjoyment out of your hobby if you collect the items that appeal to you personally. That is the first, most important rule of collecting.

2. WHERE DO I FIND IT?

With Star Trek merchandise sitting on store shelves at every turn, the answer to this question may seem obvious. That is until you try and find that one, certain action figure you've been looking for or that out-of-print book you've heard about. And with so much Star Trek merchandise being produced these days, even stores that do carry, for instance, toys or books, rarely carry the manufacturer's or publisher's entire line, not to mention items that have been out of production for years. To complicate matters even further, Star Trek collecting is so popular that the most sought after items never even make it out of the stock room. There are always eager store employees ready to snap up that hard-to-find goody for themselves or a friend. Though you definitely should check out regular retail outlets for your purchases (if they do have an item they will probably be the most economical source), the time will come when you will have to seek out more specialized sources to expand your collection. When this happens, there are several possibilities you might try.

First, there are local specialty stores. These days, almost every town of any size has a store that specializes in Star Trek and other science fiction items, and larger cities usually have several. Try looking in the phone book under headings such as "Books," "Comic Books," and "Toys" and then see if any of these also advertise that they carry science fiction items. A quick call can confirm whether they have much in the way of Star Trek merchandise. The advantages to shopping at local stores is that they often have very reasonable prices on merchandise because they are aware of competition from discount chains and other specialty stores that may be in the area. In addition, since it is to their advantage to build up a regular clientele, they often offer services to good customers (subscription services, special discounts, search services, or waiting lists, etc.) that other sources would not. The disadvantages of local stores, especially with out-of-production merchandise that must be purchased on the

11

secondary market, is that since they are only drawing from a set location they often will not have the best selection.

Second, you might try shopping in the dealers' room at a Star Trek convention. These days, there is a Star Trek convention held somewhere in the country virtually every weekend. Larger cities often hold several in the course of a year. For the price of admission, these functions offer actors and other personalities from the shows as guest speakers, plus other events and exhibits and, of course, the dealers' room. Though the size of these conventions varies greatly, even a modest one usually has several dealers both local and from out of town. The advantages of shopping at a convention are that you are likely to see a much broader selection of merchandise than at a local store, and dealers are often willing to negotiate prices, especially toward the end of the show. The disadvantages of conventions are that you may have to travel to attend one, and the larger ones with the most to offer usually are located only in big cities and have rather steep admission fees. Also, at many of the busier conventions you may find that a lot of the choice items in the dealers' room are snapped up in the first frantic rush of customers.

A third option, open to virtually everyone no matter how remote your location or limited your travel ability, is mail order. Numerous mail order companies specializing in media science fiction merchandise exist, including several very well-established and reputable ones. Companies offering Star Trek merchandise often run ads for merchandise and/or catalogs in media-oriented science fiction magazines or (for the computer literate) have ads on the Internet. The advantages of mail order are that it is convenient and mail order companies often have the best selection of merchandise of any of the purchasing possibilities. The disadvantage is that since you are buying blind, you should investigate the company you are planning to make your purchases from before you plop down your money. While very few blatantly dishonest mail order companies exist in the world of Star Trek collectibles, there have been a great many fan-run companies that ran into trouble simply because their enthusiasm outmatched their business sense. For this reason the best choice is usually well-established, professional companies. Ask some simple questions of them before you buy—how long have they been in business, what are their business credentials (for instance, are they rated in Dun & Bradstreet), and what are their policies concerning sales? By law a mail order company must refund your money if you are dissatisfied with a product as long as it is returned in the same condition in which it was sent to you and as long as it is returned to the company within a reasonable amount of time. Any company that doesn't offer you this option should be suspect.

Lastly, you have the option of buying from private individuals either through yard sales and flea markets or by answering classified ads. This can be the source of some great bargains but it can also be very risky, especially if you are buying from individuals through the mail. People, particularly if they are not experienced collectors, often misrepresent the condition of a piece, usually out of ignorance rather than a deliberate attempt to deceive. And unlike a regular business, individuals are unlikely to be willing to refund your money once they have it. Be sure to ask direct questions about items you are interested in to be sure they are as advertised. Better yet, have the seller send you a snapshot of the item or items. As for yard sales and flea markets, unless you really enjoy attending them, you are probably better off shopping elsewhere. Everyone has heard stories of the super-rare piece bought for pennies at a garage sale, but it is far more common to spend hours and drive miles only to find a sad array of worn and incomplete items that could only be considered collectible in the broadest sense of the word.

3. WHAT DO I LOOK FOR?

How do you determine whether or not an item is (or is likely to become) collectible? While, of course, no one can determine beyond a shadow of a doubt whether or not a piece will increase in value, there are a couple of good guidelines to steer you in the right direction. Let's start first with those things that almost certainly will not become collectible. If it is easy and inexpensive to manufacture in small numbers, the chance of an item ever accruing much value is almost nil. The reason why is obvious. Once an item increases in value to a point where a significant profit can be had simply by reproducing it, some enterprising entrepreneur is going to do just that. Licensed merchandise that fits into this category is no safer from counterfeiting than any other item; temptation far outweighs the risk of any legal retribution the license may offer. What kind of items fit into this category? Almost any item that involves a simple printing process, whether it is made of paper or some other material. This would include scripts, fanzines, T-shirts, most mugs, blueprints, bumper stickers, paper badges, and almost all stationery items. Even more complex printed material (those items requiring color separations and printing presses capable of handling this process) are now beginning to be victimized by bootleggers because larger printers are making their services available to a wider range of customers than in the past. Counterfeit copies of color posters, books, and trading cards have all shown up on the market in recent years. Other types of items that are unlikely ever to become collectible are photos and slides, buttons, prop reproductions, videos, computer software, and costume jewelry because these kinds of items can all be easily reproduced either by an individual or through readily available manufacturing services.

So, if easy-to-reproduce items are bad collectible investments, does this mean that hard-to-reproduce items are good ones? Not always, but it is a good starting point. Two other important criteria to consider include collector demand and scarcity. They are, to a point, connected to one another. If an item is scarce, there are going to be fewer of them to go around and as long as there are more potential buyers than there are items to buy, the price is going to escalate. Generally, as soon as a product goes out of production, its value starts to rise. Obviously some items go out of production quicker than others, either because they are not profitable for the manufacturer, the license runs out, or because they are deliberately limited. Be careful, however, not to be deceived by clever marketing techniques into believing a product is limited when it is not, or that the limit on the "limited edition" is so high as to be inconsequential. Also there are more factors involved than intentionally limiting a product that might make it in short supply. One of these is crossover collectibility—that is, being in demand by more than one sector of the market. A good case in point is Star Trek action figures. Action figures are one of the most popular collectible items among Star Trek fans, but in addition to that, collecting action figures in general is one of the hottest fields of collectibles in America today. With both Star Trek collectors and action figure collectors trying at the same time to purchase one area of merchandise, it's no wonder that the price of Star Trek action figures has risen so dramatically. Other areas that have strong collector markets outside of Star Trek include toys, books, movie memorabilia, plates, records, comics, trading cards, and watches. Collectibles from any of these categories have the potential to be in demand by more than one segment of the population.

Now that it has been determined what *kind* of items are collectible, there is still one more very important factor that makes a particular toy or book valuable and another virtually worthless. This factor is condition. It is more important today than ever before because there are more knowledgeable collectors than ever before. And it is more important in the Star Trek field because so much of what is collectible in Star Trek is relatively new and therefore more likely to exist in excellent condition. It might be expected that a 100-year-old doll looks a little worse for the wear, but should an action figure that's not even five yet look the same?

So what constitutes condition? Ideally, an item should look as close as possible to the condition it was in when it was new. If it came in a display box (as opposed to a plain mailer), the box should still be present. Discard a box and in most cases you are discarding 50% of the value of the item. If the item originally had an instruction sheet or interior packaging (cardboard or Styrofoam) and it is still present, so much the better. The same for items with decal sheets. It is not nearly as serious to apply the decals to a toy, for example, as to throw away the box, but leaving them on the original decal sheet is an added bonus. If an item is packaged on a blister card, it should stay there. Opening the blister card in any way devalues the item almost as much as if the package had been discarded.

Items must, of course, be undamaged. A broken toy, a written-in book, a chipped ceramic piece, or almost any item with significant smoke or water damage is unacceptable.

To be in truly collectible condition items must be complete. This one fact has been the source of a great deal of disappointment to all those attic and garage scroungers who have run across, say, an old collection of Mego dolls and found that when the vacuum sucked up Scotty's phaser or the dog chewed up McCoy's uniform that the figure's potential value disappeared too. Even the relatively minor wear and tear of storage can make a difference in collectible value.

Scuffing, minor creases and wrinkles, and yellowing due solely to age can all make a significant difference in value.

SELLING

The time may come when you want or need to sell your collectibles. Just as with buying, there are several options open to you. In many respects they are much the same as those available to individuals wishing to buy, but from a different perspective.

1. SELLING TO LOCAL STORES

This is often the first option many people try. However, before you load up your car and start driving around town, you should make a few preparations. First of all, call around to see which stores, if any, are buying. If an owner doesn't have the cash or the space for more stock, or what you are selling doesn't fit in with their line of merchandise, you'll need to look elsewhere to sell your items.

If they are interested, try and make an appointment to show your pieces when the store is less busy and the owner or buyer can give you his or her undivided attention. Next take a little time to prepare your goods to be seen to best advantage. Put paper items and small pieces in bags and boxes intended for collectibles, make sure the larger items are organized and free of dust, and package all items carefully for the journey to the store. Not only will this ensure that your collectibles arrive in the best possible condition but it will also impress upon the store owner that you are aware of their value as collectibles. Decide in advance if you will sell individual pieces separately or if you only wish to sell the collection in its entirety. Many store owners will balk at the latter, either because they lack the capital or space, or they simply don't like selling certain lines of merchandise. Keep in mind that the store owner is buying these items to resell, so you will not get full value for your pieces. Most merchants pay anywhere between 30% and 60% of full retail price for items depending on how badly they need a particular piece and what their economic situation is at the moment. If the store owner doesn't want to buy your collectibles outright, you might try asking if you could leave some pieces in the store on consignment, though many dealers won't want to bother, especially with lower-priced items. If the store owner does agree, be sure to work out all details in advance. Set a definite time period in which to leave your items and have a clear understanding of the amount you expect to receive from the sale of your pieces.

2. SELLING TO LARGE DEALERS

If you live in a remote area or have a very large collection you wish to sell, this may be your only practical option since large dealers routinely buy collections through the mail and they are generally the only ones with enough capital to invest in large quantities of stock that may take them months to sell. Unless you are lucky enough to have a large dealer located near to where you live and are able to take your collection to him, you will have to be prepared to deal with him sight-unseen. For this reason take care to choose a well-established, reputable dealer that you feel you can trust. Since no dealer is going to pay you in advance of receipt of the merchandise and virtually none will allow you to send merchandise COD, you will have to depend on his sense of integrity to give you a fair deal. Once you have chosen a dealer, you will need to start by making a list of your individual pieces. Give a brief description of each item listing pertinent information that the dealer will need to make you an offer. Is the piece complete? Is it in the original package? What is its condition? Be honest in your assessment of your collectibles. The dealer is making an offer on your pieces based on the conditions you describe. If, when he or she receives them, they are not as stated, the dealer will not feel obligated to honor the original offer. Be sure to state your preferences concerning the shipping arrangements if you decide to accept the dealer's offer. If the dealer is to pay the shipping cost, it will probably be reflected in his offer, especially if the bulk of your collection is made up of particularly large or heavy items. If you are selling items in order to raise cash for another collectible that this particular dealer carries, be sure to mention this fact as most dealers give more generous offers in trade credits than in cash.

Once you have accepted an offer, package your items very carefully for shipment. Keep in mind that the offer was made for items as originally described. If the items don't arrive to the dealer in this condition, he will not feel obliged to pay for them whether it's your fault or the shipper's. In most cases UPS is the best shipping option. They insure packages up to $100 in value automatically (additional value is available for a small fee), have an excellent system for tracking packages, and are convenient to most locations. The U.S. Post Office will sell you insurance for your packages but collecting from them is a long and frustrating process. Also, be sure to request a return receipt (there is a small additional fee for these) for any package sent by the Post Office to be sure that your item actually reached its intended destination. Unless you have made prior arrangement with a dealer to be paid in installments (this is usually done only in the case of very expensive collections), you should be sent your check or credits as soon as the dealer has received your collectibles and examined them to see they are as described. If there is a problem, you should similarly be promptly notified.

3. SELLING THROUGH CLASSIFIED ADS

The advantage to selling through classified ads is that you get retail price for pieces whereas a dealer will only give you wholesale. The disadvantage is that there is an initial outlay of cash that is irretrievably lost if your pieces don't sell. Also, since it is impractical to list a great many items in a classified ad, this form of selling is practical only if either the item(s) you are selling are fairly expensive or the ad is very cheap. In the case of classified ads, you pretty much get what you pay

for. An ad in a local paper is cheap but very unlikely to get results unless there just happens to be a buyer for that particular item in your area that just happens to read that particular classified ad on that particular day. Ads left on message boards on the Internet have much the same problem. Items in fan publications are inexpensive but most have very small circulations. Major media science fiction publications have large circulations but their ads are much more expensive (usually $100 or more per column inch).

If you do run an ad, take time to word it in as concise a way as possible that still gives all the pertinent information. Describe the piece or pieces clearly and indicate their general condition. Be sure to list your address and FAX or E-Mail numbers if you have them. If you are listing a phone number, be sure to state times you will be available since most people who call will be doing so to ask questions.

If, as in most cases, you must send your items to the buyer, don't risk sending pieces for inspection or COD. After you do receive payment, wait until checks clear the bank before you send out the item or items. Package pieces very carefully, make sure they have sufficient insurance, and request a return receipt (especially if you are sending an item by the U.S. Post Office) so that you know for sure that your package reached the buyer. Hold on to the cash for at least a month. Remember, just as in the case of large mail order companies, you are obliged to refund their money if they request it as long as it is done within a reasonable period of time.

4. SELLING ITEMS AT A CONVENTION

The advantage to setting up at a convention is that you will be face-to-face with a large number of avid potential buyers, many of whom find the dealers' room a major attraction. This is an especially attractive option if you have ever had a yen to become a professional dealer. As an additional bonus, you will have the fun of attending the convention. The disadvantages are that this is by far the most expensive option and is viable only if you have a large amount of items to sell. It is also by far the most complicated. To start with, you will need to contact the convention to arrange to buy table space. These days, a table at a worthwhile convention of even modest size is at least $200 and must be paid in advance. Conventions are typically two days long (a few are three or four) and the table fee is for the entire convention. Daily rentals are generally not allowed. Try and make arrangements as early as possible in order to assure that space is still available. Be sure and ask about location (near entrances and along walls are usually considered choice spots), especially if it is a large room, but remember that all of the best locations will have already been reserved long ago by professional dealers. To save money, you might ask about a fan rate, which is usually significantly lower than what professional dealers are charged. Many conventions make no distinction, however, and if they do have fan tables they often have restrictions concerning location and number of tables that may be purchased.

Remember that any permits (such as sales tax) and licenses (such as studio merchandise licenses) involved are purely the responsibility of the individual dealer and not the convention organizer or the convention center or hotel.

Several hours are usually allotted for dealers to set up their displays either the morning of the show or sometimes the day before. Try to come early to ascertain which table(s) you have been assigned and to (as much as possible) avoid the confusion as the dealers move in. Be prepared to transport your goods to your location yourself. Conventions are usually held either in convention centers or large hotels. Few convention centers provide handtrucks and hotels usually only have bellmen who, of course, expect a generous tip. Try to arrange your items in an attractive and eyecatching manner. Remember, though, that the room will be crowded at times. Don't leave your table unattended. Try to keep small items where you can keep an eye on them and keep especially fragile and/or valuable items out of reach. You can always hand them to serious potential buyers for inspection. Before the convention opens to the public, make sure you have small bills and coins for making change, paper and pens for making notes, and cards to hand out so that someone interested in potential future sales is able to contact you. You will increase your potential for sales if you accept personal checks but make sure they include the individual's address and phone number and verify that they are correct by checking them against other forms of ID.

Though the busiest day for sales is usually the first one, most dealers elect to stay for the entire show (which is what they paid for after all) and in some cases, moving out early is not even allowed. Though the dealers' room is usually locked over night and some form of at least nominal security provided, responsibility for the merchandise left in the room is strictly in the hands of the individual dealer. Bring something to cover your merchandise at night (old sheets work nicely) as cloths are rarely provided by the convention, and try and take very valuable items with you.

Finally, be especially vigilant when packing up. This is when the room is at its most confusing and this confusion can create a perfect opportunity for thieves.

USING THIS BOOK

In this book I have tried to keep technical terms and inside Trek jargon to a minimum in order to make the information offered as clear to as many people as possible. Even so, it would have been impossible not to assume at least a casual knowledge of the TV series and movies. If you think "dilithium crystal" is a brand of glassware or that Bajor used to be part of Yugoslavia it might be a good idea if you study up a little more on the Star Trek saga before you attempt to jump into the world of Star Trek collectibles.

Because Star Trek collecting encompasses such a wide range of different types of items, it has been necessary to arrange chapters on different kinds of items in different ways so that the information in each chapter can be accessed in the easiest possible manner. Be sure to read the Section Notes at the beginning of each chapter to find out which format the chapter you are referencing uses. An overall view of the particular category of items, a few suggestions on Care, and an

Investment Potential rating (either excellent, good, fair, or poor) are listed there also. We hope you find these tips to be of some use.

It has been assumed in all cases, unless specifically stated otherwise, that the values given here are for complete items in excellent condition and in their original packaging (if applicable). In other words, basically new. If you offer a piece to a collector or dealer in any other condition and expect him to assess the item's worth at anywhere near what's quoted in this book, you are certain to be disappointed.

Last but not least, please keep in mind that this is a price *guide*, not the absolute last word on the worth of Star Trek collectibles. Star Trek collecting, even more than most collectible fields, is a dynamic, ever-changing process and to glom onto certain figures and treat them like they were chiseled in stone would seriously hamper your abilities as either a buyer or a seller.

ACTION FIGURES

Action figures in general, and Star Trek action figures in particular, comprise one of the hottest fields in collectibles today. The current line of figures being produced by Playmates caters as much to the collector as it does to children. Figures are individually numbered and the selection changes constantly by older figures going out of production and newer ones being produced on a regular basis. This also tends to focus the collector's attention on older figure series that he or she may wish to add to their collection. Prices on both the older and the newer figures especially are very volatile and the collector is advised to keep as up to date as possible. Because of the popularity of action figures, unpackaged action figures are also very popular but retain only about 50% of the value of a packaged figure, and then only if complete with all accessories. Incomplete, damaged, or very badly worn figures are of little value to the serious collector.

INVESTMENT POTENTIAL
Excellent.

CARE
To preserve maximum collectibility do not discard or damage boxes and never remove a carded figure from the plastic bubble. The package is as important as the figure itself. Store figures so that the least possible wear occurs to the box or header card. Creases, tears, nicks, and scratched or yellowed plastic bubbles all decrease the value of packaged figures. Store unpackaged figures in plastic bags or boxes to ensure that all accessories remain with the figures and that they are protected from dirt and fading.

SECTION NOTES
The section is organized chronologically by date of manufacture. Prices are for packaged figures in excellent condition. Look under Toys, Housewares (Figurines), and Pewter for other types of figures.

ORIGINAL STAR TREK ACTION FIGURES
(Mego Corp., 1975)

Figures approx. 8″ tall. These were issued in three different series and values are based primarily on scarcity of each series. A small hoard of first series dolls surfaced in Canada in 1985, keeping values for these early dolls comparatively low, especially for the Kirk, Spock, and Klingon figures that comprised the majority of the cases. All are fully costumed with removable cloth outfits and have movable joints and hand equipment. Very early figures of the first series had metal rather than plastic joints but are not noticeably more valuable. Figures came blister-packed on color display cards showing artwork insets of characters for first series and planetscapes for second and third series.

First Series

Capt. Kirk—Yellow shirt, black pants and boots with phaser, communicator, and belt. ....$35–$50
Dr. McCoy—Blue shirt, black pants and boots with communicator, belt, and tricorder. ....$100–$175
Klingon—Brown pants, black boots, brown tunic with orange phaser and communicator, and belt. ....$40–$60
Lt. Uhura—Red tunic with tricorder. ....$100–$175
Mr. Scott—Red shirt, black pants and boots with phaser, communicator, and belt. ....$100–$175
Mr. Spock—Blue shirt, black pants and boots with phaser, communicator, belt, and tricorder. ....$35–$50

Second Series

Cheron—Black and white alien, black and white jumpsuit. ....$200–$300

Gorn—Brown reptilian alien, brown pants, black boots, and brown tunic with orange phaser and communicator, and black belt. ....$250–$350

Keeper, The—Blue alien, long white robe with orange trim. ....$200–$300

Neptunian—Green amphibian with removable webbed feet and hands, green and red jumpsuit. ....$200–$300

Third Series

Andorian—Blue, antennaed alien, silver metallic pants, brown tunic and belt. ....$750–$1000

Mugato—Horned, white apelike alien, red pants, green top with black belt. ....$600–$850

Romulan—Gold helmet, silver and black jumpsuit, brown boots with orange phaser and communicator, and black belt. ....$900–$1200

Talos(ian)—Yellow jumpsuit, orange shoes, black belt and collar. ....$500–$750

STAR TREK: THE MOTION PICTURE FIGURES
(Mego Corp., 1979)

Figures approx. 12″ tall. All are fully costumed with removable outfits and have posable joints and hand equipment. Boxes had movie logo and color artwork of Enterprise and crew with clear plastic window and dark blue cardboard inserts. *Note*: The plastic used in the faces of this series of dolls has a tendency to discolor with long exposure to sunlight.

Arcturian—Wrinkled head, beige pants, white tunic. ....$85–$125

Capt. Kirk—Dark blue and white uniform with phaser and belt buckle. ....$85–$125

Decker—Gray uniform with phaser and belt buckle. ....$150–$250

Ilia—Short white dress, orange necklace, phaser. .....$75–$100

Klingon—Black and silver Klingon uniform with belt, breastplate, and Klingon weapon. ....$150–$250

Mr. Spock—Gray uniform with phaser and belt buckle. ....$85–$125

STAR TREK: THE MOTION PICTURE FIGURES
(Mego Corp., 1979)

Figures approx. 3³/₄″ tall, posable. Came blister-packed on color cards depicting logo, ship, and characters. No hand equipment.

First Series

Decker—Yellow uniform. ....$20–$30
Dr. McCoy—White shirt, gray pants. ....$35–$50
Ilia—Gray and white uniform. ....$15–$20
Kirk—Gray and white uniform. ....$35–$50
Scotty—Gray uniform. ....$20–$30
Spock—Gray uniform. ....$35–$50

Second Series

Made primarily for overseas markets. Some were available in the United States through Sears mail order but these did not come on cards.

Arcturian—Wrinkle-faced alien, yellow outfit. ...$100–$150
Betelgeusian—Silver body, black hair, red robe. .$225–$300
Klingon—Black and silver Klingon uniform. ......$150–$200
Megarite—Multilipped, black outfit and robe. ....$225–$300
Rigellian—Purple-skinned, white Starfleet uniform. ....$100–$150
Zaranite—Silver mask, gray outfit. ....$200–$275

STAR TREK: THE MOTION PICTURE SOFT POSABLE FIGURES
(Knickerbocker, 1979)

Figures 13″ tall, plastic head, soft body in *Star Trek: The Motion Picture* uniform. Came boxed in window box without plastic. Photo of Kirk, Spock, and movie Enterprise on box.

Kirk. ....$40–$60
Spock. ....$40–$60

STAR TREK III: THE SEARCH FOR SPOCK
(ERTL, 1984)

Figures 3¾″ tall, fully posable. Came blister-packed on color card depicting logo and characters; included hand equipment for each figure.

Capt. Kirk—with communicator. ....$25–$40
Klingon—with pet. ....$15–$25
Mr. Scott—with phaser. ....$15–$25
Mr. Spock—with phaser. ....$25–$40

STAR TREK PORCELAIN DOLL COLLECTION
(Ernst, 1988)

Collector series of original TV dolls from Ernst—13″ tall, porcelain head, arms, and feet. Soft bodies with cloth uniforms. Dolls came with to-scale accessories* and metal doll stand. Packaged in white cardboard boxes with blue Star Trek log and illustration of original TV Enterprise.

Chekov—No accessories. ....$200–$300
Kirk—With metal phaser and communicator. .....$200–$300
McCoy—With orange and clear plastic beaker. ...$200–$300
Scotty—With metal phaser and communicator. ...$200–$300
Spock—With metal phaser and communicator. ...$200–$300
Sulu—With metal phaser and communicator. ......$200–$300
Uhura—With earrings. ....$200–$300

This was one of the last lines of merchandise produced by Ernst before they went out of business. Toward the end of the production run accessories were not always included with the figures.

STAR TREK: THE NEXT GENERATION
(Galoob, 1988)

Posable, 3¾″. Came blister-packed on blue card with logo, ship, and photo of individual character. These figures were released in mixed cases with very unbalanced distribution. Prices reflect scarcity of figures. Galoob originally intended to release two additional figures, Wesley Crusher and a

Romulan. Though these are pictured on the packages of many original Galoob *Next Generation* products, they were never produced.

Enterprise Crew

All come with tricorder.

Capt. Picard. ....$25–$35
Comdr. Riker. ....$8–$15
Lt. Comdr. La Forge. ....$15–$25
Lt. Data*. ....$35–$50
Lt. Worf. ....$15–$25
Lt. Yar.** ....$30–$40

There are several variations on Data's face coloration, including "speckled" and "blue" or "white." These sell for up to twice the value of the regular Data depending on the variation and the preference of the individual collector. The white/blue variation is usually considered the rarest.
**Contrary to popular belief, they did not discontinue production of the Yar figure when the character was dropped from the show. The same number of Yars as Datas were produced by the company.*

Aliens

Antican—Felinoid, gray outfit. ....$45–$75
Ferengi—Striped vest, olive pants, and blue whip. ....$85–$100
"Q"—Black outfit, red hat. ....$85–$100
Selay—Green reptilian. ....$45–$75

STAR TREK: THE NEXT GENERATION, DEEP SPACE NINE (DS9), VOYAGER, AND ANNIVERSARY FIGURES
(Playmates, 1992–present)

Figures are approx. 5″ high, fully posable, and highly detailed with numerous pieces of hand equipment and other accessories for each figure, including a base with each figure's name in the shape of the symbol most appropriate to the figure (i.e., Starfleet symbol for Enterprise characters, Klingon symbol for Klingons, etc.). All figures are numbered on the bottoms of the feet and lower numbers are desirable to many collectors. Distribution of figures in cases was very uneven. Cases of the same assortment shipped at one time or to one area may have been low on a figure when the same figure was common in other areas or in other shipments. Variations in colors of hand equipment, variations of package backs, and, later, variations in the promotional trading cards included with the figures (plain card vs. Space Cap card) make collecting for the completest extremely difficult. All figures are blister-carded on colorful header cards. Differences in cards are described at the beginning of each series.

NOTE: Many of the figures made by Playmates were marketed in Europe by Ban Dai. In Great Britain the packaging was similar to the U.S. style (i.e., blister-carded) but German figures were packaged in small window boxes. Prices for carded foreign figures are comparable to U.S. prices and for boxed versions are slightly higher.

Star Trek: The Next Generation

First Series, 1992

Card shows Enterprise in straight-on view with logo. Figure is below with accessories displayed to his left. Card has standard punch-type slot for hanging. Back pictures other figures and has information about character and equipment.

Borg—Black and silver Borg armor, bionic laser arm, mechanical manipulator arm, shield generator coils (4), connecting coils (2). ....$25–$35
Capt. Jean-Luc Picard—Red uniform jacket over gray shirt, phaser, tricorder, PADD, personal view screen, bonus Captain's Log adventure booklet. ....$25–$35
Comdr. William T. Riker—Red collar-style uniform with tears in shirt and pants, phaser, tricorder, Away Team field kit, directional U.V. source. ....$20–$30
Ferengi—Gray outfit with yellow, black, and white vest and boots, energy whip, hand-blaster, Ferengi rifle, dilithium crystal. ....$25–$35
Gowron the Klingon—Silver, gray, and black Klingon uniform, ceremonial club, Targ (piglike animal), painstick, Klingon disrupter. ....$40–$50
Lt. Comdr. Data—Gold collar-style uniform, opening arm panel, phaser, tricorder, diagnostic testing unit. ....$20–$30
Lt. Comdr. Deanna Troi—Gray jumpsuit with pink trim, phaser, tricorder, PADD, desktop viewer, portable computer gear. ....$40–$50
Lt. Comdr. Geordi La Forge—Gold collar-style uniform, phaser, tricorder, Away Team computer gear, dilithium crystals, bioengineering tools (2). ....$25–$35
Lt. Comdr. Geordi La Forge (removable visor variation)—Same figure as above except with removable visor, information on back of package describes the visor as removable while package of the above figure does not. ....$100–$125
Lt. Worf—Gold collar-style uniform with silver Klingon sash, phaser, tricorder, bat'telh, Klingon dagger. ......$25–$35
Romulan—Gray Romulan uniform, phaser rifle, Romulan PADD, disrupter. ....$40–$50

Star Trek: The Next Generation

Second Series, 1993

Same general packaging as First Series. All figures now have a promotional card of the character (from Skybox) included in the package. Later production runs had Space Cap cards (cards with a punch-out pog in the center).

Adm. McCoy—Black pants and shirt, gray cardigan sweater with epaulets, medical monitor, medical tricorder, portable medical kit, hypo spray. ....$8–$15
Amb. Spock—Gray pants and gray Romulan-style top, Klingon monitor, Romulan phaser(?), Romulan phaser rifle, Vulcan book. ....$8–$15
Borg—Black Borg armor with silver trim, hydraulic mechanical ram arm, multifunctional rotation arm, shield generator coils (3). ....$8–$15
Cadet Wesley Crusher—Black and red Starfleet cadet uniform, portable tractor beam, Starfleet carrying case, tricorder. ....$8–$15
Capt. Jean-Luc Picard (First Season Uniform)—Hand phaser, tricorder, personal view screen, PADD. ....$8–$15
Capt. Scott—Movie-uniform vest and black pants, dilithium crystal, engineering monitor, multirange light source, bioengineering tools (2). ....$8–$15
Comdr. Sela—Gray Romulan uniform, Romulan PADD, Romulan phaser, Romulan phaser rifle, Romulan knife. ....
....$8–$15
Comdr. William T. Riker (Second Season Uniform)—Same collarless style as first season uniforms, phaser, tricorder, directional U.V. source, field kit, analyzer. ....$8–$15
Counselor Deanna Troi (Second Season Uniform)—Red jumpsuit, PADD, portable computer, desktop viewer, tricorder. ....$8–$15
Dathon—Heavyset alien with orange markings on head, light green jumpsuit, gray vest and knife scabbard, dagger, logbook, flaming branch, Tamarian knife. ....$8–$15
Dr. Beverly Crusher—Blue collar-style uniform and blue medical coat, portable medical kit, monitor, hypo spray, medical tricorder. ....$8–$15
Guinan—Red outfit and hat, tray, mug, glass, chess set. ....
....$8–$15
K'Ehleyr—Female Klingon, black jumpsuit with orange spots on one side, spiked glove, life support mask, ceremonial Klingon sword. ....$8–$15
Klingon Warrior Worf—Klingon armor and Klingon ceremonial robe, Klingon pain stick, disrupter, Klingon spiked club. ....$25–$35
Locutus—Picard in black Borg armor, cybernetic hand, cybernetic manipulator, shield generator coils (2). ....$15–$20
Lore—Brown boots, pants, shirt, and vest, phaser, tricorder, field kit and hand-held laser. ....$8–$15
Lt. Comdr. Data (First Season Uniform)—Access panel on arm, phaser, tricorder, diagnostic testing unit. ....$8–$15

Lt. Comdr. Geordi La Forge in Dress Uniform—Long gold uniform dress jacket, phaser, tricorder, desktop viewer, plaque of medals. ....$8–$15

Lt. (JG) Geordi La Forge—First season uniform style, phaser, tricorder, dilithium crystal, Away Team computer gear, engineering tools (2). ....$15–$20

Lt. (JG) Worf—Phaser, tricorder, bat'telh, Klingon knife, Klingon sword. ....$8–$15

Mordock the Benzite—Alien with blue-accented skin, black pants, blue and silver shirt, silver breathing device attached to chest, phaser, tricorder, scanner monitor. ....$8–$15

Q—Red, collar-style Starfleet captain's uniform, miniature Enterprise, miniature Earth, dilithium crystal, scepter. ....
....$8–$15

Vorgon—Ridge-faced alien with orange, gold, and blue markings on head, brown jumpsuit with silver accents, Tox Uthat artifact, dilithium crystal, hex, Vorgon scanner. ....
....$8–$15

Star Trek: The Next Generation

Early Third Series, 1994

Slight changes in package design. Artwork of Enterprise and background is slightly different and now there is a slotted "J" for hanging the card instead of a punch hole. All Skybox promotional cards are now Space Caps (a punch-out pog in the center of each card) and there is a gold foil "Collector Series 7th Season" sticker on each package.

Capt. Jean-Luc Picard as Dixon Hill—Gray 1940s-style suit and hat with red patterned tie, floor lamp, pistol, rotary telephone. ....$15–$20

Capt. Picard as a Romulan—Picard with Romulan features and long brown Romulan robe, Romulan bowl, Romulan disguise kit, Romulan phaser, Romulan PADD. ....$10–$15

Capt. Picard in Duty Uniform (No Trading Card)—Red collar-style Starfleet uniform, phaser, tricorder, Starfleet monitor, mug. ....$15–$20

Comdr. Riker as a Malcorian—Riker with heavy brow ridges, blue pants and blue jacket, Malcorian medical scanner, Malcorian syringe, Malcorian monitor, phaser. ....$8–$15

Dr. Noonian Soong—White hair, brown pants and vest, long brown coat, human motion simulacrum, sub-processor surgical tool, crystalline test tubes. ....$10–$15

Ens. Wesley Crusher (No Trading Card)—Red, collar-style Starfleet uniform, scanner, monitor, PADD, dilithium crystal. ....$20–$25

Esoqq—Red mane, toothy jutting lower jaw, brown jumpsuit with gold collar, belt and gloves, knife, knife leg sheath, food ration, Chalnoth communicator. ....$50–$65

Gowron in Ritual Klingon Attire (No Trading Card)—Black and silver Klingon armor and long brown sleeveless robe with gray and gold trim, bat'telh, Klingon dagger, Klingon sword, Klingon painstick. ....$20–$25

Hugh Borg—Black Borg armor with silver and gold accents, mechanical telescoping arm, power regulator, scanner. ....
....$10–$15

Lt. Barclay—Gold, collar-style Starfleet uniform, engineering tool, antigravity pallet, fencing foil, cryo container. ....
....$8–$15

Lt. Comdr. Data as a Romulan—Data with Romulan features and long gray Romulan robe, Romulan rifle, Klingon monitor, phaser, Romulan PADD. ....$15–$20

Lt. Comdr. Data as seen in "Redemption" (Red Uniform—No Trading Card—Portable tractor beam, tricorder, science kit, hand laser. This was a special promotion figure only available through a send-in offer. ....$400–$800

Lt. Comdr. Data in Dress Uniform (No Trading Card)—Long gold Starfleet dress coat, tricorder, Starfleet monitor, PADD, plaque. ....$15–$20

Lt. Comdr. Deanna Troi in Sixth Season Uniform—Regular, teal, collar-style Starfleet uniform, monitor, portable computer gear, PADD, tricorder. ....$15–$20

Lt. Comdr. La Forge as a Tarchannen III Alien—Brown body accented with blue "veins," searchlight, field kit, U.V. source, medical monitor. ....$15–$20

Lt. Thomas Riker (No Trading Card)—Gold collar-style uniform, phaser, portable computer gear, duffel bag, tricorder.
....$250–$500

Lt. Worf in Starfleet Rescue Outfit—Black jumpsuit with silver and gold belt, backpack, Klingon spear and ring, explosive charges, homing device. ....$8–$15

Q in Judge's Robes—Long red robe with black accents, black hat, gold necklace, gavel, scepter, scroll, lion statue. ....
....$15–$20

Ro Laren—Red collar-style Starfleet uniform, Bajoran earring, phaser, tricorder, monitor, duffle bag. ....$35–$45

Star Trek: The Next Generation

Later Third Series, 1994/1995

Top of header card which had been rounded off in previous issues is now straight. View of Enterprise has changed from head-on to side view. Equipment is now displayed on figure's right instead left. Skybox trading cards are again present. Though some figures are represented in *Generations* movie uniforms, logo on packaging is still *Star Trek: The Next Generation*. Packaging for later figures sometimes has subtitles for various subsets of figures.

NOTE: Some earlier Third Series figures have been repackaged in later package style.

Amb. Sarek—Gray-haired Vulcan, tan robe, gold necklace with red jewels, Vulcan gong, Vulcan harp, Vulcan book, IDIC medallion. ....$15–$20

Capt. Jean-Luc Picard as Locutus (Metallic Armor)—Holodeck Series subtitle, Picard as Locutus with shiny silver-colored breastplate, cybernetic hands (2), hoses (2). ....$15–$20

Dr. Beverly Crusher in Starfleet Duty Uniform—Standard teal series-style collar uniform, phaser, tricorder, medical kit and Starfleet container. ....$10–$15

NOTE: Though this figure is pictured on the card backs of early Combined Series figures, the card style is consistent with the later Third Series figures.

Jean-Luc Picard Retired Starfleet Captain—"All Good Things" Series subtitle, Picard with gray beard, blue and tan shirt, tan hat and dark gray pants with suspenders and black belt, gardening tool, scanner, and carrying case. ......$10–$15

Lt. Comdr. Data in Movie Uniform—Black and gold movie-style uniform and insignia, phaser, tricorder, Starfleet monitor, isolinear chips (2). ....$15–$20

Lt. Comdr. Data in 1940's Attire—Holodeck Series subtitle, Data in black suit with gray shirt, gray hat, and black and red tie, pistol, typewriter, cocktail glass, and champagne bottle. ....$10–$15

Lt. Comdr. Geordi La Forge in Movie Uniform—Black and gold movie-style uniform and insignia, engineering monitor, isolinear chips (2), multirange light source, engineering tools (2). ....$15–$20

Lt. Natasha Yar—Gold first season uniform, phaser, tricorder, flashlight, PADD. ....$15–$20

Lt. Worf in Ritual Klingon Attire (Metallic Armor)—Holodeck Series subtitle, Worf in Klingon battle dress with shiny silver breastplate, Klingon disrupter, spiked war club and Klingon painstick. ....$10–$15

Lwaxana Troi—Black-haired woman, long brown skirt, gold top, wine glass, gong, suitcase, talking gift box. ....$15–$20

Nausicaan, The—Alien with long black hair and prominent upper fangs, reddish brown pants and jacket with black and brown trim, Nausicaan knife, Dom-Jot cue, bottle, mug. ....$15–$20

Star Trek: Deep Space Nine

Series I, 1993

Cardboard header is square-topped with "J"-type slot hanger. Logo in front of artwork of Space Station with center of Space Station above logo. All include appropriate insignia stand for figure and Skybox promotional trading card. Trading cards and hand equipment are displayed on figure's left. Reverse has pictures and information about character and equipment and pictures other figures in series.

Chief Miles O'Brien—Gold DS9 uniform with sleeves rolled up, engineering kit, laser drill, phaser, fire extinguisher. ....$10–$15

Comdr. Benjamin Sisko—Black and red DS9 uniform, phaser, PADD, DS9 monitor, Bajoran orb case. ....$10–$15

Comdr. Gul Dukat—Dark gray Cardassian pants and breastplate with gold trim, Cardassian rifle, Cardassian pistol, Cardassian PADD, Cardassian field control unit. ....$10–$15

Dr. Julian Bashir—Black and teal DS9 uniform, PADD, phaser, medical tricorder, medical kit, DNA scanner. ....$15–$20

Lt. Jadzia Dax—Black and teal DS9 uniform, trill, tricorder, bio sample collector, hypo spray, portable computer. ....$10–$15

Maj. Kira Nerys—Reddish brown and brown Bajoran jumpsuit, Bajoran pistol, Bajoran tricorder, Bajoran PADD, duffle bag. ....$10–$15

Morn—Heavyset long-faced alien, brown pants and vest, sandy brown sleeves with gold gloves, laser pistol, pyramid dice, gold pressed latinum bars (2), square glass. .....$10–$15

Odo—Brown pants, brown and reddish brown top, Bajoran Padd, DS9 monitor, Bajoran tricorder, sleeping bucket. ....$10–$15

Quark—Green pants, brown boots, brown jacket with gray accents and black and gold trim, reptilian pet, Ferengi blaster, Ferengi head cane, bottle, bold pressed latinum bars (2). ....$10–$15

Star Trek: Deep Space Nine

Second Series, 1994/1995

Package shape remains the same. Artwork has changed slightly. Center of Space Station is now below logo. Trading card and hand equipment are now displayed on figure's right. Artwork on back is changed but still contains basic information about character and equipment and pictures of other figures in series.

Capt. Jean-Luc Picard in DS9 Uniform—Red DS9 uniform with old-style communicator pin, tricorder, phaser, field kit, directional U.V. light source. ....$10–$15

Chief Miles O'Brien in Starfleet Duty Uniform—Gold collar-style uniform with old-style communicator pin, phaser, engineering kit, laser drill, fire extinguisher. ....$10–$15

Comdr. Benjamin Sisko in Dress Uniform—Sisko in standard red Starfleet dress jacket with old-style insignia, monitor, 3-D chess set, Salah'na clock and carrying case. ....$15–$20

Dr. Julian Bashir in Starfleet Duty Uniform—Teal collar-style uniform with old-style communicator pin, PADD, medical tricorder, medical kit, DNA scanner, phaser. ....$15–$20

Jake Sisko—Dressed in light brown longsleeve turtleneck outfit with dark brown boots and short dark brown sweater, book bag, baseball mitt, Jum Jum stick, and monitor. ....$25–$35

Lt. Jadzia Dax in Starfleet Duty Uniform—Teal collar-style uniform with old-style communicator pin, trill, tricorder, bio sample collector, hypo spray, portable computer gear. ....$15–$20

Lt. Thomas Riker in DS9 Uniform—Gold DS9 uniform with old-style communicator pin, tricorder, phaser, scanner, DS9 monitor. ....$15–$20

O'Brien in Dress Uniform—O'Brien in gold standard Starfleet dress jacket with old-style insignia, phaser, pattern enhancer, carrying case, and cello and bow. ....$10–$15

Q in DS9 Uniform—Red DS9 uniform with old-style communicator pin, orb case, PADD, phaser, DS9 monitor. ....
....$10–$15

Rom, Ferengi Brother of Quark—Ferengi with black pants, brown and gold shirt, and short green jacket, Nog mini-action figure, lock pick and magnesite drops. ....$30–$40

Tosk—Tan-skinned, scaled, reptilian alien, red-brown jumpsuit and tan scaled gloves, rifle, mug, and collar, and leash. ...
....$20–$25

Vedek Bareil—Dark-haired Bajoran man in long red robe with brown trim, black belt, and Bajoran earring, orb case, candleholder, snake and ceremonial encasement. ....
....$25–$35

Star Trek: Generations

1994

Cardboard header has a wavy die-cut top and "J"-shaped hanging slot. Artwork shows Picard and Kirk on either side of the new logo Paramount has adopted to represent all forms of Star Trek. A Starfleet delta shield insignia appears inside of an ellipse. Movie logo is below artwork of characters. All figures come with promotional movie mini-poster, appropriate stand, and hand equipment which is displayed to figure's left. Back has information about character and equipment and pictures other characters in the series. Many major Enterprise-D characters from this series are depicted wearing uniforms with gold stripes on the sleeves and a flap-type top with rank pins below the collar on the figure's right. This is a costume that was designed for the movie but ultimately not used. Figures are also now using the new double-bar–type communicator pin design.

B'etor—Klingon woman in long gray skirt with wide belt and Klingon armor, war club, Klingon disrupter, Klingon knife, Klingon sword. ....$25–$35

Beverly Crusher—Teal, unused Generations movie uniform, medical kit, phaser, medical tricorder, Starfleet thermos.
....$20–$25

Data—Gold, unused Generations movie uniform, phaser, tricorder, Starfleet monitor, isolinear chips (2). ....$10–$15

Deanna Troi—Teal, unused Generations movie uniform, PADD, Starfleet monitor, portable computer gear, tricorder. ......
....$20–$25

Dr. Soran—Dark gray hair, black jumpsuit with gray collar, Klingon disrupter, pocket watch, PADD, multirange light source. ....$20–$25

Geordi La Forge—Gold, unused Generations movie uniform, engineering monitor, multirange light source, engineering tools (2), isolinear chips (2). ....$15–$20

Guinan—Light purple pants, tunic and hat with darker trim, tray, glasses (2), Starfleet monitor. ....$25–$35

James T. Kirk—Classic Star Trek movie uniform, classic phaser, communicator, and tricorder. ....$20–$25

James T. Kirk in Space Suit—Silver suit with black boots, gloves and harness, multipurpose light source, helmet, engineering tools (2), champagne bottle. ....$25–$35

Jean-Luc Picard—Red, unused Generations movie uniform, phaser, tricorder, family album, Starfleet monitor. ...$10–$15

Lursa—Klingon woman in long gray skirt with narrow belt and Klingon armor, Klingon disrupter, Klingon sword, bat'telh, isolinear chip. ....$25–$35

Montgomery Scott—Classic Star Trek movie uniform, classic phaser, communicator, and tricorder. ....$45–$60

Pavel A. Chekov—Classic Star Trek movie uniform, classic phaser, communicator, and tricorder. ....$45–$60

William Riker—Red, unused Generations movie uniform, Starfleet scanner, field science kit, phaser, isolinear chips (2).
....$15–$20

Worf—Gold, unused Generations movie uniform, U.V. light source, phaser rifle, tricorder, phaser. ....$15–$20

Worf in 19th-Century Outfit—Tan pants, yellow vest, white shirt, black and gold boots, shackles, sword, pike, scroll. ....$15–$20

Classic Star Trek
Collector Figure Set

1993

Originally sold only as a set. Set of seven figures from the original TV series (Kirk, Spock, McCoy, Scotty, Uhura, Sulu, and Chekov) in original series costumes displayed in a large window box with the interior designed to look like the bridge from the original Enterprise. Each figure is equipped with appropriate insignia stand, classic phaser, and classic communicator.

Set. ....$150–$250
Individual Complete Unpackaged Figures:
　Chekov. ....$25–$30
　Kirk. ....$25–$35
　McCoy. ....$25–$30
　Scotty. ....$25–$30
　Spock. ....$25–$30
　Sulu. ....$25–$30
　Uhura. ....$25–$30

Star Trek Teenage Mutant Ninja Turtles

1994

This is a crossover between classic Star Trek and Playmates other incredibly successful toy line. Figures are of the four Turtle characters dressed in classic Star Trek outfits. Cardboard header is square-topped "J"-slot hanger type with classic Star Trek logo over Turtles logo and pictures of characters. Hand equipment, stand, and (non-Skybox) trading card are shown on figure's left. Back has information on characters and equipment.

Capt. Leonardo—Yellow, command shirt, blue trim, classic phaser, classic communicator, classic tricorder, futurized Ninja sword. ....$15–$20
Chief Engineer Michaelangelo—Red, engineering shirt, orange trim, classic phaser, classic communicator, classic tricorder, nunchakus. ....$15–$20
Chief Medical Officer Raphael—Blue, science shirt, red trim, classic phaser, classic communicator, classic tricorder, sais. ....$15–$20
First Officer Donatello—Blue, science shirt, purple trim, classic phaser, classic communicator, classic tricorder, up-dated battle bo. ....$15–$20

Classic Star Trek (Movie Series)

1995

Header card is straight-topped with "J"-shaped hanging slot. Color artwork depicts original Enterprise flying at an angle with classic Star Trek logo under saucer section of ship. Back has movie info, equipment info, and lists other characters in series. Figure is packaged in front of round *Star Trek: The Motion Picture*-style insignia stand with equipment to figure's immediate left and long, horizon-tally formatted color Skybox trading card further to figure's left.

Adm. Kirk—Dark gray and white Star Trek: The Motion Picture-style uniform, phaser, wrist communicator, Captain's Log, and mini Voyager component. ....$10–$15
Comdr. Kruge—Klingon in standard black and gray military attire with silver breastplate, dark gray sash, and gold accents, Klingon communicator, Klingon tricorder, Klingon disrupter, and Klingon rifle. ....$15–$20
Comdr. Spock—Light gray Star Trek: The Motion Picture-style uniform, tricorder, engineering tool, Vulcan kolinahr necklace, Voyager spacecraft. ....$10–$15

Dr. McCoy—Gray, open collar Star Trek: The Motion Picture-style uniform, medical tricorder, medical kit, neurological scanner, mini Voyager spacecraft. ....$15–$20
Gen. Chang—Bald Klingon with small mustache and eye-patch, light gray pants, dark blue-gray boots and jacket with black trim, dark red collar, gold and silver sash, Klingon communicator, Klingon disrupter, Klingon staff, glass of Romulan ale. ....$10–$15
Khan—Gray-haired with two-tone brown pants, brown boots and red-brown top with darker brown belt and silver ornaments, one black glove on right hand, phaser, Genesis torpedo, control box, bowl of Ceti Eels, and grabbing wand. ....$10–$15
Lt. Saavik—Black and red Star Trek II–through VI-style movie uniform, tricorder, phaser, communicator, duffel bag. ....$10–$15
Lt. Sulu—Tan Star Trek: The Motion Picture-style uniform, phaser, wrist communicator, tricorder, and Voyager spacecraft. ....$10–$15
Lt. Uhura—Tan Star Trek: The Motion Picture-style uniform, tricorder, wrist communicator, PADD, Voyager spacecraft. ....$15–$20
Martia—Dark-skinned female with short curly black and red hair, light gray boots, long black coat, long gray scarf, laser drill, flare, drilling mask, leg irons. ....$15–$20

Star Trek Combined Series

1995

Straight-topped card with "J" hanger. Motion picture-style "Star Trek" word logo on space background. Figures from all series may now appear in this packaging. Subtitled subsets such as "Interstellar Action Series" or "Holodeck Series" are included and do not distinguish between programs. Figures may or may not include regular or Space Cap cards.

NOTE: A Kirk in early original TV series-style uniform was also manufactured but was available only as an accessory to Playmates Shuttlecraft Galileo toy. See Toys.

Adm. Riker from "All Good Things"—Gray beard and hair, red admiral's uniform with future communicator, PADD, desk monitor, phaser, and tricorder, includes card. ....$15–$20
Borg with "Interstellar Action" (STNG)—Firing cybernetic arm, black Borg armor with metallic blue and gray highlights, phaser beam, laser scanner, and Borg hoses (3). ... .$20–$25
Capt. Christopher Pike from "The Cage" (Original TV Series)—Gold early-style uniform, Rigelian spear, shield, communicator, and laser. ....$20–$25
Capt. James T. Kirk in Casual Attire (Original TV Series)—Black pants, green wraparound top, classic phaser,

communicator, tricorder, and Captain's Log, includes card. .....
....$15–$20
Capt. Picard as Galen (STNG)—Brown pants and top, alien monitor, alien PADD, Hano disrupter, stone of Gol, includes card. ....$20–$25
Capt. Picard from "Tapestry" (STNG)—Movie-style maroon Starfleet uniform, special 30th anniversary limited production run of 1701 pieces. ....$700–$1000
Christine Chapel (Original TV Series)—Blue medical mini-dress uniform and black boots, medical scanner, tricorder, anabolic protoplaser, and hypo spray, includes card. ....
....$15–$20
Comdr. Benjamin Sisko—Red, regular collar-style Starfleet uniform, no equipment, no package, figure was available only through a promotional mail-in program. ....$300–$600
Comdr. Sisko from "Crossover" (DS9)—red-brown pants, brown and tan shirt, phaser, Klingon disrupter, alien knife, and liquid nutriment bottle, includes card. ....$15–$20
Deanna Troi from "A Fist Full of Datas" (STNG)—"Holodeck Series" subset, red-brown pants and shirt with sleeves rolled up, dark brown hat, silver revolver, rifle, revolver, keys, clock, includes card. ....$20–$25
Dr. Beverly Crusher from "The Big Goodbye" (STNG)—"Holodeck Series," light tan 1940's-style skirt and jacket, black hat, pistol, handbag, compact, parasol, includes card. ...
....$20–$25
Dr. Katherine Pulaski (STNG)—Teal, no collar-style uniform, medical scanner, tricorder, monitor, medical case, includes card. ....$20–$25
Elim Garak (DS9)—Cardassian in black pants and brown tunic with red-brown trim, tailor's tape, Cardassian PADD, isolinear rods (2), and Cardassian phaser. ....$20–$25
Geordi La Forge from "All Good Things" (STNG)—Blue pants, purple shirt, brown belt, no visor, tricorder, monitor, book, cup of tea, includes card. ....$20–$25
Gov. Worf from "All Good Things" (STNG)—Graying hair and beard, "All Good Things" future Klingon attire, Klingon disrupter, knife, monitor, and bat'telh, includes card.
....$20–$25
Grand Nagus Zek (DS9)—Wrinkle-faced Ferengi, black boots, navy blue jumpsuit, short tan jacket with gold accents, Ferengi bottle, Ferengi cane, latinum bars (2), includes card.
....$15–$20
Hunter of Tosk (DS9)—Light gray face with wrinkled forehead and black hair, red jumpsuit with high, dark gray boots, gloves, belt, and bandolier, rifle, helmet, and scanner, includes card. ....$20–$25
Jadzia Dax from "Blood Oath" (DS9)—Klingon knife, Klingon bat'telh, cups, and tray, includes card. ....$20–$25
Jem'Hadar (DS9)—Black boots, dark and light gray jumpsuit, Jem'Hadar handgun, rifle, and knife. ....$15–$20
Lt. Comdr. Worf (DS9)—Red DS9 uniform with silver Klingon sash, type II phaser, duffel bag, Klingon knife and battle blade, includes card. ....$15–$20
Lt. Geordi La Forge with "Interstellar Action" (STNG)—

Firing phaser rifle, gold early no-collar uniform, phaser rifle, phaser bolt, Away Team gear. ....$20–$25
Lt. Natasha Yar from "Yesterday's Enterprise" (STNG)—Gold collar-style uniform, type II phaser, Enterprise-C phaser, tricorder, isolinear optical chips (2), special 30th anniversary issue of only 1701 pieces. ....$600–$900
Lt. Reginald Barclay from "Projections" (Voyager)—Gold later-style (with turtleneck) uniform, phaser, PADD, tricorder and desktop monitor, limited to 3000 pieces. ....$300–$600
Mr. Spock from "The Cage" (Original TV Series)—Blue, early style uniform, monitor, specimen case, communicator, and laser. ....$20–$25
Odo from "Necessary Evil" (DS9)—Brown shirt, gray vest and pants, Bajoran tricorder and PADD, list of traitors and DS9 monitor. ....$15–$20
Orion Animal Woman from "The Cage" (Original TV Series)—Green skin, brown hair, gold outfit and armband, fountain and torch. ....$20–$25
Rand (Original TV Series)—Red uniform mini-dress and black boots, original phaser, communicator, tricorder, and PADD, includes card. ....$15–$20
Sheriff Worf from "A Fist Full of Datas" (STNG)—"Holodeck Series" subset, brown pants and vest, red shirt, black hat, pistols (2), shot glass, Alexander mini-action figure, includes card. ....$20–$25
Talosian from "The Cage" (Original TV Series)—Large bald head, silver-gray longsleeved robe, Talosian view screen, vial and gas sprayer. ....$20–$25
Traveler, The (STNG)—Heavy brow ridge, balding, brown hair with three-fingered hand, light blue turtleneck jumpsuit, engineering monitor and stool, includes card. ....$20–$25
Vash (DS9)—Short blue dress with gold-color trim, duffle bag, dagger, statue and crystal egg with encasement, includes card. ....$20–$25

Star Fleet Officers Collectors Set

1995

Set of six figures, two each from *Star Trek* (original TV series), *Star Trek: The Next Generation*, and *Star Trek: Deep Space Nine*. Figures were originally sold only as a set which included a black and silver plastic stand for figures. Each figure included two pieces of hand equipment. Came packaged in a window box with "Star Trek" logo located below display window.

Set. ....$100–$150
Individual Complete Unpackaged Figures:
   Kira in Duty Uniform. ....$8–$10
   Kirk in Dress Uniform. ....$15–$25
   Picard in Dress Uniform. ....$15–$25
   Riker in Dress Uniform. ....$15–$25

Sisko in Duty Uniform. ....$8–$10
Spock in Dress Uniform. ....$15–$25

NOTE: The Sisko and Kira figures are identical to the First Series Deep Space Nine Sisko and Kira figures.

Voyager Series

1995

Straight-top header cards with "J"-style hanging slot. Artwork shows side view of ship below word logo. Yellow-orange planet in background. Hand equipment and Skybox trading card is displayed to figure's right.

B'Ellana Torres—Standard black and gold uniform, phaser, engineering case, tricorder, test cylinder. ....$20–$25
B'Ellana Torres the Klingon—Dark gray pants and shirt, black belt, Klingon knife, sword, weapon, and Vidian scanner/phaser. ....$10–$15
Capt. Kathryn Janeway—Standard black and red uniform, phaser, tricorder, monitor, PADD. ....$25–$35
Chakotay—Standard black and red uniform, phaser, medicine bundle (3 pieces), and sims beacon. ....$10–$15
Chakotay the Maquis—Brown pants and vest, red, white, and blue-striped shirt, brown belt and holster, tricorder, phaser, and medicine bundle (wing, stone, and akoonah). ......
....$10–$15
Doctor, The—Standard black and teal uniform, medical tool, hypo spray, PADD, monitor. ....$10–$15
Ens. Seska—Standard black and gold turtleneck-style Starfleet uniform, tricorder, phaser, engineering tools (2), trajector device. ....$10–$15
Harry Kim—Standard black and gold uniform, tricorder, field kit, antipolaric armband and polaric generator. ....
....$10–$15
Kazon—Brown pants, black boots, light gray vest, dark gray harness and gloves, dark skin and hair, Kazon rifle, pistol, and canteen. ....$10–$15
Lt. Carey—Standard black and gold turtleneck-style Starfleet uniform, PADD, test cylinder, phaser, engineering diagnostic. ....$10–$15
Ocampa, The (Kes)—Short, brown single-strap tunic over red-brown shortsleeve jumpsuit, PADD, tricorder, monitor, and biological scanner. ....$15–$20
Talaxian, The (Neelix)—Pink, blue, and white suit, phaser, tricorder, beacon, cooking pan. ....$10–$15
Tom Paris—Standard black and red uniform, phaser, Away Team gear, PADD, and phaser rifle. ....$10–$15
Tuvok—Standard black and gold uniform, phaser, phaser rifle, tricorder, beacon. ....$10–$15
Vidiian—Tan, lumpy-skinned alien with patches of purple and green on head, gray-green pants and shirt, lavendar harness, gray boots, tricorder, hypo spray, medical tool, Vidiian scanner/phaser. ....$10–$15

Collector Series—Command Edition

1994

Figures are approx. 9″ tall, fully articulated with removable clothing and hand equipment. Includes insignia-shaped stand appropriate to character, collector card, and certificate of authenticity. Comes packaged in window box wider at the top than at the bottom. Character's name and UFP seal appear at top and character's ship at bottom. Box has pink and purple cardboard liner.

Capt. James T. Kirk (Original TV series)—Original TV uniform with gold top and black pants, classic tricorder, communicator, and phaser. ....$75–$100
Capt. Jean-Luc Picard—Red, collar-style Starfleet uniform, phaser I, PADD, and tricorder. ....$25–$35
Comdr. Benjamin Sisko—Black and red DS9 uniform jumpsuit, phaser II, PADD, and tricorder. ....$25–$35

Collector Series—Movie Edition

1994

Approx. 9″ tall, fully articulated with removable clothing and hand equipment. Includes movie insignia–shaped stand, certificate of authenticity, and mini-poster. Comes packaged in window boxes wider at the top than at the bottom with character's name at top. Bottom has movie logo. Box liner has starscape with Nexus effect.

Capt. James T. Kirk—Red Star Trek II to VI-style movie uniform, phaser II, multirange light source, champagne bottle.
....$75–$100
Capt. Jean-Luc Picard—Black and red movie uniform jumpsuit, phaser II, family album, isolinear chips (2). ....
....$25–$35
Lt. Comdr. Data—Black and gold movie uniform jumpsuit, tricorder, phaser II, U.V. light source. ....$25–$35
Lt. Comdr. Geordi La Forge—Black and gold movie uniform jumpsuit, tricorder, engineering kit, engineering tools (2).
....$25–$35

Collector Series—

Starfleet/Federation/Alien Edition

1995/1996

Approx. 9″ tall, fully articulated with removable clothing and hand equipment. Includes insignia stand appropriate to the character and Playmates (not Skybox) Space Cap trading card. Comes packaged in window box wider at top than at the bottom with "Star Trek Collector Series" logo at top and appropriate character insignia and name of character below figure.

Borg—Black cloth bodysuit with black and gray plastic Borg cybernetic appliances, collective connector tubes (3). ....
....$35–$45

Capt. James T. Kirk in Dress Uniform—Black pants and green satin dress jacket with gold trim from original TV series, classic tricorder, communicator, and phaser from original TV series. ....$25–$35

Capt. Picard in Dress Uniform—Black pants, long red tunic with black shoulders and gold collar braid, phaser, tricorder, and PADD. ....$35–$45

Comdr. Deanna Troi—Black and teal collar-style uniform, PADD, tricorder, portable computer gear. ....$35–$45

Comdr. Spock—Black pants and blue tunic from original TV series, classic tricorder and phaser, Vulcan harp. ....
....$25–$35

Comdr. William Riker—Black and red collar-style uniform from Star Trek: The Next Generation TV series, phaser rifle, U.V. light source, and type II phaser. ....$25–$35

Dr. Beverly Crusher—Black and teal collar-style uniform from Star Trek: The Next Generation TV series and long blue lab coat, hypo spray, medical tricorder, and medical kit. ....
....$35–$45

Dr. McCoy—Black pants and blue tunic from original TV series. ....$35–$45

Guinan—Blue tunic over longsleeve blue bodysuit, blue hat and shoes, tray, goblet, and glass. ....$25–$35

Lt. Comdr. Data—Black and gold collar-style TV series uniform, tricorder, laser light, isolinear chips (2). ....$25–$35

Lt. Comdr. Geordi La Forge—Black and gold collar-style TV series uniform, tricorder, PADD, multirange light source.
....$35–$45

Lt. Uhura—Red original series mini-dress, original-style tricorder, phaser, and communicator. ....$25–$35

Worf—Deep Space Nine uniform, bat'telh, tricorder, and phaser rifle. ....$35–$45

Worf—Dressed in Klingon uniform, bat'telh, Klingon disrupter, Klingon knife. ....$35–$45

Space Talk Series
1995

Approx. 7″ tall, fully articulated with small button on the back of each figure to activate talking feature. Each figure says three different things in the actual voice of the actor who played the character. Figures come blister-packed on header cards with logo at top and accessories to figure's right. Back shows other figures in series, info on accessories, and has small hole to allow access to speech button on figure.

Capt. Jean-Luc Picard—Red, black, and dark gray uniform with jacket from TV series, type I phaser, PADD, and Adventure Booklet. ....$10–$15

Comdr. Riker—Red and black collar-style TV uniform, type II phaser, tricorder, and Adventure Booklet. ....
....$10–$15

Borg—Gray, black, and silver Borg armor, Borg scanner, Borg connector tubes (2), and Adventure Booklet. ....:.........
....$25–$30

"Q"—Red and black collar-style Next Generation TV show Starfleet uniform, gavel, scepter, and Adventure Booklet. .....
....$25–$30

STAR TREK KEN AND BARBIE
Mattel, 1996

Special Star Trek 30th anniversary collectors' edition. Standard 12″ Ken and Barbie dolls with original Star Trek TV series uniforms; gold shirt and black pants for Ken and red mini-dress for Barbie. Ken has phaser and communicator accessories and Barbie has tricorder and communicator. Packaged as a set with bridge backdrop.

Set. ....$100–$150

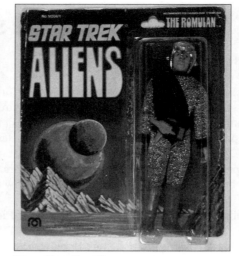

Mego Mugato Figure

Mego Romulan Figure

Mego *Star Trek: The Motion Picture* 3³/₄″ Arcturian Figure

Mego *Star Trek: The Motion Picture* 3³/₄″ Betelgeusian Figure

Mego *Star Trek: The Motion Picture* 3³/₄″ Megarite Figure

Mego *Star Trek: The Motion Picture* 3³/₄″ Rigellian Figure

ERTL *Star Trek III* 3³/₄″ Scotty Figure

Ernst Porcelain Captain Kirk Doll

Galoob *Star Trek: Next Generation* 3³/₄″ Antican Figure

Galoob *Star Trek: Next Generation* 3³/₄″ "Q" Figure

Playmates Toys *Star Trek: Next Generation* **Action Figure (early packaging**

Playmates Toys Third Series Action Figure (early packaging)

Playmates Toys *Deep Space Nine* **Action Figure (early packaging)**

Playmates Toys *Star Trek Generations* **Action Figure**

Playmates Toys Classic *Star Trek Movie* **Action Figure**

Playmates Toys Picard Action Figure (from "Tapestry")

Playmates Toys *Star Trek: Voyager* **Action Figure**

Playmates Toys Tasha Yar Action Figure (from "Yesterday's Enterprise")

Playmates Toys Captain Kirk 9″ Figure (Command Edition)

Playmates Toys Captain Kirk 9″ Figure (Movie Edition)

Playmates Toys Captain Kirk 9″ Figure (Dress Uniform)

Playmates Toys Borg "Space Talk" Figure

Playmates Toys Data Figure (from "Redemption")

Playmates Toys Thomas Riker Figure (rarer version)

ARTWORK

It would be improper to write a book about collectibles without mentioning original works of art. At the same time, it is impossible to catalog art because it is, by nature, unique. When considering Star Trek art as a collectible, it is, first of all, best to use the same criteria you would use for any other category of collectible: Does it appeal to you personally? Choosing a piece of Star Trek art can be a challenging experience because Star Trek art is so diverse. When most people think of art they think of a painting, but this overlooks a vast assortment of skills and crafts. At a large Star Trek convention you can find sculptures, ceramics, jewelry, needlepoint, leatherwork, and much more that fits into the category of art.

When buying an item with an eye toward future collectibility, however, you may wish to consider a few things. Is the piece well made? Is the person who made it a good craftsman as well as a good artist? Does the piece have a unique quality? Does it fit in with your other collectibles? Is the artist well known in his or her field? Has the work ever been published, say as a book cover or trading card? Some very well-known artists in the fantasy and science fiction art field have done the original artwork for published Star Trek items.

Prices for artwork can range from a few cents for a fan-made craft item to several thousand dollars for a painting by a nationally known artist. Whether you purchase a piece that increases in value astronomically with time or one that is never worth more than you paid for it depends entirely on your skill as an art critic. The good news is that as long as you enjoy your find you win either way.

Original Artwork (painting) used on cover of FASA Star Trek Role-Playing Game by famous fantasy artist Rowena

AUTOGRAPHS

Autograph collecting is a well-established hobby in its own right, which, because of the obvious celebrity status of the actors involved, makes it a natural tie-in with Star Trek collecting. Unfortunately, because of the high demand for Star Trek autographs and the well-known fact that so much money changes hands in the Star Trek collectibles field, forgeries, which have always been somewhat of a problem for autograph collectors, are especially prevalent in the Star Trek branch of the field. Some experts believe that for every genuine Star Trek autograph in circulation there may be as many as 10 fakes being offered as authentic. The best way for a collector to assure that his or her autographs are genuine is, of course, to be present when the person is signing them. If this isn't possible, the next best solution is to buy from a source that plausibly had access to the people whose signatures appear on the merchandise (for instance, convention organizers who have hired the particular individual as a guest). Keep in mind that even many "authorized" sources (i.e., the studio) may not be sending you an actual signature. Fan mail is often signed by someone other than the actor or a stamp may be used. When purchasing autographs on the secondary market, try to buy only from reputable dealers who buy their autographs through reliable sources and offer a guarantee. Certificates of authenticity look nice in a frame but, practically speaking, are only worth as much as the paper they are printed on.

Guidelines for the value of authentic autographs are fairly clear cut. As a general rule, the more famous the individual, the more valuable the autograph. The other primary factor affecting collectibility is that for one reason or another, some people simply don't sign as much as others. Also keep in mind that two authentic autographs from the same individual may not match exactly. Many people change their signatures during the course of their lives and they may at times use abbreviated signatures (for instance, during autograph sessions when they know they will have to sign for several hours).

INVESTMENT POTENTIAL
Good.

CARE
Care of autographs depends a great deal on the item that has been signed. Since autographs appear on everything from T-shirts to plates and toys (not just paper items), the first requirement is to properly care for the item itself. Particular considerations for the actual autograph are to avoid fading caused by too much exposure to direct sunlight and to prevent smearing, which can be a special problem with smooth surfaces such as plastic, metal, or glass. Protective glass or plastic covers or frames are probably the best solution in most cases.

SECTION NOTES
The following is, for practical considerations, no more than a guideline for the value of Star Trek autographs. First of all, as was previously mentioned, autographs can be found on practically any object, therefore the value (either actual or intrinsic) of the item itself must be considered as part of the whole. A very common example is an autographed photo which has been mounted onto a plaque. At least two-thirds the value of autograph plaques is found in the presentation of the piece, and not in the autograph itself. Second, the long history of Star Trek includes not just the major actors we are all familiar with but thousands of other individuals who made guest appearances (many of whom went on to become major stars in their own right and some of whom have since died, both value boosters in the autograph field) and many other individuals (writers, directors, technical people, etc.) who have contributed in some way.

For comparison purposes, all of the autographs listed below shall be considered to be on a standard 8″ × 10″ photograph. The section is organized chronologically by show and alphabetically by individual.

ORIGINAL STAR TREK

James Doohan. ....$30–$40
DeForest Kelly. ....$75–$100
Walter Koenig. ....$20–$30
Nichelle Nichols. ....$20–$30
Leonard Nimoy. ....$75–$100
Gene Roddenberry. ....$100–$125
Majel Barrett Roddenberry. ....$20–$30
William Shatner. ....$75–$100
George Takei. ....$20–$30
Grace Lee Whitney. ....$15–$25

STAR TREK: THE NEXT GENERATION

Levar Burton. ....$35–$45
Denise Crosby. ....$25–$35
Michael Dorn. ....$25–$35
Jonathan Frakes. ....$50–$75
Gates McFadden. ....$25–$35
Diana Muldaur. ....$40–$50
Marina Sirtis. ....$25–$35
Brent Spiner. ....$50–$75

Patrick Stewart. ....$75–$100
Wil Wheaton. ....$25–$35

STAR TREK: DEEP SPACE NINE

René Auberjonois. ....$25–$35
Avery Brooks. ....$50–$75
Siddig El Fadil (Alexander Siddig). ....$25–$35
Terry Farrell. ....$25–$35
Cirroc Lofton. ....$15–$25
Colm Meany. ....$25–$35
Armin Shimmerman. ....$25–$35
Nana Visitor. ....$25–$35

STAR TREK: VOYAGER

Robert Beltran. ....$25–$35
Roxann Dawson. ....$25–$35
Jennifer Lien. ....$25–$35
Robert Duncan McNeill. ....$25–$35
Kate Mulgrew. ....$50–$75
Ethan Phillips. ....$25–$35
Robert Picardo. ....$25–$35
Tim Russ. ....$25–$35
Garrett Wang. ....$25–$35

Autographed Photo

Autographed Record Plaque

BADGES

The word "badge" is used here to denote either hard plastic pinback badges with the subject affixed or engraved on the surface or the printed paper kind that is either inserted loose or laminated into a plastic holder. Most of these kinds of items are basically fan-made and produced in small quantities or even as one-of-a-kind items. Though they are popular convention items, the collectible value of fan-made badges is virtually nil due to their ease of reproduction, and they have not been included in this section.

The items listed here are all licensed and employ professional manufacturing processes. For other items that might be considered badges see Buttons for metal pinbacks and Jewelry for cloisonné or enameled pins.

INVESTMENT POTENTIAL
Fair.

CARE
Except for the loose paper kind which must be protected from moisture and creasing the same as any other paper item, badges are very durable and require minimal care.

SECTION NOTES
Being essentially handmade items, fan-manufactured badges can be made in infinite variety and therefore cannot, in any practical sense, be cataloged. For this reason, only licensed badges will be presented in this section. The section is organized alphabetically by manufacturer.

A.H. PRISMATIC
(British, 1992)

Plastic pinback badges approx. 2″ square with diffraction-grating-type holographic stickers affixed to front. Affixed to

3″ × 4¾″ paper header cards with either "Star Trek," "Star Trek: The Next Generation," or "Star Trek: Deep Space Nine" logos above. Three series.

Original Star Trek Series

Enterprise. ....$3–$4
Group—Kirk, Scotty, and Chekov. ....$3–$4
Group—Spock, McCoy, Sulu, and Uhura. ....$3–$4
Kirk and Landing Party on Planet. ....$3–$4
Klingon and Klingon Ship. ....$3–$4
Spock, giving Vulcan salute. ....$3–$4
"Star Trek," with Enterprise. ....$3–$4
"Star Trek," with movie-style command symbol. ....$3–$4
Transporter Scene. ....$3–$4

Star Trek: The Next Generation

Bridge Scene, with Romulan ship on view screen. ...$3–$4
Data and Worf. ....$3–$4
Enterprise-D and "Star Trek: The Next Generation.".......
....$3–$4
Enterprise-D and Ringed Planet. ....$3–$4
Group—Picard, Geordi, Troi, and Wesley. ....$3–$4
Group—Riker, Data, Worf, and a Benzite. ....$3–$4
Picard and Geordi on Planet. ....$3–$4
Picard, Troi, and Dr. Crusher. ....$3–$4
Two Ferengi and Ferengi Ship. ....$3–$4

Star Trek: Deep Space Nine

Cardassian Ships, Space Station, and Logo. ....$3–$4
Runabout. ....$3–$4
Runabout and Logo. ....$3–$4

Space Station. ....$3–$4
Space Station and Logo. ....$3–$4
Space Station and Runabout. ....$3–$4

NOTE: This company has employed diffraction-grating holo-
grams in a variety of other Star Trek products including
pins, boxes, stickers, magnets, keychains, bookmarks, pens,
and pencils. See Buttons, Housewares, Decals, Jewelry,
and School and Office Supplies sections of this book for
these items.

DUFORT & SONS
(British, Star Trek: The Next Generation, 1995)

Color, plastic, die-cut buttons with name of character beneath
photo image with appropriate symbol as background.

Borg. ....$3–$4
Command Insignia, no background or title. ....$3–$4
Data. ....$3–$4
Dr. Crusher. ....$3–$4
Enterprise. ....$3–$4
Geordi. ....$3–$4
Picard. ....$3–$4
Riker. ....$3–$4
Troi. ....$3–$4
Worf. ....$3–$4

NOTE: These 10 badges were also sold as a set with a card-
board display stand. ....$35–$40

ICONS
(1992)

Laminated, two-sided, color photo badges, 2³/₄″ × 4³/₄″. A
hole in one end was provided for either a lanyard or a key

ring, one of which was provided with each badge. Packaged
in plastic bags with cardboard header for hanging which displayed company logo. Two series.

Original Star Trek Series

One side of all badges shows color photo of original Enterprise orbiting planet with "Space . . . the Final Frontier" and
"Star Trek" below. Other side displays quote and subject.

Captain, the Engines Canna Take Anymore, Enterprise in
Tholian web. ....$4–$6
Energize, crew in transporter. ....$4–$6
Illogical/Logical, Spock. ....$4–$6
Live Long & Prosper, Spock doing Vulcan salute. .....$4–$6
Mind Meld, mirror, universe, Spock, and McCoy. ......$4–$6
Scotty, I Need More Power!, bridge scene. ....$4–$6
Set Phasers on Stun, Spock and Kirk with phaser. .....$4–$6
To Boldly Go . . . Where No Man Has Gone Before,
Enterprise. ....$4–$6
To Explore Strange New Worlds, Enterprise and Kirk. ....
....$4–$6
We Come in Peace, crew members. ....$4–$6

Star Trek: The Next Generation

One side of all badges shows color photo of Enterprise-D
with "Star Trek: the Next Generation" above and "United
Federation of Planets Starfleet Flagship Galaxy Class USS
Enterprise NCC-1701-D" below. Other side displays subject
and information.

Bridge Scene. ....$4–$6
Data. ....$4–$6
Dr. Crusher. ....$4–$6
Geordi. ....$4–$6
Guinan. ....$4–$6
Picard. ....$4–$6
Riker. ....$4–$6
Troi. ....$4–$6
Worf. ....$4–$6

A.H. Prismatic Holographic Badge

Icons Badge

BLUEPRINTS

This line of merchandise gained popularity in 1975 when Ballantine published a deck-by-deck schematic of the Enterprise originally drawn as a fan publication by Franz Joseph. It was such a hit with the many technically oriented fans of the show that it produced a rash of similar products, almost all unlicensed. Though almost always referred to as "blueprints," a process used most commonly to reproduce architectural drawings, plans of the type most fans are familiar with from conventions and specialty stores are usually printed in the standard offset manner. They vary greatly in quality and detail and generally come packed in printed envelopes or sometimes in the case of one-sheet designs merely rolled or folded, although a few fan blueprints do come in plastic pouches. Though they are very popular novelty items with fans, they are also probably the best example of a category of merchandise that will almost certainly never increase in value due to the extreme ease with which they can be reproduced. In this section we are presenting only an overview of unlicensed blueprints. For the few existing licensed plans and other technically oriented publications, see Books and Posters.

INVESTMENT POTENTIAL
Poor.

CARE
Like all paper items, plans need protection from moisture and fading caused by sunlight. Plastic collectors' bags, which come in a variety of sizes, provide the best protection from the elements and also help prevent accidental tearing. Cardboard poster tubes are excellent for storing one-sheet designs.

SECTION NOTES
Like fanzines, it would be very difficult to make a complete listing of blueprints because so many amateur artists have drawn sets as a labor of love and then reproduced a few sets either for friends or, in the case of some of the better sets, sold their designs to dealers to sell on a wider scale. Virtually every ship that ever appeared in Star Trek and a great many imaginary ones, as well as space stations, starbases, and all manner of weapons, equipment, and other items have, over the years, appeared in blueprint form. The only attribute that all unlicensed plans unfortunately share is that as collectibles they are practically valueless. Even the original fan version of the Franz Joseph Enterprise plans, which one would think should be collectible, was being widely reproduced in a form indistinguishable from the original well before the licensed Ballantine version ever appeared.

The determining factors that do exist in the price of blueprints are commonly the size and complexity of the set. A simple exterior representation of a ship from several angles does not require as much work as deck-by-deck detail, and this is usually reflected in the price. Packaging is also an expense that can be passed along to the customer. An envelope printed in two colors is more expensive than a one-color envelope, and a tube or plastic pouch more expensive yet. No fan-made blueprint, however, should cost more than $20 and most are much cheaper.

NOTE: Since quality varies so much in unlicensed blueprints, it is always best to inspect them before you buy. If a vendor offers only sealed plans (they are almost never initially packaged that way) there is probably a reason.

BOOKS (Comic Books, Convention Program Books, and Novels and Reference Books)

COMIC BOOKS

Star Trek comics were first issued while the original TV show was still on the air, making them one of the oldest types of collectibles. Several publishers have produced Star Trek comics over the years, with Paramount Publishing currently starting up several new series.

INVESTMENT POTENTIAL
Good.

CARE
Being printed on inexpensive pulp paper makes preserving your comic book collection an exercise in "beating the elements." The bad things for any book collection are the acid in the paper (which causes paper to become brittle), temperature, humidity, and sunlight. Comics should be stored in a dark place with a controlled environment, i.e., inside your climate-controlled house, not in the garage or attic. Comics should be stored in acid-free containers so as not to add to the speed with which the paper decays. Mylar holders are best but can be fairly expensive, i.e., up to $1 each. Regular comic book plastic bags are good but need to be replaced every few years as they tend to turn yellow with age. Be sure that if you use backing boards that you get acid-free or neutral ones.

SECTION NOTES
The listings here are chronological by publisher. Values listed are per book and for books in near mint condition. Except for the very early issues (1960s and 1970s) issues, books in less than near mint condition are generally not collectible.

Star Trek
(Gold Key Comics, 1967–1979)

This series featured original stories based on the Star Trek characters. Most of the series was drawn by an artist who had never watched Star Trek. The lower value is for books in good condition and the higher value for books in near mint condition.

#1 (Photo Cover). ....$100–$400
#2–5. ....$50–$200
#6–9 (Last Photo Cover). ....$35–$150
#10–20. ....$25–$75
#21–40. ....$15–$50
#41–61. ....$10–$30

Star Trek
(Dan Curtis Giveaways, 1974)

3″ × 6″, full-color, 24-page reprints of Gold Key.

#2 Star Trek—Enterprise Mutiny. ....$8–$20
#6 Star Trek—Dark Traveler. ....$8–$20

Star Trek: The Enterprise Logs
(Gold Key, 1976–1977)

Golden Press. Each of these reprints eight of the previously mentioned Gold Key comics. A warehouse fire destroyed much of the print run on these.

#1 (Reprints #1–8 Comics). ....$15–$25
#2 (Reprints #9–17 Comics). ....$15–$25
#3 (Reprints #18–26 Comics). ....$20–$30
#4 (Reprints #27, 28, 30–34, 36, 38 Comics). ....$20–$30

Star Trek

(Dynabrite Comics, 1978–1979)

Full-color, 48-pages, cardboard cover reprints of Gold Key.

#11357 Star Trek, #33 and #41. ....$8–$20
#11358 Star Trek, #34 and #36. ....$8–$20

Star Trek

(Marvel Comics, 1980–1982)

Starts with adaptation of Star Trek: The Motion Picture and then continues with original stories.

#1. ....$3–$8
#2–7. ....$2–$6
#8–17. ....$3–$8
#18 (Last Issue). ....$6–$30
Marvel Super Special #15 (Magazine Size, Adapts Complete Movie)
    $1.50 Cover price. ....$5–$10
    $2 Cover price (scarce). ....$10–$20

Star Trek Classic

(DC Comics, 1984–1988)

This series had original stories based on the movie crew of the Enterprise with flashbacks and references to characters from the TV show.

#1 (Sutton Art Begins). ....$5–$15
#2–10. ....$3–$8
#11–18, 20–33. ....$2–$6
#19 (Written by Walter Koenig). ....$4–$8
#34–55. ....$2–$5
#56 (Last Issue). ....$3–$9
Annual #1–3. ....$3–$6
Who's Who in Star Trek #1, 2. ....$5–$10

Star Trek Movie Specials

(DC Comics, 1984–1989)

#1 Adapts Star Trek III. ....$5–$10

#2 Adapts Star Trek IV. ....$3–$6
#1 Adapts Star Trek V. ....$3–$6

Star Trek Classic

(DC Comics, 1989–1996)

Original stories based on the movie Star Trek crew.

#1. ....$5–$15
#2–9. ....$3–$9
#10–50. ....$2–$6
#51–80. ....$2–$5
Annual #1. ....$5–$10
Annual #2–6. ....$3–$6
Special #1–3. ....$3–$6
Star Trek 25th Anniversary Special. ....$3–$6
Modala Imperative #1–4. ....$2–$4
Star Trek VI Movie Adaptation. ....$3–$6

Star Trek: The Next Generation Mini-Series

(DC Comics, 1988)

This was a six-issue mini-series based on the Next Generation TV show.

#1. ....$5–$15
#2–6. ....$4–$9

Star Trek: The Next Generation

(DC Comics, 1989–1996)

Original stories based on Next Generation characters.

#1. ....$5–$15
#2–9. ....$3–$9
#10–50. ....$2.50–$6
#51–80. ....$2–$5
Annual #1. ....$2.50–$5
Annual #2–6. ....$3–$6
Specials #1–3. ....$3–$6
Ill Wind #1–4. ....$2–$4
Modala Imperative #1–4. ....$2–$4
Shadowheart #1–4. ....$2–$4
Series Finale. ....$3–$6

Star Trek: Next Generation/ Deep Space Nine Mini-Series

(DC Comics)

#1, 2. ....$3–$5

Star Trek: Generations

(DC Comics)

Prestige Format. ....$4–$8
Regular Format. ....$2–$4

Star Trek: Deep Space Nine

(Malibu)

#1. ....$3–$6
#2–10. ....$2.50–$5
#11–28. ....$2–$4
Special #1. ....$2.50–$5
Hearts and Minds #1–4. ....$2.50–$5
The Maquis #1–4. ....$2–$4
Terok Nor #0. ....$2–$4

Star Trek: Deep Space Nine/The Next Generation

(Malibu)

#1, 2. ....$3–$5

Parodies

There have been several parodies of Star Trek in other comics and magazines. An issue of *Mad* magazine or *Cracked* with a Star Trek parody is worth between $5 and $10 (see Magazines). Individual comics such as *Elf Trek* or *Imagi-Nation* with Star Trek parodies are worth between $2 and $5.

CONVENTION PROGRAM BOOKS

In the early days of Star Trek conventions it was common practice to produce souvenir program books. Rising production costs have discouraged the more complex programs and in recent years most conventions have supplied only simple schedules to their attendees. The few program books that have become truly collectible are primarily from the very early conventions ('72, '73, '74). In future years, as they become a little older (and scarcer), programs from the big anniversary conventions could easily increase in value. As with most printed collectibles, quality paper and especially color covers and/or interior photos tend to distinguish the more collectible program books.

INVESTMENT POTENTIAL
Fair.

CARE
Since convention program books are essentially magazines, their care is identical. Keep books intact. Protect them from moisture, tearing, and scuffing with plastic collectors bags, and use cardboard inserts in the bags to prevent creasing, especially when storing them vertically.

NOTE: Books often came in a convention "package," a printed plastic convention bag which sometimes contained other items—badges, pocket programs, stickers, etc. These types of items generally have minimal collector value, usually no more than $2–$5.

NOVELS AND REFERENCE BOOKS

Anyone who hasn't noticed the incredible profusion of Star Trek books in recent years hasn't walked into a bookstore lately. Many stores have separate Star Trek sections complete with a selection of the most popular reference books and the latest *Star Trek Classic*, *Star Trek: The Next Generation*, *Star Trek: Deep Space Nine*, and *Star Trek: Voyager* novels (with perhaps a young reader novel or special hardbound novel thrown in for good measure). While this is, of course, a testimony of fan loyalty to written Star Trek (novels consistently make the *New York Times* paperback bestseller list), Paramount's acquisition of Pocket Books several years ago certainly didn't hurt either. As collectibles, books hold up very well as long as they are (and remain) out of print. To date, few current books have done so; there is simply too much demand for them by readers. Many older books, however (those written before the mid-'80s), are out of print and have respectable collectible value. At the same time, it should be noted that unlike some other collectible fields—rare mainstream books and comic books, for example—there are very few Star Trek collectors who are willing to pay more than a very small premium for first editions. While they will gladly pay whatever is necessary to add a particular book to their library, if the book is reprinted the demand (and value) of the original tends to slump sharply.

INVESTMENT POTENTIAL
Good.

CARE

Books are, in general, fairly durable and only need the obvious protection from moisture and fading that is necessary for all paper collectibles. Plastic collector bags in a variety of sizes suitable for books are available for this purpose. To best maintain collectible value, never discard the dust jacket to a hardback. With paperback books, take care to keep the cover free from creases and never break the spine of the book (often done so that the book remains open more easily) or dog-ear corners to mark a place.

SECTION NOTES

This section is generally organized alphabetically by the specific publisher and then by title. Exceptions have been made, however, in cases where a series of books has been numbered by the publisher. In these cases they are listed in their original numerical order. Please note that by "specific" publisher we mean the first one listed on the cover and/or spine of the book. Large publishers often consist of a number of subsidiary companies. For example, Pocket Books is a division of Simon and Schuster but Pocket is the name that you would see on the cover of most current novels and is the name we would use to place the book alphabetically.

Two categories of books which may have collector interest have been intentionally omitted. The first is fan-published technical books. These are very popular among fans but, since they are not produced by a regular publishing house, they more properly fit into the category of fanzines despite the better-than-average production values of many of these books. The second is non–Star Trek books written by Star Trek personalities. Leonard Nimoy's photography and poetry books have been mentioned because of their long-standing acceptance as collectible books, however William Shatner (*Tek* novels), George Takei (*Mirror Friend, Mirror Foe*), Walter Koenig (*Buck Alice and the Robot Actor*), and Nichelle Nichols (*Saturn's Child*) have all authored novels.

NOTE: As it is used in the book industry, the term paperback here refers to the size book (cover dimension, not thickness) common to most paperback novels, while "trade" paperback refers to any oversize paperback book.

Ace

Shatner: Where No Man Has Gone Before—1979. W. Shatner, S. Marshak, and M. Culbreath. Biography, paperback. ....$40–$60

Alpha Books

Star Trek: The Next Generation 20th-Century Computers—1993. Jennifer Flynn. Computer guide written as a Starfleet text. Trade paperback. ....$18–$20

Anima

Meaning in Star Trek—1977. Karen Blair. Explains Star Trek's popularity through Jungian psychology.
    Hardcover. ....$20–$30
    Paperback (see Warner)

Archway

Monsters of Star Trek (see Pocket)
Phaser Fight (Which Way Book #24)—1986. Barbara Siegel and Scott Siegel. ....$5–$10
Star Trek: Voyage to Adventure (Which Way Book #15)—1984. Michael J. Dodge. Plot-Your-Own-Adventure. Carousel (British) edition has different cover art. ....$5–$10

Ballantine

Letters to Star Trek—1977. Susan Sackett. ....$12–$20
Making of Star Trek, The—1968. Stephen Whitfield and Gene Roddenberry. History of the making of the original TV series.
    First Edition. ....$15–$30
    Later Editions (changed to Del Rey, a division of Ballantine). ....$8–$15
Starfleet Medical Reference—1977. Eileen Palestine (editor). Trade paperback size.
    Ballantine edition, blue cover, originally came shrink-wrapped with silver cover sheet. ....$50–$75
    The above book is based on an earlier fan edition with a white cover that is very scarce. ....$75–$150
Starfleet Technical Manual. Franz Joseph.
    Original Edition—1975. Trade paperback with red cover in black binder. ....$35–$85
    Reprint Versions—1986 to Present. Trade paperback with black cover, no binder. ....$12–$15
Star Trek Blueprints—1975. Franz Joseph. Twelve-sheet, deck-by-deck reproduction of the original Enterprise. Came packaged in a brown plastic pouch with clear front panel and cover sheet. ....$40–$65
Star Trek Concordance—1976. Bjo Trimble. Cross-referenced information directory.
    Trade paperback with index wheel on cover. ....$35–$75
    Reprint (Citadel, 1995). Trade paperback with some additional information on the movies not in original version. ....$20–$23

NOTE: The fan version of this book, two volumes in offset print format, had considerable collectors' value at one time. Counterfeiting has made this publication virtually worthless.

Star Trek Log Books. All by Alan Dean Foster. (Log Nine, Log Ten, and all reprints are Del Rey.) These are novelizations of the Star Trek animated series. Original editions of one through eight had cover art from the series. Nine and ten and subsequent printings of the other numbers had solid-color covers with pictures of the Enterprise until 1992 when they changed to artwork of space scenes. One through six contain several episodes in each volume. Seven through ten have one story per book.

Log One—1974. ....$3–$8
Log Two—1974. ....$3–$8
Log Three—1975. ....$3–$8
Log Four—1975. ....$3–$8
Log Five—1975. ....$3–$8
Log Six—1976. ....$3–$8
Log Seven—1976. ....$3–$8
Log Eight—1977. ....$3–$8
Log Nine—1977. ....$3–$8
Log Ten—1978. ....$5–$10

NOTE: Log Books were also published as compilations (see Del Rey).

Trek or Treat—1977. T. Flanagan and E. Ehrhardt. Humorous captioned photo book. Horizontal format, Spock on cover. ....$3–$5
Trouble with Tribbles—1973. David Gerrold. Making of the episode. (Reprints were Del Rey.). ....$10–$15
World of Star Trek—1973. David Gerrold. (Reprints were Del Rey.) Regular paperback format. ....$10–$15

NOTE: There was an up-dated version printed in 1984 (see Bluejay).

Bantam

Bantam Novels

This was an early series of Star Trek novels. All have been reprinted at one time or another since their original publication dates with different cover art. As prices indicate, some are much more common than others. Published in the United Kingdom by Corgi.

Death's Angel—1981. Kathleen Sky. ....$15–$20
Devil's World—1979. Gordon Eklund. ....$10–$15
Fate of the Phoenix, The—1979. S. Marshak and M. Culbreath. Sequel to *Price of the Phoenix*. ....$5–$7
Galactic Whirlpool, The—1980. David Gerrold. ...$10–$15
Mudd's Angels—1978. J.A. Lawrence. ....$15–$20
Perry's Planet—1980. J. Haldeman II. ....$10–$15
Planet of Judgment—1977. Joe Haldeman. ....$5–$7
Price of the Phoenix—1977. S. Marshak and M. Culbreath.
....$5–$7
Spock Messiah—1976. Theodore Cogswell and Charles Spano. ....$5–$7
Spock Must Die—1970. James Blish. ....$5–$7

Starless World—1978. Gordon Eklund. ....$10–$15
Trek to Madworld—1979. Stephen Golkin. ....$8–$12
Vulcan—1978. Kathleen Sky. ....$15–$20
World Without End—1979. Joe Haldeman. ....$8–$12

Blish Novelizations

These are adaptations of the original TV episodes by James Blish. Published in the United States by Bantam and in the United Kingdom by Corgi. There were numerous printings and cover art often varied between editions. The final book, #12, was co-authored by J.A. Lawrence, James Blish's wife, because Mr. Blish died before the book could be completed.

No. 1—Jan. 1967. ....$3–$6
No. 2—Feb. 1968. ....$3–$6
No. 3—April 1969. ....$3–$6
No. 4—July 1971. ....$3–$6
No. 5—Feb. 1972. ....$3–$6
No. 6—April 1972. ....$3–$6
No. 7—July 1972. ....$3–$6
No. 8—Nov. 1972. ....$3–$6
No. 9—Aug. 1973. ....$3–$6
No. 10—Feb. 1974. ....$3–$6
No. 11—April 1975. ....$5–$8
No. 12—Nov. 1977. ....$8–$10

Blish Compilations (1991)

These are reprints of the original Blish adaptations compiled into three volumes and organized by seasons.

The Classic Episodes Vol. 1. ....$6–$8
The Classic Episodes Vol. 2. ....$6–$8
The Classic Episodes Vol. 3. ....$6–$8

NOTE: The Blish adaptations were also published in four hardback volumes between 1970 and 1974 (see Dutton).

Fotonovels

These are scene-by-scene, color adaptations of the original TV show. Series of 12.

No. 1—City on the Edge of Forever, Nov. 1977. .....$10–$15
No. 2—Where No Man Has Gone Before, Nov. 1977. ....
....$10–$15
No. 3—The Trouble with Tribbles, Dec. 1977. ....$10–$15
No. 4—A Taste of Armageddon, Jan. 1978. ....$10–$12
No. 5—Metamorphosis, Feb. 1978. ....$10–$12
No. 6—All Our Yesterdays, March 1978. ....$10–$15
No. 7—The Galileo 7, May 1978. ....$12–$18
No. 8—A Piece of the Action, June 1978. ....$12–$18
No. 9—Devil in the Dark, July 1978. ....$15–$20
No. 10—Day of the Dove, Aug. 1978. ....$15–$20

No. 11—The Deadly Years, Sept. 1978. ....$15–$20
No. 12—Amok Time, Oct. 1978. ....$20–$30

NOTE: This popular series of books has been translated into several languages by foreign publishing houses. Foreign language editions may have slightly higher values than U.S. editions.

Miscellaneous

Official Star Trek Cooking Manual, The—1978. Ann Piccard. ....$40–$60
Star Trek Intergalactic Puzzles—1977. James Razzi. Trade paperback. Silver Cover. (*Note: Worked puzzles devalue book considerably.*) ....$15–$25
Star Trek Maps—1980. Two 29″ × 40″ two-sided color star maps plus 32-page technical booklet. Packaged in color cardstock envelope. ....$150–$250
Star Trek Puzzle Manual. J. Razzi. Black cover with artwork of Enterprise (both formats). (*Note: Worked puzzles devalue books considerably.*)
    Trade Paperback—1976. ....$15–$25
    Regular Paperback Size—1977. ....$10–$15
Star Trek: The New Voyages—1976. Edited by Sondra Marshak and Myrna Culbreath. Anthology of fan-written fiction. ....$5–$10
Star Trek: The New Voyages 2—1977. Edited by Sondra Marshak and Myrna Culbreath. ....$5–$10

BBC Productions

(Western Publishing)

Star Trek Annuals—1970 to present. BBC British. Comics and articles in oversize hardcover editions.
    1970–1972. ....$50–$75
    1973–1975. ....$40–$50
    1976–1980. ....$30–$40
    1981–1983. ....$20–$30
    1984–1990. ....$15–$25
    1991 up. ....$10–$15

Bible Voice

Star Wars, Star Trek and the 21st Century Christians—1978. Winkie Pratney. ....$10–$15

Bluejay

World of Star Trek—1984. David Gerrold. Updated version of book earlier published by Ballantine. Trade paperback. .....
....$15–$20

Books Americana

Encyclopedia of Trekkie Memorabilia—1988. Chris Gentry and Sally Gibson Downs. Trade paperback. ....$10–$12

Boulevard Books

Beyond Uhura—1994. Nichelle Nichols. Paperback. A hardcover edition was also published (see Putnam). ....$6–$8

Celestial Arts

I Am Not Spock. Leonard Nimoy. Autobiography of the Spock/Nimoy relationship.
    Trade Paperback, Celestial Arts—1975. ....$35–$60
    Regular Paperback Size, Del Rey—1977. ....$15–$30

Leonard Nimoy also did a series of poetry and photography books which, while not technically Star Trek books, are still in demand as collectibles. They are as follows:

Will I Think of You. Celestial Arts (1st ed.). ....$25–$35
Will I Think of You. Dell. ....$15–$25
You and I. Celestial Arts (1st ed.). ....$25–$35
You and I. Avon. ....$15–$25
Thank You for Your Love. Blue Mountain. ....$45–$60
Come Be with Me. Blue Mountain. ....$45–$60
These Words Are for You. Blue Mountain. ....$45–$60
We Are All Children Searching for Love. Blue Mountain.
....$45–$60
Warmed by Love. Blue Mountain. Hardback, excerpts from other books. ....$16–$20

Chatham River

Star Trek: The Next Generation Starship Enterprise Make A Model—1990. David Woodroffe, Jon Sutherland, and Nigel Gross. ....$10–$15

Cinemaker Press

Charting the Undiscovered Country—1992. Mark A. Altman, Ron Magid, and Edward Gross. Making of the movie. Trade paperback. ....$15–$20
Exploring Deep Space and Beyond—1992. Mark A. Altman and David Ian Solter. Trade paperback. ....$15–$20

Citadel

Starfleet Academy Entrance Exam, The—1996. Peggy Robin. Trivia book. Trade paperback. ....$10–$12
Star Trek Concordance (see Ballantine).

Creative Education

Star Trek, TV and Movie Tie-ins—1979. James A. Lely. Hardback. ....$15–$25

Dell

The Nitpickers Guide for Classic Trekkers—1994. Phil Farrand. Trade paperback. ....$13–$15
The Nitpickers Guide for Next Generation Trekkers—1993. Phil Farrand. Trade paperback. ....$13–$15
The Nitpickers Guide for Next Generation Trekkers Volume II—1995. Phil Farrand. Trade paperback. ....$13–$15

Del Rey

I Am Not Spock (see Celestial Arts).
Log Books. Novelizations of the Star Trek animated series (see Ballantine).
Making of Star Trek (see Ballantine).
Star Trek Log Compilations—1993. Alan Dean Foster. Books contain three regular Log Books in each volume. Log Ten is not included.
　　Log One/Log Two/Log Three. ....$5–$8
　　Log Four/Log Five/Log Six. ....$5–$8
　　Log Seven/Log Eight/Log Nine. ....$5–$8
Trouble with Tribbles (see Ballantine).
World of Star Trek (see Ballantine).

Donning

On the Good Ship Enterprise—1982. Bjo Trimble. Humorous anecdotes from Star Trek fandom. Trade paperback. ....
....$25–$40

Doubleday

Making of the Trek Conventions, The. Joan Winston. Photographs and behind-the-scenes descriptions.
　　Hardcover, Doubleday—1977. ....$40–$60
　　Regular Size Paperback, Playboy Press—1979. .....$25–$35

Dutton

Star Trek Readers were hardback compilations of the Star Trek original episode adaptations by James Blish. They were done in both regular and bookclub editions, which are not as thick and use slightly courser paper stock.
　　Vol. I—1970, 21 episodes. ....$15–$25
　　Vol. II—1972, 19 episodes. ....$15–$25
　　Vol. III—1973, 19 episodes. ....$20–$30
　　Vol. IV—1974, 12 episodes plus "Spock Must Die." ....
....$20–$30

Futura

Star Trek: The Motion Picture—1979. Futura (British). G. Roddenberry (novelization). Same as Pocket's American edition except for color photo section. ....$10–$15
Star Trek Speaks—1979. Susan Sackett, Fred Goldstein, and Stan Goldstein. Trade paperback. ....$15–$25

Greenberg

Greenberg's Guide to Star Trek Collectibles—1992. Christine Gentry and Sally Gibson-Downs. Three volumes. Trade paperbacks.
　　A–E. ....$20–$25
　　F–P. ....$20–$25
　　P–Z. ....$20–$25

Grosset & Dunlap

Star Trek Catalog—1979. Gerry Turnbull.
　　Trade Paperback Size. ....$7–$10
　　Regular Paperback Size. ....$4–$6

Harper

Star Trek Memories—1993. William Shatner and Chris Kreski.
　　Hardback. ....$20–$25
　　Paperback. ....$7–$10
Star Trek Movie Memories—1994. William Shatner and Chris Kreski.
　　Hardback. ....$20–$25
　　Paperback. ....$7–$25
Ultimate Unauthorized Star Trek Quiz Book, The—1994. Robert W. Bly. Trade Paperback. ....$10–$12

Heritage

Who Was That Monolith I Saw You With?—1976. Michael Goodwin. Trade paperback. Cartoon strip compilation.
....$5–$10

Hyperion

I Am Spock—1995. Leonard Nimoy. Sequel to his 1975 autobiography *I Am Not Spock* (see Celestial Arts). Hardback.
....$25–$30

NOTE: This book was published by Century in the U.K. with a different dust jacket photo than the U.S. version. This jacket was withdrawn after a very short time at the author's request, making it a good potential future collectible.

Image

Deep Space Nine Log Book, The—1994. Mark A. Altman and Edward Gross. Trade paperback. ....$12–$15
Great Birds of the Galaxy—1992. Edward Gross and Mark A. Altman. Trade paperback. ....$15–$20
Making of the Trek Films, The—1992. Edited by Edward Gross. Trade paperback. ....$15–$20
New Voyages (Volume I)—1991. Edward Gross and Mark A. Altman. Trade paperback. ....$15–$20
New Voyages (Volume II)—1992. Mark A. Altman and Edward Gross. Trade paperback. ....$12–$15
Trek Classic—1991. Edward Gross. ....$12–$15

Intergalactic Press

Chekov's Enterprise (see Pocket).

McFarland & Company

Star Trek: An Annotated Guide—1991. Susan R. Gibberman. Library reference book. Hardbound. ....$40–$60

Marvel Comics

Star Trek: The Motion Picture—1979. Issues 1 and 2 of the comic movie adaptation in paperback form. ....$3–$5

NOTE: For other booklike Star Trek comic adaptations see Comics section of this book.

Merrigold

See Wanderer and Whitman.

Parkers Run

Giant Coloring Books—1978. 22″ × 17″.
   Uncharted World. ....$25–$35
   War in Space. ....$25–$35

Pioneer

Formerly Schuster and Schuster. All books from this publisher are unlicensed trade paperbacks. Production quality varies considerably.

Best of Enterprise Incidents: The Magazine for Star Trek Fans—1992. Edited by James Van Hise. ....$10–$15
Deep Space Nine, A Celebration—1993. James Van Hise.
....$15–$20
Deep Space Nine Crew Book—1993. James Van Hise. ....
....$15–$20
History of Trek, The—1992. James Van Hise. ....
....$15–$20
Let's Trek: The Budget Guide to the Federation—1994. James Van Hise. ....$15–$20
Man Between the Ears: Star Trek's Leonard Nimoy—1992. James Van Hise. ....$15–$20
Man Who Created Star Trek: Gene Roddenberry, The—1992. James Van Hise. ....$15–$20
New Trek Encyclopedia—1992. (Includes at least one revision.) ....$20–$22
New Trek Encyclopedia—1994. Updated version of earlier encyclopedia. ....$20–$22
Next Generation Crew Book, The—1994. James Van Hise.
....$15–$20
Trek Crew Book, The—1989. James Van Hise. .....$10–$15
Trek: Deep Space Nine—1993. Scott Nance. ....$15–$20
Trek: Deep Space Nine, The Unauthorized Story—1993. James Van Hise. ....$20–$22
Trek Fan's Handbook, The—1992. James Van Hise. ....
....$10–$15
Trek in the 24th Century—1994. James Van Hise. ....
....$15–$20
Trek: The Lost Years—1992. Edward Gross. ....$13–$15
Trek: The Making of the Movies—1992. James Van Hise.
....$15–$20
Trek: The Next Generation—1991. James Van Hise. ....
....$15–$20
Trek: The Next Generation Tribute Book—1993. James Van Hise. ....$15–$20
Trek: The Printed Adventures—1993. James Van Hise. ....
....$15–$20

Trek: The Unauthorized Next Generation—1992. James Van Hise. ....$15–$20
Twenty-fifth Anniversary Trek Tribute—1991. James Van Hise. ....$15–$20
Trek vs. Next Generation—1993. James Van Hise. ....$15–$20

Playboy Press

Making of Star Trek Conventions, The (see Doubleday).
Startoons—1979. Joan Winston. Comic strips compiled into paperback form. ....$15–$25

Pocket

This company, owned by Paramount, is the sole publisher of Star Trek novels and studio-approved reference books at this time.

Reference Books

Art of Star Trek, The—1995. Judith and Garfield Reeves-Stevens. Hardback. ....$50–$65
Captain's Log: Star Trek V, The Final Frontier—1989. Lisabeth Shatner. A personal account of the making of the movie. Trade paperback. ....$9–$11
Chekov's Enterprise—1980. Walter Koenig. A personal journal of the making of Star Trek: The Motion Picture. Paperback. ....$25–$40
    Reprint—1991. Intergalactic Press. Trade paperback. ....$10–$15
Ferengi Rules of Acquisition, The—1995. Ira Steven Behr. ....$6–$8
Inside Star Trek—1996. Herbert F. Solow and Robert H. Justman. Hardcover. ....$30–$35
Klingon Dictionary—1985. Mark Okrand. English/Klingon Klingon/English. Paperback. ....$5–$7
Klingon Way, The—1996. Mark Okrand. Trade paperback. ....$12–$15
Make It So—1995. Wess Roberts, Ph.D., and Bill Ross. Hardback. ....$22–$25
Making of Star Trek: Deep Space Nine—1994. Judith and Garfield Reeves-Stevens. Trade paperback. ....$20–$25
Making of Star Trek II: The Wrath of Khan—1982. Allan Asherman. Trade paperback. ....$20–$35
Monsters of Star Trek, The—1980. D. Cohen. Reprints are published by Archway, a division of Pocket Books. .....$2–$5
Mr. Scott's Guide to the Enterprise—1987. Shane Johnson. Trade paperback. ....$10–$12
Official Star Trek Quiz Book, The—1985. Mitchell Magilo. Trade paperback. ....$8–$15
Official Star Trek Trivia Book, The—1980. Rafe Needleman.
    Paperback. ....$8–$12
    Hardcover. ....$10–$15

Star Trek Chronology—1993. Michael Okuda and Denise Okuda. Trade paperback. ....$16–$20
Star Trek Compendium, The—1993. Allan Asherman. Trade paperback. ....$13–$15

NOTE: This current book has a white cover and covers material through Star Trek VI: The Undiscovered Country. Two earlier versions (red and black covers) exist but have little collectible value.

Star Trek Encyclopedia, The—1994. Michael Okuda, Denise Okuda, and Debbie Mirek. Trade paperback (also available as hardback). ....$20–$25
Star Trek Interview Book—1988. Allan Asherman. Trade paperback. ....$7–$9
Star Trek: The Motion Picture Photostory—1980. Richard J. Anobile. Color throughout. ....$12–$20
Star Trek: The Next Generation Companion—1995. Larry Nemecek. Trade paperback. ....$16–$20

NOTE: This current edition has a red cover and covers all seven seasons of the series. An earlier, blue-covered edition exists but has little collectible value.

Star Trek: The Next Generation Technical Manual—1991. Rick Sternbach and Michael Okuda. ....$13–$15
Star Trek: The Next Generation U.S.S. Enterprise NCC 1701-D Blueprints—1996. Rick Sternbach. Thirteen folded sheets and a 16-page booklet in a boxed set. ....$20–$25
Star Trek II: The Wrath of Khan Photostory (published by Methuen in the U.K.)—1982. Black and white. .....$5–$10
Star Trek III: The Search for Spock Storybook—1984. Lawrence Weinberg. Oversized hardback and trade paperback formats. ....$6–$10
Star Trek "Where No One Has Gone Before"—1994. J.M. Dillard. Hardcover. This book was available with two different dust jacket options—one picturing the movie version Enterprise and one picturing the Enterprise 1701-D. Neither version is more prevalent than the other. A Star Trek: Generations bookmark was also included. ....$45–$55
Strange and Amazing Facts About Star Trek—1986. Daniel Cohen. ....$2–$4
To the Stars—1994. George Takei. Hardcover. ....$22–$25
Worlds of the Federation—Pocket. 1989. Shane Johnson. Trade paperback. ....$11–$13

Star Trek Novels

Pocket keeps virtually all books in their numerous ongoing series in print at all times. Books in the regular series are numbered and are presented here by number, which is also the chronological order in which they were published. Novels deemed outstanding by the publisher for one reason or other are not numbered and appear alphabetically following the numbered books. Many of the books were also printed in hardback form, either as an earlier release or as book club editions.

Hardback Star Trek novels generally have values two to three times that of their paperback counterparts. Foreign editions are common and have the same approximate value.

NOTE: Many Star Trek novels have also been released in audio formats read by various stars of the series. See Records, Audio Tapes, and Compact Discs section of this book.

ORIGINAL STAR TREK NOVELS, NUMBERED

#1 Star Trek: The Motion Picture—1979. Gene Roddenberry. Regular Edition. ....$5–$8
Special Autographed Hardcover, with slipcase (limited to 500 copies). ....$150–$250
#2 The Entropy Effect—1981. Vonda McIntyre. ......$5–$8
#3 The Klingon Gambit—1981. Robert Vardeman. ....$5–$8
#4 The Covenant of the Crown—1981. Howard Weinstein. ....$5–$8
#5 The Prometheus Design—1982. S. Marshak and M. Culbreath. ....$5–$8
#6 The Abode of Life—1982. Lee Corey. ....$5–$8
#7 Star Trek II: The Wrath of Khan—1982. Vonda McIntyre. ....$5–$8
#8 Black Fire—1982. Sonni Cooper. ....$5–$8
#9 Triangle—1983. S. Marshak and M. Culbreath. ....$5–$8
#10 Web of the Romulans—1983. M.S. Murdock. ..$5–$8
#11 Yesterday's Son—1983. A.C. Crispin. ....$5–$8
#12 Mutiny on the Enterprise—1983. Robert Vardeman. ....$5–$8
#13 The Wounded Sky—1983. Diane Duane. ....$5–$8
#14 The Trellisane Confrontation—1984. David Dvorkin. ....$5–$8
#15 Corona—1984. Greg Bear. ....$5–$8
#16 The Final Reflection—1984. John M. Ford. ....$5–$8
#17 Star Trek III: The Search for Spock—1984. Vonda McIntyre. ....$5–$8
#18 My Enemy, My Ally—1984. Diane Duane. ....$5–$8
#19 The Tears of the Singers—1984. Melinda Snodgrass. ....$5–$8
#20 The Vulcan Academy Murders—1984. Jean Lorrah. ..
....$5–$8
#21 Uhura's Song—1985. Janet Kagan. ....$5–$8
#22 Shadow Lord—1985. Laurence Yep. ....$5–$8
#23 Ishmael—1985. Barbara Hambly. ....$5–$8
#24 Killing Time—1985. Della Van Hise. Original printings of this book (distinguishable by raised lettering in the title) contained several paragraphs which were objectionable to Paramount and were removed from later printings.
First Printing. ....$10–$15
Subsequent Printings. ....$5–$8
#25 Dwellers in the Crucible—1985. Margaret W. Bonanno.
....$5–$8
#26 Pawns and Symbols—1985. Majliss Larson. .....$5–$8
#27 Mindshadow—1986. J.M. Dillard. ....$5–$8
#28 Crisis on Centaurus—1986. Brad Furguson. ......$5–$8
#29 Dreadnought!—1986. Diane Carey. ....$5–$8
#30 Demons—1986. J.M. Dillard. ....$5–$8

#31 Battlestations!—1986. Diane Carey. ....$5–$8
#32 Chain of Attack—1987. Gene DeWeese. ....$5–$8
#33 Deep Domain—1987. Howard Weinstein. ....$5–$8
#34 Dreams of the Raven—1987. Carmen Carter. ....$5–$8
#35 The Romulan Way—1987. D. Duane and P. Norwood.
....$5–$8
#36 How Much for Just the Planet?—1987. John M. Ford.
....$5–$8
#37 Bloodthirst—1987. J.M. Dillard. ....$5–$8
#38 The IDIC Epidemic—1988. Jean Lorrah. ....$5–$8
#39 Time for Yesterday—1988. A.C. Crispin. ....$5–$8
#40 Timetrap—1988. David Dvorkin. ....$5–$8
#41 The Three-Minute Universe—1988. Barbara Paul. .....
....$5–$8
#42 Memory Prime—1988. Gar and Judith Reeves-Stevens. ....$5–$8
#43 The Final Nexus—1988. Gene DeWeese. ....$5–$8
#44 Vulcan's Glory—1989. D.C. Fontana. ....$5–$8
#45 Double, Double—1989. Michael Jan Friedman. ..$5–$8
#46 The Cry of the Onlies—1989. Judy Klass. ....$5–$8
#47 The Kobayashi Maru—1989. Julia Ecklar. ....$5–$8
#48 Rules of Engagement—1990. Peter Norwood. ...$5–$8
#49 The Pandora Principle—1990. Carolyn Clowes. ....
....$5–$8
#50 Doctor's Orders—1990. Diane Duane. ....$5–$8
#51 Enemy Unseen—1991. V.E. Mitchell. ....$5–$8
#52 Home Is the Hunter—1991. Dana Kramer-Rolls. ....
....$5–$8
#53 Ghost Walker—1991. Barbara Hambly. ....$5–$8
#54 A Flag Full of Stars—1991. Brad Ferguson. ....$5–$8
#55 Renegade—1991. Gene DeWeese. ....$5–$8
#56 Legacy—1991. Michael Jan Friedman. ....$5–$8
#57 The Rift—1991. Peter David. ....$5–$8
#58 Face of Fire—1992. Michael Jan Friedman. ....$5–$8
#59 The Disinherited—1992. P. David, M.J. Friedman, and R. Greenberger. ....$5–$8
#60 Ice Trap—1992. L.A. Graf. ....$5–$8
#61 Sanctuary—1992. John Vornholt. ....$5–$8
#62 Death Count—1992. L.A. Graf. ....$5–$8
#63 Shell Game—1993. Melissa Crandall. ....$5–$8
#64 The Starship Trap—1993. Mel Gilden. ....$5–$8
#65   Windows on a Lost World—1993. V.E. Mitchell. ......
....$5–$8
#66 From the Depths—1993. Victor Milan. ....$5–$8
#67 The Great Starship Race—1993. Diane Carey. .$5–$8
#68 Firestorm—1994. L.A. Graf. ....$5–$8
#69 The Patrian Transgressions—1994. Simon Hawke. ....
....$5–$8
#70 Traitor Winds—1994. L.A. Graf. ....$5–$8
#71 Crossroad—1994. Barbara Hambly. ....$5–$8
#72 The Better Man—1994. Howard Weinstein. ......$5–$8
#73 Recovery—1995. J.M. Dillard. ....$5–$8
#74 The Fearful Summons—1995. Denny Martin Flinn. ....
....$5–$8
#75 First Frontier—1995. Diane Carey and Dr. James L. Kirkland. ....$5–$8

#76 The Captain's Daughter—1995. Peter David. ...$5–$8
#77 Twilight's End—1996. Jerry Oltion. ....$5–$8
#78 The Rings of Tautee—1996. D.W. Smith and K.K. Rusch. ....$5–$8

ORIGINAL STAR TREK NOVELS, UNNUMBERED

Ashes of Eden, The—1996. William Shatner. ....$5–$8
Best Destiny—1993. Diane Duane. ....$5–$8
Enterprise—1986. Vonda McIntyre. ....$5–$8
Federation—1995. Judith and Garfield Reeves-Stevens. ......
....$5–$8
Final Frontier—1988. Diane Carey. ....$5–$8
Lost Years, The—1990. J.M. Dillard. ....$5–$8
Prime Directive—1990. Garfield and Judith Reeves-Stevens.
....$5–$8
Probe—1992. Margaret Bonanno. ....$5–$8
Return, The—1996. William Shatner. ....$5–$8
Sarek—1994. A.C. Crispin. ....$5–$8
Shadows on the Sun—1994. Michael Jan Friedman. ....
....$5–$8
Spock's World—1988. Diane Duane. ....$5–$8
Star Trek IV: The Voyage Home—1986. Vonda McIntyre.
....$5–$8
Star Trek V: The Final Frontier—1989. J.M. Dillard. ....
....$5–$8
Star Trek VI: The Undiscovered Country. ....$5–$8
Strangers from the Sky—1987. Margaret Bonanno. ....
....$5–$8

STAR TREK: THE NEXT GENERATION NOVELS, NUMBERED

#1 Ghost Ship—1988. Diane Carey. ....$5–$8
#2 The Peacekeepers—1988. Gene DeWeese. ....$5–$8
#3 The Children of Hamlin—1988. Carmen Carter. .$5–$8
#4 Survivors—1989. Jean Lorrah. ....$5–$8
#5 Strike Zone—1989. Peter David. ....$5–$8
#6 Power Hungry—1989. Howard Weinstein. ....$5–$8
#7 Masks—1989. John Vornholt. ....$5–$8
#8 The Captain's Honor—1989. P. David and D. Dvorkin.
....$5–$8
#9 A Call to Darkness—1989. Michael Jan Friedman. ....
....$5–$8
#10 A Rock and a Hard Place—1990. Peter David. ....
....$5–$8
#11 Gulliver's Fugitives—1990. Keith Sharee. ....$5–$8
#12 Doomsday World—1990. C. Carter, P. David, M.J. Friedman, and R. Greensberger. ....$5–$8
#13 The Eyes of the Beholders—1990. A.C. Crispin. ....
....$5–$8
#14 Exiles—1990. Howard Weinstein. ....$5–$8
#15 Fortune's Light—1991. Michael Jan Friedman. ....
....$5–$8
#16 Contamination—1991. John Vornholt. ....$5–$8
#17 Boogeyman—1991. Mel Gilden. ....$5–$8
#18 Q-in-Law—1991. Peter David. ....$5–$8
#19 Perchance to Dream—1991. Howard Weinstein. ....
....$5–$8

#20 Spartacus—1992. T.L. Mancour. ....$5–$8
#21 Chains of Command—1992. W.A. McCoy and E.L. Flood. ....$5–$8
#22 Imbalance—1992. V.E. Mitchell. ....$5–$8
#23 War Drums—1992. John Vornholt. ....$5–$8
#24 Nightshade—1992. Laurell K. Hamilton. ....$5–$8
#25 Grounded—1993. David Bischoff. ....$5–$8
#26 The Romulan Prize—1993. Simon Hawke. ....$5–$8
#27 Guises of the Mind—1993. Rebecca Neason. .....$5–$8
#28 Here There Be Dragons—1993. John Peel. ....$5–$8
#29 Sins of Commission—1994. Susan Wright. ....$5–$8
#30 Debtors' Planet—1994. W.R. Thompson. ....$5–$8
#31 Foreign Foes—1994. D. Galanter and G. Brodeur. ....
....$5–$8
#32 Requiem—1994. M.J. Friedman and Kevin Ryan. ....
....$5–$8
#33 Balance of Power—1995. Dafydd Ab Hugh. ......$5–$8
#34 Blaze of Glory—1995. Simon Hawke. ....$5–$8
#35 Romulan Stratagem—1995. Robert Greenberger. ....
....$5–$8
#36 Into the Nebula—1995. Gene DeWeese. ....$5–$8
#37 The Last Stand—1995. Brad Ferguson. ....$5–$8
#38 Dragon's Honor—1996. Kij Johnson and Greg Fox. ....
....$5–$8
#39 Rogue Saucer—1996. John Vornholt. ....$5–$8
#40 Possession—1996. J.M. Dillard and K. O'Malley.
....$5–$8

STAR TREK: THE NEXT GENERATION NOVELS, UNNUMBERED

All Good Things—1995. Michael Jan Friedman. ....$5–$8
Crossover—1995. Michael Jan Friedman. ....$5–$8
Dark Mirror—1994. Diane Duane. ....$5–$8
Descent—1993. Diane Carey. ....$5–$8
Devil's Heart, The—1994. Carmen Carter. ....$5–$8
Encounter at Farpoint—1987. David Gerrold. ....$5–$8
Imzadi—1993. Peter David. ....$5–$8
Metamorphosis—1990. Jean Lorrah. ....$5–$8
Q-Squared—1995. Peter David. ....$5–$8
Relics—1992. Michael Jan Friedman. ....$5–$8
Reunion—1991. Michael Jan Friedman. ....$5–$8
Star Trek: Generations—1995. ....$5–$8
Unification—1991. Jeri Taylor. ....$5–$8
Vendetta—1991. Peter David. ....$5–$8

STAR TREK: DEEP SPACE NINE NOVELS, NUMBERED

#1 Emissary—1995. J.M. Dillard. ....$5–$8
#2 The Siege—1993. Peter David. ....$5–$8
#3 Bloodletter—1993. K.W. Jeter. ....$5–$8
#4 The Big Game—1993. Sandy Schofield. ....$5–$8
#5 Fallen Heroes—1994. Dafydd Ab Hugh. ....$5–$8
#6 Betrayal—1994. Lois Tilton. ....$5–$8
#7 Warchild—1994. Esther Friesner. ....$5–$8
#8 Antimatter—1994. John Vornholt. ....$5–$8
#9 Proud Helios—Melissa Scott. ....$5–$8
#10 Valhalla—1995. Nathan Archer. ....$5–$8

#11 Devil in the Sky—1995. G. Cox and J.G. Betancourt.
....$5–$8
#12 The Laertian Gamble—1995. Robert Scheckley. ....
....$5–$8
#13 Station Rage—1995. Diane Carey. ....$5–$8
#14 The Long Night—1996. D.W. Smith and K.K. Rusch.
....$5–$8
#15 Objective Bajor—1996. Diane Carey. ....$5–$8

STAR TREK: DEEP SPACE NINE NOVELS, UNNUMBERED
Search, The—1994. Diane Carey. ....$5–$8
Warped—1996. K.W. Jeter. ....$5–$8
Way of the Warrior, The—1995, Diane Carey. ....$5–$8

STAR TREK: VOYAGER NOVELS, NUMBERED
#1 Caretaker—1995. L.A. Graf. ....$5–$8
#2 The Escape—1995. D.W. Smithe and K.K. Rusch. ....
....$5–$8
#3 Ragnarok—1995. Nathan Archer. ....$5–$8
#4 Violations—1995. Susan Wright. ....$5–$8
#5 Incident at Arbuk—1995. Gregory Betancourt. ......$5–$8
#6 The Murdered Sun—1996. Christie Golden. ....$5–$8
#7 Ghost of a Chance—1996. M. Garland and C. McGraw.
....$5–$8
#8 Cybersong—1996. S.N. Lewitt. ....$5–$8

Star Trek: The Next Generation Starfleet Academy Novels (Young Readers):
#1 Worf's First Adventure—1993. Peter David. ......$4–$6
#2 Line of Fire—1993. Peter David. ....$4–$6
#3 Survival—1993. Peter David. ....$4–$6
#4 Capture the Flag—1994. John Vornholt. ....$4–$6
#5 Atlantis Station—1994. V.E. Mitchell. ....$4–$6
#6 Mystery of the Missing Crew—1995. Michael Jan
Friedman. ....$4–$6
#7 Secret of the Lizard People—1995. Michael Jan Friedman.
....$4–$6
#8 Starfall—1995. Brad and Barbara Strickland. ....$4–$6
#9 Nova Command—1995. Brad and Barbara Strickland.
....$4–$6
#10 Loyalties—1996. Patricia Barnes Svarney. ....$4–$6
Star Trek: Generations (Young Readers Movie Adaptation)—1994. John Vornholt. ....$4–$6

Star Trek: Deep Space Nine Novels (Young Readers):
#1 The Star Ghost—1994. Brad Strickland. ....$4–$6
#2 Stowaways—1994. Brad Strickland. ....$4–$6
#3 Prisoners of Peace—1994. John Peel. ....$4–$6
#4 The Pet—1995. Mel Gilden and Ted Pedersen. .....$4–$6
#5 Arcade—1995. Diana G. Gallagher. ....$4–$6
#6 Field Trip—1995. John Peel. ....$4–$6
#7 Gypsy World—1996. Ted Pederson. ....$4–$6
#8 Highest Score—1996. Kem Antilles. ....$4–$6

Putnam

Beyond Uhura—1994. Nichelle Nichols. Hardcover. ....
....$22–$25

Random House

Giant in the Universe—1977. Kay Wood. Oversized hard-back pop-up book. ....$35–$60
Prisoner of Vega—1977. S. Lerner and C. Cerf. Hardback children's book. Glossy or rough-textured library binding. ....
....$30–$45
Star Trek Action Toy Book—1976. James Razzi. .....$20–$30
Trillions of Trilligs—1977. C. Cerf and S. Lerner. Oversized hardback pop-up book. ....$35–$60
Truth Machine, The—C. Cerf and S. Lerner. Hardback children's book. Glossy or rough-textured library bindings. ....
....$30–$45

Roc

Best of Trek (see Signet).

Running Press

Crossword Puzzle—1976. In the form of large color poster. Puzzle is shaped like Enterprise. Comes in envelope with color artwork. ....$6–$10

Saalfield

Star Trek Coloring Books—1975.
    #1 (Spock and Kirk covers). ....$10–$15
    #2 (Spock close-up cover). ....$10–$15
Star Trek Punch-Out and Play Album—1975. ....
....$15–$25

Schiffer

A Trekker's Guide to Collectibles—1996. Jeffrey B. Snyder. Trade paperback. ....$25–$30

Schuster and Schuster

All trade paperbacks. This publisher later changed their company name to Pioneer and had previously published magazines as New Media Publishing.

Creating the Next Generation—1988. Edward Gross. ....
....$15–$20

Making of the Next Generation (Part One)—1988. Edward Gross. ....$15–$20
Making of the Next Generation (Part Two)—1988. Edward Gross. ....$15–$20
Next Generation, The Complete Guide—1988. Edward Gross. ....$15–$20

Sheed, Andrews, and McNeel

Star Trek: Good News in Modern Images—1976. Sheed, Andrews, and McNeel. Betsy Caprio.
    Hardback. ....$35–$60
    Paperback. ....$25–$50

Signet

Best of Trek, The—1978–1991. Walter Irwin and G.B. Love. Based on "Trek," a high-quality fan-published magazine from the '70s. Each book is a collection of articles from different sources concerning Star Trek characters, actors, fan activities, etc. (#15 and #16 were published by ROC).
    #1 1978. ....$10–$15
    #2 1980. ....$10–$15
    #3 1981. ....$10–$15
    #4 1981. ....$10–$15
    #5 1982. ....$10–$15
    #6 1983. ....$10–$15
    #7 1984. ....$10–$15
    #8 1985. ....$10–$15
    #9 1985. ....$10–$15
    #10 1986. ....$10–$15
    #11 1986. ....$10–$15
    #12 1987. ....$10–$15
    #13 1988. ....$10–$15
    #14 1988. ....$10–$15
    #15 1990 (ROC). ....$6–$10
    #16 1991 (ROC). ....$4–$6
Best of the Best of Trek—1990. Trade paperback. ....$15–$25
Best of the Best of Trek II—1992. Trade paperback. ....$12–$15
Star Trek Quiz Book—1977. B. Andrew with B. Dunning. Later reprints are titled *Trekkie Quiz Book.* ....$10–$12

St. Martins

Star Wreck Parodies—1990–1994. Leah Rewolinski.
    Star Wreck: The Generation Gap—1990. ....$4–$6
    Star Wreck 2: The Attack of the Jargonites—1992. .$4–$6
    Star Wreck 3: Time Warped—1992. ....$4–$6

    Star Wreck 4: Live Long and Profit—1993. ....$4–$6
    Star Wreck 5: The Undiscovered Nursing Home—1993. ....$4–$6
    Star Wreck 6: Geek Space Nine—1994. ....$4–$6

Star

Who's Who in Star Trek—1984. John Townsley. .....$2–$5

Wallaby

Make Your Own Costume Book—1979. Lynn Edelman Schnurnberger. Simplified costume patterns from Star Trek: The Motion Picture.
    Oversized Hardback. ....$15–$25
    Trade Paperback. ....$10–$20
Making of Star Trek: The Motion Picture—1980. Susan Sackett with Gene Roddenberry.
    Trade Paperback. ....$30–$40
    Hardcover. ....$40–$60
Star Trek Compendium. Allan Asherman. Trade paperback.
    Original edition—1981. Wallaby. Blue cover. ....$10–$15
    British (Star) edition—1983. Purple cover. ....$10–$15
    First U.S. revision—1986. Pocket. Red cover. .....$10–$15
    Second U.S. revision—1989. Pocket. Black cover. ....$10–$15
Star Trek Spaceflight Chronology—1980. Stan Goldstein and Fred Goldstein. Trade paperback. ....$50–$75
Star Trek: The Motion Picture Blueprints—1980. David Kimble. Fourteen sheets of ship and set schematics from the movie. Packaged in a blue plastic pouch with a clear front panel and cover sheet. ....$35–$45
Star Trek: The Motion Picture Peel-Off Graphics Books—1979. Lee Cole. Peel-off stickers and designs from the movie. ....$35–$45

Wanderer

Coloring Books.
    Star Trek Giant Coloring Book #1—1979. STTMP. ....$10–$15
    Star Trek Giant Coloring Book #2—1979. STTMP. ....$10–$15
    Star Trek Activity Book—1986. ....$5–$10
    Star Trek Adventure Coloring Book—1986. ....$5–$10
    Star Trek Alien Coloring Book—1986. ....$5–$10
    Star Trek Puzzle Coloring Book—1986. ....$5–$10

NOTE: Reprints were done by Merrigold Press (both companies are subsidiaries of Western Publishing).

Star Trek II Biographies—1982. William Rotsler. Trade paperback. ....$10–$15

Star Trek II Distress Call—1982. William Rotsler. Trade paperback. A plot-your-own-adventure story. ....$10–$15

Star Trek II Short Stories—1982. William Rotsler. Trade paperback. ....$10–$15

Star Trek III Movie Trivia—1984. William Rotsler. Shrink-wrapped with pen. ....$10–$15

Star Trek III: The Search for Spock, More Movie Trivia—1984. Comes with pen to reveal answers. ....
....$10–$15

Star Trek III Short Stories—1984. William Rotsler. Five stories. Trade paperback. ....$10–$15

Star Trek III: The Vulcan Treasure (Ravette in U.K.)—1984. William Rotsler. Plot-Your-Own-Adventure. ....
....$10–$15

Star Trek IV: The Voyage Home—1986. Photo story book.
....$15–$20

Star Trek Make-a-Game Book—1979. Bruce and Greg Nash. ....$15–$25

Star Trek: The Motion Picture Pop-Up Book—1980. Tor Lokvig and Chuck Murphy. ....$15–$35

Star Trek: The Motion Picture Bridge Punch-Out Book—1979. ....$15–$25

Star Trek: The Motion Picture U.S.S. Enterprise Punch-Out Book—1979. ....$25–$35

Warner

Meaning in Star Trek—1977. Karen Blair. Paperback version of the hardback published by Anima. ....$20–$25

Western

Mission to Horatius—1968. Mack Reynolds. Hardback. First professional Star Trek novel. ....$50–$75.

Whitman

Coloring Books—1978. Books had original TV artwork covers.
A Blast of Activities. ....$5–$10
A Launch into Fun. ....$5–$10
Far-Out Fun. ....$5–$10
Futuristic Fun. ....$5–$10
Jeopardy at Jutterdon (sticker book). ....$5–$10
Planet Ecnal's Dilemma. ....$5–$10
Rescue at Raylo. ....$5–$10

NOTE: Books were re-issued in abridged form in 1979 by Merrigold (both Whitman and Merrigold are divisions of Western Publishing) with Star Trek: The Motion Picture covers. Prices are the same.

William Morrow and Company

Boldly Live as You've Never Lived Before—1995. Richard Raben and Hiyaguha Cohen. Life lessons from Star Trek. Hardback. ....$15–$17

Vulcan Books

My Stars—1980. M.C. Goodwin. Collection of comic strips about Star Trek and the Enterprise. ....$15–$25

Zebra Books

Trivia Mania, Star Trek—1985. Xavier Einstein. ....
....$15–$25

Ballantine Books Star Trek Blueprints

Star Trek Log Books, original and reprint

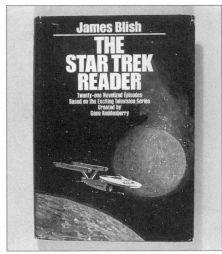

Star Trek Episode Adaptations by James Blish, hardcover

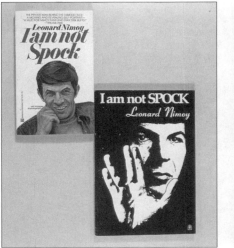

Celestial Arts (right) and Del Rey (left) "I Am Not Spock" Books

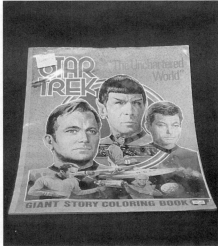

Giant Coloring Book

Trek: *Deep Space Nine*

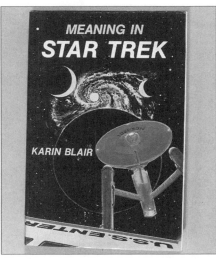

"Meaning in Star Trek" Hardcover Book

"Make It So" Hardcover Book

Next Generation Young Reader Novel

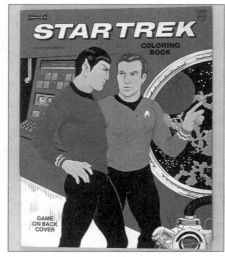

Saalfield Coloring Book

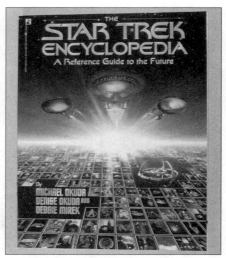

Star Trek Encyclopedia

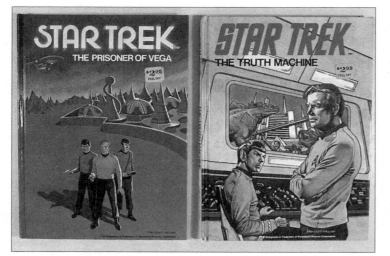

Children's Books

Gold Key Star Trek Comic Book #1 (photo cover)

Golden Press Enterprise Log #1

DC Comics Star Trek Comic Book

Star Trek Parody Comic Book

BUMPER STICKERS

Simple bumper stickers, printed in a variety of colors and styles onto paper, vinyl, or mylar (a shiny plastic material), come in a variety of sizes and styles. They can be quickly and easily manufactured, are very popular, inexpensive novelty items, and are virtually worthless as collectibles. The ones listed below are all licensed (or at least tolerated) by Paramount. There are, of course, many, many more unlicensed ones.

INVESTMENT POTENTIAL
Poor.

CARE
Be careful to keep the backing on any bumper sticker or decal you do not intend to apply to a surface. If you fold it for storage be sure the sticky surface is inside the crease to avoid having it stick to other items at the seam of the backing. Paper bumper stickers are not very durable. In addition to deteriorating when wet, they tend to fade.

SECTION NOTES
Section is organized alphabetically by manufacturer. All are bumper stickers unless otherwise noted.

Aviva

(1979)

This series of stickers, made at the time of Star Trek: The Motion Picture, were two or three colors printed on vinyl.

Beam Me Up Mr. Spock. ....$2–$3
Dr. McCoy Doesn't Make House Calls. ....$2–$3
Federation Vehicle Official Use Only. ....$2–$3
I Am a Trekkie. ....$2–$3

Live Long and Prosper. ....$2–$3
Star Trek: The Motion Picture. ....$2–$3

Creation

Ongoing series has three- or four-color artwork on white vinyl.

Beam Me Up Scotty/Star Trek, pictures Scotty. ....$2–$3
Federation Shuttlecraft NCC-1701/7 Galileo. ....$2–$3
"Hailing Frequencies Open"/Star Trek, pictures Uhura. ....
....$2–$3
"He's Dead Jim"/Star Trek, pictures McCoy. ....$2–$3
Kirk/Spock in '92. ....$2–$3
Kirk/Spock in '96. ....$2–$3
Live Long and Prosper, hand with Vulcan salute. ......$2–$3
My Other Vehicle Is a Federation Starship. ....$2–$3
My Other Vehicle Is a Klingon Bird of Prey. ....$2–$3
My Other Vehicle Is a Romulan Warbird. ....$2–$3
Picard/Riker in '92. ....$2–$3
Picard/Riker in '96. ....$2–$3
Starfleet Academy, pictures Academy symbol. ....$2–$3
Starfleet Academy/San Francisco, Earth "Ex Astris, Scientia" (with Starfleet symbol), window decal, two-color on clear plastic backing. ....$2–$3
This Vehicle Travels at Warpspeed, pictures Enterprise-D.
....$2–$3
United Federation of Planets Delegate, with UFP seal. ....
....$2–$3
United Federation of Planets Galaxy Class Starship/USS Enterprise NCC-1701-D. ....$2–$3
USS Enterprise NCC-1701. ....$2–$3
USS Enterprise NCC-1701-A. ....$2–$3
Vulcan Science Academy . . . for the logical education, pictures IDIC. ....$2–$3
Vulcan Science Academy (with IDIC), window decal, two-color on clear plastic backing. ....$2–$3

Lincoln Enterprises

All black lettering on colored background.

Bring Back the Enterprise. ....$1–$2
Don't Tailgate, This Is a Klingon War Cruiser. ....$1–$2
Government Vehicle, Vulcan Embassy. ....$1–$2
The Human Adventure Is Just Beginning. ....$1–$2
I Am a Carbon Unit. ....$1–$2
I Grok Spock. ....$1–$2
Jaws Is a Klingon Minnow, with picture. ....$1–$2
Live Long and Prosper. ....$1–$2

Mr. Spock for President. ....$1–$2
Mr. Spock Phone Home. ....$1–$2
Star Trek Lives. ....$1–$2
Support the Right to Arm Klingons. ....$1–$2
Vote Yes on Star Trek. ....$1–$2
We Want Star Trek III. ....$1–$2
Smile (picture) **If You Like Star Trek.** ....$1–$2
Don't Tailgate—This Is a Ferengi War Cruiser. .....$1–$2
**Star Trek The Next Generation—The 24th Century Is
Just Beginning.** ....$1–$2
I Am Fully Functional—Data. ....$1–$2
Support Your Local Android—Data. ....$1–$2

Creation Star Trek Bumper Sticker

BUTTONS

The primary thing to consider about collecting buttons is the ease of manufacture. Simple button-making machines are available to the hobbyist for about $20. In addition, there are companies that will produce relatively small quantities of buttons for a modest price. Word buttons are particularly easy. They can be hand-lettered or run off cheaply at any local Quickprint. As for picture buttons, it is easy and perfectly legal to cut any picture out of a magazine and incorporate it into a button. For this reason we are only including licensed buttons in this section. It is arguable whether certain other buttons may have collector value, especially those from conventions, but because they could be so easily duplicated it is unlikely they would ever become very valuable. "Button" here is used to refer to items printed directly onto a metal pinback surface or printed onto paper affixed to a pinback. For cloisonné, enamel, or epoxy surfaced pins sometimes referred to as buttons, see the Jewelry section of this book.

INVESTMENT POTENTIAL
Poor.

CARE
Buttons are fairly durable and require little in the way of care outside of protecting them from moisture, which may cause them to warp or rust.

SECTION NOTES
Section is organized alphabetically by manufacturer.

Aviva

From Star Trek: The Motion Picture. 1979. Color licensed buttons, 2¼″. All have logo in addition to picture.

Group Shot, on the bridge. ....$2–$3

Kirk, in gray uniform. ....$2–$3
Kirk, standing, blue background. ....$2–$3
Kirk, Spock, and McCoy. ....$2–$3
Spock, in uniform. ....$2–$3
Spock, in Vulcan attire. ....$2–$3

Button-Up

(Original TV Series)

These are 1½″ licensed color buttons. 1984.

Capt. Kirk, close-up of head. ....$1–$2
Enterprise. ....$1–$2
Group Shot, Dr. McCoy, Lt. Uhura, and Chekov. ....$1–$2
Group Shot, Capt. Kirk, Dr. McCoy, and Mr. Spock. .$1–$2
Kirk and Dr. McCoy, head shots. ....$1–$2
Kirk and Mr. Spock, close-up from "Errand of Mercy." ......
....$1–$2
Lt. Sulu, close-up of head. ....$1–$2
Starships, the Enterprise and Constellation. ....$1–$2

Button-Up

(Star Trek III: The Search for Spock)

These are 1½″ licensed color buttons. 1984. All have logo in addition to photo.

Capt. Kirk, close-up of head. ....$1–$2
Capt. Kirk, head and shoulders shot. ....$1–$2
Comdr. Chekov, close-up of head. ....$1–$2

Comdr. Sulu, close-up of head. ....$1–$2
Comdr. Uhura, holding a phaser. ....$1–$2
David Marcus, head and shoulders shot. ....$1–$2
Dr. McCoy. ....$1–$2
Kruge, Klingon, close-up of head. ....$1–$2
Lt. Saavik, close-up of head. ....$1–$2
Logo from Star Trek III. ....$1–$2
Spock, in Vulcan garb. ....$1–$2

Creation Entertainment

Rectangular color photo or word buttons, 2″ × 3″. 1992/1995.

Borg. ....$1–$3
Borg Ship. ....$1–$3
Crew (original), in movie uniforms. ....$1–$3
Data. ....$1–$3
Dax. ....$1–$3
Deep Space Nine Space Station. ....$1–$3
Dr. Crusher. ....$1–$3
Enterprise (original). ....$1–$3
Enterprise-A. ....$1–$3
Enterprise-D. ....$1–$3
Ferengi. ....$1–$3
Kira. ....$1–$3
Kirk and Spock. ....$1–$3
Klingon. ....$1–$3
Klingon Bird-of-Prey. ....$1–$3
Odo. ....$1–$3
Picard. ....$1–$3
Quark. ....$1–$3
Romulan. ....$1–$3
Romulan Bird-of-Prey. ....$1–$3
Troi. ....$1–$3
UFP Delegate Badges
    Earth (United Nations symbol). ....$1–$3
    Klingon (Klingon symbol). ....$1–$3
    Visitor. ....$1–$3
    Vulcan (IDIC symbol). ....$1–$3
Vulcan. ....$1–$3
Worf. ....$1–$3

Image Products

From Star Trek: The Wrath of Kahn, 3″ buttons. 1982. Color.
Logo and photo. Licensed.

Enterprise. ....$2–$3
Group Shot. ....$2–$3
Khan. ....$2–$3
Kirk. ....$2–$3
Spock. ....$2–$3

Langley & Associates

An early manufacturer of licensed merchandise, now out of
business. 1976. 2¼″. Color.

Capt. Kirk, close-up of head. ....$1–$2
Capt. Kirk, in dress uniform. ....$1–$2
Capt. Kirk, in "Trouble with Tribbles." ....$1–$2
Capt. Kirk, ready to beam down. ....$1–$2
Capt. Kirk, with communicator. ....$1–$2
Capt. Kirk, hand reaching out through cell bars. ....$1–$2
Capt. Pike, the original commander of the Enterprise. ....
....$1–$2
Dr. McCoy, close-up of face. ....$1–$2
Dr. McCoy, looking puzzled. ....$1–$2
Dr. McCoy, speaking. ....$1–$2
Enterprise, captioned "Star Trek." ....$1–$2
Enterprise, looming over planet. ....$1–$2
Enterprise, rear view. ....$1–$2
Enterprise, shooting phasers. ....$1–$2
Enterprise, with red planet. ....$1–$2
Khan, original character. ....$1–$2
Klingon ship, overhead shot. ....$1–$2
Lt. Uhura, with headset on. ....$1–$2
Lt. Uhura, leaning on communication equipment. ......$1–$2
Mr. Chekov, flanked by crew. ....$1–$2
Mr. Chekov, in a deep frown. ....$1–$2
Mr. Chekov, on the bridge. ....$1–$2
Mr. Chekov, smiling. ....$1–$2
Mr. Scott, close-up of head. ....$1–$2
Mr. Spock, as Science Officer. ....$1–$2
Mr. Spock, close-up profile. ....$1–$2
Mr. Spock, laughing. ....$1–$2
Mr. Spock, looking logical. ....$1–$2
Mr. Spock, smiling. ....$1–$2
Mr. Spock, talking on the bridge. ....$1–$2
Mr. Spock, tight close-up of head. ....$1–$2
Mr. Spock, with beard. ....$1–$2
Mr. Sulu, the navigator. ....$1–$2
Mr. Sulu, close-up shot of head. ....$1–$2
Mr. Sulu, looking up. ....$1–$2
Nurse Chapel, close-up shot. ....$1–$2
Yeoman Rand, with plaited hair. ....$1–$2

Paramount

Promotional Button. 1989. Star Trek V: The Final Frontier.
Blue rectangular with logo. ....$2–$3

Pocket Books

Promotional Button. Pictures Spock, "Star Trek: The Only
Logical Books to Read." ....$1–$2

Taco Bell

Promotional buttons. 1984. Star Trek III: The Search for Spock. 3″. Blue and yellow.

    Beam Home with the Enterprise Crew. ....$2–$3
    Beam Home with T'Lar. ....$2–$3

    Beam Home with Spock. ....$2–$3
    Beam Home with Kruge. ....$2–$3

Universal Studios

Promotional buttons. 1989. Color photo of Enterprise with words "Paramount Pictures Star Trek Adventure" underneath.
....$3–$5

Creation Rectangular Button

Star Trek II **Licensed Button**

CALENDARS

Though Lincoln Enterprises produced a few early calendars, the high-quality calendars first produced by Ballantine in 1976 were the first truly collectible Star Trek calendars. At least one professionally produced calendar has appeared every year since then and, in recent years, one calendar for each of Star Trek's different incarnations has been made. Though they may not be as active an area of collectibles as some other Star Trek fields, calendars are still a part of many collections and escalate in value reasonably well.

INVESTMENT POTENTIAL
Good.

CARE
All of the Ballantine calendars and the first Pocket calendar (1980) came packaged in mailing boxes. Ideally, these should be unopened and in good condition, free from writing or other damage. If the calendar has been opened, it is still better if the box is present and hopefully has been opened by ungluing a flap rather than by pulling the perforated tab originally intended to open the box. After 1980, calendars were simply shrink-wrapped in plastic and removing this does not significantly detract from the value of the calendar. Tears and writing in the calendar or other obvious damage, however, make a calendar unacceptable to most collectors. As with all paper collectibles, storage in plastic collectible bags is recommended for protection from moisture (bags made for records fit most calendars). Exposure to direct sunlight should also be avoided as it may cause the calendar to fade.

SECTION NOTES
Fan-produced calendars have been omitted from this section because the simple printing process used to manufacture them make them very easy to reproduce and therefore unlikely to attain any collectible value. Section is organized chronologically.

1973, Lincoln Enterprises—Color photos from the original TV show. ....$10–$15
1974, Lincoln Enterprises—Color photos from the Star Trek animated series. ....$10–$15
1976–1978, Lincoln Enterprises—Three-year calendar. Color photos from the original TV series. ....$15–$20
1976, Ballantine Books—Photos from the original TV series, color, Kirk and Spock on cover with light blue border, boxed. ....$35–$50
1977, Ballantine Books—Color photos from original TV show, Kirk and Spock on cover with black border, boxed. ....$30–$40
1977, Franco—Cloth hanging calendar, vertical design printed on white cloth, came packaged in envelope. ....$35–$60
1978, Ballantine Books—Color original TV photos, Kirk, Spock, McCoy with blue border on cover, boxed. ....$25–$35
1979, Ballantine Books—Color original TV photos, Spock with silver border on cover, boxed. ....$25–$35
1980, Pocket Books—Color photos from Star Trek: The Motion Picture, Enterprise and main characters on cover, last year for boxed calendars (future calendars came shrink-wrapped). ...
....$20–$30
1980, Wallaby (Division of Pocket Books)—The Official USS Enterprise Officer's Date Book, Star Trek: The Motion Picture, spiralbound 5½″ × 8″ desk calendar, cover has color photo of Kirk, Spock, and Enterprise with blue border, interior has color and black and white photos from movie. ......$15–$25
1981, Pocket Books—Color photos from Star Trek: The Motion Picture, Enterprise in space dock on cover. ....$25–$35
1982, Pocket Books—Color photos from Star Trek: The Motion Picture, Enterprise, Kirk, and Spock on cover. ....$25–$35
1983, Pocket Books—Color photos from Star Trek II: The Wrath of Khan, Enterprise approaching Regula I space station on cover. ....$25–$35

1984, Pocket Books (Timescape)—Color photos from original TV show, Kirk and Spock on cover. ....$15–$25

1985, Pocket Books—Color photos from Star Trek III: The Search for Spock, Enterprise approaching space dock on cover. ....$15–$25

1986, Pocket Books—Color photos of characters from the movies done to date, group shot of characters on cover. ....$15–$25

1987, Pocket Books—Color photos from original TV show, Kirk, Spock, McCoy, and Uhura on cover. ....$15–$25

1988, Pocket Books—Color photos from the original TV series and from the first four movies. ....$15–$25

1989, Pocket Books—Star Trek Celebration Calendar. Color photos from original TV series, Kirk, Spock, and Scotty on cover. ....$15–$25

1989, Pocket Books—Star Trek: The Next Generation Calendar, color photos from the first season of the Next Generation, group shot on cover. ....$15–$25

1990, Pocket Books—Star Trek V: The Final Frontier Calendar, color photos from Star Trek V, group shot on cover. ....$15–$20

1990, Pocket Books—Star Trek: The Next Generation Calendar, color photos from the Next Generation, Enterprise-D on cover. ....$15–$25

1991, Pocket Books—Star Trek Classic Calendar, color photos from all five movies, movie Enterprise and Excelsior on cover. ....$15–$20

1991, Pocket Books—Star Trek: The Next Generation Calendar, color photos from the third season, crew on bridge on cover. ....$15–$20

1992, Pocket Books—Star Trek 25th Anniversary Calendar, color photos from original series, Kirk, Spock, and McCoy on cover. ....$15–$20

1992, Pocket Books—Star Trek: The Next Generation Calendar, color photos from all seasons, Enterprise-D on cover. ....$15–$20

1993, Pocket Books—Star Trek VI: The Undiscovered Country Calendar, color photos from the movie, Enterprise-A on cover. ....$15–$20

1993, Pocket Books—Star Trek: The Next Generation Calendar, color photos from show's fifth season, group shot on cover. ....$15–$20

1994, Pocket Books—Star Trek (original TV) Calendar, color photos from original series, Kirk, Spock, and McCoy in transporter on cover. ....$10–$15

1994, Pocket Books—Star Trek: The Next Generation Calendar, color photos from series' sixth season, group shot on cover. ....$10–$15

1994, Pocket Books—Star Trek: Deep Space Nine Calendar, color photos from series, space station on cover. ......$10–$15

1995, Applause—Star Trek: The Next Generation Desk Calendar, black plastic desk calendar approx. 5½″ × 4½″, revolving face has color photo of Enterprise-D on one side and 1995 calendar on other, "Stardate" is above face and a digital clock is below. ....$15–$25

1995, Pocket Books—Star Trek (original TV) Calendar, color photos from original series, Kirk and Spock on cover. .. ..$10–$15

1995, Pocket Books—Star Trek: The Next Generation Calendar, color photos from the show's seventh season, Enterprise-D and shuttlecraft on cover. ....$10–$15

1995, Pocket Books—Star Trek: Deep Space Nine Calendar, color photos from the series, space station, runabout, and wormhole on cover. ....$10–$15

1996, Bastei (German)—Star Trek Stardate Year Planner, 216 pages with color pictures from all series and films, cover shows Enterprise-D and hologram title. ....$20–$30

1996, Pocket Books—Star Trek 30th Anniversary Calendar, color photos from original TV series, Kirk and Spock on cover. ....$10–$15

1996, Pocket Books—Star Trek: The Next Generation Calendar, color photos from "All Good Things" and "Generations," group shot on cover. ....$10–$15

1996, Pocket Books—Star Trek: Deep Space Nine Calendar, color photos from the series, group shot on cover. ....$10–$15

1996, Pocket Books—Star Trek: Voyager Calendar, color photos from the series, group shot on cover. ....$10–$15

1997, Pocket Books—Star Trek, close-up photos of Kirk and Spock on cover. ....$11–$13

1997, Pocket Books—Star Trek: The Next Generation Calendar (10th anniversary edition), Enterprise-D orbiting planet on cover. ....$11–$13

1997, Pocket Books—Star Trek: Deep Space Nine Calendar, crew shot (minus Bashir) on cover. ....$11–$13

1997, Pocket Books—Star Trek: Voyager Calendar, Tuvok, Janeway, and Chakotay on cover. ....$11–$13

1997, Pocket Books—Star Trek Stardate 1997 Calendar, desk calendar with black and white photo for each day and blue plastic base, box art has new style UFP seal. ....$9–$11

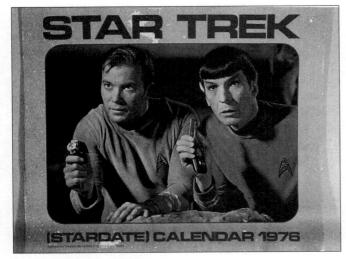

Star Trek Calendar, 1976

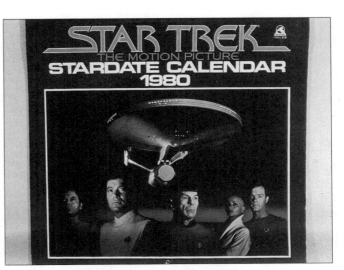

Star Trek: The Motion Picture **Calendar, 1980**

CELS AND STORYBOARDS

Cels are the transparencies on which the action parts of an animated film are printed. Storyboards are the preliminary sketches made for an animated story. There are hundreds of storyboards and thousands of cels for each half hour of an animated Star Trek episode. Until fairly recently, the value of cels as original art had gone largely unrecognized by the general public. This has changed dramatically and the price of cels has skyrocketed. Although Filmation, the company which made the Star Trek animated episodes, is better known for being prolific than for the quality of their artwork, due to the subject matter, Star Trek must be considered one of their more select products. Desirable features in cels are complete well-centered figures and, of course, main characters and groups. Authentic cels seldom have backgrounds since one backdrop could serve for many "action" sequences. A storyboard should sell for between $50–$100 and a good quality cel for $75–$200.

INVESTMENT POTENTIAL

Authentic Cels—Good. Reproduction Cels—Fair.

CARE

Cels and storyboard drawings need to be cared for in a manner consistent with other forms of artwork. This entails keeping them safe from moisture, scratching, scuffing, and heat. Since most cels come framed or at least matted for display purposes, further protective measures are rarely necessary.

SECTION NOTES

Since authentic cels are, by their nature, unique, the listings below are all for cel reproductions. Section is organized alphabetically by manufacturer.

Filmation

(1977)

In 1977 Filmation released a series of 14 cel reproductions from the Star Trek animated series. These came in 14″ × 18″ mats and included a seal of authenticity.

1A	The Crew of the Enterprise.	$50–$100
5	Yesteryear.	$50–$100
6	More Tribbles, More Troubles.	$50–$100
9	The Ambergris Element.	$50–$100
11	Jihad, composite of aliens.	$50–$100
12	Spock, the boy atop L'Chaya.	$50–$100
14	The Time Trap.	$50–$100
15	The Enterprise and the Aqua Shuttle.	$50–$100
16	Beyond the Farthest Star.	$50–$100
20	Kukupkan and the Enterprise.	$50–$100
22	Time Warp.	$50–$100
23	About to Battle a Klingon.	$50–$100
25	The Counter Clock Incident.	$50–$100
00	Title Scene From Star Trek.	$50–$100

Lincoln Enterprises

(1983)

These are 4″ × 8″ copies of character cels on acetate.

Chapel.	$2–$3
Enterprise.	$2–$3
Kirk.	$2–$3
Lt. Arex.	$2–$3
Lt. M'Hress.	$2–$3

McCoy. ....$2–$3
Scotty. ....$2–$3
Spock. ....$2–$3
Sulu. ....$2–$3
Uhura. ....$2–$3

Royal Animation Art, Inc.

(1989, re-issued in 1994)

These are 11½″ × 8½″ (cell size without matt). Reproductions of original animation cels with backgrounds. Limited to 500 pieces. Numbered. Includes certificate of authenticity. Value reflects issue price.

S96A Spock and Kirk, waist up. ....$200–$250
S96B McCoy, waist up on planet. ....$200–$250
S96C Spock, waist-up action pose. ....$200–$250
S96D Scotty, holding tricorder. ....$200–$250
S96E McCoy and Kirk, with machinery. ....$200–$250
S96F Spock and Kirk, in transporter. ....$200–$250
S96G Arex and Scott. ....$200–$250
S96H Alien and Crew member. ....$200–$250
S96I Kirk, holding communicator. ....$200–$250
S96J Sulu, waist up. ....$200–$250
S96K Sulu, machinery in background. ....$200–$250
S96L Scott, waist up. ....$200–$250
S96M Kirk and McCoy, with hypo. ....$200–$250
S96N Spock, with machinery. ....$200–$250
S96O Spock, waist up. ....$200–$250
S96P McCoy, behind window. ....$200–$250
S96Q Kirk, waist-up action pose. ....$200–$250
S96R Kirk, waist up. ....$200–$250
S96S Spock, with two aliens. ....$200–$250
S96T Chapel and Kirk. ....$200–$250
S96U Kirk, full figure. ....$200–$250
S96V Kirk and Spock, on planet. ....$200–$250
S96W Scott, on bridge. ....$200–$250
S96X Kirk and Spock, on bridge. ....$200–$250

CERAMICS AND GLASSWARE

In recent years production of Star Trek ceramics aimed specifically at the collector market has boomed. The enthusiasm for this line of merchandise probably resulted from the success enjoyed by earlier Star Trek ceramic collectibles, most notably the eight-plate Episode series produced by Ernst and marketed by Hamilton between 1987 and 1989. The success as an investment of these plates, much rarer than the same company's earlier character series, is well known to Star Trek collectors and well appreciated by collectible ceramic manufacturers. Manufacturers are very aware of their market and try hard to cater to their customers. Plates, for instance, are usually done in numbered limited editions. Even if, as sometimes happens, the number manufactured is relatively high, ultimately only so many exist. As usually happens with any collectible item produced in series, sales often drop off late in a series and each *new* series on the same general subject can expect fewer initial sales than the one before. For this reason, fewer of the later plates are usually produced. This means that the items that ultimately end up being the best collectibles are often the last ones produced.

INVESTMENT POTENTIAL
Good.

CARE
Except for ensuring that they do not get broken or chipped, ceramics and glassware require very little special treatment. They do not fade or scuff easily, are not bothered by sunlight or moisture, and are easily cleaned. Furthermore, unlike toys, action figures, and many other collectibles, most do not come in special packaging which needs to be carefully preserved.

SECTION NOTES
Section is organized alphabetically by subject matter and chronologically by TV series or film (starting with earliest if more than one is covered in a category).

BOTTLES

Saurian Brandy Bottle. Curved-neck bottle equipped with a leather harness and wooden stopper seen in several episodes of the original *Star Trek* as well as in *Star Trek: Deep Space Nine* (at Quark's Bar). Actually a commemorative "Powder Horn" whiskey bottle manufactured by the George Dickel Distillery in Tennessee. Bottles came in several sizes and had variations in glass color—clear to dark amber—and decorative harness design. In demand by bottle as well as Star Trek collectors.

Nipper Size.	$35–$50
Fifth Size.	$50–$75
Quart Size.	$50–$75
Gallon Size, rare limited edition.	$400–$750

CANDY DISH

Star Trek VI Candy Dish—Pfaltzgraff, 1993. White and blue stoneware approx. $9^{1}/_{2}''$ long at its longest dimension. Shaped like a movie version command insignia; blue and yellow USS Enterprise NCC-1701-A insignia emblem in bottom of dish. Comes boxed in flat, dark blue box with insignia on top and two sides and product information on two sides. ....$30–$45

CHIP AND DIP SET

Star Trek VI Chip'n Dip—Pfaltzgraff, 1993. White stoneware two-piece set. Chip bowl is approx. $11^{1}/_{4}''$ in diameter with three blue and yellow USS Enterprise NCC 1701-A insignia emblems equally spaced around bottom, with blue and yellow lines around edge and raised center platform for dip bowl. Dip bowl is white with blue and yellow lines around edge. Comes boxed in dark blue box with insignia on top and two sides and product information on two sides. ......$40–$60

COASTER SET

Star Trek VI Coaster Set—Pfaltzgraff, 1993. Set of four white stoneware coasters. Blue and yellow USS Enterprise 1701-A insignia emblem in center; blue line around edge. Comes boxed with insignia on top and two sides and product information on other two sides. Originally sold only in sets. Set value. ....$25–$40

COOKIE JARS

Original (30th Anniversary) Television Cookie Jars—Star Jars, 1996. Jars are from 14″ to 16″ high detailed with metallic glazes and cloisonné insets. Limited to 1000 pieces each.
    #1 Enterprise and UFP Logo, with "Space the Final Frontier." ....$250–$300
    #2 Spock and Kirk (in front of jar), with "These are the Voyages of the Starship Enterprise." ....$375–$400
    #3 Crew Members and Enterprise, with "It's five-year mission . . . To explore new worlds." ....$375–$400
    #4 Alien Ships and Starfleet Insignia, with "To seek out new life and civilizations." ....$275–$300
    #5 Vulcan Salute, with "To Boldly go where no man has gone before." ....$275–$300

Star Trek VI Cookie Jar—Pfaltzgraff, 1993. White stoneware. Approx. 8″ tall with lid. Blue and yellow USS Enterprise 1701-A insignia emblem on one side. Blue line around lip, yellow line around base. Plain white lid. Comes in dark blue box with insignia on top and two sides and product information on two sides. ....$50–$75

DECANTERS

Full-Figure Spock Liquor Decanter—Grenadier, 1979. Spock standing, 13″ tall, gold metallic glaze. Some came with dark blue satin display box. Probably never held liquor. ....
....$700–$1000
Spock Bust Liquor Decanter—Grenadier, 1979. Star Trek: The Motion Picture uniform, 10″ tall. Came in window display box, originally held Cielo liquor. Decanters still containing liquor and those with boxes are more collectible. ....
....$50–$100

NOTE: Some Spock bust decanters display white insignia patches instead of the orange that is correct for the char-
acter, but neither design seems more prevalent. White patch decanters may originally have been intended for Kirk decanter heads but except for prototypes, none were ever produced.

DINNERWARE

Star Trek VI Enterprise Buffet Set—Pfaltzgraff, 1992. Three-piece white bone china set; dinner plate, teacup, and saucer. Plate has USS Enterprise NCC-1701-A insignia emblem in blue and gold in center, cup has small movie-style command insignia and "USS Enterprise NCC-1701-A" in blue and gold on one side. All three pieces have blue, gold, and red rim design. Plate has additional gold accent ring and cup has gold ring at base. Limited to 3000 pieces. Numbered on back. Comes boxed in dark blue box with insignia on top and product information on one side. Certificate of Authenticity included. ....$400–$500
Star Trek VI Dinner Plate—Pfaltzgraff, 1992. White bone china dinner plate approx. 10¾″ in diameter. Similar to plate in limited edition Star Trek VI Buffet Set but without red accents in border design and not numbered on back. Comes in flat white box with logo and product information on top. ....
....$50–$65
Star Trek: Deep Space Nine Buffet Set—Pfaltzgraff, 1993. White bone china three-piece set. Triangular plate approx. 10″ at longest dimension. Center has triangular blue and purple emblem; starfield with small Next Generation–style command insignia at top. "Bajor Sector" and "Deep Space Nine" around starfield. Flaring blue, black, and purple accent stripes around edge of plate which is bordered in gold. Triangular saucer with matching edge pattern of plate. Handleless cup has smaller emblem on either side bordered by flaring blue, black, and purple stripes. Rimmed in gold. Comes in purple box with sticker placed so insignia is on top and product information is on side. Limited to 10,000 sets. Certificate of Authenticity included. ....$125–$140
Star Trek VI Buffet Set—Pfaltzgraff, 1993. Three-piece white stoneware set; dinner plate, small mug/cup, and saucer. Plate and mug have blue and yellow USS Enterprise insignia emblem. All three pieces are accented with blue and yellow lines. Comes boxed in dark blue box with insignia on top and two sides and product information on other two sides. ....
....$35–$50
Star Trek VI Excelsior Buffet Set—Pfaltzgraff, 1993. White three-piece bone china set. Similar to the Star Trek VI Enterprise bone china buffet set but with Excelsior insignia emblem (USS Excelsior NCC-2000) instead of Enterprise. Insignia on cup is all blue instead of blue and gold as in Enterprise set. Comes in dark blue box with sticker placed so insignia is on top and product information is on one side. Limited to 10,000 sets. Certificate of Authenticity included.
....$115–$125
Captain's Service Dinner Plate—Pfaltzgraff, 1994. White

bone china dinner plate with three scalloped indentations set equidistant around edge of plate. Gold, silver, and blue insignia emblem in center with "USS Enterprise * Constitution Class * NCC-1701" around original TV command symbol. Blue and gold line around edge with stars at each indentation. Limited to 5000 pieces. ....$40–$50

Generations USS Enterprise NCC-1701-D Buffet Set—Pfaltzgraff, 1994. White three-piece bone china set. Plate is approx. 10³/₄″ in diameter. Gold, silver, and blue new-style insignia emblem in center with "USS Enterprise NCC-1701-D." Plate is bordered in blue, gold, and red. Gold accent stripe further toward center of plate. White triangular saucer with gold rim. Teacup has "USS Enterprise NCC-1701-D" in blue above gold and silver insignia emblem. Cup rim matches plate. Gold line around base. Comes in silver box with sticker placed so that insignia is on top and product information is on side. Limited to 3000 pieces. Certificate of Authenticity included. ....$125–$140

Star Trek VI Large Cup and Saucer Set—Pfalzgraff, 1994. Oversize white stoneware cup with saucer. Blue and yellow Enterprise-A insignia emblem on side of cup. ....$20–$25

USS Enterprise NCC 1701 Buffet Set—Pfaltzgraff, 1994. White bone china three-piece set consisting of a dinner plate, saucer, and teacup. Plate and cup are decorated with a gold, blue, and red three-insignia design showing original TV command, science and engineering emblems with the command emblem centered and larger than the other two, and "USS Enterprise NCC-1701." Complementary border designs. Limited to 5000 pieces. A J.C. Penney exclusive. ....$115–$135

DOLLS, PORCELAIN

See Action Figures

DRINKING GLASSES

Star Trek Animated Series Glasses—Dr. Pepper Promotional, 1976. Set of four with color waist-up artwork of three characters and the Enterprise from the animated Star Trek series. Back of glass has short description of subject.

Enterprise.	$20–$25
Kirk.	$20–$25
McCoy.	$20–$25
Spock.	$20–$25
Set of All Four.	$150–$175

Original Star Trek Glasses—Dr. Pepper Promotional, 1978. Set of four with color waist-up artwork of three characters and Enterprise. Artwork is not from animated Star Trek series and can be further distinguished from earlier Dr. Pepper set by the presence of background artwork behind subject. Short description of subject on back.

Enterprise.	$25–$30
Kirk.	$25–$30
McCoy.	$25–$30
Spock.	$25–$30
Set of All Four.	$175–$200

Star Trek: The Motion Picture Glasses—Coca-Cola Promotional, 1979. Set of three glasses with color artwork on front and short description on back. A printing error caused the colors on some of the glasses to be applied in the wrong order giving the artwork a somewhat muddy appearance. Coca-Cola never found a franchise to carry these glasses and they were not widely distributed.

Decker and Ilia.	$15–$20
Enterprise.	$15–$20
Kirk, Spock, and McCoy.	$15–$20
Set of All Three.	$65–$95

Star Trek III: The Search for Spock—Taco Bell Promotional, 1984. Set of four flair-bottomed glasses with color artwork depicting scenes from the movie.

Enterprise Destroyed.	$5–$10
Fal-Tor-Pan.	$5–$10
Lord Kruge.	$5–$10
Spock Lives.	$5–$10
Set of All Four.	$25–$50

Star Trek VI: The Undiscovered Country Cooler Set—Pfaltzgraff, 1993. Set of four 6¼″ tall glasses with USS Enterprise NCC-1701-A movie-style command insignia printed on one side in blue and yellow. Blue and yellow stripes around top of glass. Set came boxed in dark blue box with printed sticker placed so that insignia is on top of box and contents information is on one side. Originally sold only in sets. Set value. ....$35–$50

Star Trek VI: The Undiscovered Country Double Old Fashion Set—Pfaltzgraff, 1993. Set of four 4¼″ tall glasses with USS Enterprise NCC-1701-A movie-style command insignia printed on one side in blue and yellow. Blue and yellow stripes around top of glass. Set came boxed in dark blue box with insignia printed on two sides and contents information printed on other two sides. Originally sold only in sets. Set value. ....$35–$50

UFP Cocktail Glass—Creation, 1994. Short frosted glass tumbler with the Next Generation–style United Federation of Planets emblem printed on both sides. White-edged gold bands around top and bottom repeat "United Federation of Planets." ....$8–$10

FIGURINES

Star Trek Figurine Collection—Danbury Mint, 1991. Painted cold cast porcelain original Star Trek TV figurines varying between 4½″ and 5½″ in height. Character is posed on to-scale silver replica of a transporter pad. Sticker with manufacturer's information is affixed to bottom of base. Originally intended to be purchased in installments. A blue plastic 13″ ×

20″ two-tier display box with Enterprise in space backdrop was included at no extra charge.

Andorian.	$25–$40
Chekov, with tribbles.	$25–$40
Khan.	$25–$40
Kirk, holding communicator.	$25–$40
Klingon.	$25–$40
McCoy, with tricorder and hypo spray.	$25–$40
Romulan.	$25–$40
Scotty, holding phaser.	$25–$40
Spock, with tricorder, giving Vulcan salute.	$25–$40
Sulu, with fencing foil.	$25–$40
Talosian.	$25–$40
Uhura, seated.	$25–$40

MUGS AND STEINS

Flat ceramic mugs with simple silk-screen designs of only a few colors are produced by souvenir manufacturers for just about every imaginable subject and Star Trek is no exception. Like any category of merchandise that can be made inexpensively in small quantities, unlicensed Star Trek mugs are overly abundant. Also for this reason, it is extremely unlikely that this kind of mug will ever attain much collectible value. If, for some reason, one did start to climb in price, some intrepid entrepreneur would simply make up a new batch indistinguishable from the originals. Therefore, to keep this section to a manageable size, we will only list licensed mugs. Please keep in mind, however, that a mug is a mug, licensed or otherwise, and licensed ones that fit into the above category are just as easy to reproduce. (Also see Dinnerware in this section.)

Star Trek II: The Wrath of Khan Character Steins—Image Products, 1982. Character's features molded into front of stein, 6″ tall, logo on back, dark blue glaze lining.

Kirk.	$150–$200
Khan.	$350–$500
Spock.	$150–$200

Official Star Trek Fan Club Mug—1986. 20th anniversary and fan club logos. ....$8–$15

Original TV Character Mugs—Hamilton/Ernst, 1986. Same designs with Susie Morton artwork as first series character plates manufactured by this company. Originally sold only in sets of eight. Re-issued in 1991 with slightly smaller mugs by Presents (Hamilton). Originals may be slightly more desirable than re-issues.

Beam Us Down, Scotty.	$10–$15
Chekov.	$10–$15
Kirk.	$10–$15
McCoy.	$10–$15
Scotty.	$10–$15
Spock.	$10–$15
Sulu.	$10–$15
Uhura.	$10–$15

Steins—Ernst, 1986. Sepia tone line drawings, 6¼″ tall, individually numbered.

Kirk.	$40–$60
Spock.	$40–$60

Star Trek Magic Mugs—Image Design Concepts, 1989/1994. Heat sensitive design allows figures in mug illustration to "disappear" when hot beverage is added, leaving background visible. Images return as mug cools. Process necessitates simple artwork. Sometimes packaged in boxes with starfield background and various Star Trek ships. "Official Star Trek Magic Mug" in red and yellow on front and lid.

Capt. Picard.	$11–$13
Comdr. Riker.	$11–$13
Counselor Troi.	$11–$13
Deep Space Nine and Wormhole.	$11–$13
Dr. Crusher.	$11–$13
Enterprise D and Klingon Bird-of-Prey.	$11–$13
Enterprise Evolution, Original and NG ships.	$11–$13
Guinan.	$11–$13
Holodeck Data as Sherlock Holmes.	$11–$13
Holodeck Picard and Data as Musketeers.	$11–$13
Holodeck Picard as Dixon Hill.	$11–$13
Kirk, Spock, and McCoy on Transporter.	$11–$13
Lt. Comdr. Data.	$11–$13
Lt. Geordi La Forge.	$11–$13
Lt. Worf.	$11–$13
Wesley Crusher.	$11–$13
Worf is a Merry Man.	$11–$13

Star Trek VI Logo Mug—Creation, 1991. Black mug with blue, red, and silver word logo on one side. ....$10–$15

Star Trek: The Next Generation Photo Mugs—Presents (Hamilton), 1992. Photo on either side of white mug. Bordered in red with logo between two pictures. Comes packaged in light blue box with logo on all sides and lid and photo of character on mug on two sides.

Crew.	$8–$12
Data.	$8–$12
Enterprise-D.	$8–$12
Picard.	$8–$12
Troi.	$8–$12
Worf.	$8–$12

This Vehicle Travels at Warp Speed Mug—Creation, 1992. Black wide-based mug with saying and line drawing of Enterprise-D in silver. Small logo under saying. ......$15–$20

Starfleet Academy Mug—Creation, 1992. White mug with dark red, black, and gold Starfleet Academy logo on one side; Star Trek: The Next Generation word logo on other side. ......
............$10–$15

Star Trek: The Next Generation Ship Mugs—Creation, 1992. Color artwork of ship on one side with identification or slogan beneath ship. Logo on other side of mug in blue and white.

Enterprise-D.	$10–$15
Klingon Bird-of-Prey.	$10–$15
Romulan Warbird.	$10–$15

Star Trek: Deep Space Nine Logo Mug—Image Design

Concepts (for Creation), 1992. Black mug with gold and silver word logo on one side and drawing of space station in silver on other side. ....$10–$15

Star Trek Logo Mug—Creation, 1993. Black mug with original Star Trek word logo in red and silver on both sides. ....$8–$12

Star Trek Evolution Mug—Creation, 1993. Black mug with purple planet and star background on one side. Color artwork of original, movie, and Next Generation Enterprises and Deep Space Nine space station. "To Boldly Go Where No One Has Gone Before" and "Star Trek" to side. ....$8–$10

Double Photo Mugs—Centric, 1993. Each mug has two color photos, one on each side, of characters and ships. Appropriate slogan: "To Boldly Go Where No One/Man Has Gone Before" printed on bottom. Box has space scene on sides with slogan around top. Lid has names of characters/ships on mug.

    Data/Worf. ....$10–$15
    Enterprise-D/Romulan Warbird. ....$10–$15
    Kirk/Spock. ....$10–$15
    Movie Enterprise/Klingon Bird-of-Prey. ....$10–$15
    Picard/La Forge. ....$10–$15
    Riker/Troi. ....$10–$15

Star Trek VI Tankard—Pfaltzgraff, 1993. White stoneware tankard with NCC-1701-A ship logo emblem in blue and yellow on one side and "USS Enterprise NCC-1701-A" and small blue and yellow movie-style command symbol on other side. Blue rim. Yellow line around base. Comes in dark blue box with emblem on top and two sides and product information on two sides. ....$25–$30

Star Trek VI Stoneware Mug—Pfaltzgraff, 1993. Same basic design as the above tankard but on a 4¼"-high white stoneware mug. Packaging is also similar to the stoneware tankard. ....$10–$15

Star Trek VI Bone China Mug—Pfaltzgraff, 1993. Similar in design to the stoneware mug but with a slightly flared, gold-edged rim. No yellow line around base. Comes in dark blue box with sticker placed so emblem is on top and product information is on one side. ....$35–$40

Star Trek VI Glass Tankard—Pfaltzgraff, 1993. Clear 5½"-high glass tankard with blue and yellow command insignia–style USS Enterprise NCC-1701-A ship logo emblem on one side. Comes boxed in dark blue box with dark blue sticker placed so sticker is on top and product information is on one side. ....$25–$30

USS Enterprise NCC-1701-A Mug—Creation, 1993. Gray mug with blue command insignia–style ship logo emblem. ....$10–$15

Star Trek VI Excelsior Mug—Pfaltzgraff, 1993. White stoneware mug with yellow and blue Excelsior insignia emblem from movie. Blue rim. ....$10–$15

Star Trek VI Excelsior Bone China Mug—Pfaltzgraff, 1993. White mug with gold and blue insignia emblem for Excelsior (USS Excelsior NCC-2000) on one side. Slightly flared rim is bordered in gold. ....$30–$40

Galaxy Class Starship Development Project Mug—Cre-

ation, 1993. White mug with blue, gold, and red shipyard logo on one side and Star Trek: The Next Generation logo in red on other side. ....$10–$15

Star Trek: The Next Generation Pewter Logo Mugs—Creation, 1993. Black mugs with pewter and enamel emblems. Similar but not identical to Rawcliffe pewter mugs.

    Delta Shield (NG Insignia) Mug. ....$15–$20
    Starfleet Academy Logo Mug. ....$15–$20

Star Trek: The Next Generation Logo Mug—Creation, 1993. Black mug with blue and silver word logo on both sides. ....$10–$15

United Federation of Planets Mug—Creation, 1993. Black mug with silver Next Generation–style UFP logo (starfield bracketed by a wreath design) on both sides. "United Federation of Planets" above. Silver rim. ....$10–$15

Ferengis, Klingons, and Borgs ... Oh My! Mug—Promotional (Star Trek Science Exhibit), 1993. Caption under color artwork of three aliens on white mug. ....$15–$20

Star Trek: Deep Space Nine Coffee Mug—Pfaltzgraff, 1993. White stoneware mug featuring triangular blue and purple emblem with starfield below small Next Generation–style command insignia surrounded by "Bajor Sector" and "Deep Space Nine." Flaring blue, purple, and black accent lines originating at emblem. ....$10–$15

Star Trek: Deep Space Nine Bone China Mug—Pfaltzgraff, 1993. Same basic design as the previous stoneware mug but on a white bone china mug with a gold rim. ....$30–$35

USS Enterprise Insignia Emblem Mug—Pfaltzgraff, 1994. White stoneware mug with original TV command, science and engineering insignias, and "USS Enterprise NCC-1701" in a circular red, yellow, and blue emblem design. Other side has words over insignias without circular emblem design. Blue stripe around top, red stripe around base. Comes in maroon box with insignia emblem on top and two sides and product information on two sides. ....$15–$20

Captain's Cabin Coffee Mug—Pfaltzgraff, 1994. White bone china mug with scalloped bottom and triangular handle. Gold and blue original TV command insignia in silver circle. Wide blue and yellow accent stripe originates from center of design and circles mug at approximate middle. ....$25–$30

Star Trek Original Cast Stein—CUI (for Catch-a-Star), 1994. White stein 6½" tall with color photo reproduction of crew portrayed around body of stein. Characters are bordered on one side by picture of original Enterprise and "Star Trek" in gold, and on the other by "To Boldly Go Where No Man Has Gone Before," also in gold. Stein has metal flip-up lid with white ceramic inset depicting gold command symbol. Comes with Certificate of Authenticity. ....$50–$75

Character Tankards—Hamilton, 1994. White stein 6½" tall. Dark blue star background with the Thomas Blackshear portraits used on the Hamilton 25th anniversary plate series on one side and "Star Trek" over a command insignia and character name in gold on the back. Gold decoration around the rim and base of the stein and on the handle. Each. ....$35–$50

Star Trek Original TV Mugs—Enesco, 1994. Same color, Todd Treadway artwork as the Enesco plates. Artwork is reproduced on both sides with logo in middle and to sides. Comes boxed in black horizontal format window box with logo on top and sides.

    Crew. ....$8–$12
    Enterprise. ....$8–$12
    Kirk. ....$8–$12

Ships and Logos Mug—Creation, 1994. Black mug with an original TV Enterprise, an Enterprise-D, a Runabout, a Deep Space Nine space station, and two Next Generation–style UFP logos in gold around mug. "Star Trek" repeated in gold bands above and below design. ....$10–$15

Ships and Logos Glass Stein—Creation, 1994. Same design as previous mug but on a frosted glass stein. ....$15–$20

Star Trek Figural Mugs—Applause, Inc., 1994/1996. Approx. 5½″ high full-color mugs shaped like the head and shoulders of the respective character. Packaged in boxes with appropriate logo on lid and all-over star motif. Character name appears on bottom of mug and box. Certificate of Authenticity included.

    Borg. ....$15–$20
    Capt. Kirk. ....$15–$20
    Cardassian. ....$15–$20
    Comdr. Riker. ....$15–$20
    Comdr. Spock. ....$15–$20
    Dr. Crusher. ....$15–$20
    Gorn. ....$15–$20
    Lt. Comdr. Data. ....$15–$20
    Lt. Worf. ....$15–$20
    Lt. Comdr. La Forge. ....$15–$20
    Lt. Comdr. Troi. ....$15–$20
    McCoy. ....$15–$20
    Neelix. ....$15–$20
    Proprietor Quark. ....$15–$20
    "Q." ....$15–$20
    Security Chief Odo. ....$15–$20

Star Trek Pewter Logo Mugs—Rawcliffe, 1994. 4½″ tall, dark blue mug, silver band around rim and base. Pewter and enamel emblem applied to one side of mug. Packaged in silver window box with logo on front, sides, and lid. Product info on back.

    Borg Symbol. ....$15–$20
    Ferengi Symbol. ....$15–$20
    Original Klingon Symbol. ....$15–$20
    Next Generation Command Symbol. ....$15–$20
    Next Generation Enterprise. ....$15–$20
    Next Generation UFP Symbol. ....$15–$20
    Original Enterprise. ....$15–$20
    Original TV Command Symbol. ....$15–$20
    Original TV Engineering Symbol. ....$15–$20
    Original TV Science Symbol. ....$15–$20
    Romulan Symbol. ....$15–$20
    Star Trek: Generations Logo. ....$15–$20
    Starfleet Academy Symbol. ....$15–$20
    Voyager Ship. ....$15–$20

Star Trek Insignia Mug—Pfaltzgraff, 1994. White mug with Motion Picture–style command insignia in red, yellow, and black on both sides of mug. ....$10–$15

Movie Poster Artwork Mugs—Bee International, 1994. A 10 oz. mug with full-color reproduction of theatrical promotional posters from the first six movies. Came packed with candy. Originally sold and most commonly packaged in gift sets of all six mugs.

    Star Trek: The Motion Picture. ....$10–$15
    Star Trek II: The Wrath of Khan. ....$10–$15
    Star Trek III: The Search for Spock. ....$10–$15
    Star Trek IV: The Voyage Home. ....$10–$15
    Star Trek V: The Final Frontier. ....$10–$15
    Star Trek VI: The Undiscovered Country. ....$10–$15
    Gift Set in Display Box. ....$75–$100

Star Trek: The Next Generation Schematic Mug—Pfaltzgraff, 1994. Blue background with white, labeled, schematic drawings of Enterprise-D. Logo and "U.S.S. Enterprise NCC-1701-D" in yellow. ....$10–$15

Star Trek: Deep Space Nine Episode Mugs—Applause, 1994. Space background with photo of two characters on one side and artwork of space station and logo on other side. Inset panel to right of photo identifies characters and episode of photo. Packaged in box with space background, photo of space station, and logo on front and on lid. Certificate of Authenticity included.

    "Babel" (Kira and O'Brien). ....$8–$12
    "Move Along Home" (Odo and Quark). ....$8–$12
    "Q-Less" (Dax and Sisko). ....$8–$12

USS Enterprise NCC-1701-D Mug—Pfaltzgraff. 1994. White stoneware mug with Enterprise-D, Generations-style insignia logo in blue, yellow, and silver on one side and "USS Enterprise NCC-1701-D" and smaller insignia on other. Blue line around rim. Light blue band around base. Came packaged in silver box with insignia logos on top and two sides and product information on other two sides. ....$10–$15

USS Enterprise NCC-1701-D Tankard—Pfaltzgraff, 1994. Same basic design as above mug but on white stoneware tankard. No blue line around rim. Packaging is also similar. .. ..$25–$30

USS Enterprise NCC-1701-D Bone China Mug—Pfaltzgraff, 1994. Same basic design as stoneware mug but on high quality bone china. Gold edging on edge of rim instead of blue line. Rim is slightly flared. No line around base. Silver box with dark blue sticker placed so design is on top and product information is on back. ....$35–$40

Star Trek: The Next Generation Tumble-Not Mugs—Promotions International (British), 1995. Wide-based mugs with "Star Trek: The Next Generation" and insignia in metallic silver.

    Klingon Symbol, on black mug. ....$15–$20
    Romulan Symbol, on black mug. ....$15–$20
    Starfleet Logo (Command Insignia), on blue mug. ....$15–$20
    UFP Seal, on blue mug. ....$15–$20

Quark's Bar Mug—Creation, 1995. White mug with stylized portrait of Quark on one side and Quark's Bar logo on other side in red, yellow, black, and gold. Star Trek: Deep Space Nine logo in gold around bottom of design. ....$10–$15

Star Trek: Generations Mugs—Applause, 1995. Three photo-scene and one logo mug. Photo-scene mugs each have three photos—one action scene with two character photos on either side. Logo under center photo. Nexus effect background. Logo mug has small photo of Enterprise and two logos (one on either side of mug) on Nexus-effect background. Box has Nexus-effect background with logo on front and lid. Certificate of Authenticity included.

> "Capt. Kirk Meets Capt. Picard." ....$8–$12
> "Crew Scene." ....$8–$12
> Generations Logo. ....$8–$12
> "Villains." ....$8–$12

Star Trek: Generations Logo Mug—Creation, 1995. Dark blue mug with red logo. ....$10–$15

Voyager Mug—Creation, 1995. Black mug with Voyager ship in silver on one side and logo in gold and silver over white planetscape on other. Starscape pattern background. Gold and silver bands above and below design. ....
....$15–$20

Captain's Commemorative Mugs—Applause, 1996. Color wraparound collages of character. Name of character at top and short history on back.

> Janeway. ....$7–$10
> Kirk. ....$7–$10
> Picard. ....$7–$10
> Sisko. ....$7–$10

PLAQUES

Plaques are by Willitts Design. Triangular with blunt ends, slightly concave, approx. 8″ at longest dimension. Color artwork with metallic gold borders. Come in six-sided wooden, glass-fronted display boxes approx. 2″ deep. Can be hung on wall with frame or displayed with or without frame with built-in easel. Packaged in boxes with color photo of plaque on cover with metallic title lettering and space backdrop. Product information is inset on back.

"Voyage of the Starship Enterprise"—1993, Artist: Mark Newman. Limited to 9500 pieces. Numbered on back. Shows artwork of original TV Enterprise in space. Small placard underneath has "Star Trek" in gold. Black frame. ....
....$75–$100

"Star Trek: The Next Generation Commemorative Plaque"—1994, Artist: Jason Palmer. Artwork shows heads of seven major cast members with Enterprise-D underneath. Small placard below has raised Next Generation–style insignia with dates "1987" and "1994" to either side. Dark gray frame. ....$75–$100

PLATES
(Artwork)

All plate series here were issued one plate at a time over a period of months. All are numbered and low numbers are more desirable. Most come with Certificates of Authenticity which, in actuality, add little or nothing to the value. Merchandisers of collectible plates like to emphasize that their product is limited in number by reminding potential customers that the plates are only produced for a certain number of "firing days." While this sounds very impressive, it should be noted that this statement excludes more exacting information such as how many plates can be made in a "firing day" and are the "firing days" consecutive? For functional dining plates see Dinnerware in this section.

Classic Character Plates—Ernst/Hamilton, 1985 through 1987, Artist: Susie Morton. Diameter 8½″. Characters in original TV uniforms. Blue borders with "The Voyages of the Starship Enterprise" and "To Boldly Go Where No Man Has Gone Before."

> Beam Us Up Scotty (Group). ....$60–$75
> Chekov. ....$60–$75
> Kirk. ....$60–$75
> McCoy. ....$60–$75
> Scotty. ....$60–$75
> Spock. ....$60–$75
> Sulu. ....$60–$75
> Uhura. ....$60–$75

Enterprise Collector's Plate—Ernst/Hamilton, 1987, Artist: Susie Morton. Diameter 10¼″. Depicts Enterprise with heads of seven major characters around lower edge of plate. Gold edging with embossed words "USS Enterprise NCC 1701" at top and character names below. Produced after the last plate in the character series was released. There were two versions—an unsigned and a signed edition which had reproduction signatures of the seven actors plus Susie Morton and Gene Roddenberry around the back rim. Although advertised as a "special" edition, there is a good possibility that more signed than unsigned plates exist. Both versions are numbered on the back. ....$150–$250

Twentieth-Year Anniversary Collection—Ernst/Hamilton, 1987. Nine-plate set. Eight 9¼″ plates with same artwork as regular Classic Character Series plus one 10½″ plate with the same artwork as the Enterprise Collector's Plate. Plates have 1″ platinum border embossed with "Twentieth Year Anniversary Collection," "Star Trek," "NCC 1701," and star design. Most plates have simulated autograph of actor who depicted character on reverse (Gene Roddenberry for "Beam Us Down" artwork and artist Susie Morton for larger plate). This special series was limited to 1701 matching number sets and were sold only as sets. Value is for set of nine. ....
....$1500–$2000

Episode Plates—Ernst/Hamilton, 1987–1989, Artist: Susie

Morton. Hamilton did extensive research and customer surveys to determine not only which episodes but which scenes from the episodes were most popular. The fact that this colorful series is generally considered more attractive than the earlier character series and that far fewer of this series were produced has made it the more desirable of the two. Plates are 8½″ in diameter with embossed gold edging, with small Enterprises and words "Star Trek" and "The Commemorative Collection." Numbered on reverse.

Amok Time.	$100–$150
City on the Edge of Forever.	$250–$400
Devil in the Dark.	$100–$150
Journey to Babel.	$100–$150
Menagerie.	$100–$150
Mirror, Mirror.	$200–$350
Piece of the Action.	$100–$150
Trouble with Tribbles.	$100–$150

Star Trek: The Next Generation Portrait Plates—Ernst/Hamilton, 1989–1990, Artist: Susie Morton. Plate, 8½″, with platinum embossed edging with words "Star Trek: The Next Generation." Numbered on back. Ernst lost the license to do plates after the first two in this planned series of eight were finished. Only about 4000 of each were made compared to approx. 40,000 each of the blue-border character series, which was also manufactured by Ernst.

Data.	$200–$250
Picard.	$200–$250

Classic Character Mini-Plates—1991, Presents (Hamilton). Porcelain plates, 4¼″, reproducing the artwork from the original 1985 Classic Character plate series. Came packaged in small, flat, dark green boxes with logo on side and clear lids to show plate. Plastic plate stand included. Series was not limited.

Chekov.	$5–$10
Enterprise (not original Character Series artwork).	$5–$10
Group (Beam Us Down artwork).	$5–$10
Kirk.	$5–$10
McCoy.	$5–$10
Scotty.	$5–$10
Spock.	$5–$10
Sulu.	$5–$10
Uhura.	$5–$10

Star Trek 25th Anniversary Commemorative Collection—1991, Hamilton, Artist: Thomas Blackshear II. Portrait plates, 8½″, with stylized original series command symbol and words "Star Trek" embossed in gold border. Number and 25th Anniversary symbol on back of plate.

Chekov.	$45–$65
Kirk.	$45–$65
McCoy.	$45–$65
Scotty.	$45–$65
Spock.	$45–$65
Sulu.	$45–$65
Uhura.	$45–$65
USS Enterprise.	$45–$65

Star Trek 25th Anniversary Commemorative—1991, Hamilton, Artist: Thomas Blackshear II. Gold-rimmed plate,

9¼″. Artwork shows all seven major characters in various action poses with original Enterprise and planets in background. Border is embossed with "To Boldly Go Where No Man Has Gone Before," "1966 * Star Trek * 1991," and stylized command symbols. Numbered on back. ....$150–$250

NOTE: After 1992, Hamilton Gifts began operating as Enesco, a separate company from the Hamilton Collection. From this point on, both companies produced plate series.

Star Trek: The Next Generation Mini-Plates—Hamilton, 1992. Mini-plates, 4″, featuring a photo on a star background. Borders have plate title at top and "Star Trek: The Next Generation" at bottom flanked on either side by Next Generation command insignia. Come boxed in flat plate box with clear plastic lid. Small plate stand included. Series not limited.

Capt. Picard.	$5–$10
Continuing Voyages, The (Crew).	$5–$10
Counselor Troi.	$5–$10
Lt. Comdr. Data.	$5–$10
Lt. Worf.	$5–$10
USS Enterprise NCC 1701-D.	$5–$10

Classic Crew—Enesco, 1993, Artist: Todd Treadway. Gold-rimmed plate, 8½″. Crew in various poses in foreground below Enterprise. Logo located lower right. "These are the Voyages of the Starship Enterprise" and planet motif embossed around rim. Numbered on back. ....$25–$30

Star Trek: The Next Generation Crew—Enesco, 1993, Artist: Todd Treadway. Gold-rimmed plate, 8¼″. Collage of crew members and Enterprise with logo located in lower right. Rim is embossed with "To Boldly Go Where No One Has Gone Before" at top and "Star Trek: The Next Generation" at bottom. Numbered on back. ....$25–$30

The Voyagers Collection—Hamilton, 1993/1994, Artist: Keith Birdsong. Gold-rimmed plates, 8″. Spaceship series covering all Star Trek through the Next Generation. Rims are embossed with dots and dashes pattern and have "Star Trek" at bottom. Numbered on back.

Cardassian Galor Warship.	$35–$45
Ferengi Marauder.	$35–$45
Klingon Battle Cruiser.	$35–$45
Klingon Bird-of-Prey.	$35–$45
Romulan Warbird.	$35–$45
Triple Nacelled USS Enterprise.	$35–$45
USS Enterprise NCC-1701.	$35–$45
USS Enterprise NCC-1701-A.	$35–$45
USS Excelsior.	$35–$45

Star Trek: The Next Generation 5th-Anniversary Collection—Hamilton, 1993/1994, Artist: Thomas Blackshear II. Gold-rimmed plates, 8¼″. Rims are embossed with wreath motif and "Star Trek: The Next Generation" at top. Numbered on back.

Capt. Picard.	$35–$45
Comdr. Riker.	$35–$45
Counselor Troi.	$35–$45
Dr. Crusher.	$35–$45

Lt. Comdr. Data. ....$35–$45
Lt. Geordi La Forge. ....$35–$45
Lt. Worf. ....$35–$45
Wesley Crusher. ....$35–$45

Star Trek: The Movies Collection—1994/1995, Hamilton, Artist: Morgan Weistling. Gold-rimmed plates, 8¼". Plates have a collage of scenes from the respective movie. Rims are embossed with movie commander insignias with movie number at top and title at bottom. Scene plates use simply "Star Trek" in title location. Numbered on back. Plates were not released in chronological order by movie.

Title Plates:
Star Trek: The Motion Picture. ....$35–$40
Star Trek II: The Wrath of Khan. ....$35–$40
Star Trek III: The Search for Spock. ....$35–$40
Star Trek IV: The Voyage Home. ....$35–$40
Star Trek V: The Final Frontier. ....$35–$40
Star Trek VI: The Undiscovered Country. ......$35–$40
Scene Plates:
Destruction of the Reliant (STII). ....$35–$40
Triumphant Return (Bird-of-Prey from STIV). ....
....$35–$40

Star Trek: The Next Generation Episode Collection—Hamilton, 1994/1995, Artist: Keith Birdsong. Gold-rimmed plates, 8¼". Each plate shows collage of scenes from the respective episode. Rims are embossed with staggered wreath design with "Star Trek: The Next Generation" at bottom. Numbered on back.

All Good Things. ....$35–$45
Best of Both Worlds, The. ....$35–$45
Big Goodbye, The. ....$35–$45
Descent. ....$35–$45
Encounter at Farpoint. ....$35–$45
Relics. ....$35–$45
Unification. ....$35–$45
Yesterdays Enterprise. ....$35–$45

Star Trek: Deep Space Nine Collection—Hamilton, 1994/1995, Artist: Morgan Weistling. Series of 8¼" plates. Plates have predominantly gold borders with purple and turquoise stripes embossed with "Star Trek" at top and "Deep Space Nine" at bottom. Border is uneven in width making the picture area of the plate elliptical. Numbered on back.

Chief Miles O'Brien. ....$35–$45
Comdr. Sisko. ....$35–$45
Dr. Julian Bashir. ....$35–$45
Lt. Jadzia Dax. ....$35–$45
Maj. Kira Nerys. ....$35–$45
Odo. ....$35–$45
Quark. ....$35–$45
Space Station. ....$35–$45

Enterprise—Enesco, 1995, Artist: Todd Treadway. Gold-rimmed plate, 8½". Original Enterprise with logo and "USS Enterprise NCC-1701" located in lower right. "These are the Voyages of the Starship Enterprise" and planet motif embossed around rim. Numbered on back. ....$25–$30

Capt. James T. Kirk—Enesco, 1995, Artist: Todd Tread-way. Gold-rimmed plate, 8½". Collage of Kirk from original TV show. Logo located in lower left. "These are the Voyages of the Starship Enterprise" and planet motif embossed around rim. Numbered on back. ....$25–$30

Star Trek Classic Mini-Plates—Enesco, 1995, Artist: Todd Treadway. Mini-plates, 4", with same artwork as larger Enesco plates. Blue borders with planet motif. Each comes in small flat box with clear lid. Small plate stand included. Series not limited.

Crew. ....$5–$10
Enterprise. ....$5–$10
Kirk. ....$5–$10

USS Enterprise NCC-1701-D—Enesco, 1995, Artist: Todd Treadway. Gold-rimmed plate, 8¼". Head-on view of Enterprise in foreground with logo in lower right. Rim is embossed with "To Boldly Go Where No One Has Gone Before" at top and "Star Trek: The Next Generation" at bottom. Numbered on back. ....$25–$30

Capt. Jean-Luc Picard—Enesco, 1995, Artist: Todd Treadway. Gold-rimmed plate, 8¼". Collage of Capt. Picard with logo in lower left. Rim is embossed with "To Boldly Go Where No One Has Gone Before" at top and "Star Trek: The Next Generation" at bottom. Numbered on back. .....$25–$30

Star Trek: The Next Generation Mini-Plates—Enesco, 1995, Artist: Todd Treadway. Mini-plates, 4", with same artwork as the larger Next Generation Enesco plates but with purple instead of gold borders. Each plate comes boxed in a flat plate box with clear plastic lid and includes a small plate stand. Series not limited.

Capt. Picard. ....$5–$10
Enterprise NCC 1701-D. ....$5–$10
Next Generation Crew. ....$5–$10

Star Trek: Generations Collection—Hamilton, 1995, Artist: Keith Birdsong. Series of 8¼" plates. Plates have gold borders embossed with Generations-style delta shield insignia. Numbered on back. Kirk's Final Voyage. ....$35–$45

Star Trek: The Original Series Collection—1996, Hamilton, Artist: Jack Martin. Plates with blue and gold borders, 8¼". "Star Trek" and "To Boldly Go . . ." in gold at top and bottom of borders respectively. Numbered on back.

Tholian Web. ....$35–$45
Turnabout Intruder. ....$35–$45
Space Seed. ....$35–$45

Space, The Final Frontier Collection—1996, Hamilton, Artist: Michael David Ward. Horizontal format, oval plates, 8¼" wide at widest dimension. Narrow gold rims. Numbered on back.

Second Star from the Right. ....$45–$50
To Boldly Go. ....$45–$50

The Power of Command Collection—1996, Hamilton, Artist: Keith Birdsong. Gold-rimmed plates, 8¼", with abstract design of horizontal and vertical dashes embossed in rim. Numbered on back. Adm. Kirk and the USS Enterprise NCC-1701. ....$35–$40

Star Trek: Voyager Collection—Hamilton, 1996, Artist: Dan Curry. Narrow gold border with inset gold detail line running through image and logo at top in gold. Numbered on back. The Voyage Begins (crew members and ship). ....$35–$45

SHOTGLASS

UFP Shot Glass—Creation, 1993. Frosted glass with Next Generation–style UFP symbol printed on both sides in gold. White-edged gold bands with "United Federation of Planets" repeated around top and bottom. ....$4–$8

TOBY JUGS

Star Trek Figural Toby Jugs—Kevin Francis (British), 1995. Figures are between 8″ and 10″ high and are "jugs" only in the sense of having a very small opening in the top. Very limited editions. Numbers produced are given in parenthesis. Characters have color glaze and are presented in various action poses. Numbered. Includes Certificate of Authenticity.

    Borg (350). ....$750–$950
    Capt. Kirk (750). ....$450–$700
    Cardassian (450). ....$550–$800
    Counselor Troi (400). ....$550–$800
    Dr. McCoy (450). ....$600–$850
    Ferengi (350). ....$700–$900
    Geordi (400). ....$550–$800
    Lt. Worf (400). ....$600–$850
    "Q" (500). ....$600–$850
    Spock (750). ....$450–$700

NOTE: A very few (less than 30) Capt. Picard jugs were made but never went into general production due to licensing difficulties.

TRADING CARDS, PORCELAIN

Star Trek Classic Porcelain Trading Cards—Presents (Hamilton), 1991. Approx. 4½″ high white porcelain. Gold, original TV insignia. Round, color, Susie Morton artwork character portrait inserted over insignia. Character name and "Star Trek" below portrait. Comes in flat window box. Small plastic stand included.

    Kirk. ....$10–$15
    Spock. ....$10–$15

Star Trek: The Next Generation Porcelain Trading Cards—Presents (Hamilton), 1992. Rectangular porcelain plaque approx. 5½″ high. Blue background with character photo portrait framed in red superimposed on Next Generation–style command insignia. Enterprise-D, character name, and "Star Trek: The Next Generation" below character portrait. Packaged in flat window box. Small stand included.

    Data. ....$10–$15
    Enterprise. ....$10–$15
    Picard. ....$10–$15
    Troi. ....$10–$15
    Worf. ....$10–$15

Star Trek: The Next Generation Card Collection—Hamilton Collection, 1996. Set of 12 different 2½″ × 3½″ rectangular porcelain "cards" with color artwork by Sonia Hillios of characters and ships from the series. Gold and silver Next Generation–style command-insignia-shaped plaque provided free upon completion of set. Price per card. ....$20–$25

Star Trek: The Voyagers Card Collection—Hamilton Collection, 1996. Set of 12 different 2½″ × 3½″ rectangular porcelain "cards" with the same Keith Birdsong color artwork of ships from various Star Trek productions that appears on plates by the same company. Oval gold and silver display plaque with current overall Star Trek logo insignia provided free upon completion of set. Price per card. ....$20–$25

Pfaltzgraff Cookie Jar

Spock Bust Liquor Decanter

Pfaltzgraff Bone China *Star Trek VI* Buffet Set

Pfaltzgraff Bone China *Deep Space Nine* Buffet Set

1978 Dr. Pepper Promotional Glasses

Riker "Magic" Mug

Janeway Captain's Mug

***Star Trek III* Movie Poster Art Mug**

Spock Character Stein

20th Anniversary Collector's Plates

Ernst Episode Plate

Classic and *Next Generation* Mini-Plates

25th Anniversary Commemorative Plate

"Space Seed" Episode Plate

***Star Trek II* Movie Plate**

Ernst (left) and Hamilton (right) Picard Plates

"Yesterday's Enterprise" Episode Plate

First Plate in *Voyager* Series

CLOTHING AND ACCESSORIES

With the exception of a very few items, mostly the more elaborate (and more expensive) jackets, most Star Trek clothing items are not particularly good collectible investments. The vast majority of Star Trek clothing, about 90% of which is T-shirts, is simply bought to be worn and enjoyed. Accessories fair a little better, perhaps because they may fit well into collections of other three-dimensional items such as toys and housewares, but have still, to date, been one of the weaker fields of Star Trek collectibles. Unlicensed items have been omitted entirely from this section, partially because of the enormous amount that has been produced, particularly in the early days of Star Trek fandom (mostly T-shirts and T-shirt transfers), and partially because they have even less collectible potential than their licensed counterparts. Also excluded are items that are Star Trek related but do not require a license (such as convention T-shirts and parody T-shirts) for much the same reasons.

INVESTMENT POTENTIAL
Fair.

CARE
The best way to preserve clothing items is to not wear them. Unfortunately, with a great many T-shirts even this does not guarantee their long-term preservation. The inks used in printing the designs, especially on many black shirts, seem to make them unusually susceptible to dry rot. Accessory items hold up somewhat better but are still best left unused if it is hoped that they will accrue any value as collectibles.

SECTION NOTES
Section is organized alphabetically by item and then alphabetically by manufacturer, if known. For clothing items designed primarily as costumes, costume accessories such as ears, and patterns for costumes see the Costumes, Costume Patterns and Accessories section. For jewelry accessories see Jewelry section.

BELTS

Lee—1976. Elastic cloth belt with original Enterprise and "Star Trek" repeated in fabric. Assorted colors. ....$35–$50
Lee—1979. Star Trek: The Motion Picture. Blue stretch cloth with "Star Trek" woven in red and white. Small rectangular red enamel buckle with "Star Trek." ....$25–$40
Lee—1982. Brown leather belt with Star Trek character names and ships embossed in color the length of belt. ....
....$30–$45

NOTE: Lee marketed several of their Star Trek buckles which were also sold separately with plain, removable belts attached. See "Buckles" in Jewelry section of this book.

Rarities Mint—1989. Reversible brown/black leather belt with silver USS Enterprise (picture of original TV ship and Star Trek logo) in gold-plated buckle. ....$40–$60

CAPS

The following are all baseball-style caps with designs that are either silk-screened on or embroidered into the fabric of the cap. Caps with applied embroidered patches have been omitted from this section because, while many patches were manufactured specifically for hats (for example, all Star Trek patches made by the Thinking Cap Co.), *any* patch can be applied to a hat and even those designed for hats ultimately were sold most commonly as separate patches. (See Patches section of this book.)

American Needle—1994

All are fully embroidered.

Character Caps (crew from original TV series)—Color portrait on front, word logo in silver thread on side, name in large letters on back.

    Bones, on dark green cap. ....$15–$18

    Capt. Kirk, on navy cap. ....$15–$18

    Chekov, red cap. ....$15–$18

    Khan (portrait from movie), on navy cap. ....$15–$18

    Mr. Spock, on lavendar cap. ....$15–$18

    Mr. Sulu, on red cap. ....$15–$18

    Scotty, on red cap. ....$15–$18

    Uhura, on red cap. ....$15–$18

Character Caps (crew from Star Trek: The Next Generation)—Color portrait on front, word logo on side in silver thread, name in large letters on back.

    Capt. Picard, on navy cap. ....$15–$18

    Riker, on·red cap. ....$15–$18

    Worf, on red cap. ....$15–$18

Enterprise Cap—Side view of ship from original TV show in white on black cap. ....$15–$18

Logo Caps—Word logos on front of hats.

    Star Trek (original TV), "Space . . . The Final Frontier" on back, white embroidery on black hat. ....$15–$18

    Star Trek: Deep Space Nine, gold and silver on navy cap. ....$15–$18

    Star Trek: Generations, red on tan cap. ....$15–$18

    Star Trek: The Next Generation, silver on purple cap. ....$15–$18

Symbol Caps—Symbol embroidered on front, appropriate word logo on side and name on back.

    Borg, on tan cap. ....$15–$18

    Command Emblem (original TV), on lavender or black cap (no name on back). ....$15–$18

    Ferengi, on light green cap. ....$15–$18

    Klingon (original three-color symbol), on lavender cap. ... .$15–$18

USS Enterprise NCC-1701-D—In gold on front of black cap. Next Generation word logo in gold on back. .....$15–$18

Creation—1995

Star Trek logo caps. Embroidered on fronts of black or white caps.

Starfleet Academy Emblem Logo, red, yellow, white, and black embroidery. ....$12–$15

Star Trek: Deep Space Nine, gold and silver metallic embroidery. ....$12–$15

Star Trek: Generations, red embroidery. ....$12–$15

Star Trek: The Next Generation, red, purple, turquoise, and white embroidery. ....$12–$15

Star Trek: Voyager, silver and gold metallic embroidery. ... .$12–$15

Miscellaneous

Official Star Trek Fan Club—1986. Star Trek IV. Corduroy hat embroidered with movie logo. ....$12–$15

Paramount—1989 (Promotional). Star Trek V. White or black cap with silver and red logo. ....$10–$20

Paramount Special Effects—1989. Star Trek crew. Black cap with original TV letter logo in white embroidered lettering and "Crew" below in smaller letters. ....$15–$20

Ralph Marlin—1991. Painters caps. All-over designs. Color artwork screen-printed on black backgrounds. Three different.

    Enterprise NCC-1701-A, ship and small 25th anniversary logos. ....$10–$15

    Star Trek: The Next Generation, ships and logos. $10–$15

    25th Anniversary, large anniversary logo and movie ships. ....$10–$15

Ralph Marlin—1994. Silver embroidery on black caps.

    "Star Trek." ....$10–$15

    "Star Trek: The Next Generation." ....$10–$15

Thinking Cap Co.—1982. Vulcan Ear Hat. Rubber pointed ears attached to sides. (Also came with embroidered "Spock Lives" patch.) ....$15–$25

Thinking Cap Co.—1982. Star Trek II: The Wrath of Khan. Color logo silk-screened on cap. ....$10–$15

Ultra Graphics—1996. Silver holographic appliqué of Next Generation ship and word logo on black hat. ....$15–$20

Ultra Graphics—1991. Color appliqué designs on fronts of hats. Three designs. Assorted hat colors.

    "Star Trek," with movie Enterprise. ....$10–$15

    25th Anniversary Logo. ....$10–$15

    USS Enterprise 1701, with NG command emblem. ....$10–$15

IRON-ON TRANSFERS

Primarily used for T-shirts. Though very popular in the 1970s, almost all T-shirts made in recent years have silk-screened designs.

AMT—1968. Color artwork from original TV show. Approx. 6″ × 9″. Offered in promotion with this company's model kits.

    Assortment of Small Transfers—Insignias, USS Enterprise (words), How's Your Tribble (with picture), and Vulcan Power with Vulcan hand salute. ....$3–$5

    Keep on Trekkin', with Enterprise. ....$3–$5

    Klingon Power, with Klingon ship. ....$3–$5

    Star Trek Lives. ....$3–$5

General Mills—1979. Star Trek: The Motion Picture. Promotional. Five different. Originally sold only as set.

    Blank (make own design). ....$2–$4

    Enterprise and Logo. ....$4–$6

    Kirk and Logo. ....$4–$6

    Kirk, Spock, and Logo. ....$4–$6

Spock and Logo. ....$4–$6

Lincoln Enterprises—1980. Poor quality color photo reproductions. All from original TV show.

Enterprise, firing phasers. ....$1–$2
Kirk, in dress uniform. ....$1–$2
Kirk, with phaser. ....$1–$2
Kirk and Spock, from "Patterns of Force." ....$1–$2
Kirk and Spock, from "Spock's Brain." ....$1–$2
Kirk and Spock, looking down. ....$1–$2
Kirk and Spock, with phaser. ....$1–$2
Kirk, Spock, and McCoy, from "Patterns of Force." ....
....$1–$2
Spock, with lyre. ....$1–$2
Spock (Vulcan salute). ....$1–$2

Lincoln Enterprises—1984. Star Trek III: The Search for Spock logo. ....$1–$2

McDonald's (Promotional)—1979. Star Trek: The Motion Picture. Color glitter transfer. Two small transfers on one sheet. Spock standing and a red movie-style uniform emblem with movie logo. Originally given away as Happy Meals premiums. ....$1–$2

Pacific Transfer—1982. Star Trek: The Wrath of Khan color photo transfers.

Khan, from Wrath of Khan. ....$1–$2
Kirk, from Wrath of Khan. ....$1–$2
Spock, from Wrath of Khan. ....$1–$2
Wrath of Khan Logo. ....$1–$2

Paramount (Promotional)—1989. Star Trek: The Final Frontier logo. ....$3–$4

Roach—1979. Star Trek: The Motion Picture. Color glitter photo transfers. Marketed primarily already applied to shirts.

Enterprise, Kirk, Spock, and Logo. ....$1–$2
Enterprise and Logo. ....$1–$2
Glitter Enterprise and Logo. ....$1–$2
Ilia and Enterprise. ....$1–$2
Kirk, Enterprise, and Logo. ....$1–$2

JACKETS

Creation—1995. Denim jackets. Blue denim with embroidered designs on back and appropriate small pocket logo on front.

Star Trek: Deep Space Nine, Gold and silver logo. ....
....$50–$75
Star Trek: The Next Generation, multicolored logo. ....
....$50–$75
USS Enterprise NCC-1701-D, with ship. ....$50–$75
United Federation of Planets, with seal. ....$50–$75

Creation—1995. Black wool jackets with leather suede sleeves in assorted colors. Embroidered design on back and appropriate smaller logo in breast pocket area.

Starfleet Academy, color emblem. ....$200–$250
Star Trek, word logo. ....$200–$250
Star Trek: Deep Space Nine Space Station. .....$200–$250

Star Trek: Deep Space Nine, word logo. ....$200–$250
Star Trek: The Next Generation Logo, multicolor. ....
....$200–$250
Star Trek: Voyager, word logo. ....$200–$250
United Federation of Planets, with seal. ....$200–$250
USS Enterprise NCC-1701-D, with ship. ....$200–$250

D.D. Bean & Sons—1979. Star Trek: The Motion Picture. Lightweight silver material with movie-style insignia on front. ....$100–$125

D.D. Bean & Sons—1979. Star Trek: The Motion Picture. Deluxe L.E.D. jacket UFP patch on front. Back has movie title logo over Enterprise outline embellished with red flashing L.E.D.'s. ....$150–$200

Great Lakes—1974. Light blue nylon with black collar and cuffs and two white accent stripes on arms. Shoulder pocket on left sleeve. Leatherette original TV science emblem. Promotional item sold through AMT model company. ..$50–$75

Great Lakes—1974. Silver nylon with embroidered original UFP design. ....$40–$60

Lincoln Enterprises—1984. Star Trek III: The Search for Spock. Lightweight jacket with white trim. Embroidered STIII patch on front and "U.S.S. Enterprise" on back.

Black Nylon. ....$25–$30
White or Blue Satinique. ....$50–$60

Lincoln Enterprises—1986. Star Trek IV: The Voyage Home crew jacket. White satin trimmed in navy. Back has fully embroidered Star Trek IV logo design showing Enterprise, Golden Gate bridge, and whales. ....$125–$150

Lincoln Enterprises—1986. Star Trek IV: The Voyage Home. Lightweight windbreaker in white, black, or navy with patch depicting Bird-of-Prey over Golden Gate Bridge and whales. USS Enterprise on back.

Nylon. ....$30–$35
White, black, navy, gray, or red satinique. ....$50–$60

NOTE: Similar windbreakers and jackets came with patch showing Enterprise over whales.

Lincoln Enterprises—1986. Twentieth anniversary windbreaker. Lightweight black, white, or navy jacket with patch showing Enterprise and "Star Trek—20th Anniversary." "U.S.S. Enterprise" on back.

Nylon. ....$30–$35
White, black, navy, gray, or red satinique. ....$50–$60

Official Star Trek Fan Club—1986. Star Trek IV jacket. Silver satin with two-color Star Trek IV logo on back. ....
....$40–$50

Paramount Special Effects—1989. Star Trek: The Next Generation jean jacket. Airbrushed Enterprise and Star Trek logo on front. "U.S.S. Enterprise" down arm. ....$180–$200

Paramount Special Effects—1989. Star Trek: The Next Generation satin jacket. Silver, black, or navy with insignia logo on front and large insignia on back. ....$90–$100

Paramount Special Effects—1989. Star Trek V denim jacket. Embroidered logo strip over front pocket. .....$75–$80

Paramount Special Effects—1989. Star Trek V satin jacket.

Black satin embroidered front and back with logo in silver, black, and red. ....$75–$80

Top Line—1991. This company produced fully embroidered designs on a variety of different jacket styles. The most common are listed.

Enterprise—Ship from original TV series embroidered in color on back of jacket. Original command emblem embroidered in black and gold metallic thread in breast pocket area.

Black Wool Jacket (with or without assorted color leather sleeves). ....$225–$300

Blue Denim Jacket. ....$85–$125

Star Trek: The Next Generation Logo—In red on back of jacket. Next Generation–style command insignia embroidered in metallic thread in breast pocket area.

Black Denim Jacket. ....$85–$125

Black Satin Jacket. ....$85–$125

Black Wool Jacket (with or without assorted color leather sleeves). ....$225–$300

Star Trek 25th Anniversary Logo—Large multicolored design on back of jacket with extensive use of gold and silver metallic thread. Metallic gold and black original command insignia design in breast pocket area.

Denim Jacket (blue or black). ....$85–$125

Satin Jacket (assorted colors). ....$85–$125

Wool Jacket (black with or without assorted color leather sleeves). ....$225–$300

PANTS

Creation—1995. Gray sweatpants with "Property of Starfleet Academy Athletic Department" and Starfleet Academy seal on left leg. ....$20–$25

RAINGEAR

Fabil—1977. Yellow plastic slicker with Star Trek logo on front and original Enterprise on back. Children's size. ....$65–$80

Swell Wear—1979. Silver and white plastic slicker decorated with Star Trek: The Motion Picture Enterprise and crew. Children's sizes. ....$50–$75

SCARF

Ralph Marlin—1995. Red and black silk approx. 35″ square. Dark red background with black universal Star Trek logo in all-over design and 2³⁄₄″ black border. ....$30–$40

SHIRTS

Creation—1995. Medical scrubs. Green with "Starfleet Medical Corps" and caduceus on breast pocket. ....$20–$25

Creation—1995. Polo shirts. Embroidered pocket designs on black shirts.

Star Trek: The Next Generation, color word logo. ....$25–$30

Star Trek: Generations, logo. ....$25–$30

USS Enterprise NCC-1701-D, with ship. ....$25–$30

United Federation of Planets, with seal. ....$25–$30

Funatics (Canadian)—1993. Children's Star Trek: The Next Generation shirts.

Data. ....$15–$25

Final Frontier. ....$15–$25

USS Enterprise. ....$15–$25

Worf. ....$15–$25

GEM—1995. Hockey jersey. Black mesh with red neck and red, gray, and orange stripes on lower part of shirt and sleeves. Large red and orange Klingon emblem with white and black embroidered edges on front of shirt and "Klingon Empire" embroidered in red on gray body stripe. .....$50–$60

GEM—1996. Hockey jersey. Blue mesh with lighter blue neck and light blue and gray stripes on lower part of shirt and sleeves. Light blue, gray, and black movie-style command emblem on front of shirt. ....$50–$60

Huk-a-Poo Clothing—1978. Button front collar-style shirt. Original TV Kirk, Spock, and Enterprise in all-over blue, white, and brown design. ....$50–$75

SHOES AND SHOELACES

Shoes—1968. Children's plastic slip-ons. Tan plastic with red linings. Decorated with Spock, Enterprise, and logo. ....$65–$95

Shoes—1979. Blue rubber beach sandals with white straps. Top of sole has "Star Trek" and lenticular position changing Enterprise. Plastic lenticular medallion on straps changes from red Motion Picture–style command insignia to color artwork of Kirk, Spock, and McCoy in Motion Picture uniforms. ....$60–$75

Shoelaces—1991. White laces with "USS Enterprise NCC-1701" and outline of ship repeated in black. ....$10–$15

SHORTS

Dawnelle—1979. Short and shirt sets. Star Trek: The Motion Picture. Blue shorts and tank tops with color artwork decals. Three different designs.

Enterprise and Crew. ....$25–$40
Kirk and Spock. ....$25–$40
Spock. ....$25–$40

Ralph Marlin—1991. Boxer shorts with all-over color artwork designs.
Star Trek: The Next Generation, logo and ship. ...$15–$20
25th Anniversary Logo. ....$15–$20

Ralph Marlin—1995. Boxer shorts with all-over color artwork designs.
Star Trek: Deep Space Nine, space station, "Star Trek" and faces of various aliens on black background. ....
....$15–$20
Star Trek Ships, gold and blue schematics of various ships on black background. ....$15–$20
Star Trek: The Next Generation, word logo and various symbols on blue background. ....$15–$20

Ralph Marlin—1996. Silk boxer shorts with all-over design of new-style double bar communicator insignia. Two-color schemes. Blue and gray or red and gray. Adult sizes. ....
....$25–$35

SLEEPWEAR

Funantics (Canadian)—1993. Children's Star Trek: The Next Generation pajamas.
Data. ....$20–$30
Enterprise and Crew. ....$20–$30
Uniform. ....$25–$35

Nazareth Mills—1976. Two-piece children's pajamas with color artwork of Enterprise above logo. ....$45–$65

Nazareth Mills—1979. Two-piece toddler's pajamas. Star Trek: The Motion Picture. Pajamas decorated with color artwork from movie. Packaged in bags with line art of movie Enterprise and logo in corner.
Enterprise. ....$30–$45
Kirk. ....$30–$45
Spock. ....$30–$45

Pajama Corp. of America—1979. Star Trek: The Motion Picture. Child's sizes. Two-piece pajamas with color photos from the movie. Packaged in bags with artwork of Kirk, Spock, and movie Enterprise and logo.
Enterprise. ....$35–$50
Kirk. ....$35–$50
Kirk, Spock, and McCoy. ....$35–$50
Spock. ....$35–$50

Pajama Corp. of America—1989. Star Trek: The Next Generation. Two-piece children's pajamas with black pants and tops in assorted colors designed to resemble Next Generation uniforms with black shoulders and oversized insignia. ....
....$25–$35

Paramount Special Effects—1989. Sleep shirt. Long black T-shirt with "Star Trek Crew" on front in silver. ......$25–$35

SOCKS

John Batts Co.—1976 Original TV character iron-on on white tube socks with character name and logo.
Crewman Phasering Alien. ....$25–$35
Enterprise and Crew Beaming Down. ....$25–$35
Kirk. ....$25–$35
Spock. ....$25–$35

Carolina Casuals—1989. Original TV word logo embroidered in white on black socks. ....$25–$35

Charleston Hosiery—1979. Star Trek: The Motion Picture. White tube socks with cuff stripes in assorted colors. Iron-on photo of character with name and logo above.
Decker. ....$20–$30
Enterprise. ....$20–$30
Ilia. ....$20–$30
Kirk. ....$20–$30
Spock. ....$20–$30
Kirk and Spock. ....$20–$30

No-Comment International (Swiss)—1995. Knitted in original TV series designs with Star Trek logo.
Enterprise. ....$10–$15
Enterprise, 3 views. ....$10–$15
Spock. ....$10–$15
Starfleet Logo (repeated motif). ....$10–$15
Transporter Room. ....$10–$15

Paramount Special Effects—1989. White tube socks with Star Trek: The Next Generation command insignia logo embroidered in blue, black, and gold metallic threat. ....
....$25–$35

SWEATSHIRTS

Creation—1993/95.
Property of Starfleet Academy Athletic Department, with color emblem on gray shirt. ....$20–$30
Starfleet Academy, with emblem on black shirt. ....
....$20–$30
Star Trek: Deep Space Nine, logo on black shirt. ....
....$20–$30
Star Trek: Generations, red logo on black shirt. ....
....$20–$30
Star Trek: The Next Generation, color word logo on black shirt. ....$20–$30
United Federation of Planets, with seal on black shirt. ......
....$20–$30
USS Enterprise NCC-1701-A, in green with command emblem on back of gray shirt, "Star Trek" on breast pocket area. ....$20–$30

Great Southern—1989. Star Trek V: The Final Frontier. Color silk-screened picture of Klaa with letter logo on front and Klingon Bird-of-Prey and "Keep on Trekking" on back of black shirt. ....$20–$25

Great Southern—1989. Star Trek: The Next Generation. Enterprise and logo on front. Call Letter energy burst design on back. Color silk-screen. ....$20–$25

Novel Teez (Canadian)—1986. White sweatshirt with color silk-screened artwork.

Kirk and Enterprise (Original TV), "Scotty Beam Me Up . . . There's No Intelligent Life on Earth!" ....
....$15–$20

Spock and Kirk in Car (Star Trek IV), "Spock, If You Don't Like the Way I Drive . . . Get Off the Sidewalk! ....$15–$20

Spock and McCoy (Star Trek IV), "Damn It, Spock . . . Keep Your Volcanic Space Farts to Yourself." ....
....$15–$20

Spock, Vulcan Salute (Original TV), "Live Long and Prosper." ....$15–$20

Star Trek IV Logo. ....$15–$20

Paramount (Promotional)—1991. 25th anniversary logo embroidered in color on front of gray shirt. ....$40–$45

Paramount Special Effects—1989. "Star Trek" in white Star Trek: The Motion Picture–style movie lettering logo embroidered on black shirt. ....$20–$25

Paramount Special Effects—1989. Star Trek: The Next Generation. Logo with insignia on white or blue sweatshirt. ....$20–$25

T-SHIRTS

Changes—1991/92. All designs are color unless otherwise stated.

Belt Prints, all-over front and back artwork prints in black and blue on white shirts.

Original TV, Kirk, Spock, McCoy, Enterprise, and logo. ....$15–$20

Star Trek: The Next Generation, Enterprise, and logo. ....$15–$20

Crew Shirts, photo group shot of respective crew with Enterprise above and logo below on black shirt.

Original TV. ....$15–$20

Star Trek: The Next Generation. ....$15–$20

Enterprise, two-sided shirt has front view of original ship on front of shirt with "Star Trek" above ship, "Space . . . the Final Frontier" below. Back of shirt has rear view of ship and mirror image of words. Silk-screen on black shirt. ....$15–$20

Enterprise/Klingon Cruiser, artwork of ships from original TV series, one on front, one on back. ....$15–$20

Progressive Images, four artwork squares on white shirts arranged to show different phases of action in a scene from the original TV series. "Star Trek" above and appropriate caption underneath on white shirts.

Characters Transporting. ....$15–$20

Enterprise. ....$15–$20

Spock. ....$15–$20

Spock, full-shirt artwork on front. ....$15–$20

Star Trek VI: The Undiscovered Country, photo designs silk-screened onto black shirts.

"Klingons," with characters from movie. ....$15–$20

Movie Poster Artwork. ....$15–$20

Scenes From the Movie (collage). ....$15–$20

"Starfleet," with Kirk, Spock, and McCoy. ....
....$15–$20

Trial Scenes. ....$15–$20

Star Trek: The Next Generation Character Shirts, portrait of character in front of appropriate background artwork above logo on black shirts.

Data. ....$15–$20

Geordi. ....$15–$20

Ferengi. ....$15–$20

Picard. ....$15–$20

Riker. ....$15–$20

Worf. ....$15–$20

25th Anniversary T-Shirt, color photo collage from original TV series and 25th anniversary logo on white. ....
....$15–$20

25th Anniversary T-Shirt, artwork of original Enterprise orbiting planet with small 25th anniversary logo in lower corner. ....$15–$20

Creation—1991. 25th anniversary T-shirt. Movie and Next Generation Enterprises above NG-style command symbol with "Star Trek" above and "25 Years 1966–1991 The Continuing Voyages of the Enterprise" below in blue. Color artwork silk-screened on black shirt. ....$15–$20

Creation—1991. Silver anniversary tour shirt. Front has "Star Trek 25" being circled by original Enterprise in red, blue, black, and silver. Back has list of conventions. Silk-screened on white shirt. ....$15–$20

Creation—1994/95. Silk-screened T-shirts. Photo or artwork designs are color unless otherwise specified.

Character History, character faces progress down right side of shirt. Black and white photos on black. ......$15–$20

Enterprise-D, artwork and logo. ....$15–$20

Enterprise-D, photo with energy burst on black. .....$15–$20

Enterprise-D, schematic red on white, logo back. ....
....$15–$20

"Galaxy Class Starship" and "USS Enterprise NCC-1701-D," with color artwork of ship on black. ....$15–$20

Imzadi T-Shirt, Riker, Troi "Imzadi," and logo. ....
....$15–$20

"Join Starfleet See the Universe," artwork on black. ....
....$15–$20

Kirk and Spock, black and white photo on black. ....
....$15–$20

Klingon Bird-of-Prey, artwork front, Klingon script back on black. ....$15–$20

Klingon Cruiser (Original TV), artwork front, Klingon symbol back on black. ....$15–$20

Legacy of Star Trek, Ships and "To Boldly Go, etc." in front of Earth on black. ....$15–$20

"Lursa & B'etor The Duras Sisters," with photo on black. ....$15–$20

Planet Travel Labels, simulated suitcase labels in black and white all-over design. ....$15–$20

"Q," photo on black. ....$15–$20

Quark and Odo, photo on black. ....$15–$20

Romulan Warbird, artwork front, Romulan symbol back on black. ....$15–$20

"Starfleet Academy," with emblem front, logo back on gray. ....$15–$20

Star Trek: Deep Space Nine, logo and artwork of space station on black. ....$15–$20

Star Trek: Generations, logo on black. ....$15–$20

Star Trek: Generations, logo and collage photo on black. ....$15–$20

Star Trek: Generations, logo and photo of Kirk and Picard on black. ....$15–$20

Star Trek: Generations, movie poster artwork on black. ....$15–$20

"Star Trek: The Next Generation Excuse Shirt," with list on black shirt. ....$15–$20

Star Trek: The Next Generation 5th Anniversary Shirt, with list of episodes on black. ....$15–$20

"Star Trek Excuse Shirt," with list on black. ....$15–$20

"10-Forward," with command insignia on white. ....
....$15–$20

"The Future of Health Care," three doctors photos on black. ....$15–$20

"The Borg," photo on black. ....$15–$20

"The Borg," reproductions of mechanical appliances in white on black. ....$15–$20

"The Women of Star Trek," photo on black. ....$15–$20

"To Boldly Go, etc." and "Star Trek," circular design on black shirt. ....$15–$20

"United Federation of Planets," blue and silver on black. ....$15–$20

"United Federation of Planets," with seal, white on blue shirt. ....$15–$20

"Vulcan Science Academy," with IDIC on white. ....
....$15–$20

Creation—1996. Campaign T-shirts. Color silk-screen on white shirts.

Kirk/Spock '96. ....$15–$20

Picard/Riker '96. ....$15–$20

Edwards Teez—1995. Two-sided shirts with oversized photo of the face of the character made up of dot patterns silk-screened on black shirts.

Data (black on white shirt). ....$15–$20

Kirk. ....$15–$20

Picard. ....$15–$20

Spock. ....$15–$20

GEM—1995. One-sided color silk-screen designs.

"Borg . . . Resistance Is Futile," with ship. ....$15–$20

"Klingon Bird-of-Prey" above, "Klingon Defense Force" below picture of ship on black shirt. ....$15–$20

Klingon Symbol, with Klingon writing in gray and silver on black shirt. ....$15–$20

"Star Trek: Voyager," with universal logo in red and orange on black shirt. ....$15–$20

Voyager Ship Schematic, in green on black. ....$15–$20

Great Southern—1989. Two-sided color silk-screened designs on black T-shirts.

Star Trek V: The Final Frontier, group on front, ship and "Crew" on back. ....$10–$15

Star Trek V: The Final Frontier, Klaa on front; Bird-of-Prey and "Keep on Trekkin" on back. ....$10–$15

Star Trek V: The Final Frontier, Ship and logo on front, logo on back (originally designed for theater sales only). ....$10–$15

Star Trek: The Next Generation, Enterprise and logo front, starfield back. ....$10–$15

Star Trek: The Next Generation, Enterprise and logo front; call letters in energy burst design on back. ....$10–$15

Image Design—1991. Heat-sensitive ink applied to white shirt. Line artwork of Kirk, Spock, and McCoy from original show "beams" away when worn due to body heat. ....
....$15–$20

Lincoln Enterprises—1981. Color silk-screened artwork on T-shirts and tank tops in a variety of colors.

Enterprise (original), with "Star Trek Lives." ....$5–$10

Promo Art, early NBC design. ....$5–$10

Lincoln Enterprises—1987. Color silk-screened artwork on white or black T-shirts.

Enterprise-A, with "She Lives." ....$9–$15

Enterprise-A, whales and "The Ultimate Voyage." ....
....$9–$15

25th Anniversary, Enterprise and insignia design. ....
....$9–$15

Lincoln Enterprises—1987. Puffy silk-screen designs on T-shirts.

Enterprise-D with NG logo (white on navy). ....$15–$20

UFP Seal (new style), white and navy on tan. ....
....$15–$20

"United Federation of Paramount," Enterprise-D flying around company's mountain trademark. ....$15–$20

Official Star Trek Fan Club—1986. Star Trek IV: The Voyage Home. Movie logo on black shirt. ....$10–$15

Official Star Trek Fan Club—1986. Finalized version of official 20th anniversary logo. ....$15–$20

Official Star Trek Fan Club—1995. Color silk-screen of Next Generation–style UFP emblem superimposed on starfield on back of black shirt. Command emblem on front breast pocket area. ....$15–$20

Paramount (Promotional)—1986. "The Next Generation." Silver silk-screened on black shirt. Included in early promo kit. ....$15–$20

Paramount (Promotional)—1986. Early version of 20th anniversary logo. ....$15–$20

Paramount (Promotional)—1990. Star Trek V: The Final Frontier logo silk-screened on white or black shirts. ....
....$15–$20

Paramount Special Effects—1989. Color artwork designs silk-screened on T-shirts.

Aliens, collage of original TV aliens on black. ....$15–$20

Gorn, from original TV show on white shirt. ....$15–$20

Ralph Marlin—1994. Deep Space Nine space station. Color silk-screen on black shirt with all-over blue pattern. ....$15–$20

Ralph Marlin—1994. Deep Space Nine space station. Color silk-screen on black shirt. ....$15–$20

Stanley Desantis—1996. Color silk-screened designs on black shirts.

Enterprise (Original), with "Star Trek." ....$15–$20

Kirk, waist up. ....$15–$20

McCoy, waist up. ....$15–$20

Spock Face (Front), 30th anniversary logo back. ....$15–$20

Spock, Vulcan salute. ....$15–$20

Spock, waist up. ....$15–$20

"Star Trek 5 Year Mission" (Front), stardates back. ....$15–$20

30th Anniversary (Pocket Logo Front), original Enterprise back. ....$15–$20

30th Anniversary (Pocket Logo Front), original Enterprise and Tholian web schematic back. ....$15–$20

Voyager, crew and logo. ....$15–$20

Voyager, logo front, ship back. ....$15–$20

Voyager, ship and logo. ....$15–$20

TAG—1993. All designs are color silk-screens on black shirts unless otherwise noted.

Character Shirts, portrait with suitable background artwork, characters name and logo, one sided.

Cardassian. ....$15–$20

Odo. ....$15–$20

Quark (Quark's Bar). ....$15–$20

Riker. ....$15–$20

Sisko. ....$15–$20

Troi. ....$15–$20

Worf. ....$15–$20

"Energize!" above original characters on transporter, logo below. ....$15–$20

Enterprise (Original), orbiting planet with "To Boldly Go Where No Man Has Gone Before" above and "Star Trek" below. ....$15–$20

Enterprise-D, head-on view in front of planet with logo above and call letters below. ....$15–$20

"Live Long and Prosper," with Spock and "Star Trek." ....$15–$20

Star Trek (Original TV Series) Belt Prints, full-shirt prints on both sides of shirts.

Capt. Kirk. ....$15–$20

Spock. ....$15–$20

"Star Trek," in yellow, with character faces and opening monologue from original series in white on black. ....$15–$20

Star Trek: Deep Space Nine, crew above logo. ....$15–$20

Star Trek: Deep Space Nine, space station and logo. ....$15–$20

Star Trek: Deep Space Nine, space station schematic and logo. ....$15–$20

Star Trek: The Next Generation, crew below logo. ....$15–$20

"The Trouble with Tribbles," above Kirk and tribbles, logo below. ....$15–$20

Ultra Graphics—1995. Line artwork of ships done in holographic foil on black shirts.

Enterprise (Original). ....$15–$20

Enterprise-D. ....$15–$20

Klingon Bird-of-Prey. ....$15–$20

Romulan Warbird. ....$15–$20

Winterland—1994. Silk-screened designs on black shirts.

"Borg," with sepia-tone photo of character. ....$15–$20

Schematic, of ships and symbols in purple. ....$15–$20

Three Captains Shirt, color photos of Kirk, Picard, and Sisko with their respective ships. ....$15–$20

TIES

Lee—1976. Clip-on ties with Enterprise ships, "Star Trek," and "NCC 1701" repeated in diagonal stripes. Ties came in blue, brown, or red. ....$35–$50

Ralph Marlin—1993/96.

Cotton Tie:

Star Trek: The Next Generation, word logos and ships. ....$15–$20

Polyester Ties:

Amok Time, two scenes from episode. ....$15–$20

Borg Collage. ....$15–$20

Crew Collage (Original). ....$15–$20

Crew Collage (Next Generation). ....$15–$20

Crew Collage (Deep Space Nine). ....$15–$20

Deep Space Nine, alien collage. ....$15–$20

Deep Space Nine, space station. ....$15–$20

Enterprise (Original), with gold planet. ....$15–$20

Enterprise (Original), with pink planet. ....$15–$20

Enterprise 1701-D, with gold planet. ....$15–$20

Kirk (Original TV). ....$15–$20

Kirk (On Opening Monologue Background). ....$15–$20

Kirk, Spock, and McCoy, three faces. ....$15–$20

Klingon Collage. ....$15–$20

McCoy (Original TV). ....$15–$20

Menagerie, two scenes from episode. ....$15–$20

Mirror, Mirror, two scenes from episode. ....$15–$20

Picard. ....$15–$20

Quark. ....$15–$20

Spock (Original TV). ....$15–$20

Star Trek (Original) Club Tie, word logo and command

symbols in horizontal stripes on dark blue tie. ....
.................................$15–$20

Star Trek: The Next Generation Club Tie, word logo and command symbols in horizontal stripes on dark blue tie. ....$15–$20

Tholian Web, two scenes from episode. ....$15–$20

Worf. ....$15–$20

Voyager, crew and ship. ....$15–$20

Silk Ties:

Enterprise Blueprint (Original TV). ....$20–$25

Enterprise (Original TV). ....$20–$25

Enterprise and Klingon Ships (Original TV). ....
.................................$20–$25

Four Captains, photos of Kirk, Picard, Sisko, and Janeway. ....$20–$25

Insignia (new style), all-over design in gray, black, and red. ....$20–$25

Kirk (Original TV). ....$20–$25

Ship Schematics (Enterprises and DS9 Station). ....
.................................$20–$25

Star Trek Logo (Universal), black all-over design on red tie. ....$20–$25

30th Anniversary Logo, all-over design. ....$20–$25

Tie Rack (British)—1993. Silk ties. Both styles have several color variations.

Enterprise (Original TV), repeated. ....$25–$35

Montage Tie, faces of Kirk and Spock repeated. ....
.................................$25–$35

TOTE BAGS

Aviva—1979. Star Trek: The Motion Picture. Vertical-format blue canvas with one outside zippered pocket and color artwork transfer on side.

Enterprise. ....$35–$50

Kirk. ....$35–$50

Spock. ....$35–$50

NOTE: These same three transfers were used by Aviva on a variety of different style canvas totes—open shopping type, one zipper athletic bags, etc. Values for all are approximately the same.

Creation—1995. Open-topped canvas totes with handles. Design on side.

Starfleet Academy, color emblem on tan tote. ....
.................................$20–$25

"Star Trek," white on black tote. ....$20–$25

"Star Trek: The Next Generation," red and yellow on black tote. ....$20–$25

"United Federation of Planets," with seal in white on blue tote. ....$20–$25

Creation—1995. Sports bag. Black and red nylon. Horizontal format with handles and three outside pockets. Voyager logo in gold and silver on side pocket. ....$50–$60

Sears—1975. Black and gray zippered tote. Approx. 12″.

Enterprise. ....$45–$75

Kirk. ....$45–$75

Spock. ....$45–$75

UNDERWEAR

Nazareth Mills—1979. Star Trek: The Motion Picture. T-shirt and underwear set in boys sizes. ....$35–$45

UMBRELLAS

Shaw Creations—1993. Black umbrellas decorated with spacescapes, logos, opening monologues, and Enterprise and Klingon ships from their respective TV series.

Star Trek (Original TV). ....$35–$45

Star Trek: The Next Generation. ....$35–$45

WALLETS

Larami—1977. Original Star Trek television Enterprise and Romulan Bird-of-Prey decal on brown zippered wallet. ....
.................................$35–$45

Larami—1979. Star Trek: The Motion Picture. Blue plastic snap-shut wallets with Star Trek: The Motion Picture motifs on front. Came blister-carded on color header with photo of Kirk, Spock, and Enterprise at top.

Enterprise (Artwork) and Logo. ....$25–$35

Kirk, Spock, Enterprise (Photo) and Logo. ....$25–$35

Klingon Hockey Jersey

Ultra Graphics *Next Generation* Holographic T-Shirt

Ralph Marlin *Deep Space Nine* Shorts

From left: Galoob *Star Trek: Next Generation* 3³/₄″ Ferengi
Figure; Playmates Toys *Deep Space Nine* Action Figure, later
design (with earlier design for comparison)

Mego Andorian Figure

Dufort & Sons *Next Generation* Badges

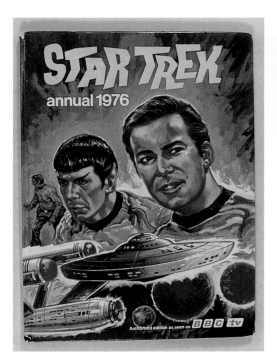

British Star Trek Annual

Pocket Books Star Trek Novels

Star Trek Steins

Ernst 20th Anniversary Star Trek Plates, Rare Platinum Bordered Edition (center) and Regular Blue Bordered Edition (right)

Quark _Deep Space Nine_ Plate

Celebrity Star Trek Stamp Packets

Lightrix Holographic Sticker set (uncut sheet)

WM McKinney & Sons Holographic Sticker Set

Hasbro Star Trek Board Game, 1974

Random House Greeting Card, large size

Milton Bradley *Star Trek: The Motion Picture* Board Game

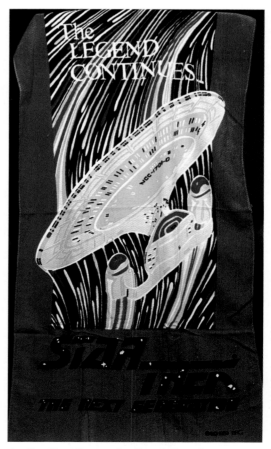

Classic Star Trek Original Series Trivia Game

Jupiter *Next Generation* Beach Towel

Triangle Merchandise Bags

Magazine

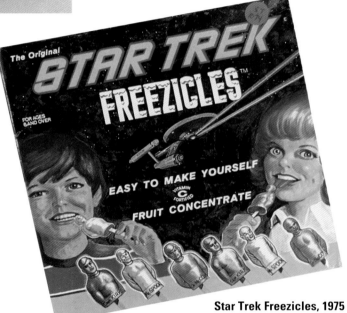

Star Trek Freezicles, 1975

Assortment of Typical Keychains

Magazine

Prime Press Original Star Trek Postcard Book

AMT/ERTL Vinyl Scotty Model Kit

Schmid Next *Generation* Jigsaw Puzzle

Japanese *Star Trek IV* Movie Poster

Moustrak Mousepad

TEC Card Telephone Cards

**Applause *Deep Space Nine*
and *Generations* (first) Figure Sets**

Triangle *Next Generation* Stand-Me-Up

**Playmates *Next Generation* Innerspace
Phaser Playset**

South Bend Electronic Enterprise

COINS AND MEDALLIONS

Coins vary in quality from simple novelties and costume jewelry pieces to some of the rarest (and most expensive) of Star Trek collectibles. The gold and silver Star Trek coins which have been minted over the years have not been given the attention by collectors that they probably deserve, perhaps because their issue price was always considerably above the value of the precious metals they contained. This is beginning to change as many collectors begin to realize that unlike many other "limited" Star Trek collectibles, most coins actually are relatively rare. The reason for this is simple economics on the part of the coin manufacturers. No hoards of unsold Star Trek coins ever languished in the back room at the mint waiting to be re-discovered by some lucky collector. Precious metals are too expensive to leave lying around collecting dust. Instead they would have long ago been melted down and recycled into another more "salable" product.

INVESTMENT POTENTIAL
Good.

CARE
Collectible coins are produced by a special minting process intended to give the surface of the coin a lustrous shine. To preserve its value, the coin should be handled only by the edge in order not to mar this surface finish. Protective plastic coin holders in a variety of sizes and styles are readily available at hobby stores and should definitely be obtained if your coins did not already come in them. Silver coins are subject to a process called "toning" where the surface of the coin tarnishes with age. As long as this coloring was caused naturally, it is not considered a defect and should not be removed. Several Star Trek collector coins come in special folders that should remain with the coin and be cared for appropriately. On the other hand, the little velveteen boxes that the coins are often placed in are simple generic packaging and add no value to the piece.

SECTION NOTES
Section is organized alphabetically by manufacturer.

Chicagoland Processing

25th Anniversary Commemorative Coins—1991. Coins are 1 oz. limited edition silver or silver with gold trim numbered on front under subject. Back of all coins shows 25th anniversary logo. Coins came in a 6″ × 4″ blue suede holder with metal reinforced corners and the Star Trek 25th anniversary logo embossed in silver on the corner. Coin in plastic holder is held in center leaf which can be turned to view back of coin. Included color information booklet held by red, white, and blue ribbon to inside front cover of folder and 25th anniversary sticker. Most were sold in sets of three with matching serial numbers.

    Enterprise Silver. ....$40–$50
    Kirk Silver. ....$40–$50
    Spock Silver. ....$40–$50
    Matching number set of all three silver coins. ....
    ....$125–$150
    Gold-Trimmed Coins, subject in gold on silver background, three-coin matching number sets only. ....
    ....$200–$225

Star Trek: The Next Generation Coins—1992. Coins are 1 oz. limited edition silver or gold. Front shows subject. Reverse of all coins shows Enterprise-D with serial number of coin underneath. Packaged in blue suede folders similar to those of 25th anniversary coins but with "Star Trek: The Next Generation" embossed in silver on front and blue ribbon to hold info book. Most were sold in sets of three with matching serial numbers.

    Picard Silver. ....$40–$50
    Counselor Troi and Comdr. Riker Silver. ....$40–$50
    Worf, Data, and Geordi La Forge Silver. ....$40–$50

Matching number set of all three silver coins. ....
....$125–$150
Gold-Trimmed Coins, subject in gold on silver background, three-coin matching number sets only. ....
....$200–$225

Continental Coin Company

Movie Poster Trading Card Ingots—1992. Rectangular silver ingot approx. 2″ × 3″ with relief representation of various Star Trek movie posters. A regular paper trading card and a Certificate of Authenticity accompany each "card."
Star Trek: The Motion Picture (Advance). ....$40–$50
Star Trek: The Motion Picture (Style A). ....$40–$50
Star Trek II: The Wrath of Khan. ....$40–$50
Star Trek IV: The Voyage Home (Advance). ......$40–$50
Star Trek IV: The Voyage Home (Style A). ....$40–$50
Star Trek V: The Final Frontier (Advance). ....$40–$50
Star Trek VI: The Undiscovered Country (Advance) ....
....$40–$50
Star Trek VI: The Undiscovered Country (Style A) ....
....$40–$50

Franklin Mint

Star Trek Coins—1993. Set of 12 different solid silver coins approx. 1¹⁄₂″ in diameter containing 290 grains of silver. One side depicts portrait or scene of subject while other shows subject's symbol. Silver and blue display case was provided free upon completion of set. Each. ....$25–$30
Calendar Medals—Approx. 3″ in diameter, medals came in either silver or pewter and had theme artwork in relief on front and calendar for particular year on reverse. All came with plastic stand to display medal.
1991, Star Trek 25th Anniversary. Front shows Kirk, Spock, McCoy, and original Enterprise superimposed over command emblem.
Pewter. ....$50–$60
Silver. ....$175–$195
1992, Star Trek: The Next Generation 5th Anniversary. Front shows Picard, Riker, Data, Troi, and Enterprise-D superimposed over Next Generation–style command emblem.
Pewter. ....$50–$60
Silver. ....$175–$195
1993, Star Trek: Deep Space Nine Premiere. Front shows space station in space.
Pewter. ....$50–$60
Silver. ....$175–$195
1994, Star Trek: The Motion Picture 15th Anniversary. Front shows Motion Picture Enterprise superimposed over command emblem.
Pewter. ....$50–$60
Silver. ....$175–$195

Hanover Mint

Hanover Mint Star Trek Medallions—1974.
First Series—Serial numbers stamped on edge of coin. Came with detachable rim for necklace chain, 1¹⁄₂″ diameter. Front pictured Kirk and Spock in front of alien background. Reverse pictures original TV Enterprise.
Bronze. ....$50–$100
Gold Plating Over Silver. ....$150–$200
Silver. ....$200–$500
Second Series—Same as originals, but with serial numbers omitted. Bronze only. ....$30–$50
Third Series—Rougher strikes, featured hole for chain cast as part of coin, serial numbers on rim, bronze only. ...
....$20–$40

NOTE: Over the years, this design has been used repeatedly in a variety of unlicensed coins, keychains, necklaces, and other novelty items. These pieces are very rough strikes that can be easily distinguished from the authorized pieces. They have virtually no collectible value.

Huckleberry Designs

Vulcan Nickel—1972 (re-issued in 1975). Large wooden nickel, drawing of Spock on face, legends "In Spock We Trust" and "Leonard Nimoy Wouldn't Lie" on reverse. ....
....$5–$10

Lincoln Enterprises

Star Trek III: The Search for Spock Commemorative Medallion—1984. Lightweight metal. Front—Kirk and Spock with title around faces. Reverse—Enterprise and planet. Diameter 1¹⁄₂″. Came with coin rim and chain. ....
....$10–$15
Star Trek IV: The Voyage Home/Challenger Commemorative Medallion—1986. Front shows Enterprise over Golden Gate Bridge and whales. Reverse shows Challenger and text. Numbered at bottom, 2¹⁄₂″ with molded bezel for neck ribbon (ribbon came with coin).
Bronze. ....$20–$25
Gold Plated. ....$60–$65
Gold and Silver Plated. ....$80–$85
Pewter. ....$20–$25
Tenth Anniversary Commemorative Medallion—1976. Front shows Kirk, Spock, McCoy, and Scotty in profile with dates 1966–1976. Reverse, Enterprise orbiting planet. Diameter 1¹⁄₂″, copper color. ....$6–$8
Twentieth Anniversary Commemorative Medallion—1986. Diameter 1¹⁄₂″, Kirk and Spock on front, Enterprise and dates 1966–1986 on reverse. ....$10–$15

Nobel Studio

Voyager Medallion—1995. Round pewter medal, 4″ in diameter. Pictures ship inside of octagon design with "January 16, 1995" (premiere date) and "Star Trek: Voyager" underneath. Came with plastic display stand. ....$40–$50

QVC

25th Anniversary Medallion—Gold-plated base metal. 25th Anniversary logo on one side and original Enterprise and "USS Enterprise" on other. Originally sold with bezel and chain. ....$15–$20

Rarities Mint

Original TV Star Trek Coins—1989. Front shows character in original TV uniform in frosted relief on mirrored background. All coins have common reverse design of original TV Enterprise over Star Trek logo and metal content. Number appears around edge of coin. Numbers are deceiving as they are almost surely higher than the number of coins that exist.

1 Ounce Solid Silver Coins—Came in plastic holders inside velveteen box.

Chekov.	....$50–$75
Kirk.	....$50–$75
McCoy.	....$50–$75
Scotty.	....$50–$75
Spock.	....$50–$75
Sulu.	....$50–$75
Uhura.	....$50–$75
Set of 7.	....$400–$600

¼ Ounce Gold-Plated Silver—Came as keychain or necklace in velveteen box, Spock only. ....$35–$45

¹⁄₁₀ Ounce Silver—Came as necklaces inside velveteen box.

Kirk.	....$15–$25
McCoy.	....$15–$25
Spock.	....$15–$25

¼ Ounce Gold—Came in plastic container in velveteen box.

Chekov.	....$300–$400
Kirk.	....$300–$400
McCoy.	....$300–$400
Scotty.	....$300–$400
Spock.	....$300–$400
Sulu.	....$300–$400
Uhura.	....$300–$400
Set of 7.	....$2100–$2800

1 Ounce Gold—A special order item from the Rarities Mint. These were made only in sets which came in special embossed leather display books. Probably no more than 15 sets were ever produced. Set of 7. ....$15,000–$25,000

NOTE: This company also made coins which were incorporated into watches, desk sets, and money clips. (See Clocks and Watches, Jewelry, and School and Office Supplies).

Starland

Star Trek Insignia Medallions—Metal medallion, 2½″. Blue designs printed onto polished center surrounded by raised wreath design. Reverse has rectangle with etched number surrounded by raised wreath design. Blue neck ribbon is attached to ring molded onto top of medal. Limited to 3000 pieces each. Not licensed.

Next Generation UFP Design.	...........................$10–$20
Old UFP Design (Starfield Flanked by Faces).	.................$10–$20
United Federation of Planets/Starfleet Academy, with original command symbol.	...................................$10–$20

Huckleberry Designs Vulcan Wooden Nickel

Chicagoland Processing Silver Picard Coin in Folder

Rarities Mint One Ounce Silver Spock Coin

Rarities Mint Gold One Ounce Coins, Complete Set in Folder

COMPUTER SOFTWARE

Though Star Trek computer software is very popular among fans, its appeal is strictly in the enjoyment it provides. As a future collectible, software's potential is practically nil. The most sought after programs are the newest, most up to date. Older games are most likely sitting out in the corner of the garage with the out-of-date computers for which they were designed.

INVESTMENT POTENTIAL
Poor.

CARE
Care is the same as with any disk or CD designed for computers. Preserve any packaging that the program came with (many of them have interesting decorative boxes) as these probably represent the only means by which they may some day become collectible.

SECTION NOTES
Section is organized alphabetically by title of item. Unlicensed software, which is very common, has been excluded since it has even less collectible potential than the approved kind.

Star Trek Audio Clips—Sound Source. Includes sound effects and dialogue from the original TV series.
    Final Frontier. ....$40–$50
    Logical Collection, The. ....$40–$50
Star Trek: Deep Space Nine Entertainment Package—Sound Source, 1996. "Limited Edition CD-ROM Entertainment Utility." Games, audio clips, screen savers, etc. Includes poster and Certificate of Authenticity. Limited to 250,000. ....$40–$50
Star Trek: Deep Space Nine Episode Guide—SSI, 1996. Includes trailers from the first three seasons of the show. ....$55–$65
Star Trek: Deep Space Nine Harbinger—Viacom, 1995. Game. ....$60–$70

Star Trek: Deep Space Nine Voice Print—1996. Voice recognition system for computers. ....$60–$70
Star Trek: Generations—Micro Prose, 1996. Game based on the movie. ....$40–$50
Star Trek: Judgment Rites—Interplay, 1995. Exploration game. ....$55–$65
Star Trek: Klingon—SSI, 1996. Klingon language, customs, and culture. ....$60–$70
Star Trek Omnipedia—SSI, 1995. Reference work based on the book *The Star Trek Encyclopedia.* ....$55–$65
Star Trek Screen Posters—Berkeley Systems. Thirty-five scenes from various Star Trek movies plus Star Trek trivia. ....$20–$25
Star Trek Screen Saver—Berkeley Systems. Fifteen animated displays. ....$35–$45
Star Trek: Starfleet Academy—Interplay, 1996. Game. ....$40–$50
Star Trek: The Motion Picture Audio Clips—Sound Source. Dialogue and sound effects from the movie. ....$20–$25
Star Trek: The Next Generation "A Final Unity"—Spectrum Holobyte, 1995. Game. ....$60–$70
Star Trek: The Next Generation Audio Clips—Sound Source. Sound effects and dialogue from The Next Generation. Several different.
    Best of Both Worlds. ....$50–$60
    Encounter at Farpoint. ....$50–$60
    Virtual Data. ....$50–$60
Star Trek: The Next Generation Episode Guide—SSI, 1996. Includes trailers from all shows. ....$55–$65
Star Trek: The Next Generation Interactive Technical Manual—SSI, 1995. Allows user to go on a VR tour of the Enterprise-D. Based on the book *Star Trek: The Next Generation Technical Manual.* ....$55–$65
Star Trek: The Next Generation Screen Saver—Berkeley Systems. Thirteen animated scenarios. ....$35–$45
Star Trek: The Next Generation Stardate Calendar and

Address Book—Berkeley Systems. Eight different calendar backgrounds. Some animation. ....$40–$50

Star Trek: 25th Anniversary—Interplay. Combines space flight simulation and role-playing scenarios. ....$55–$65

NOTE: Some earlier computer games were published by Simon and Schuster: Kobayashi Alternative, Promethean Prophecy, and Rebel Universe. They have very little value on the secondary market.

Simon & Schuster Star Trek Omnipedia

COSTUMES, COSTUME PATTERNS, AND ACCESSORIES

Costumes fall into two general categories—those that were intended as inexpensive children's halloween costumes and those designed as more or less accurate replicas of costumes and uniforms designed primarily for adults. The latter, both mass produced and homemade, have always been popular items with fans who often wear them at conventions and club functions. Neither of these two categories, however, offers particularly good investment potential, the first most likely because they were designed to be inexpensive and are not of particularly high quality, and the second being because they are purchased primarily to be worn, not collected. Original costumes are, of course, extremely collectible but also incredibly rare. Collectors have long ago obtained those still existing from the original TV series and Paramount is careful not to let those from the movies and the current television series out into general circulation. An actual costume's value would vary considerably based on which Star Trek episode or movie it came from, who wore it, and its condition. Any original item would of course be very expensive and a collector would be wise to research its authenticity before the purchase.

INVESTMENT POTENTIAL
Fair.

CARE
As with all clothing items, the best way to preserve costumes as collectibles is to not wear them. In addition to the costume itself, early children's boxed costumes came packaged in thin cardboard window boxes which, although they contribute to a large percentage of the costume's collectible value, are especially flimsy and hard to maintain in good condition. Later packaging consists primarily of plastic bags with descriptive inserts which should also remain with the item but are much more durable.

SECTION NOTES
Section is organized chronologically by TV series or movie and alphabetically by manufacturer. Homemade costumes and homemade or generic appliances (i.e., pointed ears as opposed to Spock ears) have been omitted.

NOTE: See Patches and Jewelry sections for costume accessories that fit into these categories.

ORIGINAL TELEVISION SERIES

Ben Cooper—1973. Halloween costume. One-piece jumpsuit with picture of Spock and Enterprise. Came with plastic mask. Came boxed as "Super Hero" costume. ....$35–$65
Ben Cooper—1975. Halloween costume. One-piece jumpsuit picturing character and Enterprise. Came with plastic mask. Children's sizes. Came window boxed.
    Kirk. ....$35–$45
    Klingon. ....$35–$45
    Spock. ....$35–$45
Collegeville Halloween Costume—1967. Lightweight material, tie-on jumpsuit with drawing of Enterprise and "Star Trek" in felt/sparkle design on front and plastic character mask. Children's sizes. Came window boxed.
    Kirk. ....$45–$75
    Spock. ....$45–$75
Don Post/Rubies—1990. Full-head, soft plastic, adult masks with fiber hair.
    Mugatu. ....$50–$65
    Salt Vampire. ....$50–$65
Franco—1976. Vulcan ears. Came bagged with header depicting Spock. ....$20–$30
Lincoln Enterprises—1976. Patterns for standard, original TV series uniform shirts and dresses. Several sizes included in each.

Men's Uniform Shirt Pattern. ....$4–$6
Women's Uniform Pattern. ....$5–$7

NOTE: Though Lincoln did not package any of their own patterns, the patterns were often sold by other vendors that used a variety of envelope styles for these items.

Rubies—1990. Original TV uniforms. Adult size in gold, blue, and red knit material with silk-screened insignia.
Men's Shirt. ....$25–$30
Women's Dress. ....$30–$35
Simplicity—1990. Patterns for original series uniform shirts and dresses. Packaged in typical pattern envelope showing models wearing completed outfits. Several sizes in each.
Men's Shirt. ....$5–$6
Women's Dress. ....$6–$7
Starfleet Uniforms—Early 1970s. This company produced uniforms under a limited license. Virtually all sales were to the fan market. Star Trek (original) TV shirt, knit material in gold, blue, or red. Adult sizes only. ....$30–$50

STAR TREK:
THE MOTION PICTURE

Aviva—1979. Spock ears. Children's size. Came blister-carded on header with color photo of Spock. ....$25–$35
Collegeville—1979. Halloween costumes. One-piece outfit depicting characters and logo. Children's sizes. Came window boxed.
Ilia. ....$30–$40
Kirk. ....$30–$40
Klingon. ....$30–$40
Spock. ....$30–$40
Don Post—1979. Full-head, soft plastic, adult masks with fiber hair. All the masks below, with the exception of Spock, were re-issued in 1990 in conjunction with Rubies, the current costume licensee at that time. Presumably there was some licensing dispute that caused the Spock mask to be dropped in favor of the Vulcan Master.
Kirk. ....$50–$75
Klingon. ....$50–$75
Spock. ....$100–$125
Vulcan Master. ....$50–$75
Don Post/Rubies—1990. Full-head, adult, soft rubber masks in two styles. Popular, without fiber hair and deluxe with fiber hair.
Kirk (Popular). ....$35–$45
Kirk (Deluxe). ....$50–$65
Klingon (Popular). ....$35–$45
Klingon (Deluxe). ....$50–$65
Vulcan Master (Popular). ....$35–$45
Vulcan Master (Deluxe). ....$50–$65

NOTE: There was a book with simplified patterns for making your own costumes from Star Trek: The Motion Picture published by Pocket Books. See Books section.

STAR TREK II:
THE WRATH OF KHAN

Collegeville—1982. Halloween costume. One-piece outfit depicting characters, Enterprise, and Star Trek II logo. Children's sizes. Came window boxed.
Kirk. ....$35–$45
Spock. ....$35–$45
Don Post—1982. Spock ears. Came bagged on header card with color Star Trek II logo. ....$25–$35
Lincoln Enterprises—1983. Patterns. Several sizes in each pattern. No packaging.
Men's Jacket. ....$7–$10
Recreational Jumpsuit. ....$7–$10
Trousers. ....$5–$8
Turtleneck Undershirt. ....$4–$7
Women's Jacket. ....$7–$10

20TH ANNIVERSARY

Ballantine Books—1986. 20th anniversary vulcan ears. Promotional giveaway. Came bagged with 20th anniversary sticker. ....$15–$20

STAR TREK:
THE NEXT GENERATION

A.H. Prismatic—1994. Geordi's visor. Diffractive plastic in thin, silver, plastic frame. ....$4–$6

NOTE: This company continued to make this product after they lost their Star Trek license but without the Star Trek logo tag.

Ben Cooper—1988. Halloween costume. Packaged on hangers.
Ferengi. ....$10–$20
Klingon. ....$10–$20
Dekkertoys (British)—1994. "Starship Captain's Playsuit." Red, Star Trek: The Next Generation–style child's two-piece costume. Boxed with color photo of child in outfit on lid. ......
....$30–$50
Fantasy Park (British)—1994. Locutus mask. Full-head,

hand-painted, latex mask. Limited edition. Included Certificate of Authenticity. ....$250–$300

Lincoln Enterprises—1988. Patterns. Several sizes included in each. No packaging.

Men's Jumpsuit, original low-collar version. ....$10–$15
Men's Skant. ....$8–$12
Women's Jumpsuit, original low-collar version. ....
....$10–$15
Women's Skant. ....$8–$12

Lincoln Enterprises—1990. Patterns. Several sizes included in each. No packaging.

Men's Third Season Top, with collar. ....$7–$8
Pants. ....$5–$6
Womens Third Season Top. ....$7–$8

Lincoln Enterprises—1992. Patterns. Several sizes included in each. No packaging.

Picard's Duty Jacket. ....$10–$12
Troi's Dress. ....$10–$12

Rubies—1992/93. Star Trek: The Next Generation uniforms. Men's shirts and women's and children's jumpsuits in gold, blue, or red. Came with printed-on command insignias and set of cardboard rank pips. Packaged in hanging bag with color photo insert of model in costume.

Children's Jumpsuit. ....$25–$35
Men's Shirt. ....$25–$30
Women's Jumpsuit. ....$30–$35

Rubies—1994. Star Trek: The Next Generation deluxe uniforms. Adult uniforms in gold, blue, or red. Heavier weight material with detachable plastic insignia pin and metal rank pip set. Packaged in hanging bag with color photo insert of model in costume.

Men's Shirt. ....$40–$50
Women's Jumpsuit. ....$55–$65

Rubies—1995. Klingon uniforms. Adult and children's sizes. Includes silver padded top, pants, shoe tops, and belt. Packaged in hanging bag with color insert of model wearing costume.

Female Klingon. ....$50–$60
Male Klingon. ....$50–$60

Rubies—1995. Klingon makeup kits. Both include headpieces with hair, makeup, and applicators. Deluxe, Michael Westmore Signature Series has extra facial hair, makeup, and instruction booklet. Both are boxed with color photos of actual series actors and contents of kits.

Deluxe Kit. ....$40–$50
Regular Kit. ....$20–$30

Rubies—1995. Star Trek: The Next Generation adult character masks. Full-head, soft plastic masks.

Data. ....$35–$45
Geordi. ....$35–$45
Picard. ....$35–$45

Rubies—1995. Star Trek: The Next Generation PVC face masks. Thin plastic face masks held on by elastic band.

Borg. ....$4–$7
Data. ....$4–$7
Picard. ....$4–$7

Worf. ....$4–$7

Simplicity—1989. Patterns. Patterns for original low-collar style jumpsuits. Came packaged in typical pattern envelope with color photo of models in completed outfit on cover. Several sizes in each.

Children's, two children on cover. ....$6–$8
Men's Jumpsuit. ....$6–$8
Women's Jumpsuit. ....$6–$8

STAR TREK: DEEP SPACE NINE

Fantasy Park (British)—1994. Full-head latex masks.

Klingon. ....$50–$60
Odo. ....$50–$60
Quark. ....$50–$60
Romulan. ....$50–$60

Lincoln Enterprises—1994. Patterns for uniforms seen on the series. Includes several sizes in each. No packaging.

Kira's Uniform. ....$10–$12
Men's Federation Jacket. ....$10–$12
Odo's Uniform. ....$10–$12
Women's Federation Jacket. ....$10–$12

Rubies—1994. Turtleneck-style Federation uniform costumes with printed-on command insignias, separate turtleneck insert, and cardboard rank pip set. Came packaged in hanging bags with color photo insert of model wearing outfit.

Children's Jumpsuit, gold, blue, or red. ....$25–$35
Men's Shirt, gold, blue, or red. ....$25–$35
Women's Jumpsuit, blue only. ....$35–$45

Rubies—1994. Deluxe Deep Space Nine costumes. Turtleneck-style Federation uniforms seen on the series come in gold, red, or blue in adult sizes only. Heavier weight material with detachable plastic insignia pins and metal rank pip. Separate turtleneck inserts. Other character costumes come in adult and children's sizes. Packaged in hanging bags with color photo of model in costume.

Federation Men's Uniform Shirt. ....$35–$45
Federation Women's Jumpsuit. ....$55–$65
Kira's Uniform. ....$45–$65
Odo's Costume. ....$45–$65
Quark's Costume. ....$45–$65

Rubies—1994. Ferengi makeup kits. Both include headpieces, teeth, makeup, and applicators. Deluxe, Michael Westmore Signature Series kit has extra makeup and instruction booklet. Both come boxed with color photos of actors from series and contents of kits.

Deluxe Kit. ....$40–$50
Regular Kit. ....$20–$30

Rubies—1995. Full-head, soft plastic, adult masks. Came in two styles—regular and deluxe, which has more detail and is designed to blend better around eye area.

Borg. ....$35–$45
Borg (Deluxe). ....$45–$55

Cardassian. ....$35–$45
Cardassian (Deluxe). ....$45–$55
Odo. ....$35–$45
Quark. ....$35–$45

Rubies—1995. PVC character face masks. Thin plastic masks held on by an elastic band.

Odo. ....$5–$7
Quark. ....$5–$7
Sisko. ....$5–$7

VOYAGER

Rubies—1995. Turtleneck-style deluxe Federation uniforms of heavier weight material with detachable, plastic, newer-style insignia pin and metal rank pip set. All come in gold, blue, or red. Adult sizes.

Men's Shirt. ....$35–$45
Women's Jumpsuit. ....$55–$65

Franco Vulcan Ears

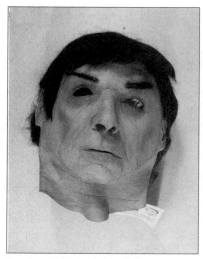

Don Post Original Spock Mask

Aviva *Star Trek: The Motion Picture* Spock Ears

Simplicity *Star Trek: Next Generation* Pattern

Rubies Ferengi Makeup Kit

CRYSTAL

The investment potential of items in this category is enhanced by the fact that there is a well-established market for crystal collectibles of all kinds in addition to the obvious appeal of these pieces to Star Trek collectors. The value of a group of items that is sought after by two separate collectible markets almost always benefits by the attention. Twice as many people competing for a limited amount of pieces means more demand and generally tends to escalate prices, especially if the pieces in question are not particularly durable (fewer and fewer pieces available to purchase as time goes on), which is certainly true in the case of crystal.

INVESTMENT POTENTIAL
Good.

CARE
Crystal is maddeningly fragile, especially when the pieces have a lot of long slender projections, as in the case of Star Trek ships. The good news is that as long as the piece breaks along a seam, it can be repaired if it is done with care. Both Super Glue and fingernail glue are close in composition to the adhesive originally used when assembling the piece, and a careful repair is often unnoticeable and does little or nothing to affect its value. When storing or transporting the piece, no amount of wrapping or padding is too much, and even then the unfortunate individual will often find their valued collectible in little bits upon unpacking. The best solution is to save the original box and interior packing. Though the box is not a display box, and therefore does little for the value of the item, the foam interior, cut specially to fit the individual piece, is the best way to protect it from damage.

SECTION NOTES
There have only been two manufacturers of Star Trek crystal to date and one of those made only one piece. Crystal from both companies is currently out of production. Section is organized alphabetically by manufacturer and then by item.

Manon

Enterprise (Original)—1990. Approx. 2″ tall. Clear crystal with red crystal accents on mirrored base. ....$125–$200

Silver Deer

Enterprise NCC-1701—1993. Approx. 4″ tall. Clear ship with red crystal accents. Base is a clear crystal pyramid turned on its side. Limited to 10,000 pieces. ....$350–$400
Enterprise NCC-1701—1993. Approx. 3³⁄₄″ tall. Clear ship with red crystal accents set on irregular-shaped, multicolored base. Limited to 1200 pieces. ....$375–$425
Enterprise NCC-1701—1993. Approx. 2¹⁄₂″ tall, mounted on clear-faceted crystal base attached at angle to multicolored mirror. ....$200–$225
Enterprise NCC-1701—1993. Approx. 1¹⁄₄″ tall. Base consists of two, clear, multifaceted crystals joined to each other at an angle. ....$50–$60
Enterprise NCC-1701-D-1993. Approx. 3³⁄₄″ tall. Clear crystal ship attached at angle to irregular-shaped, multicolored crystal base. Limited to 7500 pieces. ....$375–$425
Enterprise NCC-1701-D—1993. Approx. 3¹⁄₂″ tall. Clear crystal ship mounted at angle to multicolored, hemispherical base. Limited to 10,000 pieces. ....$350–$400
Enterprise NCC-1701-D—1993. Approx. 1³⁄₄″ tall. Clear crystal ship attached to multicolored hemispherical base. ......
....$100–$125
Enterprise NCC-1701-D—1993. Approx. 1″ tall. Clear crystal ship attached at angle to faceted, multicolored base. ....
....$50–$60
Klingon Bird-of-Prey—1993. Approx. 2″ tall. Clear crystal ship mounted at angle on faceted pear-shaped pedestal attached to multicolored mirror base. ....$125–$150

Paperweights—1993. Thick, clear, crystal disks approx. 2½″ tall. Vertically mounted on plain or multicolored mirrored bases. Each has textured sides and design etched on back.

Mirrored Base:

Enterprise NCC-1701-D. ....$80–$100

Starfleet Insignia. ....$80–$100

United Federation of Planets Emblem. ....$80–$100

Plain Base:

Enterprise NCC-1701-D. ....$50–$60

Starfleet Insignia. ....$50–$60

United Federation of Planets Emblem. ....$50–$60

Prisms—1993. Clear, four-sided crystals approx. 3″ tall with angled tops. Full figures of four different characters from respective series printed in black on each of four sides and logo printed in black on top of prisms. Separate, circular, blue mirrored base comes with each prism.

Star Trek (Original TV series). ....$85–$100

Star Trek: The Next Generation. ....$85–$100

Romulan Warbird—1993. Approx. 1¼″ tall. Clear crystal ship mounted at angle on faceted marquis-shaped pedestal attached to multicolored, mirrored base. ....$125–$150

Starcatchers—1993. Clear crystal disks approx. 2″ in diameter with assorted Star Trek symbols printed in black on one side. Ring is attached to small hole at top of each piece and ribbon for hanging is included. Twelve different.

Bajoran Symbol. ....$10–$15

Borg Symbol. ....$10–$15

Cardassian Symbol. ....$10–$15

Enterprise NCC-1701-D. ....$10–$15

Ferengi Symbol. ....$10–$15

Galaxy Class Starship Development Project Emblem. ......
....$10–$15

IDIC Emblem. ....$10–$15

Klingon Symbol. ....$10–$15

Romulan Symbol. ....$10–$15

Starfleet Academy Emblem. ....$10–$15

Starfleet Insignia. ....$10–$15

United Federation of Planets Emblem. ....$10–$15

DECALS, STAMPS, AND STICKERS

This section covers a wide range of different items utilizing a variety of different styles and materials. Included are simple "just for fun" paper and plastic stick-ons to extensive sets and actual postage stamps specifically designed for collectors. As would be expected under these circumstances, the items also exhibit a greater range in collectibility (and value) than in many other sections. Unlicensed, easily manufactured word and picture stickers have been omitted since they are extremely common, very easily duplicated, and have little chance of ever becoming collectible. Also, it should be noted that the larger, more complex sticker sets are of considerably more interest to collectors. Stickers that were intended as extensions of trading card sets can be found in the Trading Cards section of this book.

INVESTMENT POTENTIAL
Good.

CARE

The primary concern with stickers and decals made of paper is to protect them from moisture. Plastic collectibles' bags provide excellent protection but be careful to avoid placing any bagged paper collectible in direct sunlight. This could cause condensation to form, damaging your item. While this is a problem with all paper collectibles, glue-backed items are especially susceptible. Stickers, and especially stamps, retain more value if they are in their original unused state. For items that come with albums, it is far better to leave the set with the album but unapplied. As with all collectibles that come in sets, once you have completed the set, take care to keep it together. Keep any items that came packaged in the original package if possible.

SECTION NOTES
Section is organized alphabetically by manufacturer.

A.H. Prismatic

(British)

Star Trek (Original TV) Hologram Stickers—1992. Set of nine (one double image counted here as two) 2″ × 2″ diffraction holograms. Sold both as individual stickers and as an uncut sheet. Both options were packaged bagged on header cards with logo at top. Individual stickers:

    Bridge Scene A (Spock, McCoy, Uhura, Sulu). ....$1–$2
    Bridge Scene B (Kirk, Scotty, Chekov). ....$1–$2
    Command Insignia and Logo. ....$1–$2
    Enterprise. ....$1–$2
    Enterprise and Logo. ....$1–$2
    Klingon and Ship. ....$1–$2
    Kirk on Planet. ....$1–$2
    Kirk in Transporter Room. ....$1–$2
    Spock on Planet. ....$1–$2
    Uncut Sheet. ....$6–$10

Star Trek: Deep Space Nine Hologram Stickers—1993. These differ from this company's other sets in subject matter. There are fewer individual stickers (some stickers are repeated on the uncut sheet to maintain the nine-square configuration) and no characters are represented. Format and packaging remain similar in design to the previous two sets. Individual stickers:

    Runabout. ....$1–$2
    Runabout and Logo. ....$1–$2
    Space Station. ....$1–$2
    Space Station and Logo. ....$1–$2
    Space Station and Runabout. ....$1–$2
    Space Station, Logo, and Cardassian Ships. ....$1–$2
    Uncut Sheet of Nine. ....$6–$10

Star Trek: The Next Generation Hologram Stickers—1992. Nine-sticker set similar in design and packaging to the Star Trek original TV set above. Individual stickers:

Bridge Scene A (Picard, Geordi, Troi). ....$1–$2
Bridge Scene B (Riker, Worf, Data, Benzite). ....$1–$2
Data and Worf. ....$1–$2
Enterprise and Logo. ....$1–$2
Enterprise Orbiting Planet. ....$1–$2
Picard and Geordi. ....$1–$2
Picard, Troi, and Dr. Crusher. ....$1–$2
Romulan Warbird on Bridge Screen. ....$1–$2
Two Ferengi. ....$1–$2
Uncut Sheet. ....$6–$10

NOTE: A.H. Prismatic incorporated these stickers in a variety of other products including gift boxes, keychains, magnets, and pins. See appropriate chapters for these items.

Aviva

Instant Stained Glass Decals—1979. Reusable, color plastic artwork decals. Shrink-wrapped on 6½″ × 8″ blue starfield cardboard header cards with logo at top in silver.
Adm. Kirk. ....$2–$5
Enterprise. ....$2–$5
Spock. ....$2–$5
Spock Giving Vulcan Salute. ....$2–$5
Spock with Science Symbol. ....$2–$5
The Vulcan Shuttle. ....$2–$5

Puffy Sticker Sets—1979. Star Trek: The Motion Picture. Sets of colored plastic stickers featuring artwork of characters, ship, and logos from the movie. Shrink-wrapped on 6¼″ × 3½″ blue cardboard header cards with logo at top. Six stickers per set. Three variations. Price each. ....
....$5–$10

Vending Capsule Stickers—1979. Star Trek: The Motion Picture. Color photos on 2″ × 3″ stickers with orange border and logo at bottom. Originally packaged in round, clear plastic vending capsules.
Enterprise. ....$4–$8
Kirk. ....$4–$8
Kirk, Spock, and Enterprise. ....$4–$8
Spock. ....$4–$8

Celebrity Stamps

Star Trek Stamp Album—1977. Set includes 24-page album with color cardstock cover and six different stamp packet sets (sealed color cardstock envelopes) which were originally sold individually.
Set #1 (USS Enterprise). ....$15–$25
Set #2 (Capt. Kirk). ....$15–$25
Set #3 (Mr. Spock). ....$15–$25
Set #4 (Klingons and Romulans). ....$15–$25
Set #5 (Aliens of the Galaxy). ....$15–$25
Set #6 (Creatures of the Galaxy). ....$15–$25
Complete Set. ....$100–$150

Creation

Window Decals—1995. Transparent background with adhesive on front designed primarily for use in car windows.
Starfleet Academy, words in black with red and yellow academy seal in middle. "San Francisco, Earth * Ex Astris, Scientia" underneath. ....$2–$3
Vulcan Science Academy, words in blue with blue and yellow IDIC symbol at end. ....$2–$3

NOTE: A great many unlicensed window decals of this type exist but to date only this company has produced licensed ones.

Don Ling

Temporary Tattoos—1992. One- or two-color removable tattoos from either original Star Trek TV series or Star Trek: The Next Generation. Packaged in 4″ × 6″ black lightweight cardboard hanging envelopes with appropriate silver diffraction logo above picture of tattoo.
Star Trek (Original) Enterprise. ....$5–$8
Star Trek (Original) Logo. ....$5–$8
Star Trek: The Next Generation Insignia. ....$5–$8
Star Trek: The Next Generation Logo. ....$5–$8
Star Trek: The Next Generation UFP Symbol. ....$5–$8

General Mills

(Promotional)

Contest Stickers—1987. Color peel-off photo stickers of Star Trek: The Next Generation characters and ship. Cereal premium included in conjunction with a toy giveaway. Six different. Set of all six. ....$25–$50

Glow Zone

(Australian)

Glow-in-Dark Stickers—1994. Star Trek: The Next Generation. Seven different stick-on ships and a Borg figure. Packaged in a hanging envelope approx. 9″ × 6″. Vertical-format color artwork with logo, Enterprise-D, and Bird-of-Prey. ......
....$20–$30

Hallmark

Stickers—1990. Sheets of color artwork stickers depicting characters from the original TV show. Sold in sets of four sheets. Came shrink-wrapped on blue and pink header cards approx. 4″ × 7″ with logo in upper corner. ....$5–$10

Illuminations/SMFI

Glow-in-the-Dark Wall Stickers—1991. Luminous, stick-on, die-cut, cardboard stick-ons from the original TV show and Star Trek: The Next Generation.

    Star Trek Kirk and Spock, packaged on 8″ × 11″ starfield header card with logo at top. Figures approx. 8″ tall. ....$7–$10
    Star Trek: The Next Generation Enterprise, packaged on 16″ × 11″ starfield header card with logo at top. Ship approx. 16″ long. ....$10–$15
    Star Trek: The Next Generation Enterprise Orbiting Earth, packaged on 8″ × 11″ starfield header card with logo at top. Sticker approx. 8″ across. ....$7–$10
    Star Trek: The Next Generation Glow Stars, approx. 500 different astronomical shapes packaged in 8″ × 11″ black lightweight cardboard envelope with logo at top. ....$7–$10
    Star Trek: The Next Generation Klingon Battle Cruiser Orbiting Saturn, packaged on 8″ × 11″ starfield header card with logo at top. Sticker approx. 13″ across. ....$7–$10
    Star Trek: The Next Generation Space Adventure Poster Kit, kit includes poster and approx. 150 decals of ships, planets, and stars. Packaged in 16″ × 11″ lightweight cardboard envelope showing product on starfield background with logo at top. ....$10–$15

Image Marketing Ltd.

Decal Magic—1992/93. Reusable color photo decals approx. 6″ square. Earlier packaging was rectangular pink and blue window envelope with logo and other info at top. Later changed to round-topped window envelope with red and black checkerboard border.

    Deep Space Nine Crew. ....$4–$6
    Deep Space Nine Space Station. ....$4–$6
    Klingon Bird-of-Prey. ....$4–$6
    Next Generation Crew. ....$4–$6
    Next Generation Enterprise, front view. ...$4–$6
    Next Generation Enterprise, side view. ....$4–$6
    Romulan Warbird. ....$4–$6
    Worf. ....$4–$6

Langley and Associates

Circular Stickers—1976. Color photo stickers approx. 2″ in diameter. Actually adaptations of photos printed for pinback buttons by same company. Approx. 40 different characters, scenes, and ships. Price each. ....$.50–$1

Lightrix

Pictrix—1994. Set of nine 2″ × 2″ Star Trek: The Next Generation diffraction hologram stickers. Sold individually, in sets of three, or in uncut sheet of all nine. Packaged and bagged on thin cardboard header cards with logo at top. Individual stickers:

    Borg. ....$1–$2
    Command Insignia and Logo. ....$1–$2
    Enterprise. ....$1–$2
    Enterprise Firing Phasers. ....$1–$2
    Enterprise, planet in background. ....$1–$2
    Ferengi. ....$1–$2
    Klingon. ....$1–$2
    Klingon Bird-of-Prey Ships. ....$1–$2
    Romulan Warbird. ....$1–$2
    Uncut Sheet of Nine. ....$6–$10

NOTE: This company has incorporated these stickers into many other products including bookmarks, gift boxes, key rings, magnets, pins, pencil boxes, and jigsaw puzzles. See appropriate chapters for these items.

Lincoln Enterprises

Decal Sheets—1970. Water applicable two-tone artwork decals. Came in sheets divided by subject matter.

    Sheet #1, three different insignia designs. ....$1–$2
    Sheet #2, Enterprise, Klingon cruiser, Galileo. ....$1–$2
    Sheet #3, communicator, phaser, 3-D chess. ....$1–$2
    Sheet #4, NCC-1701 in various sizes. ....$1–$2
    Sheet #5, Star Trek alien. ....$1–$2
    Sheet #6 & 7, four different stars from series on each. Price each. ....$1–$2
Foil Stickers—1970. Set of three insignia stickers from original TV series. ....$2–$5
Foil Stickers—1988. Insignia design from Star Trek: The Next Generation. ....$1–$2
Stamps—1976. Twenty different color photo stamps approx. 1″ × 1″ of regular cast, guest stars, and ships. Originally produced in sheets of 40 (two of each). Price per sheet. ....$10–$15
Tenth Anniversary Sticker—1976. "Star Trektennial 1966–1976." ....$1–$2
United Federation of Planets Seal Sticker—1988. Color. Approx. 1″ × 2″. ....$1–$2

NOTE: This company also has produced a wide variety of word stickers on paper or mylar which are of very little collector value.

Ludwig Schokolade (German)

Sticker Set—1995. Promotional item. Rectangular color photo stickers with logo and number on side. Stickers were included in company's "Fritt" candy, 35 total: 15 Star Trek original TV series, 10 Star Trek: The Next Generation, and 10 Star Trek: Deep Space Nine. Price for set. ....
....$100–$125

Morris Import Sales

Sticker Set and Book (Canadian)—1975. "The Siege." Twelve-page story/sticker booklet approx. 6″ × 9″ with color artwork cover and some color interior art. Stickers come on peel-off 3″ × 4″ cards that have "Star Trek" and Enterprise on cover. Stickers vary in size. Book with complete set of 32 stickers. ....$400–$500

Panini

This Italian-based company manufactures an extensive line of sticker and album sets primarily for the European market. Because of the focus of their market, most of their products are printed in several different languages. Individual stickers are often part of two- or four-sticker mosaic picture.

Star Trek (Original TV) Album and Sticker Set—1979. Color photo sticker set, 400 pieces, 48-page album has color artwork cover depicting Kirk, Spock, McCoy, and Enterprise and two-tone interior. Price for complete set with album. ......
....$300–$500
Star Trek: The Next Generation Album and Sticker Set— 1987. Color photo sticker set, 240 pieces, 32-page album has color photo of Enterprise-D with inset photo of crew on cover and full-color planetscape background on interior pages. Originally this set was not widely marketed in the United States. Price for complete set with album. ....$50–$75

NOTE: In 1995 an album with a different cover was printed by Panini to accompany this set. Neither album significantly affects the value of the set.

Paramount

(Promotional)

Decal—Star Trek V: The Final Frontier, silver and red logo, Enterprise on starfield. ....$3–$5
Twentieth Anniversary Sticker. ....$2–$3

Pepsi

(Promotional)

Star Trek (Original TV) Stamps—1977. Perforated 4″ × 8″ sheets of seven-color photo stamps and Pepsi logo. Originally given away one per week for four weeks. Set of all four. ....
....$25–$40

Pocket Books

(Promotional)

Sticker—1986. Blue and yellow "Star Trek 20th Anniversary, the only logical books to read!" ....$2–$3

Primrose Confectionery Co., Ltd.

(British)

Stamp Set—1970. Set includes 12 different with color artwork of characters and Enterprise on thin white paper stock, 2″ × 1 3/8″, with number and descriptive paragraph on back. Probably originally intended for candy cigarettes. Virtually all in circulation today were remainders and are almost always found as complete sets. Set of all 12. ....$25–$40

SSCA

(Distributor)

Postage Stamps—1994. Three series of stamps—one from "All Good Things," one from Star Trek: Generations, and a 30th anniversary commemorative series. Stamps were issued by St. Vincent & the Grenadines and Guyana. Though these are actual postage stamps, both series were produced by their respective countries as collectible exports and were almost certainly never in actual circulation.

"All Good Things"/St. Vincent & the Grenadines Stamps

Character First Day Covers—The above set of stamps affixed to envelopes with first day cancellations. Originally sold as set only in gold embossed black cardboard folder. Certificate of Authenticity included. Set of nine. ....$55–$75
Characters Nine-Stamp Sheet—Nine different 1″ × 2″ color photo stamps sold in perforated sheet. "Commemorating Star Trek: The Next Generation 1987–1994" in top border of sheet and "All Good Things" in bottom border. ....
....$15–$20
Gift Pack—The Character Sheet and the Souvenir Sheet were also sold as a set in a gold embossed black cardboard

folder. ....$30–$40

Gold Picard Stamp—Large (3¾″ × 2″) horizontally formatted stamp coated with actual 23K gold. Embossed Enterprise-D on one side and color photo of Picard on other. Sold in set with a Crew stamped first day cover postcard, either matted or in a gold embossed plastic folder. Either format comes with Certificate of Authenticity. ....$55–$75

Group Nine-Stamp Sheet—Nine 1″ × 2″ color photo stamps of the crew (all stamps the same). "Commemorating Star Trek: The Next Generation 1987–1994" in top border and "All Good Things" in bottom border. ....$15–$20

Group Souvenir Sheet—3″ × 4″ sheet with color photo of crew. Logo is in bottom portion of sheet and actual 1¾″ × 2″ stamp is denoted by perforations in the top portion. ....
....$10–$15

Star Trek: Generations/ Guyana Stamps

Boldly Go Nine-Stamp Sheet—Nine 1″ × 2″ color stamps (all the same) of the movie logo artwork. Movie logo is in top border of sheet and "Commemorating the Motion Picture—November 18, 1994" is in the bottom border. ....
....$15–$20

Boldly Go Souvenir Sheet—3″ × 4″ color sheet depicting movie poster artwork with Boldly Go at top portion. Actual 1¾″ × 2″ stamp is denoted by perforations in the bottom portion of sheet. ....$10–$15

Gift Pack—19th-Century Scenes Sheet, 23rd-Century Scenes Sheet, and Souvenir Sheet were sold as set in a gold embossed black cardboard folder. ....$40–$50

Gold Kirk and Picard Stamp—Large (3¾″ × 2″) horizontally formatted stamp coated with actual 23K gold. Generations emblem embossed in middle between color photos of Kirk and Picard. Sold in set with a Boldly Go stamped first day cover postcard either matted or in a gold embossed plastic folder. Either format includes a Certificate of Authenticity. ....$55–$75

19th-Century Scenes First Day Covers—The above set of stamps affixed to envelopes with first day cancellations. Originally sold only as set in gold embossed black cardboard folder. Certificate of Authenticity included. ....$55–$75

19th-Century Scenes Nine-Stamp Sheet—Similar to above set but with nine different scenes from the sailing ship sequence of the movie. ....$15–$20

23rd-Century Scenes First Day Covers—The above set of stamps affixed to envelopes with first day cancellations. Originally sold only as set in gold embossed black cardboard folder. Certificate of Authenticity included. ....$55–$75

23rd-Century Scenes Nine-Stamp Sheet—Similar to the other two nine-stamp sheets but with scenes from the 23rd-century portion of the movie. ....$15–$20

Star Trek 30th Anniversary St. Vincent & The Grenadines Stamps

Crew Stamp Sheet—Nine different stamps, seven with indi-

vidual crew members, one of Kirk, Spock, and McCoy and one of the Enterprise. "Star Trek" is at top of sheet and "Commemorating 30 Years of Star Trek" at bottom. ....
....$15–$20

Gift Pack—Crew Stamp Sheet, Scenes Stamp Sheet, and Group Souvenir Sheet together in gold embossed black cardboard folder. ....$40–$50

Gold Star Trek: The Original Series Stamp—Large gold-coated, horizontally formatted stamp has color photo of Spock, Kirk, McCoy, and Scotty on one side and embossed Enterprise on other. Packaged in a black plastic folder with first day cover featuring 30-Year logo and Enterprise 1701 stamp. Gold command emblem and logo on front of folder. Includes Certificate of Authenticity. ....$55–$75

Group Souvenir Sheet—4″ × 6″ sheet with color photo of crew. Actual stamp is on right of picture denoted by perforations. ....$10–$15

Scenes Stamp Sheet—Nine different stamps each depicting a scene from and episode of the original series. "Star Trek" is at top of sheet and "Commemorating 30 Years of Star Trek" is at bottom. ....$15–$20

Swizzels Refreshers

(British)

Sticker Set—1979. 1″ × 1″ stickers with rounded corners and color photos from Star Trek: The Motion Picture. Caption is below with number on side. Premium issued with "Swizzels Star Trek Refreshers—Flavored Fizzy Sweets." Price for set. ....$30–$50

Walls Ice Cream

(New Zealand)

Stickers—1982. Six different color photos of characters from Star Trek II: The Wrath of Khan, 2″ × 3″ with product logo below photo. Price for set of 6. ....$50–$75

U.S. Postal Service

Star Trek 25th Anniversary Stamps—Set of 10 decorative (not postage) stamps approx. 1″ square. Stamps depict seven principle characters from original TV show plus Enterprise, Klingon Cruiser, and 25th Anniversary logo. Color artwork on blue, black, and metallic gold background. Sold in uncut perforated sheets of all 10. Stamps came in gray plastic folder with "Space Exploration Commemorative Stamps," "The Star Trek Commemorative Collection," and the U.S. Postal Service, Star Trek 25th Anniversary, and Paramount logos printed on front. Price for set. ....$40–$50

NOTE: The U.S. Postal Service has also issued several Star Trek–related first day cover cancellations which may be of interest to collectors.

W.M. McKinney & Sons

(British)

Holographic Stickers—1995. Small foil holographic stickers approx. ³⁄₄″ square of Star Trek: The Next Generation

subjects. All stickers have Enterprise-D as background. Color sheet with logo and Enterprise above and crew below was provided for mounting stickers. Promotion for "Oatfield Star Trek: The Next Generation Sherbet Filled Fruit Flavour Drops." Sixteen different, numbered—#1, Capt. Jean-Luc Picard; #2, Comdr. William T. Riker; #3, Lt. Comdr. Data; #4, Lt. Comdr. Geordi La Forge; #5, Lt. Worf; #6, Dr. Beverly Crusher; #7, Counselor Deanna Troi; #8, Ens. Wesley Crusher; #9, Klingon Symbol; #10, Borg; #11, Ferengi; #12, Romulan; #13, Borg Symbol; #14, Klingon; #15, Starfleet Command Logo; #16, USS Enterprise. Price for set. ....
....$50–$65

Celebrity Star Trek Stamp Album

**Illuminations Kirk and Spock
Glow-in-the-Dark Wall Stickers**

**Image Marketing Worf Decal
(reusable)**

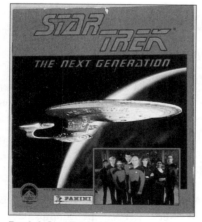

**Panini *Star Trek: Next Generation*
Sticker Album (original version)**

SSCA 30th Anniversary Stamp Folder

FANZINES

Fanzines are fan-written stories of any length printed either as individual stories or gathered into anthologies. They are published in small quantities, usually by the author or authors themselves, and often accompanied by fan artwork. Understandably they vary greatly in quality, both in physical appearance and in content. Some of them have writing and artwork by individuals who went on to become professionals in their respective fields. Others are simply abominable in every respect. The vast majority fall somewhere in between, produced by people who make up with enthusiasm whatever they may lack in talent. The common denominator in all fanzines is that they are singularly uninhibited. Released from the restraints imposed by Paramount on licensed publications, anything can and does happen in fanzine stories. The characters can marry, have children, die, become criminals, have homosexual affairs with each other, or do any number of other scintillating things that are unacceptable no-no's in the official Star Trek universe.

Fanzines have played an undoubted part in the creation of the Star Trek phenomenon. In the years between the cancellation of the original TV series and release of the first movie, they carried the torch for a multitude of fans hungry for new stories of their beloved characters that, at that time, with a few notable exceptions (primarily the 22 animated episodes), were available in no other form. In doing so they helped fuel the fire of the fan movement that would become the founding rock of the entire Star Trek industry. At one time, even new fanzines, fresh from the printer, sold for as much as $40. The most sought after out-of-print fanzines might easily cost many times that amount, if you could find someone willing to part with the particular issue.

Somewhat sadly, even the best of the old fanzines are now practically worthless as collectibles. Two factors are responsible for this. The first is technology. The very thing that allowed them to exist—easy reproduction via quick print shops—has evolved to the point where indistinguishable copies of even the more professional-looking fanzines can be easily and cheaply duplicated. Second, they are, ironically, victims of Star Trek's success. With professional writers regularly churning out new Star Trek novels, cheaply available in every bookstore, the public demand for Star Trek stories that used to be met by fanzines is now filled primarily by mainstream publishers.

INVESTMENT POTENTIAL
Poor.

CARE
As with all paper items, protection from moisture is the most important consideration. Storage in plastic collector bags best serves this purpose. Storage away from sunlight can prevent yellowing.

FILMS AND VIDEOS

FILMS

All original Star Trek episodes and all Star Trek movies do, of course, exist on film. This is, however, more and more a field for very specialized collectors. Since video cassettes have become popular, the number of individuals willing to deal with finicky projectors and bulky film libraries has dwindled considerably. In addition, since the studio did not intend for these films to be sold to the public, private collecting, especially of more recent films, exists in a sort of twilight zone of legality. Still, there is much to be said for the quality of film over that of video tape and many people still prefer this medium. For collecting purposes, the only really practical form of Star Trek film is 16mm. This pretty much limits the field to the original TV show. The movies were done either in 35 or 70mm and the projection equipment for this size film just isn't designed for home use. *Star Trek: The Next Generation* and all subsequent Star Trek series episodes are not done on film at all but stored on professional quality video tape. If you are determined to buy a Star Trek episode on film, be sure to watch it before you buy. Not only should the film be complete and free from jumps caused by splices and stretched sprockets, but original Star Trek film is coming of an age where it tends to turn red if not treated and stored properly. A good quality film should cost anywhere between $100 and $300 depending primarily on the desirability of the episode.

INVESTMENT POTENTIAL
Fair.

VIDEO TAPES

Virtually all forms of Star Trek, television and theatrical, exist on video cassettes in various formats. Paramount sees to it that new Star Trek adventures are offered for sale in a timely manner because they are more aware than anyone that if licensed videos aren't readily available, video bootleggers will soon be churning them out by the thousands. For exactly this reason, it is unlikely in the extreme that any video will ever attain any appreciable collectible value. Some special video "collections" have been aimed at the collector market but the items they offer that have collectible potential inevitably come in the form of special packaging or premiums included in the package, not the videos themselves. These days even a very hot, just-released movie video rarely costs more than $25. The price usually decreases sharply with time and drastically when offered on the secondary market.

INVESTMENT POTENTIAL
Poor.

VIDEO DISKS

Video disks have never caught on the way video tape has, despite the fact that most people feel they are of superior quality, and their adherents, while relatively few, are very devoted. Star Trek episodes, both original and Next Generation episodes, and Star Trek movies exist on video disks and the manufacturers regularly add to the selection. If they seem to proceed a little slowly it is probably at least partly because they don't feel the same sort of pressure with their product that the video tape makers do. Since video disks cannot be readily reproduced they don't have to be afraid of competition from counterfeiters. This isn't enough to make a product of such limited popularity a hot prospect as a collectible at the present, but they at least have more of a future than video tapes.

NOTE: For decorative mounted laser discs see Housewares.

INVESTMENT POTENTIAL
Fair.

CARE
The worst enemies of both film and video tape are time and use. Film, unless treated by experts with special preserva-tives, changes color and becomes brittle with age. Both film and video tape tend to stretch with use. Moisture and heat can also have disastrous effects. Disks are considerably more durable if less popular. Care should be taken to preserve the slipcovers of both tapes and disks. In the future these could easily become the most collectible feature of both.

Star Trek Videos

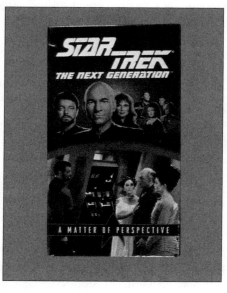

GAMES AND ACCESSORIES

From the standpoint of collectibility, the two sections in this chapter represent opposite ends of the spectrum. The appeal of gaming is almost wholly in the fun of participating in the games. Board games, on the other hand, are much more collectible, probably because most collectors tend to place them together with the very collectible category of toys.

INVESTMENT POTENTIAL
Gaming: Fair. Other Games: Good.

CARE
For the most part, Gaming items consist of magazines and books (which are best stored in plastic collectors' bags) and metal or plastic gaming pieces which are fairly durable and require little special handling. For boxed games, the most important consideration is to keep the game complete. To maximize investment potential, do not assemble games, i.e., do not punch counters or other pieces from their backings in board games. Also make sure that boxes do not get scuffed, crushed, or faded in storage as they are the major components of games.

SECTION NOTES
This chapter is divided into two sections. Gaming is organized alphabetically by manufacturer, and entries are further organized in game number order. All additions and accessories for these games are listed in this section. Other Games is listed first alphabetically by type of game and then alphabetically by manufacturer.

NOTE: For game cards other than standard card decks, see Trading Cards section of this book.

GAMING
Citadel Miniatures

1979

This company made a series of 25mm pewter gaming pieces based on Star Trek: The Motion Picture.

Sets—Andoreans, Deltans, Enterprise Crew, Ilia and Janice Rand, Klingons, McCoy, Scotty and Chekov, Security Guards, Spock, Sulu and Decker, Uhura and Chapel. Price per set. ....$5–$10

FASA
Star Trek Role Playing Game

In this game, the players assume the personalities of the characters from Star Trek and react to situations as the characters would.

Star Trek: The Role Playing Game—2001 (Deluxe Limited Edition). This game contains the Star Trek Basic Set (2004) and the Star Trek III Combat Game (2006) plus a set of three adventures and deck plans for the Constitution cruiser and the Klingon D-7 battle cruiser. ....$40–$50

　　Enterprise Deck Plans, to game 2001. ....$15–$20
　　Klingon Deck Plans, to game 2001. ....$10–$15
　　Special Autographed Edition, signed by James Doohan or Walter Koenig. ....$75–$100
　　Star Trek: The Role Playing Game, Second Deluxe Edition, no deck plans for ships. ....$25–$30

The Klingons: A Sourcebook and Character Generation Supplement—2002. This add-on module for the role playing game allows you to play the part of a Klingon. Included is a description of Klingon history and culture.

Books. ....$12–$15
Boxed Set. ....$15–$25

Star Trek II: Starship Combat Game—2003. Predecessor to Star Trek III game. Only released for a short time. ....
....$15–$20

Starship Combat Game—2003. Generic version of movie update games. Boxed. ....$18–$20

Star Trek: The Role Playing Game—2004 (Basic Set). The complete rules to role playing are contained in three easy-to-read books outlining the Star Trek universe and how to begin adventuring. ....$15–$17

The Romulans: A Sourcebook and Character Generation Supplement—2005. This add-on module for the role playing game allows you to play the part of a Romulan. Included is a description of Romulan history and culture. ....$10–$12

The Triangle—2007. Setting for a Star Trek campaign. Comes with full-color map and two books about the Triangle area. ....$10–$12

The Orions: A Sourcebook and Character Generation Supplement—2008. Includes a "Book of Common Knowledge" and a "Book of Deep Knowledge." ....$12–$15

The Federation—2011. Complete sourcebook of the United Federation of Planets. ....$10–$12

Starfleet Intelligence Manual—2014. Brings spies and secret operatives into the game. ....$10–$12

Trader Captains & Merchant Princes—2203. This rules supplement provides all the charts and rules needed for creating traders, merchants, con men, and rogues of space. A complete system for economics in the Star Trek universe is also included. ....$12–$15

More recent, Two-Book Version. ....$11–$12

Ship Construction Manual—2204. This rules supplement contains all the information and tables necessary for building your own starship. Also included is the starship combat efficiency system for rating your ship in combat.

First Edition. ....$12–$15
All Other Editions. ....$10–$12

Star Trek III: Movie Update and Sourcebook—2214. Allows players to bring their games up to the time period of the movies. Includes information necessary for adding new ships and personnel to games. ....$10–$12

STAR TREK ADVENTURE BOOKS
These add new scenarios to the Role Playing Game.

Witness for the Defense—2202. ....$7–$8
Denial of Destiny—2205. ....$8–$10
Termination: 1456—2206. ....$8–$10
Demand of Honor—2207. ....$8–$10
The Orion Ruse—2208. ....$7–$8
Margin of Profit—2209. ....$7–$8
The Outcasts—2210. ....$8–$10
A Matter of Priorities—2211. ....$7–$8
A Doomsday Like Any Other—2212. ....$7–$8

The Mines of Selka—2213. ....$7–$8
Triangle Campaign—2215. ....$8–$10
Graduation Exercise—2216. ....$7–$8
Where Has All the Glory Gone—2217. ....$7–$8
Return to Axanar—2218. ....$7–$8
Decision at Midnight—2219. ....$7–$8
Imbalance of Power—2220. ....$11–$12
Old Soldiers Never Die/The Romulan War—2221. ....
....$11–$12

A Conflict of Interest/Klingon Intelligence Briefing—2222. ....$11–$12

The White Flame—2225. A starship combat scenario pack.
....$7–$8

The Strider Incident/Regula I Deck Plans—2226. ....
....$11–$12

Deck Plans Alone. ....$7–$9

SHIP RECOGNITION MANUALS
These books contain all the game statistics for the role playing and the starship combat games. Each book contains 40 ships with a variety of variants and brief descriptions of performances and history.

The Klingons—2301. ....$7–$8
The Federation—2302. ....$7–$8
The Romulans—2303. ....$7–$8

PLAYING AIDS
Playing aids are used to add to the enjoyment of the games. None of the items are required to play but will increase the appeal of your games.

Starship Combat Hex Grid—2801. Contains three 22″ × 33″ starfield maps for use with 2006. ....$3–$5

Gamemaster's Kit—2802. Three-panel Gamemaster's screen displaying all important tables and charts; 16-page book containing all charts and tables needed by players and gamemasters. ....$6–$8

Tricorder/Sensors Interactive Display—2803. This play aid allows players to use a tricorder for scans and scientific readings. The unit is a hand-held simulated tricorder with display windows. ....$10–$12

STARSHIP MINIATURES
Scale lead of 1/3900. Come in several pieces which need glue for assembly. Blister-packed on color headers.

USS Enterprise (New)—2501. ....$4–$5
USS Reliant (Cruiser)—2502. ....$4–$5
Klingon D-7 (Battlecruiser)—2503. ....$4–$5
Romulan Bird-of-Prey (Cruiser)—2504. .....$4–$5
USS Enterprise (Old)—2505. ....$4–$5
Regula I Space Laboratory—2506. ....$4–$5
USS Larson (Destroyer)—2507. ....$4–$5
Klingon D-10 (Cruiser)—2508. ....$4–$5
Klingon D-18 (Destroyer)—2509. ....$4–$5

Gorn MA-12 (Cruiser)—2511. ....$4–$5
Orion Blockade Runner—2512. ....$4–$5
Klingon L-9 (Frigate)—2513. ....$4–$5
USS Loknar (Frigate)—2514. ....$4–$5
Romulan Winged Defender (Cruiser)—2515. ....$4–$5
USS Chandley (Frigate)—2516. ....$4–$5
USS Excelsior (Battleship, STIII)—2517. ....$10–$12
Klingon L-42 Bird-of-Prey (Frigate, STIII)—2518. ......$4–$5
USS Grissom (Research Vessel, STIII)—2519. ....$4–$5
Deep Space Freighter—2520. ....$4–$5
Romulan Graceful Flyer (Scout)—2521. ....$4–$5
Orion Wanderer—2522. ....$4–$5
Kobayashi Maru (Freighter)—2523. ....$4–$5
Romulan Gallant Wing (Cruiser)—2524. ....$4–$5
Gorn BH-2 (Battleship)—2525. ....$9–$12
USS Baker (Destroyer)—2526. ....$4–$5
Romulan Nova (Battleship)—2527. ....$11–$12
Romulan Bright One (Destroyer)—2528. ....$4–$5
Klingon L-24 (Battleship)—2529. ....$11–$12
Klingon D-2 (Missile Destroyer)—2530. ....$4–$5
Romulan Whitewind (Cruiser)—2531. ....$4–$5
USS Northampton (Frigate)—2532. ....$4–$5
USS Remora (Escort)—2533. ....$4–$5
USS Andor (Missile Cruiser)—2534. ....$4–$5

STAR TREK II: THE WRATH OF KHAN 25MM LEAD MINIATURE FIGURES

Came blister-packed on color headers.

James T. Kirk—2601. ....$2–$4
First Officer Spock—2602. ....$2–$4
Dr. McCoy—2603. ....$2–$4
Lt. Saavik—2604. ....$2–$4
Scotty—2605. ....$2–$4
Lt. Uhura—2606. ....$2–$4
Sulu—2607. ....$2–$4
Chekov—2608. ....$2–$4
Khan—2609. ....$2–$4
David Marcus—2610. ....$2–$4
Joachim—2611. ....$2–$4
Carol Marcus—2612. ....$2–$4
Capt. Terrell—2613. ....$2–$4
Khan (Ceti Alpha V)—2614. ....$2–$4
Klingon Officer—2615. ....$2–$4
Klingon Soldier 1—2616. ....$2–$4
Klingon Soldier 2—2617. ....$2–$4
Boxed Sets—Each set contains one ship and eight crew member figures.
    Enterprise and Crew—3001. ....$15–$25
    Reliant and Khan's Crew—3002. ....$15–$25
    Regula and Scientists—3003. ....$15–$25
    Klingon D-7 and Crew—3004. ....$15–$25

STAR TREK MICROADVENTURE GAMES

Small boxed games with short playing times and simple rules.

Star Trek III: The Search for Spock—5001. ....$6–$10
Star Trek III: Starship Duel 1—5002. ....$6–$10
Star Trek III: Struggle for the Throne—5004. ....$6–$10
Star Trek III: Starship Duel 2—5005. ....$6–$10

STAR TREK: THE NEXT GENERATION

Star Trek: The Next Generation Officers Manual—This book was issued and then withdrawn at the request of Paramount. Unauthorized reprints of this book do exist. Reprints have poorly printed covers.
    Original FASA Copy. ....$30–$50
    Reprint. ....$10–$15
Star Trek: The Next Generation First Year Sourcebook.
....$10–$12

Task Force Games

"Starfleet Battles." These are true war games with combat between individual ships or whole fleets. All the items listed in this section are for use with the game.

Introduction to Starfleet Battles—3000. Basic introduction to the game. ....$5–$6
Starfleet Battles Supplements. Game expansions include playing pieces and rules.
    #1 Fighters and Shuttles—3003. ....$9–$10
    #2 X-Ships—3013. ....$9–$10
    #3 Fast Patrol Ships. ....$9–$10
Starfleet Battles Reinforcements—3014. Additional playing pieces. ....$6–$7
Starfleet Battles Rules Update 1—3015. Update pages for Starfleet Battles and Supplement #1. ....$5–$6
Starfleet Battles—5001. Starting set for game. Includes 108-page Volume I Commander's Rulebook, 32-page SSD and chart book, 216 die-cut counters, and a large map. Boxed. ....$20–$25
Federation and Empire—5006. Creates the Galactic War that brought about Starfleet Battles. A larger scale game. Includes two large maps, 1080 playing pieces, 8 charts, and a rules scenario booklet. ....$35–$40
Federation and Empire Deluxe—5006. ....$40–$50
    Federation and Empire Deluxe Fleet Pack—3203. ....
    ....$12–$15
    Federation and Empire Deluxe Folio Pack—3204. ....$5–$6
Starfleet Battles Volume II—5008. Adds changes to game. Commander's Rulebook Volume II plus SSD booklet and playing pieces. Boxed. ....$20–$25
Starfleet Battles Volume III—5009. More changes to game. Includes Commander's Rulebook Volume III plus SSD booklet and playing pieces. Boxed. ....$20–$25

CAPTAIN'S LOGS

Each features a story, over 20 scenarios, and new rules for playing Starfleet Battles.

#1 3004. ....$5–$6
#2 3008. ....$5–$6

#3 3010. ....$5–$6
#4 3012. ....$5–$6

COMMANDER'S SSD BOOKS
Each contains 48 SSDs per book.

#1 3005. Federation, Andromedan, Orions, and Kzinti. ....
....$5–$6
#2 3006. Klingon, Lyran, Hydran, and Wyn. ....$5–$6
#3 3007. Romulan, Tholian, and Gorn. ....$5–$6
#4 3009. Tugs, starbases, battle stations, and freighters. ....
....$5–$6
#5 3016. Q-ships, booms and saucers, special and variant ships. ....$5–$6
#6 3018. Police ships, light tugs, survey cruisers, and space control ships. ....$5–$6
#7 3020. Tholian, Gorn, Federation, Kzinti, and Hydran ships. ....$5–$6
#8 3021. Klingon, Lyran, Orion, and Romulan ships. ....
....$5–$6
#9 3023. New Commander's SSD for all races. ....$5–$6

STARLINE 2200 MINIATURES
1/3900 scale plastic or lead miniatures. Starline 2200 Hex Sheets—7000. Four 18″ × 24″ maps.

THE FEDERATION
Federation Dreadnought—7010. ....$4–$5
Federation Heavy Cruiser—7011. ....$4–$5
Federation New Light Cruiser—7012. ....$4–$5
Federation Light Cruiser—7013. ....$4–$5
Federation Destroyer—7014. ....$4–$5
Federation Scout—7015. ....$4–$5
Federation Tug—7016. ....$4–$5
Federation Frigate (2)—7017. ....$4–$5
Federation Carrier—7020. ....$6–$8
Federation Starbase—7025. ....$6–$8

THE KLINGONS
Klingon B-10 Battleship—7040. ....$6–$8
Klingon C-8 Dreadnought—7042. ....$6–$8
Klingon D-7 Battlecruiser—7043. ....$4–$5
Klingon D-5 Cruiser—7044. ....$4–$5
Klingon F-5 Frigate (2)—7046. ....$4–$5
Klingon Tug (Carrier)—7051. ....$6–$8
Klingon PFs (6)—7053. ....$5–$6

THE ROMULANS
Romulan Condor—7060. ....$4–$6
Romulan Warbird (2)—7064. ....$4–$6
Romulan Sparrowhawk—7071. ....$4–$6
Romulan Skyhawk and Seahawk—7073. ....$4–$6

THE GORNS
Gorn Dreadnought—7080. ....$4–$6
Gorn Heavy Cruiser—7081. ....$4–$6

Gorn Light Cruiser—7082. ....$4–$6
Gorn Destroyer (2)—7084. ....$4–$6

THE KZINTIS
Kzinti Space Control Ship—7100. ....$4–$6
Kzinti Carrier—7101. ....$4–$6
Kzinti Escort Carrier—7103. ....$4–$6
Kzinti Strike Cruiser—7104. ....$4–$6
Kzinti Frigate (2)—7107. ....$4–$6
Kzinti Tug—7108. ....$4–$6
Kzinti PFs (6)—7110. ....$4–$6

THE LYRANS
Lyran Lion Dreadnought—7120. ....$4–$5
Lyran Cruiser—7122. ....$4–$5
Lyran War Cruiser—7123. ....$4–$5
Lyran Destroyer (2)—7124. ....$4–$5
Lyran PFs (6)—7126. ....$4–$5

THE HYDRANS
Hydran Paladin DN—7140. ....$4–$5
Hydran Ranger—7141. ....$4–$5
Hydran Horseman—7142. ....$4–$5
Hydran Lancer (2)—7143. ....$4–$5
Hydran Hunter/Scout (2)—7144. ....$4–$5
Hydran PFs (6)—7147. ....$4–$5

THE THOLIANS
Tholian Dreadnought—7160. ....$4–$5
Tholian Cruiser (2)—7161. ....$4–$5
Tholian Patrol Cruiser (2)—7164. ....$4–$5
Neo-Tholian Dreadnought—7172. ....$4–$5
Neo-Tholian Cruiser (2)—7174. ....$4–$5

THE ORIONS
Orion Heavy Cruiser—7181. ....$5–$6
Orion Salvage Cruiser—7182. ....$5–$6
Orion Raider (2)—7183. ....$5–$6
Orion Slaver (2)—7184. ....$5–$6

ALL RACES
Small Freighter (2)—7200. ....$4–$5
Battle Station—7211. ....$4–$5

THE ANDROMEDANS
Andromedan Intruder—7221. ....$5–$6
Andromedan Satellite Ships (3)—7222. ....$5–$6
Andromedan Conquistador and Python—7223. ......$5–$6

THE INTERSTELLAR CONCORDIUM
ISC Dreadnought—7250. ....$5–$6
ISC Star Cruiser—7252. ....$5–$6
ISC Destroyer and Frigate—7256. ....$5–$6
Starline 2220 Starships—7300. Boxed set. Includes one each of Federation Heavy Cruiser, Klingon D-7 Battlecruiser,

Klingon F-5 Frigate, Gorn Destroyer, and Romulan Warbird.
....$10–$13

Gamescience

Ships—1/3788-scale plastic gaming pieces with stands. Ships each came in white, clear, glow-in-the dark green, and glow-in-the-dark blue to represent different states in the game.

　　Cruiser—10504. ....$2–$4
　　Destroyer—10505. ....$2–$4
　　Scout—10506. ....$2–$4
　　Dreadnought—10507. ....$2–$4
　　Tug—10508. ....$2–$4

"Starfleet Battle Manual"—Starship combat game.

　　Booklet. ....$10–$12
　　Deluxe Boxed Set, includes eight plastic ships. ....
　　...$25–$30

Other Games

Arcade Games

Sega—1980. Star Trek: The Motion Picture. Standing or sitting versions made for commercial use. ....$800–$2500

Board Games (Boxed)

Cardinal—1993. Star Trek: The Next Generation Game of the Galaxies. Includes board, playing pieces, counters, die, and spinner. Black, starfield box with Enterprise-D in background and inset photo of crew. ....$20–$30

Decipher—1993. Star Trek: The Next Generation Interactive VCR Board Game. "A Klingon Challenge." Includes board, playing pieces, and video tape. White box with photos of Enterprise-D and Klingon face on space background. Limited edition. ....$40–$60

Hasbro—1974. Fold-out board. Game pieces and spinners. Box art shows animated characters on blue background. ....
....$75–$100

Ideal—1966. Includes board, four game cards, and numerous playing pieces. Color box art shows Kirk, Spock, and Uhura on bridge. ....$125–$150

Milton Bradley—1979. Star Trek: The Motion Picture. Includes board, play cards, markers, and playing pieces. ....
....$50–$75

Palitoy (British)—1975. Star Trek Game. Fold-out board and game pieces. Box has blue space scene background with Kirk, Spock, and Enterprise. ....$75–$100

West End Games—1985. Three different boxed games designed for the adult player. Each game includes maps, rules, counters, cards, and other gaming pieces.

　　Enterprise Encounter, red box with color photo of Kirk, Spock, and Scotty from original TV show. ....$20–$25

Star Trek: The Adventure Game, box art shows Kirk and Spock with Enterprise and Klingon ship in background. ....$20–$25

Star Trek III, three solitaire games in one, blue box with color art of movie Enterprise. ....$20–$25

Cartridge and Hand-Held Games (For home game systems)

General Consumer Electronics—1982. Star Trek: The Motion Picture game for their Vectrex system. ....$5–$10

Microvision (Milton Bradley)—1979. Star Trek Phaser Strike. Cartridge for hand-held game. ....$10–$20

Nintendo—1991. Star Trek 25th Anniversary Edition. ....
....$15–$20

Playmates—1992. Deep Space Nine Crossroads of Time, versions for Sega and Nintendo. ....$15–$20

Sega—1983. Home version of Sega's commercial arcade game. ....$10–$20

　　Sega—1994. Star Trek: The Next Generation. Echoes from the Past. ....$15–$25

Computer Games (See Computer Software section of this book) Party Games

Decipher—How to Host a Mystery, Star Trek: The Next Generation Version. Includes cassette tape, invitations, name tags, and various manuals and guides for the host and guests. White box with photo of Enterprise-D. ....$30–$35

Pinball Games

Azrak-Hamway—1976. Plastic toy pinball game, 12". Packaged in open window boxes with color photo of Kirk and Spock and color artwork in borders. Two versions.

　　Kirk. ....$60–$95
　　Spock. ....$60–$95

Bally—1979. Commercial electronic pinball game with Star Trek: The Motion Picture theme. Available in two different playing surfaces. ....$400–$800

Playing Cards

For card games other than regular card decks see Trading Cards section of this book.

Aviva—1979. Star Trek: The Motion Picture. Standard deck with drawing of Enterprise on back. Came blister-packed on cardboard header with Rainbow logo. ....$25–$35

Movie Players—1982. Star Trek II: The Wrath of Khan. In addition to suit and number, each card has a color picture of a character on the face. Comes boxed. Back of card and box art is color movie logo. First printing accidently omitted "II" from logo.

    First Printing. ....$20–$25

    Second Printing. ....$15–$20

Paramount/TWA—1986. Star Trek VI: The Voyage Home. Promotional give-away. Featured movie poster artwork. ....

....$10–$15

Target Games

Lincoln Enterprises. Photon Balls. Played like darts only with Styrofoam balls thrown at cloth "board." Targets are drawings of ships. ....$15–$20

Trivia Games

Classic (Score Board)—1992. Includes board, player consoles, counters, playing tokens, and cards. Box has artwork of characters from shows. Two versions.

    Star Trek (Original). ....$25–$40

    Star Trek: The Next Generation. ....$25–$40

Western Publishing—1985. Trivial Pursuit–type game. Two versions. Complete game has trivia cards, game board, and dice. Smaller version is cards only. Both come boxed with color photos from original TV show.

    Cards Only. ....$25–$40

    Complete Game. ....$35–$85

FASA *Star Trek II* Figures

SEGA Star Trek Game Cartridge

Azrack Hamway Kirk Pinball Game

GREETING CARDS

Though greeting cards are very popular novelty items they have not, to date, seemed to have caught on as collectibles. In most cases even the older and more elaborate cards are being bought at relatively low prices simply to be used and enjoyed for their original purpose. It is always possible, of course, that a stronger collectors' market could develop. At least one company, Popshots, has established a collector club toward this end (at least with their own product).

INVESTMENT POTENTIAL
Fair.

CARE
As with all paper items, greeting cards need to be protected from creasing, tears, and moisture. Any size plastic collector's bag large enough to accommodate the card or cards is suitable. If the card was originally sold with an envelope (as most were), care should be taken to keep the envelope with the card, especially for the odder size cards where finding a replacement might be difficult.

SECTION NOTES
This section has been organized alphabetically by manufacturer. Unlicensed cards and parody cards have been omitted since most are simple, easy-to-reproduce designs unlikely to ever become collectible.

California Dreamers

These are 5″ × 7″ cards with envelopes featuring color photos from the original TV series.

First Series, 1985

Chekov Screaming—"Inhuman Cossacks! Pigs! They've destroyed everything. You'll never be 29 again. Happy Birthday." ....$2–$4

Enterprise—"Space is not the final frontier . . . You are!"...$2–$4

Gorn Attacking Kirk—"Beam me up, Scotty . . . It's been one of those days." ....$2–$4

Kirk and Spock—"Fire all phasers . . . Fire all photon torpedoes . . . What the heck. It's your Birthday!"................$2–$4

Kirk as Romulan Talking into Communicator—"This is Captain James T. Kirk of the Starship Enterprise. Our mission is a peaceful one. We mean no harm . . . Sure the check's in the mail and you're 29. Happy Birthday." ....$2–$4

Kirk Looking Disgusted—"Sometimes I just want to say to hell with Starfleet, to hell with regulations and responsibility, to hell with everything. Except you!" ....$2–$4

Kirk, McCoy, and Uhura—"Phasers charged and ready. Photon torpedoes fully armed . . . Here comes Monday!"...$2–$4

Kirk, Spock, and McCoy from "Piece of the Action"—"You've got to dress for success!"................................$2–$4

Kirk Talking into Communicator—"The landing party is expendable. The ship is not. If we're not back by 0500, contact Starfleet Command, get the Enterprise out of here, and whatever you do . . . Have a good time on your Birthday!" ....$2–$4

Kirk with Arms Folded—"There's an amusing little custom we have on earth . . . Report to my quarters and I'll explain!" $2–$4

Kirk with Bow and Arrow—"I was going to shoot you with a phaser . . . But it seemed so unromantic." ....$2–$4

Kirk with the Providers from "Gamesters of Triskelion"—"Who am I? Where am I? Why do I have on these strange clothes . . . Why do I have such strange friends?"...$2–$4

McCoy Checking Instrument—"I've run every test, checked every medical reference in the galaxy, and damn it. I can't find a cure for what you've got . . . Old Age . . . Happy Birthday." ....$2–$4

McCoy (Injured)—"Listen to me. I'm a doctor. I know . . . Birthdays are hell!" ....$2–$4

Planet on Bridge Screen—"To boldly go where no man has gone before . . . or woman either. Congratulations." ....$2–$4

Scotty—"Three dilithium crystals, a tablespoon of kironide, a pinch of antimatter, and just a dash of phaser . . . I'm going to make you a birthday cake that will light up the universe . . . Happy Birthday." ....$2–$4

Spock Giving Vulcan Salute—"You were born on this day. It is therefore quite logical to wish you a Happy Birthday . . . Live long and prosper." ....$2–$4

Spock Holding Cat—"There are 3 billion worlds in the known universe, with a combined population of approximately 6,307,000,000,000 composed of carbon- and noncarbon-based life forms . . . But there's only 1 of you. Happy Birthday." ....$2–$4

Spock in Environment Suit—"The heat here is extreme. Far beyond normal ranges . . . How many candles were on that cake, anyway? Happy Birthday." ....$2–$4

Spock Looking at Bridge Instruments—"History banks indicate that inhabitants of 20th-century Earth would oftentimes undergo a strange suicidelike ritual on many of their post-30th birthdays . . . Death by Chocolate. Happy Birthday." ....$2–$4

Spock—"Readings indicate an unparalleled cosmic phenomena occurred on this day. It was in a time so ancient, the year cannot be ascertained by ship's computers . . . I guess we'll just have to look at the cake and count all those candles! Happy Birthday." ....$2–$4

Spock Seated—"It is not logical. It makes no sense . . . It must be Love!" ....$2–$4

Spock Smiling—"You make me smile!" ....$2–$4

Spock Wearing Visor—"Just because one is logical . . . does not mean one cannot be cool. You're cool. Happy Birthday." ....$2–$4

Spock with Harp—"I fail to understand the inexplicable human need to so primitively celebrate the anniversary of one's birth. Nevertheless, I offer you the words of Surak, the most revered of all Vulcan philosophers. 'Krut Toba Grig-Toba Grig.' If you party, party BIG!! Happy Birthday." ....$2–$4

Second Series, 1986

Kirk—"The universe is a big place . . . How did two great people like us ever find each other?" ....$2–$4

Kirk and Chekov on Bridge—"Damage control reports we've taken a direct hit. Power out on decks 1, 2, and 3. Life support systems functioning on auxiliary power . . . Has anybody got an aspirin? Get well soon." ....$2–$4

Kirk and Spock—"You are correct, Captain, I see them. On our right as well as our left . . . Gray hair. Happy Birthday." ....$2–$4

Kirk and Spock in Force Field—"Time is a dimension, like

height, width or depth, therefore we're getting shorter, fatter, denser and older! Happy Birthday!" ....$2–$4

Kirk in Pain—"This syndrome is like that of the madness associated with severe cases of Rigelian fever. Actually, it's something quite different . . . Love." ....$2–$4

Kirk, Spock, and McCoy (in Bushes)—"Analysis concludes that this is both the correct time and correct place . . . Throw down the blanket and let's party. Happy Birthday." ....$2–$4

Smiling Group—"A group of us got together to do something special for your birthday . . . We're having you sent into space. Happy Birthday." ....$2–$4

Spock—"Forgive me if I'm lengthy, however, mathematics is an extremely precise science . . . You're a 9.99999999999999." ....$2–$4

Spock—"It is one of the most painful of all biological phenomena . . . I've got you under my skin." ....$2–$4

Spock—"Regrettably, the laws of gravity are absolute . . . Birthdays are a drag. Happy Birthday." ....$2–$4

Third Series, 1987

Chekov—"Captain, There's an unidentified object appearing on the screen. It's blocking our path . . . Another Birthday!" ....$2–$4

Kirk and Crewman in Sickbay—"Twenty years in the fleet and I've never seen anything like it . . . 45 pieces of double fudge chocolate birthday cake! Happy Birthday!" ....$2–$4

Kirk and Spock—"You are now and shall always be . . . My best friend. Happy Birthday." ....$2–$4

Kirk and Spock—"Captain, sensors indicate that subspace interference has prevented our transmission from arriving at the intended time . . . Sorry I was late! Happy Birthday." ....$2–$4

Kirk and Spock in Chains—"Thought about in a logical fashion, current circumstances are not as desperate as they seem . . . Of course, who can think logically at a time like this. Hang in there!" ....$2–$4

Kirk at Swordpoint—"Keep your shields up!" ....$2–$4

Kirk, Spock, and McCoy at Party—"Starfleet Command has created living conditions for us in space identical to those which we experience on Earth . . . Underpaid, Overworked, Underloved." ....$2–$4

Kirk, Spock, and Uhura on Bridge—"Incoming message is extremely primitive . . . But very sincere. Happy birthday to you" (with musical notes). ....$2–$4

Kirk Talking into Communicator—"I've just ordered the ship's computers to provide me with your complete psychological profile . . . You're warped, factor-10. I like that in a person." ....$2–$4

Kirk Talking to Tellarite at Party—"Call me . . . We'll do lunch!" ....$2–$4

McCoy—"Don't quote regulations to me and don't give me any of that 'logic stuff.' Just go out there . . . And have a Happy Birthday." ....$2–$4

Spock—"It would be illogical to assume that this card is your birthday present . . . So much for logic! Happy Birthday." ....$2–$4

Spock—"Logic dictates that you recently had a birthday. Correctly applied, logic is seldom wrong . . . Sometimes late, but never wrong. Sorry I missed your birthday. Hope you had a good one." ....$2–$4

Spock—"My conclusion is that you are a magnificently superior being. My method of analysis was simple . . . It takes one to know one! Happy Birthday." ....$2–$4

Spock Reading Tricorder—"I must conclude that we are in a dimension where the laws of known physics do not apply . . . You're much too young to be that old! Happy Birthday." ....$2–$4

Spock—"These tools are extremely antiquated . . . Just like you! Happy Birthday." ....$2–$4

Spock Holding Head—"The level of pain is quite extraordinary . . . I hate being so far away on your birthday." ....$2–$4

Spock—"The thing most rare in the universe . . . A friend as good as you." ....$2–$4

Spock Wearing Headpiece—"Batteries may fail . . . but Rock and Roll will never die!" ....$2–$4

Uhura—"What I'm picking up is barely understandable. Primitive music forms. Simplistic language patterns. Assorted and wildly off-key noises. I'm not sure what it is but it sounds as if they're trying to sing . . . Happy Birthday to you." ....$2–$4

Cambridge

1979

Enterprise (front view). ....$2–$4
Enterprise (head-on). ....$2–$4
Enterprise (side view). ....$2–$4
Kirk and Spock, with Enterprise overhead. ....$2–$4
Kirk with Wrist Communicator. ....$2–$4
Kirk, Spock, and McCoy on Bridge. ....$2–$4
Spock at Science Station. ....$2–$4
Star Trek: The Motion Picture Crew, with Enterprise Overhead. ....$2–$4

Hallmark

1992/93

Color photo cards with original TV series and Star Trek: The Next Generation subjects. Cards included envelopes.

Original TV Series

Beam Me Up Scotty. ....$2–$4
Birthday Message from Mr. Spock. ....$2–$4
Bridge Crew. ....$2–$4
By Conservative Estimate (Xmas Card). ....$2–$4
Captain She's Gonna Blow (Scotty). ....$2–$4
Come On! A Klingon! Tribbles! Anything. ....$2–$4
Command Insignia on Green Foil. ....$2–$4
Enterprise and Giant Amoeba (Immunity Syndrome). ....$2–$4
He Knows You Are Sleeping? ....$2–$4
I Don't See Any Signs of Aging. ....$2–$4
I'm Sending You This Card. ....$2–$4
Jim, It's Like This. ....$2–$4
Kirk and Spock. ....$2–$4
Kirk and Spock on Foil Card. ....$2–$4
Kirk, Spock, McCoy, and Uhura. ....$2–$4
Live Long and Prosper. ....$2–$4
Negative Scotty . . . We're Not Beaming Up. ....$2–$4
Oh, Christmas Tree. ....$2–$4
Open Hailing Frequencies. ....$2–$4
Spock (Vulcan Salute). ....$2–$4
These Humans . . . They Exasperate Me. ....$2–$4
Think I'll Get Some Pointy Ears. ....$2–$4
To Boldly Go Where No Man. ....$2–$4
Valentine . . . Let's Boldly Go. ....$2–$4
Well Bones . . . What Do You Say? ....$2–$4
Would I Forget Your Stardate? ....$2–$4
You Wouldn't Happen to Be. ....$2–$4
You're Affecting My Efficiency. ....$2–$4
You've Been Married Another Year. ....$2–$4

Star Trek: The Next Generation

Anywhere, Anytime, Any Galaxy. ....$2–$4
A Warrior Does Not Cry. ....$2–$4
Being an Android, I Will Never Age. ....$2–$4
Command Insignia (Foil Design). ....$2–$4
Crew. ....$2–$4
Enterprise (Foil Card). ....$2–$4
Ferengi Carrying Bouquet. ....$2–$4
Grrr . . . (Worf and K'Ehlyr). ....$2–$4
Have a Happy Birthday. ....$2–$4
I Protest. ....$2–$4
I Sense That You Are Feeling a Little Depressed .....$2–$4
I Traveled All the Way to the Neutral Zone. ....$2–$4
I Understand That It is Customary. ....$2–$4
I'm Sensing a Strong Source of Anguish. ....$2–$4
Love, Amour, Passion. ....$2–$4
My Medical Tricorder Detects. ....$2–$4
My Visor Enables Me to See. ....$2–$4
Romulan Warbird. ....$2–$4
Sorry, I Forgot Your Birthday. ....$2–$4
Space . . . The Final Frontier. ....$2–$4
To Boldly Go Where No One Has Gone Before. ......$2–$4

Paramount Home Video—1985

Christmas Card, with Enterprise. ....$5–$10

Popshots

1993

Three-D pop-up color artwork of original TV series and Star Trek: The Next Generation subjects. Fronts of cards show artwork of either original or Next Generation Enterprise with appropriate logo above and "PopShots" below. Cards include envelope and come shrink-wrapped with color paper insert showing card in open position.

Bridge Scene with Locutus on Screen—"I am Locutus of Borg . . . Resistance is futile . . . Life as you know it is over . . . Prepare to age! Happy Birthday." ....$4–$6
"City on the Edge of Forever" Scene with McCoy Jumping Through Guardian of Forever—"There's No Escape from Your Birthday." ....$4–$6
Crew on Bridge (Next Generation)—"Happy Birthday." ....$4–$6
Kirk Buried in Tribbles—"The tribble with birthdays is they keep adding up." ....$4–$6
Kirk, Spock, McCoy, and Enterprise—"Birthday Greetings from the Starship Enterprise." ....$4–$6
Picard, Data, and Guinan in 10 Forward—"Here's to an enterprising birthday . . . Make It So!".............$4–$6

Random House

1976

Cards feature color photos from original TV series and come in assorted sizes. Larger ones have punch-out features.

Kirk—"Star light, star bright, first star I see tonight . . . I wished on a star for your birthday." ....$2–$4
Kirk—"This is your Captain speaking . . ." Inside caption ". . . Have a far-out Birthday!" ....$2–$4

Kirk Holding Rose—"The Captain and I both wish you a very happy birthday." ....$2–$4
Kirk Resting Head on Small Viewer—"COURAGE!" ....$2–$4
Kirk, Spock, Scott, Uhura, and McCoy—"Happy Birthday to a great human being!" ....$2–$4
Kirk Standing on Planet Looking Towards Earth— "There's so much space between us . . ." ....$2–$4
Kirk with Medals—"Congratulations.".....................$2–$4
Kirk with Open Communicator—"Let's Communicate." Includes a two-piece punch-out blue communicator. ....$3–$6
McCoy and Kirk—"Don't worry—You'll feel better soon." ....$2–$4
McCoy and Kirk—"Happy Birthday from one big shot. . . ." Inside caption ". . . to another." This includes a three-piece punch-out blue phaser. ....$3–$6
McCoy, Scott, Chekov, and Uhura—"Happy Birthday." ....$2–$4
Scott, Spock, Kirk, McCoy, Uhura, and Chekov—"Happy Birthday from the whole spaced out crew." ....$2–$4
Spock—"Know what I like about you?" ....$2–$4
Spock—"Sorry I blew it . . ." ....$2–$4
Spock in Dress Uniform—"It is illogical not to wish a Happy Birthday to someone so charming." ....$2–$4
Spock Listening to Headset—"I must be hard of hearing." ....$2–$4
Spock Putting Hand on Door—"Let's keep in touch!"......... ....$2–$4
Spock with Visor Giving Vulcan Salute—"Having a Birthday?" ....$2–$4
Uhura—"I hear it's your Birthday." Inside caption "Open all hailing frequencies!" ....$2–$4
Uhura and Kirk on Bridge—"Off Course." Inside caption "Hope you're back on the right Trek soon." ....$2–$4
USS Enterprise (on the front)—Caption "For your Birthday I'd like to take you on a trip to Venus." ....$2–$4
USS Enterprise Entering Orbit Around Orange Planet— "I'm sending you something from outer space . . ." Includes four-piece punch-out of the USS Enterprise. ....$4–$8
USS Enterprise Orbiting Planet—"One of the nicest earthlings in the universe . . . Inside caption "just opened this card! Happy Birthday." ....$2–$4
USS Enterprise Over Planet—"The world's a better place because of you." ....$2–$4

Random House Punch-Out Greeting Card

HOUSEWARES

This section covers a wide range of different items which, though understandably somewhat varied in collectibility, is, in general, a surprisingly active field of interest. Perhaps this is because so much of what has been produced in housewares, especially in recent years, has been aimed specifically at the collector market. The subsection "Display Items" in particular, which contains merchandise ranging from simple knickknacks to limited edition pieces, all of which have no practical function other than decoration, is made up almost entirely of items aimed directly at the collector.

INVESTMENT POTENTIAL
Good.

CARE
See individual subsections.

SECTION NOTES
Because of the great variety of items represented by housewares, this section is divided into the following subsections for ease of reference: Cloth Goods, Display Items, General Housewares, Kitchen Wares, Lunch Boxes, and Party Goods. Subsections are organized alphabetically by item.

CLOTH GOODS

CARE
Cloth goods are most desirable as collectibles when they are in their original unused condition which, in most cases, amounts to being simply wrapped in plastic with a paper or cardboard insert describing the product. The prices in this subsection represent cloth goods in this "new" condition. Unfortunately, since they are rarely to be found unused, the next best option is for them to be as near to new condition as possible. Take care when cleaning and displaying them to avoid fading, soiling, wrinkling, and other forms of wear to which fabrics are susceptible. Altered cloth goods (for instance, using a sheet to make an article of clothing) are common but of little collector value.

Afghan—Paramount Promotional, 1992. Star Trek VI: The Undiscovered Country. Approx. 4′ × 6′ fringed. Color reproduction of movie poster art. ....$250–$300
Bed Linens—Pacific Mills, 1975. Original TV Enterprise and characters in action scenes on light or dark blue background.
    Bed Spread (Twin Size). ....$100–$150
    Pillow Case. ....$20–$30
    Sheets (Twin Set). ....$60–$85
Bed Linens—Canon, 1979. STTMP. Scenes from the first movie.
    Pillow Cases. ....$15–$25
    Sheets (Twin Set). ....$50–$75
Bed Linens—Star Dream (German), 1995. Star Trek: Generations. Artwork from movie poster. Limited edition set consists of pillow case and coverlet. Price for set. ....$75–$100
Blanket—Kocomo, 1993. Tan wool blanket with USS Enterprise NCC 1701-A command insignia screenprinted in blue. Limited edition. ....$125–$150
Comforter—Aberdeen, 1986. Original TV Enterprise, characters, and scenes on dark blue background.
    Twin. ....$125–$150
    Full Sizes. ....$150–$175
Draperies—Pacific Mills, 1975 Original TV Enterprise and characters. Assorted sizes. Price for any size. ....$75–$100
Draperies—Canon, 1979. STTMP. Scenes from the first movie. Assorted sizes. Price for any size. ....$50–$75
Draperies—Aberdeen, 1986. Ships and scenes from the movies on dark blue background. Assorted sizes. Price for any size. ....$40–$75
Dust Ruffle—Aberdeen, 1986. Dark blue with star pattern. Made to match other Aberdeen Star Trek products. Star Trek packaging but no Star Trek scenes, ships, or characters on ruffle itself. ....$15–$25

Pillow Sham—Aberdeen, 1986. Ships and scenes from the movies on dark blue background. ....$10–$15
Sleeping Bag—Alp Industries, 1976. Artwork of Enterprise, scenes, and characters on blue star background. .....$60–$125
Sleeping Bag—Alp Industries, 1979. "Star Trek" and USS Enterprise with artwork of group on bridge from original TV series running full length of bag. ....$100–$150
Sleeping Bag—Ero Industries, 1987. Star Trek: The Next Generation. Pictures Worf, Data, and the Enterprise. ....
....$75–$100
Throw Rugs—1976. Small, imitation fur. Color photos and artwork from original series.
    Bridge Scene. ....$75–$100
    Crew. ....$75–$100
    Enterprise. ....$75–$100
    Episode Collage. ....$75–$100
Towel—Jupiter Beach, 1989. Beach size. Star Trek: The Next Generation. Color artwork of ship and logo on magenta background. ....$25–$35
Towels—Franco, 1975. Large size. Color artwork on white background.
    Enterprise Over Planet. ....$45–$60
    Kirk, Spock, and McCoy with Rigel Castle. ....$45–$60
    Spock Fighting Three-headed Serpent. ....$45–$60
Towels—Franco, 1976. 53″ × 29″. Color artwork on white background.
    Enterprise Fighting Klingon Cruiser. ....$40–$50
    Kirk and Spock Portraits. ....$40–$50
    Spock Holding Phaser and Communicator. ....$40–$50
Towels—Cecil Saydah Co., 1993. Beach. Vertical color artwork on black backgrounds.
    Star Trek (Original), Kirk, Spock, McCoy. ....$25–$35
    Star Trek: The Next Generation, ship. ....$25–$35
Towels—Cecil Saydah Co., 1993. Bath. Star Trek: The Next Generation. Color artwork on white background. Ship and logo.
    Horizontal Format. ....$20–$30
    Vertical Format. ....$20–$30
Washcloth—Cecil Saydah Co., 1993. Star Trek: The Next Generation. Color artwork of ship and logo on white background. ....$10–$15

NOTE: The vertical format towel and washcloth from Cecil Saydah were originally sold as a set.

DISPLAY ITEMS

CARE

Though many of the items in this subsection are somewhat fragile, they are otherwise basically durable and easy to clean. The only consideration for most is that if they come with a display box, as many do, be sure to keep the box along with any interior packaging and store it in a manner that will best preserve its original condition.

NOTE: For other items that may be considered display pieces, see Pewter, Ceramics and Glassware, Toys, and Crystal.

Data's Head (from "Time's Arrow")—Fantasy Park, 1994. Soft plastic replica of the prop used for the episode. Limited edition of 500. Includes Certificate of Authenticity. ....
....$250–$300
Die-Cast Enterprise (Original)—Franklin Mint, 1991. Painted metal replica approx. 15″ long. Removable panel in saucer section reveals details of bridge and slide-out tray in rear holds small metal shuttlecraft. Black plastic base has silver 25th anniversary insignia inset in side. ....$300–$325
Die-Cast Enterprise NCC 1701-D—Franklin Mint, 1996. Painted metal replica approx. 12″ long. Removable panel in saucer section reveals details of bridge. Removable saucer section. Black base with metal command insignia–shaped identification plaque on side. ....$300–$325
Dioramas—Applause, 1996. Three-dimensional scenes sculpted in resin approx. 7½″ high. Limited to 2500 pieces.
    Amok Time (Kirk and Spock Fighting). ....$60–$70
    Locutus. ....$60–$70
Figures—Janet D'Airo, 1995. Color painted Picard figures cut out of ⅝″ hardwood. Approx. 17″ tall. Limited to 1000 pieces each. Three different.
    Picard Standing (Starfleet Uniform). ....$60–$70
    Picard in Command Chair. ....$100–$115
    Picard in 17th-Century Naval Uniform. ....$60–$70
Figurine—Enesco, 1992. Plastic replica of Enterprise from original TV series approx. 8″ long. Attached to stand with command insignia–shaped base. Box shows photo of product on blue background with schematic of ship. ....$40–$50
Figurine—Enesco, 1995. Capt. Kirk, UFP banner from original TV series in black, and original Enterprise on command insignia base. Identifying plaque on front. Plastic, approx. 5½″ high. ....$60–$70
Figurine—Enesco, 1995. Capt. Picard, Next Generation UFP seal, and Next Generation Enterprise on Next Generation-style command insignia–shaped base. Identifying plaque on front. Plastic, approx. 5½″ high. ....$60–$70
Figurine—Enesco, 1995. Musical Star Trek: The Next Generation Enterprise. Ship orbiting planet on Next Generation command insignia–shaped base. Approx. 8″ high. Phaser-shaped remote control activates music, lights, and sound effects (4 different). ....$300–$315
Figurine—Applause, 1995. Star Trek: Generations. Kirk and Picard on horseback. Approx. 7½″ high. Movie logo on base. Limited to 5000 pieces. Comes in display box. Certificate of Authenticity included. ....$50–$60
Figurines—Applause, 1996. Cast resin figurines of characters in action poses. Figures are between 4″ and 5″ high.
    Darmok and Picard. ....$20–$25
    Gorn and Kirk. ....$20–$25
    Janeway with Command Chair. ....$20–$25
    Neelix in Kitchen. ....$20–$25
    "Q" on Throne. ....$20–$25
    Swashbuckler Sulu. ....$20–$25

Figurines—Enesco, 1993. Plastic replicas of ships from Star Trek: The Next Generation. Each approx. 7″ at longest dimension. Each comes attached to stand with base styled as an insignia appropriate to ship. Box shows color photo of ship on black space backdrop.

Enterprise 1701-D.	$40–$50
Klingon Bird-of-Prey.	$40–$50

Figurines—Franklin Mint, 1995. Ships from various Star Trek series and movies cast in sterling silver. Each is approx. 2″ in length and includes stand. Wall display with silver frame and blue, mirrored back with starfield motif was included free on completion of set.

Cardassian Warship.	$70–$80
Deep Space Nine Space Station.	$70–$80
Enterprise 1701.	$70–$80
Enterprise 1701-D.	$70–$80
Excelsior.	$70–$80
Ferengi Marauder.	$70–$80
Klingon Bird-of-Prey.	$70–$80
Klingon Cruiser (Original Series)	$70–$80
Romulan Bird-of-Prey (Original Series).	$70–$80
Romulan Warbird.	$70–$80
Shuttlecraft (Original Series).	$70–$80
Stargazer.	$70–$80

Figurines—R.S. Owens (for Paramount), 1993. Bronze Enterprise figurines approx. 8″ long with detachable black metal stands. Box has photo of item on dark blue space background. Used as promotional items by Paramount.

Enterprise 1701-D.	$95–$125
Original Enterprise.	$95–$125

Figurines—Willitts Designs, 1993. Enterprise replicas approx. 5½″ high including bases. Each has lights, musical theme, and Captain's introductory monologue appropriate to each respective TV series. Boxes have color photos of product and logo on starfield.

Enterprise 1701.	$80–$90
Enterprise 1701-D.	$70–$80

Globe—Franklin Mint, 1994. "Galaxy Globe." Pewter-rimmed glass globe approx. 7″ high. Scene of original Enterprise and two small Tholian ships from "Tholian Web." Motor swirls glitter in globe. ....$185–$210

Globes—Willitts Designs. Series of three "Star Globes" made in successive years. Each is approx. 7¼″ tall with retractable hood to enhance viewing and black base with appropriate gold embossed logo. Box has color photo of product and appropriate logo on starfield. All have battery functions; lights for all plus sound for last two years.

1992 Original Enterprise.	$65–$75
1993 Next Generation Enterprise.	$65–$75
1994 Klingon Bird-of-Prey.	$65–$75

Gold Record Plaques—California Gold, 1991. Gold-plated records mounted in frames with their album covers and numbered plaque.

Nichelle Nichols "Gene," 45 rpm.	$150–$175
Star Trek (original), 33 rpm.	$250–$275
Star Trek: The Next Generation, 33 rpm.	$250–$275

Insignia Plaque—Franklin Mint, 1995. Set of 12 silver- and gold-plated insignias approx. 3″ in size. Set was originally purchased one insignia at a time. Upon completion of set a glass-topped wooden display case was provided free of charge. Insignias include original command insignia, five-pointed movie version Admiral's rank insignia, original series UFP banner, Next Generation Romulan symbol, Next Generation UFP symbol, Klingon symbol, movie version Captain's rank insignia, IDIC, movie version Commander's rank insignia, Ferengi symbol, movie version command insignia, and Next Generation command insignia. ....
....$300–$325

Insignia Plaque—Franklin Mint, 1996. **"Trilogy Insignia Collection."** Similar to above, earlier insignia collection but with the following insignias—original Science emblem, original Engineering emblem, Starfleet Academy emblem, Tyran insignia, Bajoran military insignia, Mercenary symbol, Galaxy Class Development insignia, Lyaaran insignia, Cardassian insignia, Borg symbol, Arkarian insignia, and Bajoran emblem. ....$300–$325

Laser Disk Plaques—California Gold, 1991. Laser-etched holographic designs on framed, numbered laser disks.

Capt. Kirk.	$175–$250
Star Trek: The Next Generation.	$175–$250
Star Trek VI.	$175–$250
25th Anniversary.	$175–$250

Life Mask—Star Impressions, 1991. 25th anniversary Lt. Comdr. Data mask. Displayed in plexiglass box with black backing. Limited to 1000 pieces. Included Certificate of Authenticity. ....$800–$850

Maquette—Illusive Originals, 1996. Talosian, 15″ high hand-painted bust. Limited to 7500 pieces. Comes with Certificate of Authenticity. ....$180–$190

Plaque—Franklin Mint, 1995. Replica of commissioning plaque from Enterprise 1701-D. Bronze on hardwood base with gold- and silver-plated inset command insignia. Approx. 13½″ × 11″. ....$200–$225

Sculpture—Franklin Mint, 1995. Enterprise (original). Painted resin porcelain blend sculpture of planet in asteroid field with small plastic Enterprise attached. Black plastic base with small silver command insignia on front and glass dome to cover sculpture. Approx. 5″ high (including base and dome). ....
....$35–$45

Sculpture—Franklin Mint, 1996. Capt. Kirk (from original TV series). Painted pewter figure seated in crystal command chair on black base. Embellished with gold and colored crystal detailing. Approx. 7″ tall. ....$190–$210

Sculpture—Masterpiece Replicas, 1994. USS Enterprise 1701-D. Painted brass replica approx. 2′3″ long with interior and exterior fiber optic lighting. Comes with two-pronged stand. Limited to 5000 pieces. ....$1900–$2100

Sculptures—Franklin Mint, 1994/5. Episodes (original TV series). Individual scenes from specific episodes done in painted resin porcelain blend. Scenes are to scale with 3″ (approx.) figures. Each comes with detachable black wooden base with plaque that identifies episode.

City on the Edge of Forever, Kirk and Spock watch McCoy jump through Guardian of Forever. ......$195–$210
The Trouble with Tribbles, Kirk, Spock, and Uhura on bridge with tribbles. ....$195–$210

Sculptures—Hamilton, 1991. Plexiglass slabs approx. 7″ high with design sculpted and painted from rear to create three-dimensional effect. Identifying metal plaque on front of base. Product info and 25th anniversary symbol on bottom of base.
    Enterprise (Original Series). ....$125–$135
    Klingon Cruiser (Original Series) ......$125–$135

Sculptures—Imagine This, 1992/3. Color laser photos affixed to die-cut Plexiglas mounted on Plexiglas base with imbedded background photo for three-dimensional effect. Limited to 10,000 per piece.
    Large Size Kirk (Approx. 7½″ × 8½″). ......$30–$35
    Medium Size (Approx. 5″ × 7½″):
        Enterprise (Original). ....$30–$35
        Enterprise NCC-1701-D. ....$30–$35
    Small Size Spock (Vulcan Salute) (Approx. 1¾″ × 2¼″). ....$10–$15

Waterball—Enesco, 1992. Original series. Glitter-filled waterball approx. 2¼″ high with original Enterprise over planet. "Star Trek" and command symbols in silver on black base. Box has photos of product and logos on black starfield. ....$8–$10

Waterballs—Enesco, 1994. Next Generation. Glitter-filled waterballs approx. 2¼″ high with ships over planets. Logo in silver on black base. Boxes have photos of products and logos on blue background.
    Enterprise 1701-D. ....$8–$10
    Klingon Bird-of-Prey. ....$8–$10

GENERAL HOUSEWARES

CARE

Most of the items in this subsection are fairly durable and require only commonsense care. For items that come packaged in sets (such as bandages) or have parts that could be lost (for instance, plugs in banks), remember that complete items are far more desirable as collectibles. For items that originally came boxed, be careful to keep the box in as near original condition as possible to maintain optimum collectibility.

Bags—Triangle Enterprises, 1993. Paper gift bags with string handles. Employ color photo motifs.
    Large Next Generation Collage (10″ × 13″). ......$5–$8
    Small ST Classic Crew (7″ × 9″). ....$4–$6
    Small NG Crew (7″ × 9″). ....$4–$6
    Small NG Enterprise (7″ × 9″). ....$4–$6
    Small ST Classic Crew Die-Cut. ....$5–$8

Bandages—Adam Joseph, 1979. Star Trek: The Motion Picture. Plastic, adhesive bandages came boxed. Bandages had foil backings with artwork from movie. Bandage wrappings

had movie logo and line artwork. Boxes were orange or pink with foil line artwork and movie logo down side. Three sizes.
    10 Regular, Kirk and Spock artwork. ......$20–$30
    10 Extra Large, ships artwork. ....$20–$30
    30 Assorted Sizes, Kirk and Spock artwork. ......$20–$30

Bank (Electronic)—Thinkway Toys, 1994. Star Trek: The Next Generation. Resembles console from show. When activated has sound effects and pictures on screen. Four different effects. Packaged in open red and silver window box with description at bottom. ......$50–$60

Banks—Play Pal, 1976. Standing figures in color plastic. "Star Trek" molded into base. Slot in back to deposit coin and stopper in bottom of base for removal. Approx. 12″ tall.
    Kirk. ....$75–$100
    Spock. ....$75–$100

Banks—Thinkway Toys, 1994. Star Trek: The Next Generation. Character busts in color plastic. Slot in back to deposit coin and stopper in bottom of figure. Approx. 8″ tall. Came packaged in open window boxes with logo at top and character name at bottom.
    Borg. ....$20–$30
    Ferengi. ....$20–$30
    Klingon. ....$20–$30

Bubble Bath—Euromark (British), 1994. Plastic container is replica of Enterprise-D. Approx. 8″ long. Detachable saucer section holds liquid. Packaged in shallow open tray box with green planet in space behind product and logo below. Back has color artwork of ship in orbit. ......$25–$35

Bulletin Board—Whiting (Milton Bradley), 1979. Star Trek: The Motion Picture. "3-D Poster Bulletin Board" includes die-cut, pre-printed board, instructions, and four pens. ......$25–$40

Chair (Beanbag)—Decorion, 1976. Blue and white plastic with two-color artwork of ships. ......$200–$300

Chair (Beanbag)—Decorion, 1979. Star Trek: The Motion Picture. Yellow plastic with four-color artwork of crew. ......$150–$200

Chair (Director's)—Official Star Trek Fan Club, 1986. White metal with blue cloth Star Trek IV logo on backrest. ......$45–$55

Chair (Inflatable)—K-Mart, 1979. Star Trek: The Motion Picture. Color plastic pictures Spock on back and arms. Logo on seat. Child's size. Came boxed with picture of product on front. ......$100–$150

Christmas Ornaments—Hallmark. Part of this company's "Keepsake Ornament" line. Issued one per year since 1991 until 1995 when multiple ornaments were issued. Came boxed with color photo of ornament on front of box.
    1991 Original Enterprise, lights up. ......$350–$500
    1992 Shuttlecraft, Spock's voice. ......$30–$40
    1993 Enterprise 1701-D, lights up. ......$85–$100
    1994 Klingon Bird-of-Prey, lights up. ......$65–$75
    1995 Romulan Warbird, lights up. ......$35–$45
    1995 The Ships of Star Trek, three mini-ship set. ......$20–$30
    1995 Capt. Kirk. ......$20–$30

1995 Capt. Picard. ....$20–$30

1996 Voyager. ....$25–$35

1996 Comdr. Riker. ....$20–$30

1996 Mr. Spock. ....$20–$30

1996 30th Anniversary, die-cast metal Enterprise and shuttlecraft. ....$50–$65

Clock (Alarm)—Lincoln Enterprises. Digital travel alarm with TV command symbol in upper left corner. ....$25–$30

Clock—Official Star Trek Fan Club, 1986. White wall clock with red 20th anniversary logo on face. ....$25–$30

Clock (Alarm)—Top Banana (O.S.P.), 1994. Talking alarm clock. Original Enterprise statuette on control base with digital readout and space backdrop. Clock has "Landing party to Enterprise; beam us up Scotty" alarm feature. Packaged in window box. ....$35–$45

Clock (Alarm)—Wesco (British), 1994. Talking alarm clock. Enterprise 1701-D. Model of ship on base. Ship has detachable saucer section. Box has artwork of ship. ....$50–$60

Clock (Alarm)—Wesco (British), 1996. Talking alarm clock. Voyager. Color plastic. Base is planetscape with Voyager in relief on backboard that has color space motif. Packaged in window box with logo and color photos of ship and Janeway. ....$60–$75

Clock (Wall)—Wesco (British), 1996. Approx. 10″ across. Shaped like Next Generation command insignia. Analog with inset "Stardate" (day/month/year) digital readout. Came blister-carded. Card has logo and color artwork of Enterprise-D. ....$25–$30

Clock (Wall)—Clock-Wise, 1989. Color photo of movie Enterprise orbiting planet. Rectangular. ....$45–$55

Clock (Alarm)—Zeon Character Clocks (British), 1980. Twin bell alarm clock. Face shows color photo of Kirk and Spock with Enterprise overhead. ....$50–$75

Clock—Color photo of Kirk, Spock, and McCoy from TV series on face, no copyright date, probably unlicensed. Packaged in open-fronted tray boxes.

Alarm. ....$20–$30

Wall. ....$30–$40

NOTE: Design was also used on a pocket watch.

Clock Radio—Telemania, 1994. Shaped like Magellan shuttlecraft from Star Trek: The Next Generation on rectangular black base. ....$40–$50

Clocks (Alarm)—Centric, 1992. Round with black plastic rim and base and photo on face. No decorative packaging.

Enterprise (Original TV Series). ....$35–$45

Enterprise 1701-D. ....$35–$45

Spock (Original TV Series). ....$35–$45

Clocks (Alarm)—Centric, 1995. Gravity clock. Color photo on face of round clock suspended in circular base. Clock stays in upright position when base is turned.

DS9 Space Station. ....$35–$45

Enterprise (Original TV Series). ....$35–$45

Enterprise 1701-D. ....$35–$45

Clocks (Wall)—Centric, 1992/94. Round wall clocks with color photos on face and black plastic rims. Came boxed with picture of product on front of box.

Crew (Original TV Series) ....$35–$45

Crew (Next Generation). ....$35–$45

Crew (Voyager). ....$35–$45

Data. ....$35–$45

DS9 Space Station. ....$35–$45

Enterprise (Original). ....$35–$45

Enterprise 1701-D. ....$35–$45

Picard. ....$35–$45

Spock (Original TV Series). ....$35–$45

Voyager. ....$35–$45

Clocks (Wall)—Official Star Trek Fan Club, 1994. 9″ × 11″ rectangular. Horizontal color laser print photo faces. Beveled glass fronts.

Enterprise 1701-A. ....$40–$50

Enterprise 1701-D. ....$40–$50

Next Generation UFP Seal. ....$40–$50

Comb and Brush Set—Gabil, 1977. Oval blue plastic brush with color transfer, 6″ × 3″. Packaged in clear plastic box. ....$50–$75

Doorhangers—Antioch, 1992/95. Rectangular thin plastic doorhangers approx. 9″ × 4″. Color photos on front and "Do Not Disturb" on back of all designs.

DS9, "I've been sent to Space Station Deep Space Nine!" (Space Station). ....$2–$3

Next Generation, "Now Entering the Final Frontier" (Enterprise). ....$2–$3

Voyager, "Warning, Entering Unexplored Territory" (Ship). ....$2–$3

First Aid Kit—Adam Joseph, 1979. Star Trek: The Motion Picture. 3½″ × 4 ″ orange plastic box with black and white sticker depicting artwork of Kirk, Spock, and Enterprise. Contains various supplies and instructions. ....$40–$60

Flashlight—Azrak-Hamway, 1976. Original TV show. Small black phaser-shaped pistol, battery operated. Originally came blister-packed on header card with color artwork. ....$35–$45

Flashlight—Promotional, 1979. "Star Trek" in STTMP logo. Small, blue. Cereal premium. ....$10–$15

Flashlight—Larami, 1979. Small red and white gun-shaped hand flashlight. Came blister-packed with battery on header card with color photos from Star Trek: The Motion Picture. ....$25–$40

Knife (Pocket)—Taylor Cutlery, 1978. Swiss Army type with two blades, scissors, and tweezers. Ivory handle with Enterprise and logo. Approx. 2¼″ long. ....$75–$150

Knife (Pocket)—Taylor Cutlery, 1978. Two blades. Ivory handle with Enterprise and logo. Approx. 3¾″ long. ....$75–$150

Lamp—Franklin Mint, 1995. Replica of original TV Enterprise on curved black stand. Light comes from underside of saucer section. Approx. 16″ high. ....$80–$90

Lamp—Prestigeline. Aluminum hanging lamp shaped like a stylized Enterprise. Globe lightbulbs at front of lower section and nacelles. ....$150–$300

Light Switch Covers—Aviva, 1979. Star Trek: The Motion Picture. Color stick-ons. Four different.

Enterprise.	$5–$10
Enterprise, Kirk, and Spock.	$5–$10
Phaser Control.	$5–$10
Spock.	$5–$10

Lighter—Promotional, 1988. White plastic. "Paramount Pictures Star Trek Adventure." ....$2–$3

Magnet—Hamilton, 1991. Three-dimensional color plastic has original Enterprise superimposed on command symbol–shaped background with "Star Trek" above ship. Approx. 3″ high. ....$2–$3

Magnets—At-a-Boy, 1993. Rectangular color photos approx. 2″ × 3″ from various Star Trek films and TV series with magnetic backings.

Original TV Series:

Enterprise.	$4–$5
Group Collage, artwork.	$4–$5
Group, promo photo.	$4–$5
Group in Spacesuits.	$4–$5
Kirk on Bridge.	$4–$5
Kirk with Enterprise.	$4–$5
Kirk with Tribbles.	$4–$5
Kirk and McCoy.	$4–$5
Kirk, McCoy, and Spock.	$4–$5
Klingon Cruiser.	$4–$5
McCoy.	$4–$5
Spock, head shot.	$4–$5
Spock, Kirk, and Scotty.	$4–$5
Spock with Phaser.	$4–$5
Spock with Visor.	$4–$5
Spock, Vulcan salute.	$4–$5
Sulu and Chekov.	$4–$5

Movies:

Enterprise.	$4–$5
Kirk, Spock, McCoy, and Scotty.	$4–$5
Spock.	$4–$5

Star Trek: The Next Generation:

Data.	$4–$5
Dr. Crusher.	$4–$5
Enterprise.	$4–$5
Ferengi.	$4–$5
Geordi.	$4–$5
Group.	$4–$5
Guinan.	$4–$5
Locutus.	$4–$5
Picard.	$4–$5
Picard and Data (1940s attire).	$4–$5
"Q."	$4–$5
Riker, close-up.	$4–$5
Riker, waist-up.	$4–$5
Troi.	$4–$5
Troi, Guinan, and Dr. Crusher.	$4–$5
Wesley.	$4–$5
Worf.	$4–$5
Yar.	$4–$5

Magnets—Magnetic Collectibles, 1992. Soft color plastic die-cut magnets from the original TV series. Came packaged with paper covered display board decorated with insignia shapes at sides and "Star Trek," Enterprise, and Vulcan salute at top.

"Beam Me Up Scotty."	$4–$6
Chekov.	$4–$6
Enterprise.	$4–$6
Galileo Shuttlecraft.	$4–$6
Kirk.	$4–$6
McCoy.	$4–$6
Scotty.	$4–$6
Spock.	$4–$6
"Star Trek," on insignia.	$4–$6
Sulu.	$4–$6
Uhura.	$4–$6
Vulcan Salute.	$4–$6

Mailbox—Paramount Special Effects Merchandise, Inc., 1990. Blue with original TV Enterprise on side. Designed to be personalized. ....$75–$100

Matches—D.D. Bean and Sons, 1979. Star Trek: The Motion Picture, seven different variations on merchandise offers inside. ....$2–$4

Matches—D.D. Bean and Sons, 1982. Star Trek II: The Wrath of Khan. White with red print of movie logo on front and cap offer on back. ....$1–$2

Mirror—Lightline, 1977. Decorative frames. Two designs and sizes.

Kirk and Spock.	$30–$60
Spock.	$20–$40

Music Box—Hamilton Gifts, 1991. Lacquered 6″ × 7³⁄₄″ wood music box with color artwork portraits of five crew members from the original TV series on lid. Box art has repeating Enterprise and logo motif on space backdrop. Plays original TV theme. Limited to 25,000 pieces. Certificate of Authenticity included. ....$60–$70

Music Box—Enesco, 1993. Lacquered 5³⁄₄″ × 6¹⁄₄″ wood music box. Blue with photo of Star Trek: The Next Generation crew on lid. Box is blue with insignia logo on all sides. Plays Next Generation theme. ....$60–$70

Pennant—Image Products, 1982. Star Trek II: The Wrath of Khan. Black with movie logo, picture of Enterprise, and words "USS Enterprise" in silver, 12″ × 30″ triangle. $8–$15

Pennant—Image Products, 1982. Star Trek II logo, picture of Spock in Vulcan robes, and words "Spock Lives." Black, yellow, and red on white, 12″ × 30″ triangular. ....$8–$15

Pennant—Promotional, 1988. "Paramount Pictures Star Trek Adventure, Universal Studios Tour." Enterprise and planet. Multicolor. Odd shape approx. 9″ × 21¹⁄₂″. .....$5–$10

Road Signs—Marketfacturing, 1995. Full-size metal replicas with Star Trek sayings.

Klingon X-ing.	$35–$40
Speed Limit Warp Factor 6.	$35–$40
Starfleet Crew Member Parking Only.	$35–$40
USS Enterprise X-ing.	$35–$40

Shower Curtain—J.C. Penney, 1986. Black vinyl with movie Enterprise and Klingon ship orbiting planet. ....$25–$50

Spaceship Mobile—Mokato. Six small silver plastic ships. "Enterprise" but with third nacelle. Difference was probably to avoid licensing. Long black window box. ....$15–$25

Telephone—Kash N' Gold Ltd., 1993. Shaped like original TV Enterprise. Saucer section and part of lower section separate to become receiver. Insignia-shaped base has buttons for dialing. Box design shows product on space backdrop with "Star Trek—The Telephone," "Collector's Edition," "To Boldly Go Where No Man Has Gone Before," and color photos of characters from original show. ....$90–$125

Towlettes—Adam Joseph, 1979. STTMP. Pink and silver box of 20. Horizontal artwork of Enterprise with movie logo running down side. ....$20–$30

Tray—Aviva Enterprise, 1979. Metal lap tray with legs. Color photo of Spock from Star Trek: The Motion Picture, 17½″ wide. ....$30–$40

Tricorder—Vital Technologies Corp., 1995. TR-107 Tricorder Mark I. Actual data gathering instrument designed to resemble a Next Generation tricorder. Functions include scans for weather, electromagnetic radiation, and color spectrums. ....$375–$425

TV Remote Control—Kash N' Gold Ltd., 1996. Universal remote shaped like Next Generation phaser. Comes packaged in window box with logos and color photos of product and Enterprise 1701-D on all sides. ....$50–$60

Wall Hangings—Great Scott, 1996. Color fabric vertically formatted wall hangings. 28″ × 41″. Star Trek: The Next Generation logo below design. Two different.

    Enterprise-D, on blue starfield. ....$17–$20
    Next Generation Insignia, on black. ....$17–$20

Wallpaper—Imperial Wallcoverings, 1981. Light blue background with K-7 space station, original TV Enterprise, and other ships. Per roll. ....$50–$75

Waste Basket—Chein, 1979. Star Trek: The Motion Picture. Front features the standard motion picture "rainbow" painting, back shows photograph of the Enterprise surrounded by smaller pictures. Metal, 13″ high. ....$75–$100

Waste Basket—Chein, 1977. Black metal. Photo of the Enterprise on one side and statistics on others. Approx. 13″ tall. ....$140–$200

KITCHEN WARES

CARE

Most kitchen items are by nature durable. Plastic ware has a slight tendency to fade and scratch but usually only after extensive use. Few items have decorative packaging but it is an important part of those that do. In cases where an item is part of a set, such as for promotional tumblers, it is far more desirable to have a complete set.

NOTE: For decorative plates, glasses, ceramic mugs, steins, and accessories see Ceramics and Glassware.

Bowl—Deka, 1979. Plastic, soup. Star Trek: The Motion Picture. Color artwork of characters. ....$10–$15

Candy Boxes—Phoenix Candy, 1976. 2½″ × 5″ vertically formatted boxes of "Star Trek" candy with color photos on front.

    #1 Kirk, close-up. ....$15–$20
    #2 Spock. ....$15–$20
    #3 McCoy. ....$15–$20
    #4 Bridge Crew. ....$15–$20
    #5 Uhura. ....$15–$20
    #6 Transporter. ....$15–$20
    #7 Kirk. ....$15–$20
    #8 Enterprise. ....$15–$20

Candy Tubes—Bee International, 1993. Star Trek: The Next Generation. Clear plastic tubes approx. 13″ long. Lid consists of color plastic approx. 4″ high. Contained either hard or soft candies wrapped in colored foil with Star Trek line art. Three different.

    Borgs. ....$3–$5
    Ferengi. ....$3–$5
    Klingon. ....$3–$5

Canteen—Zak Designs, 1994. Star Trek: The Next Generation. Clear plastic glass approx. 6″ tall with lid that provides twist-up straw. Removable white carrying strap. UFP seal and logo. ....$8–$10

Canteen (Sparkle)—Zak Designs, 1994. Star Trek: The Next Generation. Same basic design as canteen above but with double walls to hold glitter-filled liquid. Clear plastic with small Enterprises and logo. ....$10–$15

Cereal Boxes—Kellogg's (British division), 1969. Color artwork on boxes of Sugar Smacks of cereal of Spock holding phaser above bowl of cereal.

    Regular Size Box. ....$40–$60
    Single Serving Size Box. ....$20–$30

NOTE: Prices are for empty boxes as it is assumed that even dedicated collector would prefer not to keep 25+-year-old perishables.

Coasters—Ritepoint. White plastic with "Star Trek" and Starfleet emblem. ....$2–$3

Decanter—BMF (German). Red, blue, or green insulated decanter. Cone-shaped approx. 10″ high with black base and screw-on lid. White cardboard box with color photos of product. After these were used in Quark's bar on Deep Space Nine, the company started applying "As seen on Star Trek: Deep Space Nine" stickers to decanter boxes. ....$35–$45

Dinnerware Set—Zak Designs, 1994. Star Trek: The Next Generation. Three-piece plastic set consists of plate, bowl, and cup. Plate and cup have color artwork of crew with Picard in foreground and Enterprise above, bowl has transporter scene. Though pieces are available as open stock, set packaging is much more prevalent. Box has color artwork of characters and photos of product. ....$18–$25

NOTE: Dinnerware sets often included premiums—trading cards or Zak Star Trek flatware.

Flatware Set—Zak Designs, 1994. Star Trek: The Next Generation. Child's flatware. Set consists of spoon and fork with plastic handles. Spoon has logo and Enterprise; fork has logo and command insignia. Packaged in window box with color artwork of ships and low header for hanging. ....$10–$15

Freezicles—Catalog Shoppe, 1975. Molds, sticks, and concentrate. Three kinds of mold in set—busts of Kirk, Spock, and McCoy. Color box art of ship and children eating product. . ...$50–$75

Marshmallow Dispenser—Kraft, 1989. Gray and blue plastic with color STV decal, plastic fork, spoon, and belt hook included in kit. ....$20–$35

Mug and Bowl Set—Deka, 1975. Original series, 10 oz. mug and 20 oz. bowl with pictures of major characters and ships. Sold as set. ....$30–$40

Mug and Bowl Set—Deka, 1979. Plastic. Star Trek: The Motion Picture. Photos of major characters, artwork of the Enterprise. ....$20–$30

Mugs—Image Products, 1982. Star Trek: The Wrath of Khan. Plastic insulated photo mugs.

    Enterprise. ....$15–$25
    Khan. ....$15–$25
    Kirk. ....$15–$25
    Spock. ....$15–$25

Softdrink Can—Warner Trade Ltd. (British, aimed primarily at German market), 1995. Warp 4 Space Drink. 250 ml aluminum pop-top can. Blue space background has artwork of original Enterprise in blue and red, and logo and product info in white and red. Product info in English and German. Originally held high-caffeine energy drink. ....$20–$30

Spoon—1988. Pewter. "Star Trek Adventure" on insignia on handle. Picture of Enterprise and word on bowl. Came in clear plastic box. ....$10–$15

Spoons—Collectors' spoons. Tally-Ho. 4½″ long with color artwork portrait on stem.

    Kirk. ....$20–$30
    McCoy. ....$20–$30
    Scotty. ....$20–$30
    Spock. ....$20–$30

Squeeze Bottle—Creation, 1992. Plastic squeeze bottle approx. 9″ tall with plastic lid/straw combination. Decorated with "Star Trek: The Next Generation" and command insignias in purple and blue. ....$5–$7

Stove Burner Covers—1995. Round steel covers in small (8″) or large (10″) sizes. White with USS Enterprise 1701-A insignia logo. Either size. ....$5–$10

Tankard—Franklin Mint, 1995. Pewter. Approx. 7″ high. Panels around tankard depict original Enterprise, Klingon Battlecruiser, and Kirk, Spock, and McCoy. Silver and gold plate command insignia is set in top of handle. ....$190–$210

Tumbler—Deka, 1979. Plastic, 11 oz., Star Trek: The Motion Picture. Photos of character and artwork Enterprise. ....
....$5–$10

Tumbler—Paramount Promotional, 1989. STV. Red plastic with insignia and logo in black and gold. ....$4–$6

Tumbler (Sparkle)—Zak Designs, 1994. Short 14 oz. double-

walled tumbler with UFP seal. Fluid filled with blue glitter between two walls of tumbler. ....$3–$6

NOTE: See Ceramics and Glassware for decorative collectors plates, mugs, glasses, etc.

Tumblers—Coca-Cola Promotional, 1979. STTMP. Three-color artwork of characters and Enterprise. Four different.

    Decker and Ilia. ....$5–$10
    Kirk. ....$5–$10
    McCoy. ....$5–$10
    Spock. ....$5–$10

Tumblers—Coca-Cola Promotional, 1986. STIV. Plastic. Four different.

    Bird-of-Prey. ....$4–$8
    Group. ....$4–$8
    Kirk. ....$4–$8
    Spock. ....$4–$8

Tumblers—K-Mart Promotional, 1987. Star Trek: The Next Generation. Five different. Color photo designs on white plastic.

    Dr. and Wesley Crusher. ....$4–$6
    Picard. ....$4–$6
    Riker. ....$4–$6
    Tasha. ....$4–$6
    Troi and Data. ....$4–$6

Tumblers—Pizza Hut Promotional (U.K. only), 1993. Original Star Trek TV series. White plastic tumblers with color silk-screened designs. Snap-on tops hold removable plastic toys. Peel-off command insignia–shaped sticker with "Official Starfleet Officer" was also originally included.

    Cup 1 USS Enterprise NCC-1701. ....$25–$30
    Cup 2 Klingon Battle Cruiser. ....$25–$30
    Cup 3 Romulan Bird-of-Prey. ....$25–$30
    Cup 4 Communicator. ....$25–$30

Tumblers—Pizza Hut Promotional (U.K. only), 1994. Star Trek: The Next Generation. White plastic tumblers with color silk-screened designs. Snap-on tops hold removable plastic toys.

    Cup 1 Tricorder. ....$10–$20
    Cup 2 USS Enterprise. ....$10–$20
    Cup 3 Communicator. ....$10–$20
    Cup 4 Phase Type 1. ....$10–$20

Tumblers (14 oz.)—Zak Designs, 1994. Star Trek: The Next Generation. Color designs silk-screened onto black or clear plastic tumblers approx. 4″ high.

    Borg Emblem. ....$3–$6
    Klingon Emblem. ....$3–$6
    Romulan Emblem. ....$3–$6
    UFP Seal. ....$3–$6

Tumblers (19 oz.)—Zak Designs, 1994. Star Trek: The Next Generation. Color designs silk-screened onto black or clear plastic tumblers approx. 6½″ high.

    Command Insignias. ....$3–$6
    Large Logo, with smaller Enterprise. ....$3–$6
    Large Enterprise, with smaller logo. ....$3–$6
    Small Enterprises. ....$3–$6

LUNCH BOXES

CARE

Older, metal boxes and thermoses should have care taken to protect them from scuffing, rust, and dents, any of which seriously reduce the value of the kit. Broken thermos liners can and should be replaced. Newer plastic kits are not subject to rust or dents but are more susceptible to scuffing because of the decals used in place of earlier silk-screened designs. Wrapping in paper or plastic bags is recommended for storage. Tray boxes should remain with Star Trek: The Next Generation character boxes.

NOTE: Lunch boxes represent an active field of collecting in their own right. Among lunch box collectors, boxes and thermoses are often bought and sold as separate pieces. However, as they were originally sold as one unit, most Star Trek collectors consider the box and thermos as one item and for this reason prices in this section will be for boxes with thermoses. A missing thermos devalues a kit by at least 50%.

Lunch Box—Aladdin, 1968. Hump back, metal. Color artwork scenes from original show on all sides and bottom of box and on thermos. ....$700–$1000
Lunch Box—Aladdin, 1978. Original TV show. Rectangular, black plastic with color artwork on cover. ......$500–$800
Lunch Box—King-Seeley Thermos Co., 1979. Metal STTMP. Shows Kirk on one side, Spock and McCoy on the other. Thermos is captioned "Star Trek."...................$45–$75
Lunch Box—Thermos, 1988. Star Trek: The Next Generation. Blue plastic with color photo decal of Next Generation cast with Enterprise in background. Comes with blue plastic thermos with silk-screened Enterprise and logo. ......$15–$25
Lunch Box—Thermos, 1990. Red or blue plastic box with photo decal of Wesley, Picard, and Data with Enterprise in background. ....$10–$15
Lunch Box (Character)—CFPF, 1993. Star Trek: The Next Generation. Color plastic replicas of the heads of three different aliens. Boxes speak when opened. Came packaged in tray boxes with plain header behind. Boxes did not come with thermoses.
    Borg. ....$25–$40
    Ferengi. ....$25–$40
    Klingon. ....$25–$40
Lunch Tote—Thermos, 1988. Star Trek: The Next Generation. Nylon with strap to hold thermos in main compartment and insulated side compartment. Clip-on shoulder strap. Color silk-screen artwork of Enterprise on front. Blue or blue-gray. Canadian distribution. ....$40–$75

PARTY GOODS

CARE

Since party goods are primarily made of paper, the primary consideration for their care is protection from moisture. The plastic wrap that most party items originally came wrapped in is sufficient protection in most cases. Also, the fact that individual pieces have very little value to collectors provides further incentive to keep the sets together in their original packaging.

Cake Decorator—Tuttle, 1976. Original TV show, with scenes of the Enterprise on centerpiece.
    10-piece set. ....$10–$20
    22-piece set. ....$15–$25
Paper/Plastic Tableware—Party Express (Hallmark), 1993/1994. Star Trek: The Next Generation theme. Color photos and artwork.
    Beverage Napkins, 16, "Ten Forward." ....$8–$10
    Cups, eight, "Set Course for Party . . . Engage.".....$8–$10
    Dinner Napkins, 16, "Ten Forward." ....$8–$10
    Invitations, eight. ....$5–$8
    Party Favors, eight. ....$5–$8
    Party Visors, eight. ....$5–$8
    Plates, 7″ or 9″ package of eight, "Party Boldly" with Enterprise-D. ....$8–$10
    Tablecloth, "Party Boldly," with Enterprise. ....$8–$10
Paper Tableware—Tuttle, 1976. White background with Kirk, Spock, Dr. McCoy, and Enterprise printed in red, white, and blue.
    Beverage Napkins, pack of eight. ....$10–$15
    Cups, pack of eight. ....$10–$15
    Dinner Napkins, pack of eight. ....$10–$15
    Plates, 7″ or 9″ package of eight. ....$10–$15
    Tablecloth, two sizes. ....$10–$15
Paper Tableware—Hallmark, 1993. Original Star Trek TV series theme. Color pictures and sayings.
    Beverage Napkins, 16. ....$8–$10
    Cups, eight. ....$8–$10
    Dinner Napkins, 16. ....$8–$10
    Invitations, eight. ....$5–$8
    Plates, 7″ or 9″ package of eight. ....$8–$10
    Tablecloth. ....$8–$10
Streamer—Portal, 1995. 7″ × 25″ color photo streamer of Deep Space Nine crew, station, and planets with "Happy Birthday from Both Sides of the Wormhole."............$10–$15
Streamer—Portal, 1995. 7″ × 25″ color photo streamer of Deep Space Nine characters giving appropriate birthday message. ....$10–$15
Wrapping Paper (Wrap-Ups)—Triangle Enterprises, 1993/94. Two sheets of 20″ × 30″ per package. Color photo collage designs.
    Star Trek (original). ....$6–$10
    Star Trek: The Next Generation. ....$6–$10

Alp Star Trek Sleeping Bag, 1976

Cecil Saydah *Star Trek: Next Generation* **Bath Towel and Wash Cloth Set**

Decorion Bean Bag Chair

Centric Wall Clocks

Magnetic Collectibles Magnets and Display

Ferengi Talking Lunch Box

JEWELRY

Most Star Trek jewelry is readily available, popular with fans, and has a confusing array of styles and different manufacturers. The vast majority is not collectible and most people buy it simply for fun. Almost all Star Trek jewelry items are easy to duplicate and most of the more popular pieces, whether licensed or unlicensed, have been reproduced numerous times by a number of different manufacturers. In addition, handmade jewelry, either as one-of-a-kind pieces or made in very small quantities, is also available and for the most part has not been included in this section. Values for fine jewelry listed in this section primarily reflect the value of the precious materials in the various pieces.

INVESTMENT POTENTIAL
Fair.

CARE
Most jewelry items are durable, do not come in special packaging that would need to be preserved, and require little in the way of care. Wearing jewelry in no way devalues the pieces. Unlike coins, tarnished jewelry items can be cleaned without adversely affecting the value.

SECTION NOTES
This section is organized alphabetically by type of item and then alphabetically by manufacturer, if known. Some items simply list variations on a particular theme (such as Enterprise jewelry) since this type of (mostly unlicensed) jewelry is extremely common and has many different manufacturers.

BADGES

The badges listed here are items made by standard jewelry manufacturing methods. For printed metal or plastic pinbacks often referred to as badges, see the Buttons section of this book.

Chrysalic Group

Borg Eyepiece—Liquid crystal pin designed to look like a Borg eyepiece. Packaged in shallow clear plastic with backing showing photo of a Borg. ....$20–$25
Klingon Medallions—1995. Set of two plastic black and silver badges. Copied after Worf's sash badges on Star Trek: The Next Generation. Packaged in shallow clear plastic with backing showing photo of Worf. ....$20–$25
Vorgon Transporter Pin—1995. Liquid crystal badge approx. 1″ square with copper-colored frame. Copy of device used by Vorgons in Star Trek: The Next Generation. ....
....$20–$25

Lincoln Enterprises

United Federation of Planets Security Badge—1986. From Star Trek IV. Hinged, two-piece, painted metal. ......$12–$18

QVC

Klingon Arm Badge—1993. Gold- and silver-plated metal approx. 3″ long. Comes packaged in plastic box with Klingon symbol (original) on lid. ....$15–$20

NOTE: See Buttons section for printed metal or plastic pinbacks often referred to as badges.

BAJORAN EARRINGS

These are the single earrings worn by all Bajorans on Star Trek: Deep Space Nine. Very popular convention item. Though licensed versions of the simple style of these are manufactured by both Hollywood Pin and Rubies Costume, the vast majority, especially of the more elaborate styles, are fan-made. Prices range from $8 or $9 for the very simple ones up to about $30 for a very elaborate earring.

BELT BUCKLES
Indiana Metal

Enterprise—On triangular enameled background. ..$20–$25
Enterprise and Saturn—Circular painted or bronze tone. Introduction to TV series impressed on back, some have "USS Enterprise" and "Star Trek." ....$10–$15

Lee Belts

Enterprise—1976. Orbiting planet, oval. ....$6–$10
Enterprise—Roughly rectangular "Star Trek" NCC-1701, 2″, brass, some with enamel trim. ....$5–$10
Kirk and Spock—1976. Rectangular brass with enamel trim. ....$4–$6
Spock—1976. Round brass, some with enamel trim, approx. 2″. ....$4–$6

Lincoln Enterprises

Command Insignia—Circular, flat, or round, gold-plated or brushed bronze reproduction of the uniform buckles worn in STII through VI. Several sizes. ....$5–$20

NOTE: This buckle is also manufactured by many other individuals.

Kirk and Spock—Looking to the left. The Enterprise and "Star Trek" at the top. Bronze, not dated, 2″ × 3″. ......$10–$12
"Star Trek, The Final Frontier"—1985. Classic movie Enterprise.
> Black Background with Gold Trim. ....$60–$65
> Brass Trim. ....$25–$30
"Star Trek III: The Search for Spock"—1984. Classic movie Enterprise. Limited edition. Numbered on back with synopsis of story. ....$20–$25
USS Enterprise Commemorative.
> Bronze with Gold Trim. ....$25–$30
> Sterling Silver with Gold Trim. ....$100–$125

Tiffany Studio

Kirk and Spock—"Star Trek" above, oval with flat corners, brass. ....$15–$20
Original TV Enterprise—Rectangular "Star Trek Lives," "USS Enterprise," and "To Boldly Go, etc." around ship. ......
....$15–$20
Original TV Enterprise—"Star Trek" above on insignia-shaped background, brass. ....$15–$20

BRACELETS
General Mills

Identification Bracelet—1979. Star Trek: The Motion Picture. Premium. Gold or silver. Children's. ....$10–$15

Hollywood Pin

Charm Bracelet—1994. Nine different charms, some enameled on gold chain. ....$20–$25

COIN NECKLACES

(See Coins and Medallions)

COMMAND INSIGNIA JEWELRY

(See also Pins and Hologram Jewelry)

Don Post Studios

Command Insignia Pin—Brushed brass. Came blister-packed on color header card. ....$25–$35

Hollywood Commemorative Pin

Command Insignia Earrings—1994. Sold as two pair, one original and one Next Generation of pierced post earrings. Packaged in faceted, clear, lucite box. For both pairs. ....
....$18–$20

Lincoln Enterprises

Command Insignia Charm—Original TV style, with 18″ chain.
> Gold Plate. ....$4–$6
> Sterling Silver. ....$15–$20
> 14k Gold. ....$90–$95
> 14k Gold and Diamonds. ....$275–$300

Command Insignia Earrings—Pierced (post or dangling) or clip-on.

    Gold Plate. ....$10–$12

    Sterling Silver. ....$30–$35

    14k Gold. ....$125–$150

    14k Gold and Diamond. ....$575–$600

Command Insignia Necklace—Classic movie style. Painted, or plated gold.

    Large Necklace. ....$5–$8

    Small Necklace. ....$4–$6

Command Insignia Pin—Same as above.

    Large Pin. ....$5–$8

    Small Pin. ....$4–$6

Command Insignia Pin—Gold-plated. ....$4–$6

Command Insignia Ring—Adjustable.

    Gold-Plated. ....$6–$8

    Sterling Silver. ....$7–$10

Insignia Wire Charm.

    Earrings, pierced (wire) or clip-on. ....$10–$12

    Necklace, with 18″ chain. ....$5–$6

Spectore

1992

Titanium jewelry. Multicolored metal.

Earrings.

    Command Symbol, original series. ....$15–$20

    Command Symbol, in circle with danglers below. ....

    ....$15–$20

Necklaces.

    Command Symbol, original series. ....$12–$15

    Command Symbol, in circle, original series. ....$20–$25

Pin, Command symbol, original series. ....$12–$15

ENTERPRISE SHIP JEWELRY

(Three-dimensional)

This has always been a popular item for the fan market. All of the below are cast metal from various manufacturers.

Lincoln Enterprises

Lincoln Enterprises has made a line of Enterprise jewelry as precious metals. These are as follows:

Movie Enterprise 14K Gold.

    Charm. ....$100–$125

    Charm with Diamonds. ....$250–$300

    Earrings. ....$200–$250

    Earrings with Diamonds. ....$500–$600

NG Enterprise 14K Gold.

    Charm. ....$100–$125

    Charm with Diamonds. ....$250–$300

    Earrings. ....$200–$250

    Earrings with Diamonds. ....$500–$600

Other

Movie Charm—Approx. 1³⁄₄″. Gold or silver plate. With or without chain. ....$10–$15

Movie Charm—Approx. 1″. Gold or silver plate. With or without chain. ....$8–$10

Movie Earrings—Approx. 1″. Gold or silver plate. Pierced or clip-on. ....$15–$20

Next Generation Earrings—Approx. 1″. Gold or silver plate. Pierced or clip-on. ....$15–$20

Original TV Charm—Approx. 1¹⁄₂″. Gold or silver plate. With or without chain. ....$10–$15

Original TV Charm—Approx. ³⁄₄″. Gold or silver plate. With or without chain. ....$6–$8

Original TV Earrings—Approx. ³⁄₄″. Gold or silver plate. Pierced or clip-on. ....$10–$15

Original TV Pin—Approx 1¹⁄₂″ long. Gold-plated original Enterprise dangles from bar with "USS Enterprise." ....

....$10–$15

Original TV Ring—Approx. 1¹⁄₂″ silver plate on adjustable ring band. ....$10–$15

Star Trek: Next Generation Charm—Approx. 1″. Gold or silver plate. With or without chain. ....$8–$10

HOLOGRAM JEWELRY

A.H. Prismatic

1992

Foil hologram jewelry. Pieces came shrink-wrapped on header card with appropriate logo at top. There are several variations in the patterns used in the hologram foil.

Data Earrings. ....$9–$12

Enterprise Cut-Out Earrings (Original Ship). ....$9–$12

Enterprise Cut-Out Earrings (NG Ship). ....$9–$12

Enterprise Earrings, ships on insignia shape (several variations). ....$9–$12

Kirk Earrings. ....$9–$12

Next Generation Command Insignia Earrings. ....$9–$12

Next Generation Command Insignia Pin. ....$5–$7

Original Series Command Insignia Pin. ....$5–$7

Picard Earrings. ....$9–$12

Spock Earrings. ....$9–$12

NOTE: There has also been several varieties of fan jewelry made utilizing designs printed on hologram foil.

IDIC JEWELRY

The IDIC, which stands for Infinite Diversity in Infinite Combinations, is a Vulcan symbol that was used in one original television episode and has been used somewhat in the movies. It consists of a gold circle with a superimposed silver triangle and a clear stone at the apex. All are metal. Several manufacturers.

Earrings—Gold and silver plate. Pierced or clip-on. Assorted sizes. ....$10–$20
    As above, 14K gold, pierced (Lincoln Enterprises). ....
....$125–$150
Necklaces—Assorted sizes ranging from ½″ to 2″. ....
....$5–$12
    As above, 14K gold (Lincoln Enterprises). ....$80–$85
Pin—Gold and silver plate. Assorted sizes. ....$6–$10
    As above, 14K gold (Lincoln Enterprises). ....$80–$85
Ring—Gold and silver plate. Men's and women's styles available. Adjustable. ....$10–$20

KEYCHAINS
A.H. Prismatic
1991/93

Foil holograms imbedded in squares of Lucite. Approx. 2″.

Original TV.
    Command Symbol and "Star Trek." ....$3–$5
    Enterprise. ....$3–$5
    Enterprise and "Star Trek." ....$3–$5
    Kirk in Transporter Room. ....$3–$5
    Kirk on Planet. ....$3–$5
    Kirk, Scotty, and Chekov. ....$3–$5
    Klingon and Ship. ....$3–$5
    Spock on Planet. ....$3–$5
    Spock, McCoy, Uhura, and Sulu. ....$3–$5
Star Trek: The Next Generation.
    Benzite, Worf, and Riker. ....$3–$5
    Data and Worf. ....$3–$5
    Enterprise and "Star Trek." ....$3–$5
    Enterprise and Ringed Planet. ....$3–$5
    Picard and Geordi. ....$3–$5
    Picard, Geordi, and Troi. ....$3–$5
    Picard, Troi, and Dr. Crusher. ....$3–$5
    Romulan Warbird on Bridge Screen. ....$3–$5
    Two Ferengi. ....$3–$5

Star Trek: Deep Space Nine.
    Runabout. ....$3–$5
    Space Station. ....$3–$5
    Space Station and Cardassian Ship. ....$3–$5

A.H. Prismatic
1994

Foil hologram keychains in round Lucite holders.

DS9 Space Station. ....$3–$5
Cardassian Warship. ....$3–$5
Enterprise (Original). ....$3–$5
Klingon Cruiser (Original). ....$3–$5
Quark. ....$3–$5
Romulan Bird-of-Prey. ....$3–$5
Runabout. ....$3–$5

Applause
1994

Characters—Soft plastic, flat keychains with stylized color representations of characters and logos from Star Trek: The Next Generation, Star Trek: Deep Space Nine, or Star Trek: Generations.
    Data. ....$3–$5
    Kirk. ....$3–$5
    La Forge. ....$3–$5
    Logo (DS9). ....$3–$5
    Logo (Generations). ....$3–$5
    Logo (Next Generation). ....$3–$5
    Lursa and B'Etor. ....$3–$5
    Odo. ....$3–$5
    Picard. ....$3–$5
    Quark. ....$3–$5
    Riker. ....$3–$5
    Sisko. ....$3–$5
    Worf. ....$3–$5
Ships—Hard plastic, three-dimensional ship representations.
    Borg Ship. ....$3–$5
    Enterprise-D. ....$3–$5
    Ferengi Marauder. ....$3–$5
    Klingon Bird-of-Prey. ....$3–$5
    Romulan Warbird. ....$3–$5
    Shuttlecraft. ....$3–$5

Aviva Enterprises
1979

Square Lucite slabs with two-sided translucent pictures, 1½″.

Enterprise. .... $2–$3
Kirk and Spock with Enterprise. .... $2–$3
Spock with "Live Long and Prosper." .... $2–$3
Spock and Uniform Insignia. .... $2–$3
Spock and "Star Trek: The Motion Picture." .... $2–$3
Mr. Spock Giving Vulcan Salute. .... $2–$3

Button Up

1980

"Beam Me Up Scotty" on yellow background. .... $2–$3

California Dreamers

1987

Color photos from original TV series in 1½″ × 2″ plastic holders.

Chekov, "I Hate Mondays." .... $2–$4
Kirk, "Beam Me Up Scotty." .... $2–$4
Kirk, "The Captain." .... $2–$4
Kirk, Spock, and McCoy, "Fire All Phaser Weapons." .... $2–$4
Kirk, Spock, and Uhura, "Keep Your Shields Up." ....$2–$4
Kirk, Spock, and Uhura, "Seek Out Strange New Worlds." .... $2–$4
Spock, "Hang in There." .... $2–$4
Spock, "I Need Space." .... $2–$4
Spock, "Spock for President." .... $2–$4
Spock, "Live Long and Prosper." .... $2–$4
Spock, "Superior Being." .... $2–$4

Fascinations

1993

Clicker viewer keychains. Twenty-four different scenes on each. Picture of character and logo on side. Came blister-packed on header cards, three different.

Aliens (Next Generation). .... $4–$6
Crew (Next Generation). .... $4–$6
Crew (Original Cast from Movies). .... $4–$6

Hamilton Gifts

1991

Enterprise—Plastic, color, original, in relief on command symbol with "Star Trek" above. .... $4–$6

Hollywood Pin

1992/96 (Cloisonné)

Borg Symbol. .... $7–$10
Command Symbol (Original Series). .... $7–$10
Command Symbol (Movie II–VI Version). .... $7–$10
Command Symbol (Next Generation), two sizes, price for either. .... $7–$10
Enterprise (Original), cut-out. .... $7–$10
Enterprise (Original), with "Star Trek." .... $7–$10
Klingon Symbol. .... $7–$10
"Make It So." .... $7–$10
Star Trek: The Next Generation, logo in command symbol, yellow and red. .... $7–$10
"Star Trek," in original typeface on command symbol in yellow and blue. .... $7–$10
"Star Trek," in movie typeface on green planetscape design command symbol. .... $7–$10
Star Trek V, logo (with Enterprise). .... $7–$10
UFP Emblem (Next Generation Version). .... $7–$10
Voyager Cut-out. .... $7–$10

Interstellar Productions

1993 to present

Electronic keychains. Various sound and light effects. Battery operated. Came blister-packed on header cards.

Communicator (Original Series). .... $10–$15
Phaser (Next Generation). .... $10–$15
Phaser II (Next Generation). .... $10–$15
Phaser (Original Series). .... $10–$15
Sound Effects (Original Series), eight different. ......$10–$15
Sound Effects (Next Generation), eight different. ....$10–$15
Tricorder (Original Series). .... $10–$15
Tricorder (Next Generation). .... $10–$15

Lincoln Enterprises

1976

Keychain Viewers—Various Star Trek TV film clips. .... $2–$3

Rarities Mint

1989

Spock—Gold-plated silver. Reverse shows original TV Enterprise. .... $30–$50

Rawcliffe

1994

Solid pewter, some with colored enamel inlay.

Arkarian Symbol.	$7–$10
Bajoran Symbol.	$7–$10
Borg Symbol.	$7–$10
Cardassian Symbol.	$7–$10
Command Insignia (Original).	$7–$10
Command Insignia (Motion Picture).	$7–$10
Communicator (Original).	$7–$10
Communicator Insignia (Original).	$7–$10
Communicator Insignia (New Style).	$7–$10
DS9 Logo.	$7–$10
DS9 Space Station.	$7–$10
Engineering Insignia (Original).	$7–$10
Enterprise 1701.	$7–$10
Enterprise 1701-A.	$7–$10
Enterprise 1701-D.	$7–$10
Ferengi Saying.	$7–$10
Ferengi Symbol.	$7–$10
Galaxy Class Development Project Logo.	$7–$10
Generations Logo.	$7–$10
IDIC, with clear stone.	$7–$10
Klingon Bat'telh.	$7–$10
Klingon Disrupter.	$7–$10
Klingon Knife.	$7–$10
Klingon Saying.	$7–$10
Klingon Symbol (Original).	$7–$10
Phaser (Next Generation Version).	$7–$10
Phaser (STI Movie Version).	$7–$10
Romulan Saying.	$7–$10
Romulan Symbol.	$7–$10
Science Insignia (Original).	$7–$10
Shuttlecraft (Next Generation Version).	$7–$10
Starfleet Academy Logo.	$7–$10
Tricorder (Original Series Version).	$7–$10
UFP Banner (From Original Series).	$7–$10
UFP Seal (Next Generation Version).	$7–$10
Voyager.	$7–$10
Voyager Logo.	$7–$10
Vulcan Hand Salute.	$7–$10
Vulcan Saying.	$7–$10

Reed Productions

1989

Black and white photos from either the original TV series or Star Trek V: The Final Frontier in plastic holders.

Original TV Series.

Kirk and Spock in Transporter.	$3–$5
Kirk and Spock with Model Enterprise.	$3–$5
Kirk, Spock, and McCoy.	$3–$5

Star Trek V: The Final Frontier.

Crew.	$3–$5
Enterprise.	$3–$5
Kirk and Spock.	$3–$5
Kirk, Spock, McCoy, and Sybok.	$3–$5

KHAN'S PENDANT

Don Post Studio

1982

Insignia in broken circle—Bronze dipped in acid to "age" piece. Came blister-packed on color cardboard header. .... $20–$30

MEDALLIONS

(See Coins and Medallions)

MONEY CLIP

Rarities Mint

1989

Clip—Gold-plated silver. Spock giving Vulcan salute. "Live Long and Prosper." .... $35–$45

NECKLACES AND PENDANTS

American Miss

1974

Flat, gold plate.

Enterprise—Orbiting ringed planet.	$15–$20
Spock.	$15–$20
"Star Trek."	$15–$20

Goodtime Jewelry

1976

Pewter medallions. Various character portraits. Poor quality.
....$10–$15

NOTE: Goodtime also did a three-dimensional pewter Enter-prise pendant.

Lincoln Enterprises

Filigree Pendants—1976. Flat, gold plated.
    Enterprise. ....$8–$10
    Rigel Castle. ....$8–$10
Mount Seleya Symbol—1985. Three-dimensional, gold plate. ....$8–$10
"Try Trekkin"—1976. Flat, gold plate. ....$8–$10
"Where No Man Has Gone Before"—1976. Flat, gold plate. ....$8–$10

Spectore

1992

Enterprise—Line drawing on oval, multicolored titanium background with silver comet design border. ....$25–$30

Star Trek Galore

1976

Phaser—Three-dimensional. Gold or silver plate. ....$8–$10
Vulcan Hand (Salute)—Three-dimensional. Gold or silver plate. ....$8–$10
Vulcan Hand (Salute)—Flat brass. ....$8–$10

PINS
(Cloisonné, Enamel, and Poly)
Aviva

1979 (Star Trek: The Motion Picture)

Poly.
    Enterprise. ....$8–$12
    Kirk. ....$8–$12
    McCoy. ....$8–$12
    Spock. ....$8–$12

    Uniform Insignia. ....$8–$12
    Vulcan Salute. ....$8–$12
Enamel.
    Kirk. ....$10–$15
    McCoy. ....$10–$15
Tie Clasps.
    Enterprise Outline, gold and black. ....$8–$12
    Mr. Spock, circular, gold and black with "Live Long and Prosper." ....$8–$12
    Uniform Insignia (Original TV), gold. ....$8–$12
    Vulcan Salute, circular, gold and black. ....$8–$12

Hollywood Commemorative Pin

1985 to Present

NOTE: Many of the more popular pins in this series were also made in a slightly smaller size in order to be sold at a more competitive price in general merchandise stores.

"100 Episodes Star Trek: The Next Generation.".....$8–$9
"Beam Me Up Scotty," with communicator. ....$6–$7
Borg Figure. ....$6–$7
"Caution Anti Matter."...$6–$7
"Caution Force Field."..$6–$7
Communicator/Insignia Pins.
    All Good Things. ....$10–$12
    Bajoran. ....$10–$12
    Future Imperfect. ....$10–$12
    Generations/Voyager, large. ....$10–$12
    Generations/Voyager, medium. ....$6–$7
    Generations/Voyager, small. ....$4–$5
    Klingon. ....$10–$12
    Next Generation, large. ....$10–$12
    Next Generation, medium. ....$6–$7
    Next Generation, small. ....$4–$5
Creatures.
    Beauregard. ....$6–$7
    Excalbian. ....$6–$7
    Gorn. ....$6–$7
    Lamatya. ....$6–$7
    Junior. ....$6–$7
    Melkotian. ....$6–$7
    Mugato. ....$6–$7
    Salt Vampire. ....$6–$7
Crew (Original TV) Standing Figure Cut-outs.
    Chekov. ....$8–$9
    Kirk. ....$8–$9
    McCoy. ....$8–$9
    Scotty. ....$8–$9
    Spock. ....$8–$9
    Sulu. ....$8–$9
    Uhura. ....$8–$9
Crew (Original TV) Faces.
    Chekov. ....$6–$7

Kirk. ....$6–$7

McCoy. ....$6–$7

Scotty. ....$6–$7

Spock. ....$6–$7

Sulu. ....$6–$7

Uhura. ....$6–$7

"Crew Member," with NG command symbol. ....$6–$7

DS9 Space Station. ....$10–$12

Earth Station McKinley Emblem. ....$8–$9

"Engage." ....$8–$9

Episode Pins, from any series, price each. ....$7–$10

Equipment.

Communicator (Original TV). ....$8–$9

Phaser (Original TV). ....$8–$9

Phaser (NG), small version. ....$6–$7

Phaser (NG), large version. ....$8–$9

Ferengi Head. ....$6–$7

"Fully Functional." ....$6–$7

Galaxy Class Starship Development Project Emblem. ......

....$6–$7

Insignia Cut-out (STTMP), small, blue, burgundy, green, orange, red, white, or yellow. ....$6–$7

Insignia Cut-out, large. ....$8–$9

Insignia Cutout (TV), black, white, red, or blue on gold.

Command. ....$6–$7

Command, pewter. ....$6–$7

Command, small. ....$5–$6

Engineering. ....$6–$7

Gamma. ....$6–$7

Medical. ....$6–$7

Pi. ....$6–$7

Science. ....$6–$7

Klingon Head. ....$6–$7

"Live Long and Prosper," Vulcan salute on blue background. ....$8–$12

As above, red background. ....$8–$12

As above, burgundy background. ....$8–$12

As above, smaller, blue background. ....$6–$10

"Live Long and Prosper," with Spock. ....$8–$9

"Make It So." ....$6–$7

Logo (Original TV).

Blue Background. ....$6–$10

White Background. ....$6–$10

Logo (Next Generation)

Blue Background. ....$6–$7

Insignia Background. ....$6–$7

Red Background. ....$6–$7

Official Logo. ....$6–$7

Rank Insignias (Klingon).

Admiral. ....$6–$7

Captain. ....$6–$7

Rank Insignias (Movies).

Admiral. ....$6–$7

Captain. ....$8–$9

Commodore. ....$8–$9

Fleet Admiral. ....$8–$9

Rank Pins (Collar)

Bajoran, four different. ....$4–$5

Maquis, two or three stripes. ....$3–$4

Starfleet, gold or black. ....$2–$3

Season Commemorative Pins, any. ....$7–$8

Series Commemorative Pins.

Original Series. ....$6–$7

Star Trek: The Next Generation. ....$6–$7

Ship Plaques.

"USS Enterprise NCC-1701." ....$6–$7

"USS Enterprise NCC-1701-A." ....$6–$7

"USS Enterprise NCC-1701-C." ....$6–$7

"USS Enterprise NCC-1701-D." ....$6–$7

Ships.

Borg. ....$8–$9

Cardassian. ....$8–$9

Defiant. ....$6–$7

Enterprise Cut-out (Original). ....$6–$7

Enterprise (Original) and Logo, on blue. ....$6–$7

Enterprise (Original), on red, large. ....$8–$9

Enterprise (Original), on red, small. ....$6–$7

Enterprise (Movie Version). ....$8–$9

Enterprise NCC-1701-C. ....$8–$9

Enterprise NCC-1701-D. ....$8–$9

Klingon Cruiser (Original TV). ....$8–$9

Klingon Cruiser (Next Generation). ....$8–$9

Romulan Warbird. ....$8–$9

Romulan Scout. ....$8–$9

Runabout. ....$8–$9

Voyager. ....$6–$7

Starbase 74. ....$6–$7

Starfleet Academy Emblem. ....$8–$9

Starfleet Command Operations, green, red, or yellow. ....

....$5–$6

Starfleet Division Insignias.

Colonial Operations. ....$8–$9

Communications. ....$8–$9

Engineering. ....$8–$9

Headquarters. ....$8–$9

Intelligence. ....$8–$9

Marines. ....$8–$9

Material. ....$8–$9

Medical. ....$8–$9

Merchant Marines. ....$8–$9

Military. ....$8–$9

Personnel. ....$8–$9

Security. ....$8–$9

Star Trek V: Final Frontier Pins.

Starfleet Insignia. ....$6–$7

Star Trek V Logo Over insignia. ....$8–$9

STV, small Enterprise. ....$8–$9

STV, large Enterprise. ....$10–$11

STV, small Galileo. ....$7–$8

STV, large Galileo. ....$9–$10

STV, Galileo logo. ....$5–$6

STV, The Final Frontier logo. ....$6–$7

Star Trek Forever. ....$8–$9
Star Trek Lives. ....$8–$9
Star Trek: Generations Logo. ....$8–$9
"Star Trek: Voyager," with ship. ....$8–$9
Symbols (Government).
    Borg, red and black. ....$8–$9
    Borg, red, black, and white. ....$8–$9
    Cardassian. ....$8–$9
    Ferengi, small. ....$6–$7
    Ferengi, large. ....$8–$9
    Klingon Symbol, small. ....$6–$7
    Klingon Symbol, large. ....$8–$9
    Klingon Symbol in Triangle. ....$8–$9
    Klingon Symbol, red and black. ....$8–$9
    Klingon Symbol, large pewter. ....$8–$12
    Maquis. ....$6–$7
    Mirror Universe. ....$6–$7
    Romulan Symbol. ....$6–$7
    Romulan Symbol (Cut-out). ....$10–$15
    Romulan, large. ....$10–$12
    Romulan, small. ....$6–$7
    Talurian. ....$6–$7
    UFP Symbol (Original TV), large cut-out. ....$8–$9
    UFP Symbol (Original TV), small cut-out. ....$8–$10
    UFP Symbol (NG), oval. ....$6–$7
    UFP Symbol (NG), shield. ....$8–$9
Thirtieth Anniversary Pins.
    Pewter Finish Logo. ....$6–$7
    Regular Logo, any color variation. ....$6–$7
Twentieth Anniversary Pins.
    Early Logo, white and blue, blue and yellow, or red, white, and blue versions. ....$10–$15
    Special Logo. ....$15–$20
    "To Boldly Go . . ." ....$10–$15
    "WOW Pin." ....$10–$15
Twenty-fifth Anniversary Pins, arrowhead design, red or green. ....$6–$7
"USS Enterprise NCC-1701-D," with ship. ....$8–$9
Vorgon Idol. ....$6–$7
Vulcan Salute. ....$4–$5

Lincoln Enterprises

1986–1991

Borg Emblem, on round background. ....$8–$10
Borg Ship and Emblem. ....$8–$10
Enterprise Cut-out. ....$6–$8
Enterprise and Statue of Liberty. ....$6–$8
Ferengi Ship Pin. ....$6–$8
Klingon Bird-of-Prey. ....$6–$8
NG Enterprise Pin, blue. ....$7–$9
    As above, white and black. ....$7–$9
    As above, white, black, and orange. ....$7–$9

NG UFP Symbol, red and black. ....$7–$9
NG Logo, rainbow. ....$7–$9
    As above, blue, silver, and white. ....$7–$9
NG Communicator Pin with Logo. ....$7–$9
Peace in Our Galaxy (IDIC). ....$6–$8
Romulan Warbird. ....$8–$10
Romulan Symbol (Next Generation). ....$8–$10
She Lives, Enterprise in Orbit. ....$7–$9
Star Trek, Gateway to a New Beginning. ....$6–$8
Star Trek: The Final Frontier. ....$6–$8
Star Trek: The Motion Picture, movie poster design. ....$6–$8
Star Trek III: The Search for Spock, commemorative. ....$6–$8
Star Trek III Enterprise in Flames. ....$6–$8
Star Trek III Movie Poster Design. ....$6–$8
Twentieth Anniversary Pin. ....$6–$8
Twenty-fifth Anniversary Pins. ....$8–$10
United Federation of Planets symbol (Movie). ....$6–$8
Star Trek IV, movie poster art. ....$6–$8
Star Trek IV, white poster art. ....$6–$8
Star Trek IV, cut-out design. ....$6–$8
Star Trek IV Logo and Whales. ....$6–$8
Whales. ....$6–$8

Paramount

Video Promotional Three-Pin Set—1991. 25th Anniversary, Enterprise and USS Enterprise NCC-1701-A crew pins given as premiums in movie video four-packs. For set of three. ....$30–$40

QVC

Phaser Range Proficiency Pin—1995. Premium given with purchase of Playmates NG Phaser. ....$4–$5

PLAQUES
Hollywood Commemorative Pin

These were designed to be used with displays of Hollywood's line of Star Trek pins.

Intro Monologue Plaque. ....$25–$30
"Star Trek." ....$10–$12
"Star Trek: The Next Generation." ....$10–$12
"Star Trek: Deep Space Nine." ....$10–$12
Star Trek Collection Plaque (Small). ....$20–$25
Star Trek Collection Plaque (Large). ....$35–$40

RINGS

Jostens

1992

Starfleet Academy Ring—Dome-topped, gold, class-style ring with command with Next Generation command insignia on top and UFP emblem on side.
    Ladies. ....$200–$250
    Mens. ....$250–$300

NOTE: A slight variation with simulated pearl backing was made for sale by QVC.

25th Anniversary Ring—Gold, flat-topped ring with 25th anniversary logo embossed on top.
    Ladies. ....$100–$150
    Mens. ....$150–$200

NOTE: See IDIC Jewelry and Command Insignia Jewelry in this section for rings which fit into these categories.

UNIFORM INSIGNIA

(See also Toy section of this book.)

Don Post

1982

STTMP Style—Bronze. Came blister-packed on cardboard header. ....$10–$15
STII–IV Movie Insignia—Circle design superimposed on bar. Bronze. Came blister-packed on color cardboard header.
....$20–$30

Hollywood Commemorative Pin

ST II–VI Movie Version—Gold-plated metal.
    Large. ....$13–$15
    Small. ....$8–$9

NOTE: See Pins for Hollywood versions of Next Generation and Deep Space Nine uniform insignias.

Lincoln Enterprises

STTMP style—See Command Insignia Pins.
STII–VI Movie Insignia—1982. Same basic design as Don Post and Hollywood versions but plated and painted. Metal. Two sizes.
    Large. ....$12–$15
    Small. ....$8–$10
STNG Communicator Insignia—1987. Metal, painted and plated. ....$12–$15

NOTE: As with all Lincoln jewelry, there are many unlicensed copies by other manufacturers. Hollywood Pin also manufactures similar pieces under their license for pins (see Pins in this section).

UNIFORM RANK INSIGNIA

Very popular for costuming. Early examples were of painted, cast fiberglass and very fragile. Those that still exist are only worth $1–$2. The following are all plated and painted metal with assorted manufacturers.

STII–IV.
    Admiral. ....$6–$12
    Captain. ....$6–$12
    Commander. ....$6–$12
    Commodore. ....$6–$12
    Fleet Admiral. ....$6–$12
    Lieutenant. ....$5–$7
    Lieutenant Commander, several varieties. ....$6–$12
    Lieutenant J G. ....$5–$7
STTNG—Collar pips, plain gold, silver, or "hollow." Plated and painted. Individuals. ....$2–$3
STTNG—Captain. ....$7–$10
STTNG—Admiral. ....$10–$15
Uniform Sleeve Pips—STII–IV, round and oblong, ridged metal, unpainted or gold plated. Numerous manufacturers.
....$2–$4
Uniform Shoulder Strap Back Pin—STII–IV, eight-sided ridged metal pin. Unpainted or gold plated. ....$3–$5

Lee Spock Belt Buckle

Lincoln Enterprises *Star Trek Final Frontier* **Belt Buckle**

Spectore Titanium Command Symbol Pin

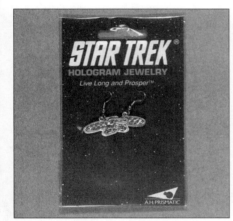

A.H. Prismatic Enterprise Earrings

A.H. Prismatic Keychain

Fascinations Clicker Viewer Keychain

Interstellar Production Classic Phaser Electronic Keychain

Don Post Studio Khan's Pendant

Aviva *Star Trek: The Motion Picture* Vulcan Salute Pins, Poly (left) and Enamel (right

Paramount Video Promotional Pin Set

MAGAZINES

Star Trek has become such a part of American culture that people who know little or nothing about Star Trek can read a casual reference to "Klingons" or "warping" and still grasp the meaning without difficulty. Articles about the TV series and movies have appeared in every kind of magazine from *Newsweek* to *Mad*. A Star Trek cover story on almost any magazine, no matter how little it is generally oriented toward science fiction, is a sure guarantee of gangbuster sales. Science fiction magazines have, of course, always depended heavily on Star Trek as a source of story material. There has, in fact, been so *much* written about Star Trek in its 30-year history that to try to catalog it all would probably fill a separate book. This is certainly not to say that just because they are so abundant, magazines aren't collectible. Virtually everyone involved in any aspect of Star Trek fandom has a cherished library of magazines with articles pertaining to their particular interest that they are happy to expand upon and this is certainly reflected in the buying habits of collectors. In this section we will try to give the reader an overview of the different kinds of magazines that tend to become collectible (and a few that may seem to fit that category but don't), and to focus on some particular magazines that are the most representative of these characteristics. This would include not only licensed publications (which have been surprisingly few) but also magazines that have devoted a considerable percentage of their content to Star Trek. We will also try, to some extent, to point out some key individual issues.

INVESTMENT POTENTIAL
Good.

CARE
Always keep magazines complete to maintain their collectible value. An intact magazine with a Star Trek article may be worth $25, but the same article cut from the magazine is practically worthless. Magazines are best stored in collectors' bags intended for this purpose (they come in regular, thick, and oversize sizes). This protects them from moisture damage, tearing, wrinkling, and fading, all of which detract from their value. Sturdy, magazine-size storage boxes are convenient for large quantities of magazines but if you intend to store your magazines standing up you may wish to insert backing boards in the bags with your magazines to prevent them from sagging.

SECTION NOTES
Since this is, of practical necessity, by no means a complete list of all publications that have contained Star Trek articles, it is prefaced by an introduction on the varieties of publications that have had articles and covers on Star Trek, along with a generalized estimate of the values of these types of magazines. The main body of the section is organized alphabetically by title and then numerically by issue. For other magazinelike publications, see Books and Comic Books sections in this book.

INTRODUCTION TO TYPES OF STAR TREK MAGAZINES

The categories listed below represent the different types of magazines that most commonly carry Star Trek articles. Since a Star Trek cover story is almost always worth more than a simple interior article, the values listed are for both types of magazines. Please remember that these values are only general estimates and that in every category there will be exceptions in both directions.

Established Genre Magazines (Slick Format)—(*Starlog, TV Zone*)—Most common source of Star Trek articles. Popular issues, including most with Star Trek covers, often either have heavy initial print runs or are frequently reprinted, tending to keep prices relatively low.

Article. ....$4–$25
Cover. ....$10–$25

Film Industry Magazines (*American Cinematographer*, *Variety*)—Quality publications, not widely distributed among the general public, with interesting, insightful articles. Good collectible potential.

Article. ....$10–$25
Cover. ....$25–$50

Limited Special Interest Magazines—Examples are gaming and computer magazines. Star Trek covers are generally used to attract buyer attention and boost sales of an issue but the content is generally of limited interest to most Star Trek fans. Usually not especially collectible.

Article. ....$2–$6
Cover. ....$5–$10

NOTE: For specific Star Trek role playing magazines see Games and Accessories section of this book.

Mainstream Magazines (Slick Format)—(*Newsweek*, *Omni*)—These well-known publications are the least common source of Star Trek articles. Good collectible potential.

Article. ....$10–$20
Cover. ....$20–$40

Newspaper Insert Magazines (Usually Sunday Supplements)—Special interest and local TV inserts are common examples. Fairly good collectible potential since they are often routinely discarded with the rest of publication, making them fairly scarce.

Article. ....$5–$10
Cover. ....$15–$25

Popular Magazines (Slick Format)—(*People*, *Us*)—Fairly common source of Star Trek articles. Tend to accrue value fairly well once they disappear from the newsstand.

Article. ....$5–$10
Cover. ....$10–$20

Science Fiction Magazines (Slick Format)—Those designed to resemble *Starlog* or *Starburst*. Often last only a few issues. Usually published simply to quickly capitalize on the popularity of a current fad. Collectibility varies and is often dependent on the quality of the content.

Article. ....$3–$8
Cover. ....$5–$15

Science Fiction Magazines (Secondary Production Quality)—(*Enterprise*, *Files Magazines*)—Mediocre collectible potential.

Article. ....$1–$5
Cover. ....$5–$10

Tabloids (Popular and Genre)—Articles are usually brief and contain little of substance that interests fans. This, combined with inherently cheap production values, gives them limited collectible potential.

Article. ....$1–$5
Cover. ....$5–$10

MAGAZINE LISTING

Specific issues of magazines and their values are listed in this section. Values assume that all magazines are complete and in excellent condition.

All About Star Trek Fan Clubs—Ego Enterprises. A series of five magazines with complete membership information plus biographies, portraits, episodes, and conventions. Began Dec. 1976. Gave early attention to fan activities.

#1. ....$8–$12
#2–6. ....$4–$8

American Cinematographer—ASC Holding Corp. A magazine primarily for technical experts in the professional film industry.

Oct. 1967, magazines premier article on Star Trek special effects. ....$25–$30
Vol. 61, No. 2, Feb. 1980, issue devoted to a look behind the scenes of "Star Trek: The Motion Picture." ....$15–$25
Vol. 63, No. 10, Oct. 1982, "Special Effects for Star Trek II." ....$10–$15
Vol. 65 No. 8, issue on Star Trek III. ....$10–$15
Vol. 67, No. 12, Dec. 1986, cover and article on Star Trek IV. ....$10–$15
Vol. 70, No. 7, cover and article on Star Trek V. ....$10–$15
Vol. 73, No. 1, special Star Trek issue. ....$10–$15

Castle of Frankenstein—Gothic Castle Publishers. Magazine devoted primarily to horror films which gave early recognition to Star Trek.

#11 1967, Star Trek issue, Spock on cover. ....$12–$20
#14 1969, Kirk and Spock cover. ....$10–$15

Cinefantastique—F.S. Clark Publishers. High quality publication focusing on science fiction and horror films and TV.

Vol. 12, No. 5/6, July/Aug. 1982, half of this print run was published with "Star Trek II" covers and half with "Bladerunner" covers. Interiors were identical. ...$15–$25
Vol. 17, No. 2, cover and article on Star Trek's 20th anniversary. ....$15–$20
Vol. 17, No. 3/4, double issue devoted to the Star Trek II, III, IV movie trilogy. ....$13–$15
Sept. 1990, first Next Generation cover. ....$8–$12
Oct. 1991, Next Generation "Zooming to a Fifth Season" cover. ....$8–$12
Dec. 1991, Star Trek 25th Anniversary Special, two different covers, character collage artwork or Roddenberry, contents are identical. ....$8–$12
Apr. 1992, Star Trek VI cover. ....$8–$12
Oct. 1992, Next Generation sixth season and Deep Space Nine preview (double issue). ....$13–$15
Apr. 1993, Deep Space Nine cover. ....$6–$10
Dec. 1994, end of Next Generation/Deep Space Nine/ Generations double issue. ....$13–$15
Feb. 1995, Star Trek VII cover. ....$6–$10
Jan. 1996, first Voyager cover, double issue. ....$13–$15

NOTE: Like many magazines, Cinefantastique tries to stay well stocked (either with heavier initial print runs or reprints) in more popular issues, including most of their Star Trek issues, in order to perpetuate back-issue sales. This tends to keep collectible prices low for as long as a particular issue of a magazine is still available from the publisher.

Cinefex—Dan Shay Publishing. Magazine devoted to special effects.

#1 March 1980, "Into V'ger Maw With Douglas Trumball," director of special effects of Star Trek. ....$75–$100
#2 Aug. 1980, "Star Trekking at Apogee." ....$60–$75
#18 "Last Voyage of Starship Enterprise." ....$30–$40
#29 1987, "Humpback to the Future." ....$25–$35
#37 Feb. 1989, Special Effects of the Next Generation. ....
....$20–$25
#42 Article on Star Trek V. ....$10–$15
#61 Article on Generations. ....$10–$15

Cracked—Globe Communications. Parody magazines with Star Trek covers are considerably more collectible than those with interior articles only.

#127 Sept. 1975, cover and article. ....$20–$25
#169 July 1980, cover and "Star Drek—The Moving Picture" parody. ....$15–$20
#228 July 1987, cover and Star Trek IV parody. .$10–$15
#232 Feb. 1987, "Star Trek—The Next De-generation," first Next Generation parody. ....$5–$10
Summer Special 1988, cover and reprint of issue #228 parody. ....$8–$10

Ebony—Johnson Publications, Jan. 1967. Prestigious black magazine interviews Nichelle Nichols. Color cover of Nichols as Uhura. ....$40–$50

Enterprise—HJS Publications. Begun April 1984 and ran 13 issues of the regular magazine. Notable as being this publisher's (the company has changed names several times) earliest primarily Star Trek–oriented effort. Color covers with black and white interiors.

#1 Apr. 1984. ....$5–$6
#2 June 1984. ....$4–$5
#3. ....$4–$5
#4–13. ....$4–$5

NOTE: There were also several special issues and reprint issues as New Media Publishing. Values are similar to regular issues.

Enterprise Incident—Science Fiction Comic Assoc. Started 1976. Notable as an early fan publication's attempt to put out a professional quality magazine.

Issue 1. ....$20–$30
Issue 2. ....$15–$20
Issue 3. ....$15–$20
Issues 4–6. ....$10–$15
Issues 7–8. ....$10–$15

Enterprise Incident—New Media Publishing. This company took over the publication of this title in 1982 and developed it as more of a commercial undertaking. Focus of the magazine became less and less on Star Trek and production values were increasingly poor.

Issue 9. ....$5–$10
Issues 10–12. ....$5–$10
Issues 13–17. ....$3–$5
Issues 18–27. ....$3–$5
Issues 28 up, name changes to *SF Movieland*, No. 36 last issue. ....$2–$3

NOTE: There were also several special and reprint issues of this magazine published. Values are similar to regular issues.

Entertainment Weekly—Time, Inc. Fall 1994 Star Trek Special. Oversize tribute edition of this offshoot of *Time* magazine devoted primarily to films. ....$10–$15

Epi-Log—Reference magazines listing episode guides to various television shows. The following are issues with Star Trek guides.

Epi-Log
#1 Original, animated, and NG seasons 1–3. .....$10–$15
#10 NG season 4. ....$6–$10
Epi-Log Journal
#5 Original, NG seasons 1–2, unmade Star Trek II series. ....$6–$10
#6 NG season 3. ....$6–$10
#7 NG seasons 4–5. ....$6–$10
#11 NG season 6. ....$6–$10
#12 NG season 6, DS9. ....$6–$10
#14 NG season 7 (part I). ....$6–$10
#15 DS9 season 2 (part I). ....$6–$10
#17 NG season 7 (part II). ....$6–$10
#18 DS9 season 2 (part II). ....$6–$10
#20 DS9 season 3 (part I). ....$6–$10
#21 Voyager season 1 (part I). ....$6–$10
#23 DS9 season 3 (part II), NG unfilmed stories. ....
....$6–$10
#24 Voyager season 1 (part II). ....$6–$10
Epi-Log Special (Primarily Reprints of other Epi-Log Guides)
#1 Original, animated, and NG seasons 1–3 (later printings revised through season 4). ....$6–$10
#2 Revised edition of #1. ....$6–$10

Famous Monsters—Warren Publications. Noted publication popular within the comic and horror industry.

#145 July 1978, Star Trek article. ....$5–$8
#187 Star Trek III cover and article. ....$5–$8

Mad Magazine—E.C. Publications. *Mad* is the best known of the comic satire magazines and has a well-defined collectible history in its own right. Star Trek issues are therefore doubly collectible.

#30 Super Special, satire on Star Trek. ....$30–$35
#64 Super Special, satire on Star Trek. ....$20–$25

#186 Oct. 1976, "The Star Trek Musical" parody and cover. ....$15–$20

#216 July 1980, STTMP parody. ....$10–$15

#236 Jan. 1983, Star Trek II parody. ....$10–$15

#251 Dec. 1984, satire on Star Trek III. ....$10–$15

#271 June 1987, cover and satire on Star Trek IV. ....
....$10–$15

#282 Oct. 1988, satire on the Next Generation. ......$10–$15

Mediascene Preview—Supergraphics. Ambitious, early, tabloid-style magazine devoted to the science fiction film industry.

#6 Feb. 1980, "Star Trek": The Motion Picture—the Enterprise encounters a most powerful obstacle, its own reputation." ....$10–$15

Vol. 1, No. 31, Dec/Jan. 1978, backstage on the Star Trek set. ....$6–$10

Media Spotlight—J. Schuster Publishers. Another publication by the same publisher as Enterprise magazine which depended heavily on Star Trek.

Issue 1, Summer, 1975, issue devoted to Star Trek, the television show, star biographies and commentaries. ....
....$8–$10

Issue 2, Fall, 1976, "Star Trek Lives Again," another issue on the television show with a photo article on Mr. Spock.
....$6–$8

Issue 3, March 1977, "The Roddenberry Tapes," "The Spirit of Star Trek." ....$6–$8

Issue 4, May 1977, Spock on the cover plus articles on "Fandom, Nichelle Nichols" and robots. ....$6–$8

Issue 5, Oct. 1977, "Kirk the Exorcist." ....$6–$8

Monster Times—Newspaper format magazine of the 70s, primarily aimed at the comic/horror audience.

#2 1974, Star Trek cover ....$10–$15

#45 Jan. 1976, Shatner cover. ....$7–$10

#46 March 1976, Kirk and Spock cover. ....$7–$10

MovieStar—Medien (German). Media magazine which has had several Star Trek special issues that include episode guides and fan information.

Star Trek—1993. ....$5–$10

Star Trek: The Next Generation—1993. ....$5–$10

Star Trek Episode Guide (Special Edition). ....$15–$20

Star Trek Guide (Special Edition). ....$15–$20

National Enquirer—Most established of the sensational tabloids. Issues with articles on Star Trek personalities are common and much less collectible than cover stories.

Jan. 1987, Nimoy cover. ....$10–$15

Jan. 1988, Shatner cover. ....$10–$15

Newsweek—Dec. 22, 1986. Spock cover and Star Trek IV article. ....$10–$15

Officers of the Bridge—1976. One-shot magazine. Blue cover with red UFP banner. Flashy souvenir fan publication includes Kelly Freas art portfolio. ....$15–$25

Omni—Mainstream. High production quality magazine focusing primarily on a mix of science fact, paranormal, and written science fiction. Feb. 1995, Voyager cover. ....
....$4–$10

Scholastic Voice—Scholastic Magazines, Inc. Publication aimed at high school students with an entertainment/education format. Two-issue article/contest designed to interest students in developing writing skills.

Jan. 29, 1973, writing contest introduction utilizing "Menagerie" script. ....$5–$10

Feb. 5, 1973, article and contest continuation, Star Trek cover. ....$15–$25

Sci-Fi Entertainment—Official Sci-Fi Channel Magazine. Dec. 1994. Star Trek cover and articles on Generations and Deep Space 9. ....$10–$15

Sci-Fi Monthly—Sportscene Publishers Ltd. British publication in color poster format. Short-lived but high quality attempt.

Issue 1, 1976, the Star Trek story, Spock's boyhood. ....
....$10–$15

Issue 2, more in the story of Spock's life, the Enterprise Blueprints, an interview with Spock's creator. ....
....$8–$10

Issue 3, Star Trek's evil empires—Klingons and Romulans. ....$8–$10

Issue 4, Enterprise Bridge Blueprints. ....$8–$10

Issue 6, Star Trek alien poster, Enterprise crew, Part 2. .....
....$8–$10

Sci-Fi Universe—HG Publications. Slick format, science fiction media magazine, first published 1994.

Sept. 1994, Next Generation (Riker) cover. ....$5–$10

Nov. 1994, Deep Space Nine Cover. ....$5–$10

Oct. 1995, Voyager cover. ....$5–$10

Starburst—Visual Imagination Ltd. Jan. 1978 to present. British publication similar in content and format to *Starlog*. Recent years have seen many more Star Trek covers and stories. Values reflect that issues after 88 are still available from the printer.

#1 First issue, Star Trek article. ....$15–$20

#2–87. ....$10–$15

#79 Mar. 1985, first Star Trek cover. ....$10–$15

#88 to present. ....$5–$10

Specials and Yearbooks (Oversize Issues). ....$8–$15

NOTE: The following issues of Starburst *had covers devoted primarily to Star Trek: 104, 106, 109, 110, 134, 147, 151, 162, 163, 170, 172, 174, 177, 182, 184, 186, 188, 194, 197, 198, 200, 202, 207, and Specials numbers 9, 13, 16, 20, 22, 23, 25, and 26.*

Starlog—O'Quinn Studios, Inc. Published Aug. 1977 to present. One of the first serious attempts to publish a high quality magazine devoted to media science fiction. Star Trek has figured prominently in virtually every issue with primarily Star Trek covers on approx. 20–25% of the issues.

#1 Star Trek cover. ....$75–$100

#2 Star Trek article. ....$35–$50

#3 Star Trek cover. ....$35–$50

#4–10 Star Trek articles. ....$10–$30

#10 Present articles and covers. ....$5–$10

NOTE: Starlog *has published a number of other magazine titles and has had several special reprints, but none except its licensed magazines (see below) have covered Star Trek as extensively as the original* Starlog *magazine.*

Starlog Star Trek Movie Special Publications—All of the below magazines are licensed publications. Through fortuitous timing on the part of the publisher, they began filling a niche in the movie industry being left vacant by the studios' decreasing desire to publish their own movie program books.

Star Trek II: The Wrath of Khan Official Movie Magazine, 1982. ....$8–$10

Star Trek III: The Search for Spock Official Movie Magazine, 1984. ....$8–$10

Stark Trek III: The Search for Spock Poster Magazine, 1984. ....$8–$10

Star Trek IV: The Voyage Home Official Movie Magazine, 1986. ....$8–$10

Star Trek IV: The Voyage Home Official Movie Special, 1986, articles plus 10 posters. ....$10–$15

Star Trek V: The Final Frontier Official Movie Magazine, 1989. ....$7–$10

Star Trek VI: The Undiscovered Country Official Movie Magazine, 1991. ....$7–$10

Star Trek: Generations Official Movie Magazine, 1994. ....$7–$10

Star Trek: Generations Official Movie Magazine, 1994, deluxe edition (lenticular cover, identical contents). ....$10–$15

Starlog Special Star Trek Television Series' Magazines— Licensed publications generally contain synopsis and articles on several different episodes of a specific series. Magazines often had bonus pull-out posters. Values reflect that all issues are kept available by the publisher.

Star Trek: The Next Generation Official Magazine Series, 1987–1994.

#1–24. ....$7–$10

#25 Special 100-page magazine anniversary issue. ....$10–$15

#26–29. ....$7–$15

#30 Special 100-page final issue. ....$10–$15

Star Trek: Deep Space Nine Official Magazine Series, 1993 to present.

#1 Special gold cover premiere issue. ....$10–$15

#2 to current. ....$7–$10

Star Trek: Voyager Official Magazine Series, 1995 to present. #1 to current. ....$7–$10

Starlog Star Trek Special Publications—Oversized, licensed, square-bound magazines. All currently out of print.

Star Trek: 25th Anniversary Special, 1991. ....$15–$25

Star Trek: The Next Generation Makeup FX Journal, 1992. ....$7–$10

Star Trek: The Next Generation Technical Journal, 1992. ....$10–$15

Star Trek Communicator (Star Trek: The Official Fan Club Magazine)—The official newsletter of the Paramount-

sanctioned Star Trek fan club. Issues up through #57 were small (5½″ × 8½″) format after which it changed to regular magazine size. After issue 100 name changed to *Star Trek Communicator.*

#1. ....$25–$35

#2–10. ....$20–$25

#11–57. ....$10–$15

#58–100. ....$7–$10

#101 to current. ....$4–$8

Star Trek Files Magazines—New Media Publishing. These are square-bound magazines with color covers. Magazines vary greatly in quality. Numbering system is inconsistent. Most magazines are poor production quality. Though it is unlikely these will ever attain much collectible value, they are of interest as providing the basic format that this publisher (as Pioneer) later applied to a profitable series of unlicensed books. (See Books section.)

#1—1985. Where No Man Has Gone Before. .....$10–$15

#1 Reprint Part 1, 1985. ....$6–$8

#1 Reprint Part 2, 1985. ....$6–$8

The Early Voyages, 1985. ....$6–$8

The Early Voyages Reprint Part 1, 1985. ....$6–$8

The Early Voyages Reprint Part 2, 1985. ....$6–$8

#2 Time Passages, 1985. ....$6–$8

#3 A Taste of Paradise, 1985. ....$6–$8

#4 On the Edge of Forever, 1985. ....$6–$8

#5 Mission Year Two, 1986. ....$10–$12

#6 Journey to Eternity, 1986. ....$6–$8

#7 The Deadly Years, 1986. ....$6–$8

#8 Return to Tomorrow, 1986. ....$6–$8

#9 Assignment Earth, 1986. ....$6–$8

#10 Enterprise Incident, 1986. ....$6–$8

#11 Tholian Web, 1986. ....$6–$8

#12 Whom Gods Destroy, 1986. ....$6–$8

#13 All Our Yesterdays, 1986. ....$6–$8

#15 The Animated Voyages Begin. ....$6–$8

#16 The Animated Voyages End. ....$6–$8

Star Trek: The Motion Picture. ....$6–$8

Star Trek: The Motion Picture Vol. 1. ....$6–$8

Star Trek: The Motion Picture Vol. 2. ....$6–$8

Star Trek II: The Wrath of Khan. ....$6–$8

Star Trek III: The Search for Spock. ....$6–$8

Star Trek IV: The Voyage Home Vol. 1. ....$6–$8

Star Trek IV: The Voyage Home Vol. 2. ....$6–$8

Star Trek: 20th Anniversary Tribute. ....$8–$10

Complete Guide to Star Trek Vol. 1. ....$6–$8

Complete Guide to Star Trek Vol. 2. ....$6–$8

Complete Guide to Star Trek Vol. 3. ....$6–$8

Complete Guide to Star Trek Vol. 4. ....$6–$8

Complete Guide to Star Trek Vol. 5. ....$6–$8

Enterprise Command Book. ....$14–$16

Star Trek Encyclopedia. ....$19–$21

Enterprise Incidents Vol. 1. ....$4–$6

Enterprise Incidents Vol. 2. ....$4–$6

Enterprise Incidents 1989 Tribute. ....$16–$18

Federation and Empire. ....$17–$19

Interviews Aboard the Enterprise. ....$18–$20
Lost Years. ....$12–$14
Monsters and Aliens Vol. 1. ....$6–$8
Monsters and Aliens Vol. 2. ....$6–$8
Star Trek Year One. ....$12–$14
Star Trek Year Two. ....$12–$14
Star Trek Year Three. ....$12–$14
Captain Kirk. ....$6–$8
Spock. ....$6–$8
McCoy. ....$6–$8
Scotty. ....$6–$8
Chekov. ....$6–$8
Uhura. ....$6–$8
Sulu. ....$6–$8
Crew File Finale. ....$6–$8
Harry Mudd. ....$6–$8
Vulcans. ....$6–$8
Romulans. ....$6–$8
Klingons. ....$6–$8
Spock and Vulcans. ....$6–$8
The Captains Before Kirk. ....$6–$8
Character Guide Vol. 1 A–D. ....$6–$8
Character Guide Vol. 2 M–R. ....$6–$8
Character Guide Vol. 3 S–Z. ....$6–$8
Star Trek Comics Vol. 1. ....$6–$8
Star Trek Comics Vol. 2. ....$6–$8
Reflections of the 60s. ....$14–$16
Special Effects. ....$4–$6
Starship Enterprise. ....$14–$16
SuperVillians. ....$6–$8
Tech Files—Star Trek Devices. ....$7–$9
Tribute Book Vol. 1. ....$12–$14
Tribute Book Vol. 2. ....$12–$14
Star Trek That Almost Was. ....$5–$7
Star Trek That Never Was. ....$5–$7
Star Trek Universe. ....$17–$19
Time Travel. ....$6–$8
Undiscovered Star Trek Vol. 1. ....$6–$8
Undiscovered Star Trek Vol. 2. ....$6–$8
Undiscovered Star Trek Vol. 3. ....$6–$8
Undiscovered Star Trek Vol. 4. ....$6–$8
Undiscovered Star Trek Vol. 5. ....$6–$8
Undiscovered Star Trek Vol. 6. ....$6–$8
Dagger of the Mind. ....$6–$8
Villains Vol. 1. ....$9–$11
Villains Vol. 2. ....$9–$11
Villains Vol. 3. ....$9–$11
Star Trek: The Next Generation Background Briefing. ......
....$14–$16
Next Generation Complete Guide. ....$19–$20
Creating the Next Generation. ....$16–$18
Guide to the Next Generation. ....$16–$18
Making of the Next Generation Part 1. ......$16–$18
Making of the Next Generation Part 2. ......$16–$18
Untold Tales of the Next Generation. ....$16–$18

NOTE: Ending this list at this point is somewhat arbitrary as the publisher continuously increased the size (and cover price) of its "magazines" until they had evolved into publications more accurately described as books.

Star Trek Poster Magazine—Paradise Press. 1976–1979. Format has interior with articles and photos opening into color poster on reverse. Early use of this now common format.

#1. ....$10–$15
#2–3. ....$8–$10
#4–10. ....$5–$8
#11–14. ....$10–$15
#15–16. ....$15–$20
#17. ....$20–$25
Star Trek: The Motion Picture. ....$10–$15

Star Trek: The Next Generation Official Poster Magazine—Visual Imagination Ltd. (British). "Magazine" interior has articles and episode guides. Fold out to 34″ × 23″ color poster.
#1–93. ....$3–$6

NOTE: Same publisher also did four issues of a "Generations" poster magazine in the same format based on the movie. Value is the same.

Star Trek II: The Wrath of Khan Official Movie Poster Magazine—Walkerprint (British). 1982. One-shot publication in regular poster magazine format. ....$10–$15
Time—Nov. 28, 1994. In-depth article on Star Trek and the Star Trek phenomena. Kirk and Picard on cover. .....$15–$20
Trek—G.B. Love and W. Irwing, 1974–1981. Fanzine turned prozine. Information about the show and the gaining of fan momentum. Series of 19 issues.
#1. ....$40–$50
#2–3. ....$10–$50
#4. ....$20–$25
#5–19. ....$8–$15
Special Issue #1, Feb. 1977. ....$8–$12
Special Issue #2, Nov. 1978. ....$8–$12
TV Guide—This weekly publication is the most widely distributed magazine in America. There is a strong collector market for the magazine itself, making Star Trek issues doubly collectible. Issues with cover stories are considerably more collectible.
Sept. 10, 1966, Fall preview issue, first mention of Star Trek. ....$75–$100
March 4, 1967, first Star Trek cover. ....$175–$250
March 24, 1967, first Star Trek review. ....$25–$40
July 15, 1967, Nichelle Nichols interview. ....$25–$40
Oct. 14, 1967, photo feature from "I, Mudd."......$25–$40
November 18, 1967, Star Trek cover. ....$100–$150
June 22, 1968, William Shatner interview. ....$25–$40
August 24, 1968, Star Trek cover. ....$75–$100
October 14, 1976, Star Trek article. ....$20–$35
March 25, 1972, Star Trek conventions article. ....
....$20–$35
Aug. 31, 1991, Kirk vs. Picard cover. ....$15–$30

Jan. 2, 1993, Sci-Fi issue, Sisko and Picard on cover. ....
....$10–$20

July 24, 1993, Sci-Fi issue, Quark on cover. ....$10–$20

July 31, 1993, Star Trek article, Stewart on cover. ....
....$10–$20

Sept. 4, 1993, Star Trek book excerpt, Kirk cover. ....
....$10–$20

Jan. 15, 1994, Sci-Fi issue, Sisko on cover. ....$10–$20

May 14, 1994, Next Generation collage on cover. ....
....$10–$20

Oct. 8, 1994, first Voyager cover. ....$5–$10

Jan. 14, 1995, Voyager cover. ....$5–$10

Oct. 7, 1995, Sisko and Worf Deep Space Nine cover. ......
....$5–$10

Feb. 17, 1996, Janeway and "Q" on cover. ....$5–$10

Aug. 24, 1996, 30th anniversary issue has four different covers: Kirk, Picard, Sisko, or Janeway (interiors identical)
Individual Magazines (any cover). ....$5–$10
Set of All four Different Covers. ....$20–$25

TV Guide Star Trek Special Publications.

Farewell to Star Trek: The Next Generation Collector's Edition—1994. TV Guide–sized magazine printed by Canadian division of the magazine. ....$10–$20

Star Trek Collectors' Edition—Spring 1995. Regular-sized magazine format. ....$10–$20

TV Zone—Visual Imagination Ltd., 1989 to present. British sister publication to *Starburst* magazine. Similar in format

and content. Virtually all issues have some Star Trek coverage. Values primarily reflect publisher's supply.

#1. ....$30–$40
#2–6. ....$25–$35
#7–8. ....$13–$15
#9–10. ....$25–$35
#11. ....$13–$15
#12. ....$25–$35
#13. ....$13–$15
#14. ....$25–$35
#15. ....$13–$15
#16. ....$25–$35
#17 to current. ....$7–$10
Specials #1–3. ....$25–$35
All Other Specials (Including Yearbooks). ....$7–$10

NOTE: The following issues have Star Trek covers: 1 (with Dr. Who), 3 (with Red Dwarf), 5, 7 (with Jupiter Moon), 11, 12, 14, 16, 22, 24, 31, 34, 37, 41, 42, 44, 48, 52, 55, 60, 62, 64, 68, 70, and Specials 1, 2, 3, 15, 16, 17, and 19 (with Babylon 5 and X-Files).

US Magazine

Dec. 1979, Spock, Star Trek: The Motion Picture cover.
....$4–$8

Jan. 1980, Star Trek: The Motion Picture cover. .....$4–$8

June 1982, Star Trek article. ....$3–$5

Magazines

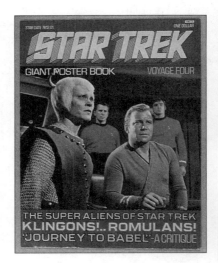

Magazines

MODEL KITS

Though models in general are usually recognized as a good field of investment for collectors, developments in the Star Trek model field have put them somewhat outside the realm of normal model collecting. AMT, the company that produced most Star Trek models until the mid '70s, was purchased by ERTL. From 1983 on, ERTL has manufactured both new models from all Star Trek movies and series with the exception of *Voyager* and re-issues of most of the original AMT Star Trek kits. Because the Star Trek line has been so successful for the company, they have kept nearly all the models from their Star Trek line in almost constant production. As a result, very few ERTL Star Trek kits have increased in value beyond their original price. In addition, because many Star Trek collectors are not as devoted to collecting "original issues," as is the case in some other collectibles fields, ERTL's re-issues have reduced the demand for many of the original AMT kits. Of course, this could all change if and when ERTL decides to let some kits go out of production.

INVESTMENT POTENTIAL
Fair.

CARE
For a model kit to retain its maximum collectibility it must remain completely unassembled and unpainted in the original box. Building a model, even a rare one, can destroy up to 90% of its value. An incomplete model is similarly valueless. Be sure that all pieces, large and small, as well as any decal sheets, instructions, stands, and electronic or other components remain unused and in the box with the kit. The condition of the box is also important in maintaining the value of the kit. Store the box so that it is protected from being crushed or scuffed, and store the box away from moisture and sunlight, which may cause warping or discoloration.

NOTE: When buying older models from a secondhand source, be careful of kits being presented as unused because they are shrink-wrapped. The contents of a model sealed in this way cannot be inspected for completeness and condition. Shrink-wrap machines are very common and an opened model could easily have been re-wrapped. Being unwrapped subtracts very little from the value of the kit.

SECTION NOTES
All model kits in this section are licensed, mass-produced products. Fan-made "garage kits" and modification kits have been omitted. Items such as these are made in such small numbers and in such variety that they more properly fit into the category of artwork than the model kits for which this section was intended. Section is organized chronologically by show and alphabetically by manufacturer. (Also look in the Toy, Action Figures, Housewares, and Games sections for other ship and figural representations.)

ORIGINAL TV SERIES
AMT/ERTL

AMT originally released its Star Trek model series in large 14½" × 10" boxes. Later editions of all models were in the smaller 8½" × 10" box. ERTL has used an assortment of box sizes for their products. Box art from both companies consisted of color representations of the items in the kits.

Cut-Away—ERTL, 1996. Model of original Enterprise with removable sections to show cross-sections of ship, 12" × 18" box shows artwork of model in space below logo. ....
....$20–$25
Enterprise (Large Box) with Lights—AMT, 1966. Very early versions had vertical box art soon replaced by horizontal format used throughout large box series. ....$175–$300

Enterprise (Large Box, No Lights)—AMT, 1968. Same box art as lighted version. Side panel describing model differentiates lighted and unlighted versions. ....$100–$150

Enterprise (Small Box)—AMT, 1968. Same box art as large version. ....$25–$50

Enterprise (Small Box)—ERTL, 1983. Early versions have same box art as AMT but with "ERTL" printed under AMT logo on side panels. ....$15–$20

Enterprise—ERTL, 1989. Current box art, but still 8½" × 10". ....$8–$10

Exploration Set (Large Box)—AMT, 1974. Featured undersized communicator, tricorder, and pistol phaser. .$100–$150

Exploration Set (Small Box)—AMT, 1974. Same box art as large box version. No ERTL re-issue. ....$75–$100

Galileo 7 (Large Box)—AMT, 1974. Art work of shuttle-craft. ....$100–$150

Galileo 7 (Small Box)—AMT, 1974. Same box art as large version. ....$100–$150

Galileo II—ERTL Re-issue, 1991. Minor name change and different artwork from earlier AMT kits. ....$8–$10

K-7 Space Station—AMT, 1976. Small box only. No ERTL re-issue. ....$75–$100

Klingon Battle Cruiser (Large Box With Lights)—AMT, 1966. Horizontal box art. Description of lights on side panel. ....$250–$400

Klingon Battle Cruiser (Large Box, No Lights)—AMT, 1968. Same basic box art as lighted version. ....$100–$150

Klingon Battle Cruiser (Small Box)—AMT. Same basic box art. ....$75–$100

Klingon Battle Cruiser—ERTL re-issue, 1991. ....$8–$10

Romulan Bird-of-Prey—AMT, 1975. Small box only. No ERTL re-issue. ....$75–$100

Mr. Spock (Large Box)—AMT, 1966. Spock phasering a serpent. ....$100–$150

Mr. Spock (Small Box)—AMT, 1968. Same box art as large version. No ERTL re-issue. ....$75–$100

Spaceship Set—AMT, 1976. Included small replicas of Enterprise, Klingon Cruiser, and Romulan Bird-of-Prey. Box 6" × 9¼". ....$20–$30

Spaceship Set—ERTL, 1983. Same box art and size as AMT version but with "ERTL" under AMT on side panel. ....
....$6–$10

Spaceship Set—ERTL, 1989. Current box art. ....$5–$7

NOTE: AMT had another ship in its early series called "Interplanetary U.F.O." Technically, it was not a Star Trek ship but is of some interest to collectors.

Special Collector's Edition Series—AMT/ERTL, 1994/1995. Vinyl character kits, 12". Packaged in 6½" × 11" boxes with vertical color photo of completed kit.

Kirk. ....$25–$30
McCoy. ....$25–$30
Scotty. ....$25–$30
Spock. ....$25–$30

USS Enterprise Command Bridge—AMT, 1975. Diorama of original TV bridge. No large box version. ....$75–$100

USS Enterprise Command Bridge—ERTL re-issue, 1991. Different box art from original. ....$8–$10

Aurora

Enterprise—1966. Same model and box art as AMT version. Made for British market. ....$75–$100

Mr. Spock—1972. Same model and similar box art as AMT version. Made for British market. ....$50–$75

ESTES

Flying model rockets—Model was fired from stand then parachuted down. Ship-shaped models originally came packaged in plastic with full-color cover sheet and header. 1975.

Enterprise. ....$25–$30
Klingon Cruiser. ....$25–$40

Re-issue Models of Above Two—1991, 10" × 20" box with horizontal color photo of toy.

Enterprise...$25–$30
Klingon Cruiser ....$25–$30

Star Trek Flying Model Rocketry Starter Kit—1976. Regular rocket with Star Trek artwork on tube. Came boxed. Color box art shows toy with characters in background. ....
....$50–$75

Medori

Enterprise—1969. Japanese model had propeller added to ship. Kirk and Spock on box art. ....$125–$200

STAR TREK MOVIES
AMT/ERTL

Star Trek: The Motion Picture models were the last made by AMT before being purchased by ERTL. Though ERTL tends to make changes in box art and packaging to reflect the most recent film, the models themselves remain basically the same.

Enterprise, STTMP—AMT, 1979. Lights in saucer section, 12" × 17" box, shows movie Enterprise with lights. ....
....$85–$125

Enterprise, STII—ERTL, 1983. Same basic box art still

showing lights, though model was not equipped with them. ....$25–$35

Enterprise, STIII—ERTL, 1984. Same model as STII. Box art now has lights removed. ....$15–$25

Enterprise, STIV—ERTL, 1986. New box art showing NCC 1701-A. Same model. ....$15–$20

Enterprise, STV—ERTL, 1989. New box art. Same model of Enterprise. Small shuttlecraft model included. ....$15–$20

Enterprise, STVI—ERTL, 1991. New box art. Same model of Enterprise with shuttlecraft still included. Introductory promotion included small, blue, plastic, two-piece Enterprise NCC-1701 D toy from Star Trek: The Next Generation which had originally been a General Mills cereal premium. A sticker placed on the outside of the boxes' shrink-wrap indicated which models contained the extra ship.

   Model With Enterprise-D Premium. ....$50–$75

   Model Without Enterprise-D Premium. ....$15–$20

Enterprise (Special Edition)—ERTL, 1991. Same basic ship as other movie models but with lights and sound effects. ....$15–$20

Enterprise-B, Generations—ERTL, 1995. 12″ × 18″ box with color artwork of ship and Generations logo. .....$15–$20

Enterprise-D, Generations—ERTL, 1995. 12″ × 18″ box with color photo of built model of movie version ship and Generations logo. ....$15–$20

Excelsior—ERTL, 1995. 12″ × 18″ box. Box art has only general Star Trek logo. ....$15–$20

Klingon Bird-of-Prey, Generations—ERTL, 1995. 12″ × 18″ box. Includes 22″ × 12″ print of the movie Enterprise. ....$15–$20

Klingon Cruiser, STTMP—AMT, 1979. Box 10″ × 12½″. ....$10–$15

Klingon Cruiser, STIII—ERTL, 1984. Same basic model as AMT kit. ....$8–$10

Klingon Cruiser, STIV—ERTL, 1991. Same basic kit as two previous models. ....$8–$10

Mr. Spock—AMT, 1979. Box 8½″ × 10″. Re-worked mold of original TV model. Different base, no serpent. ....$40–$80

Reliant—ERTL, 1995. Box 12″ × 18″. Box art has only general Star Trek logo. ....$15–$20

Vulcan Shuttle, STTMP—AMT, 1979. Box 10″ × 12½″. Model had detachable sled. ....$40–$50

Vulcan Shuttle, STIII logo—ERTL, 1984. Same basic model as AMT version. Ceased production in 1989. $30–$40

Matchbox

Matchbox and AMT were both owned by the same parent company (Lesny) at the time of STTMP and produced some models for the European market. Different box art from American models.

Klingon Cruiser—1980. 10″ × 12½″ box, instructions in several different languages. ....$45–$65

Vulcan Shuttle—1980. 10″ × 12½″ box. ....$45–$65

Musasaiya

(Japan)

Mr. Spock—1989. Box has color photo of Spock from STII and STII movie logo. ....$100–$150

STAR TREK: THE NEXT GENERATION
ERTL

Adversaries Set—1989. Includes three ships. Ferengi Marauder, Klingon Bird-of-Prey, and Romulan Warbird. Ships are to scale, 12″ × 17½″ box. ....$15–$20

Enterprise—1989. 18″ model, detachable saucer section, 12″ × 17½″ box. ....$15–$20

Enterprise (Fiber Optic)—1994. Same basic model but with components for fiber optic lighting. ....$45–$50

Enterprise Three-Piece Set—1989. Original TV, movie, and NG Enterprise. To scale, 12″ × 17½″ box. ....$15–$20

Enterprise Three-Piece Special Edition Set—1991. Same basic model as the regular Three-Piece Set but with a chrome finish. ....$20–$25

Enterprise Flight Display—1995. Same basic model as the Three-Piece Set but mounted on a clear vertical disk instead of a stand, 12″ × 17½″ box. ....$15–$20

Klingon Battle Cruiser—1991. Box 12″ × 17½″. ....$15–$20

Geometric Design

Ongoing series (1992–1995) of 12″ high vinyl character models. Earlier models in series came in 7″ × 9″ heavy cardboard boxes with color photos of completed model and logos on both sides. Current packaging has picture on one side only.

Capt. Jean Luc Picard. ....$60–$65

Counselor Deanna Troi. ....$60–$65

Comdr. William T. Riker. ....$60–$65

Ferengi. ....$60–$65

Locutus. ....$60–$65

Lt. Comdr. Data. ....$60–$65

Lt. Comdr. Geordi La Forge. ....$60–$65

Lt. Wolf. ....$60–$65

Romulan. ....$60–$65

Remco

USS Enterprise Steel Tec—1994. Metal and plastic framework model. Sound and light features. Stand, shuttlecraft, and three tools included, 13″ × 18″ box has color photo of toy on space background. Styrofoam interior packaging and instruction booklet. ....$50–$65

STAR TREK: DEEP SPACE NINE
ERTL

DS9 Space Station—1994. Box 12″ × 17½″. ....$15–$20
DS9 Space Station (Fiber Optic)—1995. Same basic model as the original but with components for fiber optics. ....$45–$50
Runabout Rio Grande—1993. Box 12″ × 17″. ......$15–$20
Special Collector's Edition Series—1995. Vinyl character kits, 12″, packaged in 6½″ × 11″ boxes with vertical color photo of completed kit.

    Odo. ....$25–$30
    Quark. ....$25–$30

STAR TREK: VOYAGER
Monogram

Well-established model manufacturer which currently holds the license for all Star Trek: Voyager models.

NOTE: Voyager models in Europe are licensed through SAT 1 (Germany) and utilize a different box style with different artwork and a cardboard flap in front that can be opened to view the unassembled model.

Voyager—1995. 12″ × 18″ box shows photo of actual production model. Completed kit approx. 20″ long. ....$15–$20
Kazon Ship—1995. 12″ × 18″ box shows photo of actual production model. Completed model approx. 12″ long. ....
....$15–$20
Maquis Ship—1995. 12″ × 18″ box shows photo of actual production model. Completed model approx. 13″ long. ....
....$15–$20
Three-Piece Set—1996. Set includes to-scale Voyager, Kazon, Maquis ships, and stand, 12″ × 18″ box shows photo of actual production models. ....$15–$20

AMT Original Star Trek *Enterprise* Model Kits, four different box versions

MUSIC, SHEET

Sheet music is a category of Star Trek merchandise that demonstrates that everything that is scarce is not necessarily in demand as a collectible. Even Star Trek sheet music that is currently in print is rarely seen in shops or at conventions, much less older pieces of music. The primary reason is not that there isn't much Star Trek sheet music around (even though there isn't) but that there is not much demand for these publications. There are sheet music collectors—just not very many that are also Star Trek collectors.

INVESTMENT POTENTIAL
Fair.

CARE
Music needs the same care as other paper collectibles such as magazines or posters. Fortunately most music, both books and individual sheets, comes in a standard 8½″ × 11″ format and so fits easily into plastic collector bags made for magazines this size. In the case of single sheets, the collector may wish to insert a backing board with the music to help prevent accidental creasing.

SECTION NOTES
Prices given are for individual pieces of music. Many variations of each piece may occur, not only for different instruments, but also for degree of difficulty. Also, entire portfolios of sheet music for concert bands, marching bands, etc. can be found. Section is organized alphabetically by publisher.

Almo Publications

Star Trek Theme (original TV)—1978. Color photo cover of enterprise. Sheet. ....$3–$5

Catapillar Music

Sing a Song of Trekkin'—1979. Book form. Blue and white cartoon cover. ....$8–$15
Visit to a Small Planet—1979. Sheet. ....$3–$5

Columbia

Star Trek (Original TV)—1970. Bruin Music. Sheet. ....$3–$5
Star Trek: The Motion Picture Main Theme—1979. Sheet. ....$3–$5
Star Trek II: The Wrath of Khan Main Theme—1982. Famous Music. Sheet assorted covers depending on arrangement. ....$3–$5
Star Trek III: The Search for Spock Music Book—1984. Famous Music. Color cover and photo section followed by several music selections. ....$10–$15
Star Trek IV: The Voyage Home—1986. Famous Music. Sheet. ....$3–$5

CPP Belwin

Star Trek: The Next Generation (Main Title)—1987. Bruin Music. Sheet. ....$3–$5
Star Trek V: The Final Frontier (The Moon's a Window to Heaven)—1989. Ensign Music. Sheet. ....$3–$5
Theme from Star Trek (Original TV)—1966 and 1970. Bruin Music. Sheet. ....$3–$5
Theme from Star Trek: Deep Space Nine—1993. Addax Music. Sheet. ....$3–$5

Hal Leonard Publishing

Selections from Star Trek: The Motion Picture—1980. Ensign Music. Portfolio for entire orchestra. ....$30–$40

Hansen House

A Star Beyond Time (Ilia's Theme) from Star Trek: The Motion Picture—1979. Famous Music. Sheet. ....$3–$5
A Star Beyond Time (Ilia's Theme) from Star Trek: The Motion Picture—1979. Famous Music. Photo cover booklet. ....$3–$8
Complete Musical Themes, Star Trek: The Motion Picture—1979. Ensign Music. Sheet. ....$3–$5
Star Trek: The Motion Picture, Hungry Five, Musical Themes—1979. Ensign Music. Portfolio. Black and white photo cover. ....$5–$10
Star Trek: The Motion Picture, Stage Band, Musical Theme—1979. Ensign Music. Portfolio. Black and white photo cover. ....$15–$20
Star Trek: The Motion Picture, Super Fun Way Concert Band—1979. Ensign Music. Color Enterprise photo cover, portfolio. ....$25–$35
Star Trek: The Motion Picture, Selections—1979. Bruin. Book format. Color photo cover. ....$5–$10
Star Trek: The Motion Picture, Selections—1979. Ensign. Roy Clark Big Note Guitar. Book format. Color photo cover. ....$4–$8

Star Trek: The Motion Picture. Elaine Sevin's Space Note Play and Color, 8½″ × 11″, horizontal book format. Color photo cover. ....$4–$8
Star Trek: The Motion Picture, Music from Outer Space and Inner Space. 8½″ × 11″ horizontal book format. Color photo cover. ....$4–$8
Star Trek: The Motion Picture, Musical Themes—1979. Ensign Music. Spiral-bound book format. Color photos throughout. ....$5–$15
Theme from Star Trek (Original TV)—1970. Bruin Music. Sheet. ....$3–$5
Theme from Star Trek/Space Race (Original TV)—1970. Bruin Music. Super Fun Way Band portfolio. ....$20–$30

Petuna Music Co.

You Are Not Alone—1967. Sheet. ....$4–$8

Studio P/R, Inc.

Main Theme from Star Trek: The Motion Picture—1980. Ensign Music. Band portfolio. Black and white cover. ....$25–$30

Warner Bros. Publications

Main Theme from Star Trek: The Motion Picture—1980. Ensign Music. Portfolio. Road Runner on cover. .....$10–$15

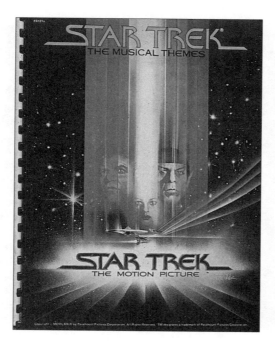

Sheet Music

PATCHES

Patches, like many other kinds of popular but easy to reproduce Star Trek merchandise, face a dim future as collectibles. The values listed for patches generally reflect current manufacturing prices. Most of the more popular designs, both licensed and unlicensed, are still in production either by the original manufacturer or others and will remain so as long as demand for them continues.

INVESTMENT POTENTIAL
Poor.

CARE
Patches, like other cloth products, tend to deteriorate fairly rapidly with use. The best protection for them is to leave them unapplied in a plastic bag. Only an early series of patches based on drawings in the original Star Trek Technical Manual and the *Star Trek: The Motion Picture* photo patches ever came packaged, so in most cases preserving the packaging is not a consideration.

SECTION NOTES
Though the original manufacturer, if known, is listed, it should be noted that the prevalence of indistinguishable, counterfeit copies of virtually all popular patches makes this information all but irrelevant. All patches in this section are embroidered unless otherwise indicated. Section is organized alphabetically by subject of patch.

Alpha Centauri Symbol—Roth. Gold and purple from Star Trek Technical Manual. Original 1975 version came packaged. ....$3–$5
Borg Symbol Patch—Lincoln Enterprises. Two variations. Red Borg symbol on either round or six-sided yellow and black ship background. ....$8–$10
Commendation Ribbons. Set of 19 small triangular patches from the original TV show. ....$10–$15
Dreadnought NCC-1707—Roth. Blue and yellow three-nacelled ship. ....$3–$5

Enterprise—Lincoln Enterprises. Oval patch with ship on black background. ....$2–$4
Enterprise. Black background with white silhouette captioned "Star Trek." ....$3–$5
Enterprise. Die-cut on black felt background. ....$3–$5
Enterprise—Star Trek Welcommittee. Orbiting planet. Six-color, fan-shaped patch approx. 4½". ....$2–$5
Enterprise—Star Trek Welcommittee. With name and number. Oval, approx. 4" on white or black background. ....$2–$5
Enterprise A. Words in circular design with movie-style command insignia in center, two variations—"Lieutenant" or "Commander" under insignia. ....$4–$5
Enterprise Cut-Out—Lincoln Enterprises. Movie version of the ship. ....$9–$12
Enterprise Cut-Out—Lincoln Enterprises. Next Generation version of the ship. ....$9–$12
Enterprise Cut-Out—Lincoln Enterprises. Next Generation version in a tiny stick-on patch. ....$1–$3
Federation—Star Trek Welcommittee. Word with Enterprise. Approx. 3". ....$2–$5
Ferengi Ship—Lincoln Enterprises. Orange die-cut. ....$6–$8

Figure Patches—Roth. Die-cuts of original TV characters on felt background. 1975. Originally came shrink-wrapped on backing card with "Star Trek" and Enterprise.
  Kirk. ....$2–$5
  McCoy. ....$2–$5
  Spock. ....$2–$5
  Uhura. ....$2–$5
Galileo—Star Trek Welcommittee. Word, number, and picture. Approx. 2" ....$2–$5
IDIC Symbol—Lincoln Enterprises. With "Peace in Our Galaxy." ....$2–$4
Insignia Patches from Original TV Series. Several minor variations in material.
  Command, black star with gold background. ....$2–$4
  Engineering, black curved symbol. ....$2–$4

*Gamma, symbol on gold background. ....$2–$4
Nursing, red cross on gold background. ....$2–$4
*Pi, symbol on gold background. ....$2–$4
Science, black circle with round symbol inside. ......$2–$4

NOTE: The Pi and Gamma designs were never used on the series but appeared in the original Technical Manual.

Insignia Patch—Roth. Original science design and "Star Trek" on square black background. Approx. 2″. Original 1975 version came packaged. ....$2–$4
Insignia Patches from Star Trek: The Motion Picture.
    Command, black star with white background. ....$2–$4
    Engineering, red background. ....$2–$4
    Medical, green background. ....$2–$4
    Operations, yellow background. ....$2–$4
    Science, orange background. ....$2–$4
    Security, silver or blue background. ....$2–$4
Insignia Patch from Star Trek: The Next Generation—Lincoln Enterprises. ....$2–$3
Keep on Trekkin'—Star Trek Welcommittee. Words on rectangular patch with red background. Approx. 3½″. ......$2–$5
Klingon—Star Trek Welcommittee. Word with picture of Klingon Cruiser, 3″. ....$2–$5
Klingon Cruiser—Lincoln Enterprises. Original TV version of ship on oval black background. ....$3–$4
Live Long and Prosper—Thinking Cap Co. Word and Vulcan salute. Circular, approx. 3″. ....$3–$6
Live Long and Prosper—Star Trek Welcommittee. Words with Vulcan hand salute. Approx. 4″. ....$2–$5
Mascot Patch. Shows tribbles. Circular. Approx. 3″. ....
....$2–$5
Medical Caduceus—Lincoln Enterprises. Green and white. ....$2–$3
Mirror, Mirror. Gold and red sword and earth design on coffin-shaped black background. Approx. 4″ long. ....
....$3–$5
Phaser Patch. Original pistol phaser. Die-cut. Original 1975 version came packaged. ....$2–$4
Photo Patches from Star Trek: The Motion Picture—Aviva, 1979. Originally came shrink-wrapped on header card with movie logo at top.
    Kirk in full dress uniform. ....$5–$10
    Spock and Kirk. ....$5–$10
    Spock in white. ....$5–$10
    Spock, Kirk, and McCoy. ....$5–$10
    Worried Adm. Kirk. ....$5–$10
Romulan Ship—Star Trek Welcommittee. Word with picture of Romulan Bird-of-Prey. Approx. 3″. ....$3–$5
Romulan Symbol—Lincoln Enterprises. Bird-of-Prey Next Generation Romulan symbol. Three color variations. ....
....$8–$10
Space Station K-7—Star Trek Welcommittee. Words and picture. Approx. 3″. ....$3–$5
Spock—Roth. With "Live Long and Prosper." Square. Original 1975 version came packaged. ....$3–$4

Spock Lives—Thinking Cap Co. 3″ circular design on blue background. ....$3–$6
61 Cygni Symbol. Planetary system symbol resembling copper-colored bird from the original Technical Manual. ......$3–$5
Star Trek: The Next Generation—Lincoln Enterprises. Word logo on curved stripes. Two color variations. Multicolored, blue and silver. ....$9–$12
Star Trek III Commemorative Patch—Lincoln Enterprises. Movie Enterprise inside of circular word logo (two minor design variations). ....$6–$8
STIV Enterprise and Whales—Lincoln Enterprises. Multicolored. Two whales inside of circular movie word logo. ......
....$9–$12
STIV Bird-of-Prey and Whale—Lincoln Enterprises. Circular multicolored design with Golden Gate bridge and movie word logo. ....$8–$10
STIV Whales—Lincoln Enterprises. Multicolored die-cut design. ....$8–$10
STV Crew—Lincoln Enterprises. Word and word logo on rectangular patch. ....$6–$8
STV Logo—Lincoln Enterprises. Enterprise and word logo on horseshoe background. ....$6–$8
Star Trek 20th Anniversary—Lincoln Enterprises. Words and movie Enterprise inside of octagon. ....$6–$8
Star Trek 25th Anniversary—Lincoln Enterprises. "Star Trek," "25," and original Enterprise on insignia-shaped background. ....$8–$10
Star Trek 25th Anniversary—Lincoln Enterprises. Enterprise-D with "Star Trek 25th Anniversary" in circle and "1986–1991" in ellipse. ....$8–$10
Star Trek 25th Anniversary—Lincoln Enterprises. Word logo and dates in circular design surrounded by original Enterprise, Enterprise-A, and Enterprise-D. ....$8–$10
Star Trek 25th Anniversary—Star Trek Official Fanclub. "Star Trek," "1991—25th Anniversary," and insignia design in red and silver on black. ....$5–$6
UFP Seal—Roth. Silver and blue circle (from original Technical Manual). Approx. 4″ Original 1975 version came packaged. ....$5–$7
UFP Seal—Thinking Cap Co. Silver and blue 3″ circle. From the movies. ....$3–$5
UFP Seal—Lincoln Enterprises. Next Generation–style. Blue and red. ....$9–$12
United Federation of Planets Banner—Roth. Silver and red or silver and black (from original TV show). Original 1975 version came packaged. ....$3–$5
USS Enterprise—Roth. Light blue background, dark blue border. Words in orange with silver original ship. Color variation has yellow background. ....$3–$5
USS Enterprise—Thinking Cap Co. Movie-style insignia and words on red. Circular, approx. 3″. ....$2–$5
USS Enterprise. Words on yellow felt background, rectangular. ....$3–$5
Zap—Star Trek Welcommittee. Word with original Enterprise firing phasers. Rectangular. Four-color. Approx. 3½″. ....$3–$5

Aviva Spock *Star Trek: The Motion Picture* Photo Patch

Roth UFP Banner Patch

PEWTER SHIPS AND FIGURES

Pewter is a soft, malleable metal, an alloy of tin and lead which, because of its nice sheen and ability to be worked into fine detail, lends itself well to artwork. Companies that make pewter figurines for the collector market abound and it was inevitable that some of them should enter the field of Star Trek collectibles. Unlike many collectible fields, (plates for instance), pewter pieces are rarely made in limited editions. The main focus of most Star Trek pewter collectors is simply to collect the pieces that appeal to them or to collect all pieces in a certain series.

INVESTMENT POTENTIAL
Fair.

CARE
Pewter does not tarnish or rust but it is a soft metal (how soft depends on the ratio of lead to tin in a particular piece). Though it is very forgiving and it is expected by the manufacturer that your piece will need some minor staightening before it goes on display, it will break if it is repeatedly manipulated in a weak area. Other care is extremely minimal. Generally, there is no special packaging to be preserved and cared for but some pieces do come with detachable stands which the collector should take care to keep with the piece.

SECTION NOTES
Section is organized alphabetically by manufacturer. At present only two companies are producing collectible Star Trek pewter but both make other, nonfigural pewter items or items that incorporate pewter that appear in other sections. In addition, other companies have, over the years, manufactured pewter or pewterlike ships and figures for gaming purposes. These have not been included in this section because their primary function is not as display pieces, as are the items in this section. For items that fit into the above categories see Jewelry (Keychains), Ceramics (Mugs), and Games.

FRANKLIN MINT

This company, well known for all sorts of collectible products, has since 1989 produced a continuing line of high quality, relatively high priced Star Trek ship replicas. Ships are between 7″ and 9″ in length and come with hardwood stands. They are embellished with gold-plated trim and crystal insets. Though this company employs an impressive advertising campaign concerning their Star Trek line that may leave the potential customer believing otherwise, these items are not limited editions. For this reason they have appreciated very little since their initial introduction and can often be bought for less than issue price on the secondary market. Franklin Mint produces many Star Trek collectibles other than the pewter ships presented here and they can be found in appropriate sections of this book (see Games, Housewares, and Coins and Medallions).

Phaser—Original TV pistol design. Approx. 8″ long. Comes with black inset hand phaser. Piece has crystal insets and gold- and silver-plated accents. Clear plastic stand with inset plaque at base. ....$190–$200
Ships (Individual).
    Borg (Type II). ....$190–$210
    Cardassian Ship. ....$190–$210
    DS9 Space Station. ....$190–$210
    Enterprise (Original TV Version). ....$190–$210
    Enterprise-D. ....$190–$210
    Excelsior. ....$190–$210
    Ferengi Ship. ....$190–$210
    Galileo II. ....$190–$210
    Klingon Bird-of-Prey. ....$190–$210
    Klingon Cruiser (Original TV Version). ....$190–$210
    Romulan Ship (Original TV Version). ....$190–$210
    Romulan Warbird. ....$190–$210
Three-Ship Set ("Beyond the Final Frontier")—Original TV

Enterprise, Romulan, and Klingon ships approx. 4″ each in size. Mounted together on a permanently attached metal stand. ....$190–$210

RAWCLIFFE

In 1988, Rawcliffe, a manufacturer of all kinds of fine pewter figurines, made a series of Star Trek ships under FASAs (see Gaming) license to produce gaming pieces. They were essentially identical to the FASA pieces except that they were made of pewter instead of base metal. Initially Paramount disagreed with this arrangement and forced Rawcliffe to temporarily cease production of the product. In 1991, after Rawcliffe had negotiated their own licensing agreement with Paramount, they resumed manufacture of most of their original FASA copies and have steadily added to their line of Star Trek products. Rawcliffe has kept most pieces in production.

Deep Space Nine Space Station—1994. Limited to 4500 pieces. Approx. 9″ in diameter. Comes with unattached triangular stone base with numbered pewter name plaque on front. Comes with Certificate of Authenticity. ....$250–$300

Delux Enterprise (Original)—Approx. 4½″ long. Gold-plated sensor dish and red crystals on nacelles. Attached stand. ....$50–$60

Delux Enterprise-A—Approx. 4½″ long. Gold-plated sensor dish and blue crystals on nacelles. Attached stand. ....$50–$60

Delux Enterprise-D—Ship comes attached to base and has removable saucer section. ....$55–$60

Delux Klingon Bird-of-Prey—Approx. 4½″ wide with movable wings and gold-plated wing guns. ....$60–$70

Large Figures—Approx. 3½″ tall with name of character on side of base. No packaging.

    Original TV.
        Kirk. ....$30–$35
        Spock. ....$30–$35
    Next Generation.
        Picard. ....$30–$35
        Worf. ....$30–$35
    Deep Space Nine.
        Odo. ....$30–$35
        Sisko. ....$30–$35

Limited Edition Enterprise-D—1993. Limited to 15,000 pieces. Approx. 4½″ long. Attached to triangular wooden base with insignia-shaped number plaque behind ship. ....$100–$125

Limited Edition Statuette, "Engage"—1996. Limited to 1701 pieces. Standing Picard figure in front of Enterprise-D on insignia-shaped attached base. Includes insignia-shaped, marble-finished stand. ....$90–$100

Limited Edition Statuette, Star Trek: Generations—1994. Limited to 4500 pieces. Kirk and Picard lying on metal bridge. Approx. 4½″ long. Comes with oval black plastic

base with name plaque on front and number plaque on back. Rectangular red and gold Generations logo keychain was originally included. ....$75–$100

Limited Edition Statuette, To Boldly Go ... —1996. Limited to 1701 pieces. Kirk (in command chair), Spock, and McCoy from original TV series. Approx. 4″ long. Comes with oval black plastic base with name plaque on front and number plaque on back. ....$90–$100

Regular Ship Series—Ships range in size from 2″ to 5″ and come with attached stand. Name of ship is imprinted on bottom of stand. Most ships come packaged in either 3″ × 2½″ or 3″ × 5½″ boxes of thin white cardboard with Rawcliffe logo on lid in blue.

    Borg Ship. ....$65–$75
    Chandley. ....$20–$25
    Enterprise (Original TV). ....$15–$20
    Enterprise-A. ....$15–$20
    Enterprise-D. ....$25–$30
    Excelsior. ....$20–$25
    Ferengi. ....$30–$35
    Grissom. ....$15–$20
    Klingon Bird-of-Prey. ....$15–$20
    Klingon Cruiser (Original TV). ....$15–$20
    Regula Space Station. ....$15–$20
    Reliant. ....$15–$20
    Romulan Warbird. ....$30–$35
    Runabout (DS9). ....$30–$35
    Voyager. ....$30–$35

Small Figures—Approx. 2¼″ tall with name of character on bottom of base. No packaging.

    Original TV.
        Chekov. ....$15–$20
        Kirk. ....$15–$20
        McCoy. ....$15–$20
        Scotty. ....$15–$20
        Spock. ....$15–$20
        Sulu. ....$15–$20
        Uhura. ....$15–$20
    Next Generation.
        Data. ....$15–$20
        Dr. Crusher. ....$15–$20
        Guinan. ....$15–$20
        Klingon. ....$15–$20
        La Forge. ....$15–$20
        Picard. ....$15–$20
        Riker. ....$15–$20
        Troi. ....$15–$20
        Worf. ....$15–$20
    Deep Space Nine.
        Bashir. ....$15–$20
        Dax. ....$15–$20
        Kira. ....$15–$20
        O'Brien. ....$15–$20
        Odo. ....$15–$20
        Quark. ....$15–$20
        Sisko. ....$15–$20

Franklin Mint *Star Trek: Next Generation Enterprise*

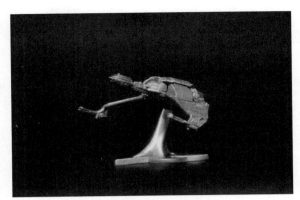

Rawcliffe Deluxe Klingon Bird-of-Prey

Rawcliffe Smaller Figures

Rawcliffe "To Boldly Go" Limited Edition Statuette

POSTCARDS

Postcards, in general, are very popular both as novelty items and as collectibles, and the same can be said for Star Trek postcards. Unfortunately, the vast majority of even the more collectible postcards never accrue much value. A major part of the appeal of postcards seems to be that they are inexpensive and they are probably destined to stay that way.

INVESTMENT POTENTIAL
Fair.

CARE
Though fortunately not as fragile as other, flimsier paper collectibles, postcards must still be protected from moisture damage, crimped corners, and creases. Plastic notebook pages suitable for postcards are readily available and a notebook is also an excellent way to store and display a postcard collection.

SECTION NOTES
Section is organized alphabetically by manufacturer. Fan-made and other unlicensed postcards which have very little collectible value have been omitted.

A.H. Prismatic (British) Lasergrams—1993. Foil hologram photo postcards. Price each. ....$3–$5
    Cardassian Ship.
    Crew (Deep Space Nine).
    Crew (Next Generation).
    Deep Space Nine Space Station.
    Enterprise (Original TV Series).
    Enterprise-D.
    Picard.
    Quark.
    Spock (Original TV Series).
    Uhura, McCoy, Spock, and Kirk (Original TV Series).

Anabas (British)—1987. Color photos from the original TV show. Two: Enterprise; Kirk, McCoy, and Uhura. Price each. ....$1–$3

Applied Holographics—1991. Subject matter printed on holographic foil background. Three: Enterprise-D and logo (on silver); Enterprise-D and logo (on gold); 25th Anniversary logo (on silver). Price each. ....$2–$3

California Dreamers—1985. Color photos with captions. Price per card. ....$1–$2
    Enterprise, "To seek strange new worlds—like you!"
    Kirk, "Screens up full, magnification 10."
    Kirk with Communicator, "Lock me in and beam me up, baby, I'm yours."
    Kirk at Party with Aliens, ". . . Call me. We'll have lunch."
    Spock, "Bizarre . . . but I like it."
    Spock Touching Wall.
    Spock with Headpiece, "Batteries may fail, but rock and roll will never die!"
    Sulu, "Control systems out, navigation out. Directional systems out . . . I'm so confused."

Classico—Color photo cards. Price each. ....$1–$2
    Original Television Series.
        Chekov.
        Chekov and Kirk.
        Chekov (I, Mudd).
        Chekov, screaming.
        Enterprise Firing Phasers.
        Enterprise (Immunity Syndrome).
        Enterprise (Tholian Web).
        Group, laughing.
        Kirk.
        Kirk and McCoy.
        Kirk as Romulan.
        Kirk at Swordpoint.
        Kirk, green shirt.
        Kirk, green shirt, close-up.

Kirk in Command Chair.
Kirk (Mirror, Mirror).
Kirk on Bridge.
Kirk (Paradise Syndrome).
Kirk, Spock, and McCoy (Plato's Stepchildren).
Kirk with Apple.
Kirk with Nomad.
Kirk with Tribbles.
McCoy.
McCoy, close-up.
McCoy, looking left.
McCoy, publicity shot.
McCoy, smiling.
McCoy with Scanner.
Mugato.
Scott.
Scott (Wolf in the Fold).
Spock and Kirk.
Spock and McCoy.
Spock (Bread and Circuses).
Spock, close-up.
Spock, looking down.
Spock, hand to head.
Spock, in front of wall.
Spock, McCoy, and Kirk, in bushes.
Spock on Bridge.
Spock (Spock's Brain).
Spock (Vulcan Salute).
Spock with Phaser, publicity photo.
Spock with Visor.
Spock with Vulcan Harp.
Sulu and Chekov.
Uhura.
Uhura and Chekov.
Uhura, McCoy, Spock, and Kirk, publicity photo.
Star Trek: The Next Generation.
Data.
Dr. Crusher.
Enterprise-D.
Ferengi Ship.
Geordi.
Group.
Group on Bridge.
Guinan.
O'Brien.
Picard.
Picard, wearing jacket.
Riker.
Romulan Warbird.
Troi, blue outfit.
Troi, gray outfit.
Troi, Guinan, and Dr. Crusher.
Wesley.
Worf, space background.
Star Trek VI: The Undiscovered Country.
Azetbur.

Chang.
Gorkon.
Kirk in Command Chair.
Kirk, Spock, McCoy, and Scott.
Movie Poster Artwork.
Sarek, Valeris, and Spock.
Spock.
Uhura.
Star Trek: Deep Space Nine.
Dax.
Dr. Bashir.
Group.
Group in Ops.
Group on Stairs.
Jake.
Kira.
Odo.
Quark.
Sisko.
Space Station.
Star Trek: Generations.
Capt. Harriman.
Chekov, Kirk, and Scott.
Data.
Data and Picard.
Dr. Soran.
Dr. Soran, close-up.
Dr. Soran, sitting.
Enterprise-B.
Enterprise-D Crew, 19th-century attire.
Kirk.
Kirk and Picard, on horseback.
Kirk, publicity photo.
Klingon.
Klingon, close-up.
Lursa.
Lursa and B'Etor.
Movie Poster Artwork.
Picard.
Picard and Data.
Picard, 19th-century attire.
Picard, space background.
Picard and Data.
Picard with Horse.
Scott.
Worf, 19th-century attire.
Star Trek: Voyager.
Capt. Janeway.
Capt. Janeway, publicity photo.
Chakotay.
Chakotay, publicity photo.
Doctor.
Group.
Group on Bridge.
Kes.
Kim.

Kim, close-up.
Kim, publicity photo.
Neelix.
Neelix, cooking.
Neelix and Kes.
Paris.
Torres.
Torres, publicity photo.
Tuvok.
Voyager, side view.
Voyager, top view.

Engale (British)—1989. Full-color photos from the original TV show and the first two seasons of the Next Generation. Backs identify them as sets of 16 but there is more than one set and not all cards are Star Trek. There are at least 30 different Star Trek cards. Price per card. ....$1–$3

Impact—1979. Movieland Wax Museum Star Trek exibit. ....$1–$2

Lincoln Enterprises—Color. Sold in sets. Three different sets. Price per set. ....$3–$5

· Original TV Series.
Chekov.
Kirk.
McCoy.
Scotty.
Spock.
Sulu.
Uhura.

Star Trek: The Motion Picture.
Chapel.

Chekov.
Decker.
Enterprise.
Ilia.
Kirk.
McCoy.
Rand.
Scotty.
Spock.
Sulu.
Uhura.

Star Trek III: The Search for Spock.
Chekov.
Kirk.
McCoy.
Saavik.
Sarek.
Scotty.
Spock.
Sulu.
T'Lar.
Uhura.

National Air and Space Museum—Color photo of original TV model now housed in museum. ....$2–$3

Prime Press, Star Trek Postcard Book—1977. Forty-eight color photo cards of the original TV series in oversize soft-cover book format. Color cover. ....$15–$20

Simon and Schuster, Star Trek III: The Search For Spock Postcard Book—1984. Twenty-two color postcards in book format. ....$6–$10

Classics Star Trek Postcards

POSTERS

The posters listed here are either mass-market posters designed to be sold to the public or commercial promotional posters such as those given away to the public in conjunction with a product. For theatrical movie posters see the Studio Promotional Material section of this book. While movie posters, which have a long-established collector market aside from the Star Trek market, are very good collectible investments, mass-market posters do not tend to accrue much collectible value. Promotional posters do a little better but the fact that most of these posters are relatively easy to counterfeit (due primarily to their smaller size compared to that of theatrical posters) tends to influence their price. Fan-produced posters printed in small quantities and limited edition art lithographs have been omitted from this section as they more properly qualify as artwork.

INVESTMENT POTENTIAL
Fair.

CARE
Posters are one of the hardest categories of collectibles to maintain in good condition. They are large, flimsy, and subject to damage by water and sunlight. The only really safe way to display a poster is in a frame with a glass or Plexiglas cover. Pin holes, tape, and glue all devalue posters as does folding and trimming. Storage is somewhat simpler. Rigid cardboard tubes that can hold several rolled posters are available where collector supplies are sold and offer excellent protection.

SECTION NOTES
Section is divided chronologically by TV series or movie and then alphabetically by manufacturer. For Star Trek posterbooks see Magazines section of this book.

ORIGINAL TV SERIES

American Cancer Society—1989. Photo of Spock (giving Vulcan salute), captioned "Don't Smoke, Live Long and Prosper." ....$15–$20
Dargis Associates—1976. 17″ × 30″ black and white.
   Door Poster, with Spock, Kirk, Enterprise, and Klingon, 6′
   ....$10–$15
   Kirk. ....$5–$10
   McCoy. ....$5–$10
   Spock. ....$5–$10
   Sulu. ....$5–$10
Dynamic Publishing Company—1976. Black light flocked posters.
   Enterprise. ....$15–$25
   Kirk. ....$15–$25
   Spock ....$15–$25
Heineken—1975. 10″ × 18″ color artwork, horizontal format. Three faces of Spock drinking beer captioned "Heineken. Refreshes the parts other beers cannot reach." British advertising promotion. Focus of a lawsuit between Nimoy and Paramount. ....$15–$25
Jeri of Hollywood—1967. 22″ × 33″ black and white posters of early promotional pictures.
   Kirk. ....$3–$5
   McCoy. ....$3–$5
   Spock. ....$3–$5
Langley Associates—1976. Manufactured an extensive line of licensed color posters, 20″ × 24″ unless otherwise noted.
   Collage. ....$4–$6
   Crew in Transporter. ....$4–$6
   Crew on Bridge. ....$4–$6
   Enterprise and Crew. ....$4–$6
   Enterprise and Klingon, two-sided, 11″ × 15″ black and white. ....$5–$8
   Enterprise Firing on Enemy Ships. ....$4–$6

Enterprise Firing Phasers. ....$4–$6
Enterprise With Enemy Ships. ....$4–$6
Kirk, 6′ door poster. ....$10–$15
Rigel Castle. ....$4–$6
Spock, 6′ door poster. ....$10–$15
Spock and Kirk. ....$4–$6
Spock and Kirk, artwork. ....$4–$6
Lincoln Enterprises
Character Collage, 16″ × 20″ color artwork. ....$4–$6
Kirk as Romulan, 17″ × 22″, artwork by Little. ....$4–$5
Kirk Collage, 2′ × 3′ color poster. ....$5–$6
Spock, two faces, three-color artwork. ....$3–$4
Spock Collage, 2′ × 3′ color poster. ....$5–$6
One Stop Publishing—24″ × 36″ color.
Crew, 1996. ....$6–$10
Kirk, 1995. ....$6–$10
Kirk, Spock, and Enterprise, 1995. ....$6–$10
Portal—1995. 24″ × 36″ color.
All I Need to Know About Life I Learned from (Spock Photo). ....$5–$10
All I Need to Know About Life I Learned from Star Trek. ....$5–$10
NOTE: All I Need to Know About Life I Learned from Star Trek was also done as a 12″ × 36″ locker poster. ....$4–$6
Door Posters, 1994. 26″ × 74 color.
Kirk. ....$10–$15
Spock. ....$10–$15
Sci-Tech—1996. 24″ × 36″ color. Enterprise Cutaway (artwork). ....$10–$15
Star Trek Galore—1976. Manufactured a line of unlicensed color posters, 19″ × 23″.
Character Collage, black and white artwork. ....$3–$5
Character Collage, black and white artwork with ship. ......
....$3–$5
City Scene, from "A Taste of Armageddon."...........$3–$4
Crew on Bridge. ....$4–$6
Enterprise Firing Phasers. ....$4–$6
Federation Recruiting Poster. ....$5–$10
Kirk. ....$4–$6
Kirk with Lirpa. ....$3–$4
Klingon Recruiting Poster. ....$5–$10
Landing Party and Klingons. ....$3–$4
Party Scene, from "Journey to Babel."................$3–$4
Spock with Harp. ....$4–$6
Star Trek Official Fan Club—1996. 30th anniversary color artwork collage. 24″ × 36″ with faces of original crew above, scenes below, and Enterprise in center. ....$15–$18
Steranko, Jim—1974. Color artwork collage of crew members and ships, 23″ × 32″. ....$6–$12

STAR TREK:
THE MOTION PICTURE

Coca Cola—18″ × 24″ color promotional. Enterprise overhead with insets of crew below. ....$5–$10

Lincoln Enterprises.
2″ × 3″.
Enterprise. ....$5–$6
Spock, crying. ....$5–$6
17″ × 22″.
Enterprise and Face. ....$3–$4
Group Shot on Bridge. ....$2–$3
Kirk. ....$2–$3
Kirk, artwork by Little. ....$3–$4
Kirk and Spock, artwork by Little. ....$3–$4
Kirk, Spock, and Enterprise. ....$2–$3
Main Characters and Ship, "Human Adventure is Just Beginning."...................................$2–$3
McCoy. ....$2–$3
Nixon and Klingon, artwork by Little. ....$3–$4
Spock, two faces, artwork by Little. ....$3–$4
Spock and Nixon, artwork by Little. ....$3–$4
Character Portfolio, twelve 11″ × 14″ color artwork posters. Sold only in sets. ....$9–$10
Proctor and Gamble—17″ × 22″ color promotional posters.
#1 Enterprise. ....$5–$7
#2 Spock and Kirk. ....$5–$7
#3 Enterprise, Crew overhead. ....$5–$7
Set. ....$15–$30
Sales Corp. of America.
Character Collage, alien landscape and ships in background.
Regular. ....$4–$6
Reversible 3-D with Glasses. ....$5–$10
Cutaway Poster, color cross-section of Enterprise.
22″ × 48″. ....$15–$25
22″ × 48″ Mylar. ....$20–$35
11″ × 23″ Coca Cola Promotion. ....$5–$10
Enterprise, Mylar 22″ × 29″. ....$10–$15

STAR TREK II:
THE WRATH OF KHAN
Lincoln Enterprises

2″ × 3″.
Group, with color insets from movie. ....$5–$6
Kirk. ....$5–$6
17″ × 22″, color artwork posters by Doug Little.
Khan, with muppet. ....$3–$4
Spock. ....$3–$4
Spock and Enterprise. ....$3–$4
Sales Corp. of America—1982. 22″ × 30″ color.
Enterprise, with insets of characters. ....$5–$8
Logo. ....$4–$6
Sega—1983. 22″ × 34″. Enterprise and Klingon ships battling with "Star Trek" above and Sega logo below. Promotional. ......
....$5–$10

STAR TREK III: THE SEARCH FOR SPOCK

Bennett—1984. 22″ × 28″ color artwork. Montage similar to foreign one-sheet artwork. ....$5–$10
Lever Bros.—1984. 16″ × 22″ color, promotional.
  Bird-of-Prey and Logo. ....$6–$10
  Enterprise and Logo. ....$6–$10
  Group. ....$6–$10
  Kirk and Kruge. ....$6–$10

STAR TREK IV: THE VOYAGE HOME

Lincoln Enterprises—Montage, 18″ × 28″ color artwork. Crew with ship and whales. ....$6–$8
  One-Sheet Artwork, 24″ × 36″.............................$5–$7
Minds Eye Press—24″ × 36″. Reprint of Enterprise Cutaway Poster updated with Star Trek IV logo. ....$10–$20
One Stop Publishing—23″ × 35″ color. Enterprise at angle with inset pictures. ....$4–$6
Sci-Tech—1996. 24″ × 36″ color. Enterprise NCC-1701-A deck plan. ....$10–$15

STAR TREK V: THE FINAL FRONTIER

Lincoln Enterprises—1989. 27″ × 40″. One-sheet artwork. ....$6–$10

STAR TREK: THE NEXT GENERATION

Door Posters—1994. Vertical 26″ × 74″ color.
  Data. ....$10–$15
  Enterprise (horizontal). ....$10–$15
  Geordi. ....$10–$15
  Picard. ....$10–$15
  Worf. ....$10–$15

Galoob—1987. Promotional. Next Generation Enterprise on one side, Galoob ad on other. ....$8–$10
JDT Associates—1991
  Enterprise 1701-D Cutaway Poster. 25″ × 48″. ......$15–$20
  Enterprise-D Cutaway—1993. 24″ × 36″ color artwork. Artwork, paper, and printing process are different from the above poster. ....$10–$15
Lincoln Enterprises—1987. 23″ × 34″ color.
  Crew in Transporter. ....$8–$10
  Next Generation Enterprise. ....$8–$10
Locker Posters—1994. Vertical 12″ × 36″ color.
  Data. ....$4–$6
  Dr. Crusher. ....$4–$6
  Enterprise (horizontal). ....$4–$6
  Geordi. ....$4–$6
  Picard. ....$4–$6
  Riker. ....$4–$6
  Troi. ....$4–$6
  Worf. ....$4–$6
One Stop Publishing—1988. 22″ × 35″. Artwork collage of characters. ....$4–$6
Portal—24″ × 36″ color.
  Aliens Collage, 1995. ....$6–$10
  Crew, 1991. ....$6–$10
  Crew Collage, 1992. ....$6–$10
  Enterprise Technical Poster, 1994. ....$6–$10
  Klingon Bird-of-Prey (Photo), 1994. ....$6–$10
  Klingon Bird-of-Prey (Artwork), 1995. ....$6–$10
  Klingon Collage. ....$6–$10
  Klingon Language Guide, 1994. ....$6–$10
  Picard Collage, 1992. ....$6–$10
Video Poster (British)—1989. 20″ × 32″ color. Promotional for release of "Encounter at Farpoint" on British video. ....
....$7–$10
Western Graphics—24″ × 36″ color.
  Enterprise, with inset crew photo, 1992. ....$6–$10
  "Resistance is Futile," Borg collage, 1995. ....$6–$10

STAR TREK: DEEP SPACE NINE

Portal.
  All I Need to Know I Learned from Quark, 1995, 12″ × 36″. $4–$6
  Crew Collage, 1994, 24″ × 36″. ....$6–$10
  Space Station, 1994, 24″ × 36″. ....$6–$10
  Space Station and Wormhole, 1994, 26″ × 74″. ....
....$10–$15
  Space Station and Wormhole, 1994, 12″ × 36″. ......$4–$6
Sci-Tech—1996. 24″ × 36″ color. Space Station Cutaway (artwork). ....$6–$10

STAR TREK: GENERATIONS

One Stop Publishing, 1994. 24″ × 36″ color.
  Collage. ....$6–$10
  Enterprise. ....$6–$10
  Two Captains. ....$6–$10

TWENTIETH ANNIVERSARY POSTERS

Anabas (British)—1987. 24″ × 35″ color. Kirk, Spock, and McCoy from original TV show. ....$5–$8
Personalities—1986. 22″ × 28″ color artwork by Gibson. Enterprise over planet with crew and logo. Heavy paper stock. ....$10–$20
Verkerkey Publishing—1986. 36″ × 24″ color. Kirk, Spock, McCoy, and Uhura from original TV. ....$6–$12

Video Poster—1987. 26″ × 39″ color artwork. Original Enterprise and characters with 20-year logo, promotional. ....
....$10–$15

TWENTY-FIFTH ANNIVERSARY

Portal—1991. 24″ × 36″ color.
  Collage and 25th Anniversary Logo. ....$6–$10
  Group Shot and 25th Anniversary Logo. ....$6–$10
Smithsonian—1991. 27″ × 40″ color. Original Enterprise reflected in faceplate of spacesuit helmet. Promotion for a 25th anniversary Star Trek exhibit. ....$15–$20

VIDEO POSTERS

Video Posters (American)—Color posters exist for all the movies and there are also several different for the television episodes. Price per poster (any). ....$10–$20

Portal Data Locker Poster

Heinekin Spock Advertising Poster

PRINTS AND HOLOGRAMS

The prints listed in this section are here because they do not properly fit into either the Stills or the Posters categories. Check these sections for other items that might be considered prints. Most items in this section were made primarily with the collectible market in mind. The holograms here are true holograms as opposed to the foil versions that can be found incorporated into products found in the Jewelry, School and Office Supply, and Trading Card sections. Very limited, high quality lithographic prints are usually considered to fit into the category of Artwork and will not be individually covered here. Of special note, however, are the artwork prints done by assorted artists for Starstruck ("Second Star to the Right," "To Boldly Go . . .", etc.) primarily because they have been licensed for use on a variety of other products.

INVESTMENT POTENTIAL
Good.

CARE
Prints and holograms are more durable than regular paper prints and in general do not require as much protection. However, it is still a good idea to place them in protective plastic bags for storage if for no other reason than to help preserve their cardboard mattes or (in the case of portfolios) envelopes.

SECTION NOTES
Section is arranged alphabetically by manufacturer.

A.H. Prismatic (British), **Holograms**—1991/93. Came in 8″ × 10″ black matt shrink-wrapped with logo/info header.
    DS9 Space Station. ....$15–$20
    Enterprise, from original series. (This was also done in a slightly smaller size.)...$15–$20
    Klingon Cruiser, from original series. ....$15–$20
Lightrix, Holograms—1994. Came in 8″ × 10″ black matt.

Packaged in cardboard envelope with window to view hologram. Logo front and info on back.
    Borg, Ferengi, Klingon three in one. ....$25–$30
    Next Generation Enterprise. ....$15–$20
    Next Generation Klingon Bird-of-Prey. ....$15–$20
MHD, Enterprise Profiles—1994. Color three-sheet (14″ × 18″) lithograph sets of various views of the ships. Three different sets. All came packaged two ways. Cardboard tubes or envelopes.
    Enterprise NCC-1701. ....$20–$25
    Enterprise NCC-1701-A. ....$20–$25
    Enterprise NCC-1701-D. ....$20–$25
Visicom, Lenticular Prints—1995/1996. "3DFX Prints," 8″ × 10″ color photos utilizing lenticular process for 3-D effect. Come matted. Includes Certificate of Authenticity.
    "Beaming to Vulcan," Kirk, Spock, and McCoy from original TV episode "Amok Time."......................$30–$35
    "Leaving Orbit," Enterprise-D over planet. ....$30–$35
    Phaser Battle," original Enterprise. ....$30–$35
Zanart, ChromArt Prints—1994–1996. Photographic prints combine color foil highlights to flat background. Both vertical and horizontal subjects typically are 11″ × 14″ and come in gray, marble-patterned matt with foil logo plaque at bottom. Certificate of Authenticity is shrink-wrapped with each piece.
    "Beam Me Up," (transporter scene from original TV. ....
    ....$15–$18
    Blueprint Series, silver on blue background.
    DS9 Space Station, side view. ....$15–$18
    DS9 Space Station, top view. ....$15–$18
    Movie Enterprise, front and back view. ....$15–$18
    Movie Enterprise, side view. ....$15–$18
    Movie Enterprise, top view. ....$15–$18
    Next Generation Enterprise, front and back view. ....
    ....$15–$18
    Next Generation Enterprise, side view. ....$15–$18
    Next Generation Enterprise, top view. ....$15–$18

Portfolio of above eight prints, unmatted. ....$25–$30
DS9 Cardassian Galor Warship. ....$15–$18
DS9 Space Station. ....$15–$18
Enterprise NCC-1701 ....$15–$18
Generations Bird-of-Prey. ....$15–$18
Generations Enterprise and Nexus. ....$15–$18
Generations Movie Logo. ....$15–$18
Movie Version Enterprise. ....$15–$18
Next Generation Enterprise. ....$15–$18
Next Generation Klingon Cruiser. ....$15–$18
Next Generation Romulan Warbird. ....$15–$18
"Phasers," original TV Kirk and Spock firing. ....$15–$18
"Profiles," Spock, Kirk, McCoy, and Scotty. ....$15–$18
Star Trek: The Motion Picture Poster Art. ....$15–$18
Star Trek II: The Wrath of Khan Poster Art. ....$15–$18

Star Trek III: The Search for Spock Poster Art. ....
....$15–$18
Star Trek IV: The Voyage Home Poster Art. ....
....$15–$18
"Trouble with Tribbles," Kirk and Tribbles. ....
....$15–$18
Voyager, Ship. ....$15–$18
Zanart, Portfolios—1994. Sets of eight 11″ × 14″ color prints on heavy card stock. Packaged shrink-wrapped in color photo covers. DS9. ....$25–$30

NOTE: This portfolio also came with a ChromArt print of the space station shrink-wrapped to cover. ....$25–$30
Star Trek VI: The Undiscovered Country. ....$25–$30
Star Trek: The Next Generation. ....$25–$30

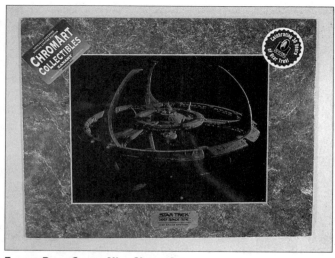

Zanart *Deep Space Nine* Chrom Art

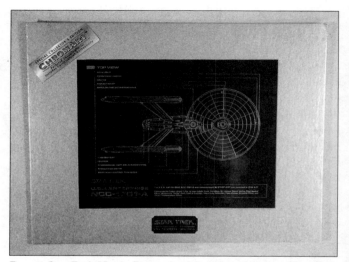

Zanart *Star Trek Movie Enterprise* Blueprint, top view from the series

PROMOTIONAL MATERIAL

Collecting movie promotional material, posters, press kits, lobby cards, and similar memorabilia is one of the best established collectible fields in existence. It is hard not to feel that to own, for example, a vintage press kit from a hit movie, an item made specifically for industry insiders, is to own a little piece of the movie itself. It's also widely acknowledged that movie memorabilia has good investment potential. Science fiction movies, in particular, have a reputation as a good source of potentially valuable collectibles.

INVESTMENT POTENTIAL
Excellent.

CARE
The items in this section are made primarily of paper and the larger items pose particularly challenging problems in preservation. This is especially important in this field where condition profoundly affects the value of the item. Press kits, program books, and press books should always be kept intact (including all stills and slides) and are best protected with plastic collector bags made for large books or oversize magazines. Folded one-sheet posters should either be stored in rigid cardboard tubes or shrink-wrapped onto large sheets of cardboard for display. About the only alternative for very large items such as standees is to try and find a place for them where they are safe from moisture, fading caused by sunlight, and being creased or crushed.

STUDIO PROMOTIONAL ITEMS
These are the items released by the studio to present an upcoming or current production to the public. Most of these items, such as press kits and lobby cards, are not designed for sales to the public but usually end up in circulation anyway since the TV stations, newspapers, and theaters have little use for them once the promotion is complete.

SECTION NOTES
Section is organized first by television series and then by movies, after which it is organized by type of item (for movies) and chronologically.

TELEVISION PROMOTIONAL MATERIAL
Original TV Series

Advance Brochure—1996. Twelve-page booklet presenting the new television series to NBC affiliates. Rare. ....$450–$600
Second Season Publicity Folder—1967. Sent to NBC affiliates to promote Star Treks second season. Rare. ......$300–$500
Star Trek Mail Call—1967. Twenty-page booklet of letters from viewers produced by NBC for network affiliates. ....$250–$400
Star Trek Syndication Package—Color folder with artwork of characters containing demographics designed to induce stations to carry Star Trek in syndication. ....$75–$150
Promotional Flyer—Early NBC promotional art where the network had the points on Spock's ears air-brushed out. ....$175–$250

NOTE: Beginning with the Next Generation, Paramount started issuing press kit–like brochures containing photos, slides, and info packets for each new season of its Star Trek *television productions. These are much rarer than their theatrical counterparts. The values listed for the season brochures are for regular press kits, many of which incorporated elaborate "gimmicks." In some cases even more involved VIP kits were also produced which would, of course, be more valuable.*

Star Trek: The Next Generation

Advance Brochure—1986. Metal folder with etched title and "Captain's Log" on cover. Contains spiral-bound book of demographics on the original show and a 20th anniversary T-shirt. Came boxed. ....$500–$750
First Season. ....$300–$500
Second Season. ....$250–$300
Third Season, picture wheel on cover. ....$300–$350
Fourth Season, audio chip. ....$300–$350
Fifth Season, "floating" Enterprise. ....$300–$400
Sixth Season, metal folder. ....$200–$300
Seventh Season. ....$200–$300
"All Good Things," rubber folder. ....$300–$400

Star Trek: Deep Space Nine

First Season, octagonal fold-out. ....$175–$250
Second Season. ....$125–$175
Third Season. ....$125–$175
Fourth Season. ....$125–$175

Star Trek: Voyager

First Season. ....$125–$175
Second Season. ....$125–$175

Universal Studios Tour,
Star Trek Adventure

Plastic Briefcase—1989. 13½″ × 16″ with color display on inside cover made to look like bridge station. ....$300–$500

MOVIE PROMOTIONAL MATERIAL
Theatrical Release Posters

The most common (and most collected) theatrical release poster is the one-sheet which is what will be listed here because it usually forms the basis for values on all other sizes of movie posters. One-sheet posters are 27″ × 41″ and come both rolled (for promotions) and folded (for mailing to theaters). Often the rolled, promotional ones are sold by Paramount to be offered for sale by theaters and dealers. Small promotional versions are also often printed as give-aways for advertising promotions and theater premiers and are generally worth about 25% of the value of the larger versions. For-

eign countries produce their own theater posters which may use different artwork from the U.S. versions. Generally they have about the same approximate value as their American counterparts. Other size domestic posters utilizing the same artwork are also made available to theaters by the studio but are not as common as one-sheets. These are generally referred to by their dimensions as compared to the standard one-sheet. A half sheet, for example, is half the size of a one-sheet. They also go the other direction (two-sheet, three-sheet, etc.) all the way up to billboard size. Their value can be estimated in roughly the same way but one-sheets are by far the most widely collected size.

Posters are often made to be displayed by theaters to promote a movie that is yet to be released and these are called "advance" posters and often have different artwork from later posters. The first regular poster released is generally referred to as "A." If the studio elects to produce more than one design (seldom the case in Star Trek movies) the lettering system is extended ("B", "C", etc.). Posters for movies re-released at a later date are similarly denoted with an "R" and usually have different artwork from the first-run posters.

Star Trek: The Motion Picture—Rainbow art.
One-sheet (Advance), "The new adventure is about to begin."
Folded. ....$65–$90
Rolled. ....$75–$100
One-sheet (regular), "There is no comparison."
Folded. ....$40–$65
Rolled. ....$50–$75
Star Trek II: Wrath of Khan—One-sheet collage.
Folded. ....$35–$50
Rolled. ....$45–$60
Star Trek III: Search for Spock—One-sheet outline of Spock in space.
Folded. ....$30–$45
Rolled. ....$35–$50
Star Trek IV: The Voyage Home.
One-sheet (Advance), dark blue with logo above San Francisco.
Folded. ....$20–$30
Rolled. ....$30–$40
One-sheet, Bird-of-Prey and Golden Gate Bridge.
Folded. ....$20–$30
Rolled. ....$30–$40
Star Trek V: The Final Frontier—One-sheet. Drew Art. Kirk, Spock, and Enterprise above horseback charge.
Folded. ....$10–$20
Rolled. ....$15–$25
Star Trek VI: The Undiscovered Country.
One-sheet (Advance), Enterprise over Klingon face.
Folded. ....$10–$20
Rolled. ....$15–$25
One-Sheet, faces coming out of explosion with space battle in foreground.
Folded. ....$10–$20
Rolled. ....$15–$25

Star Trek: Generations.
   One-Sheet (Advance), Enterprise-D on delta shield design background.
      Folded. ....$10–$15
      Rolled. ....$10–$20
   One-Sheet, Enterprise-D/delta shield design overlaid with faces of Kirk and Picard.
      Folded. ....$10–$20
      Rolled. ....$10–$20

Lobby Cards and Stills

These are the pictures designed for display in the lobbies of theaters. Lobby cards are generally 11″ × 14″. Lobby stills are 8″ × 10″. Both size sets usually employ the same pictures. There are generally eight cards in a set. Like the theatrical movie posters, they usually have foreign counterparts that are often different in content and form. German lobbies, for example, are larger sets printed on paper rather than card stock and come in perforated sheets of eight. As a general rule, foreign lobbies have the same approximate value. Though most collectors prefer sets, there is some market for individual cards, which usually sell for between $5 and $15 each, depending primarily on subject matter. The "title" card (the first card in the set) usually brings a slight premium.

Star Trek: The Motion Picture.
   Cards. ....$50–$75
   Stills. ....$40–$60
Star Trek II: The Wrath of Khan.
   Cards. ....$50–$75
   Stills. ....$40–$60
Star Trek III: The Search for Spock.
   Cards. ....$45–$60
   Stills. ....$35–$50
Star Trek IV: The Voyage Home.
   Cards. ....$40–$50
   Stills. ....$30–$40
Star Trek V: The Final Frontier.
   Cards. ....$25–$35
   Stills. ....$20–$25
Star Trek VI: The Voyage Home.
   Cards. ....$25–$35
   Stills. ....$20–$25
Star Trek: Generations.
   Cards. ....$25–$35
   Stills. ....$20–$25

Press Books and Press Kits

Press kits are the information packages given out by studios to promote an upcoming film. The general format is a folder containing stills and/or slides and biographies of the principal actors, a story outline, and additional information on produc-

ers, directors, proposed ad campaigns, etc. They can be more complex if a studio deems a particular film of sufficient importance. Press books are primarily pages of pre-made ads of different sizes. These are for use in the newspaper movie schedule section.

Star Trek: The Motion Picture.
   Book. ....$25–$40
   Giant Kit-Velcro closures. Includes novel. ......$300–$500
   Kit. ....$200–$350
Star Trek II: The Wrath of Khan.
   Book. ....$20–$30
   Kit. ....$175–$250
Star Trek III: The Search for Spock.
   Book. ....$15–$20
   Kit. ....$150–$200
Star Trek IV: The Voyage Home.
   Book. ....$20–$25
   Kit. ....$150–$200
Star Trek V: The Final Frontier.
   Book. ....$15–$20
   Kit. ....$75–$150
Star Trek VI: The Undiscovered Country.
   Book. ....$20–$25
   Kit. ....$100–$200
Star Trek: Generations.
   Book. ....$20–$25
   Kit. ....$100–$200

Standees

These are color cardboard die-cuts of figures or scenes designed for display in theater lobbies. More complex ones may have lights. These should not be confused with store standees used for promotion of various products which are much more common. Store standees will usually display a product name.

Star Trek: The Motion Picture (Lights). ....$200–$350
Star Trek II: The Wrath of Khan. ....$200–$300
Star Trek III: The Search for Spock. ....$150–$250
Star Trek IV: The Voyage Home. ....$100–$200
Star Trek V: The Final Frontier. ....$75–$125
Star Trek VI: The Undiscovered Country. ....$75–$125
Star Trek: Generations (Lights). ....$150–$200

NOTE: The Star Trek: Generations standee was recalled by Paramount because of an electrical defect. Theaters were requested to cut off the electrical cord of those already sent out.

Program Books

Unlike most other studio promotional items, program books are designed for sale to the public. Theaters sell the books right along with the popcorn and candy. In recent years, however, program books have become less popular in the United States. Foreign program books are usually identical to the U.S. version except for language and have about the same general value. Books are approx. 8″ × 11″ with color covers, usually the movie poster art, and color or black and white interior photos.

Star Trek: The Motion Picture. ....$25–$45
Star Trek II: The Wrath of Khan. ....$25–$45
Star Trek III: The Search for Spock. ....$20–$30
Star Trek IV: The Voyage Home. ....$15–$25
Star Trek V: The Final Frontier. ....$10–$20

Brochures, Cast Lists, and Newsletters

These are all simple studio promotional items handed out in theaters. Brochures can be as simple as a color "Coming Soon" flyer. Newsletters are usually a little more complex with a page or two about the film. Cast lists are often given out at the premiere of the film and are usually just a list of credits on a card stock flyer. Any of these types of items sell from between $3 and $15 regardless of the film.

Commercial Promotional Items

Though the more common and collectible promotional items made available to the public are listed in their respective categories in this book (i.e., Posters, Glasses, Trading Cards, etc.), there are many unusual items used by stores and restaurants primarily for display. These include dumps for books and video tapes, standees, mobiles, banners and plastic window displays, and counter cards and dumps for jewelry, buttons, and other small items. While these types of things are undoubtably collectible, they are very hard to assign a value to. On one hand, there are fewer of them than items manufactured for retail sale. However, on the other hand, they don't fit well into most people's collections. A counter sign may not be much of a problem but how do you display a large cardboard book rack? Probably the best rule of thumb to use is to use those criteria that apply to all collectibles. More valuable items are those that are older, in better condition, more elaborate, and the most appealing visually. This might mean a dollar or two for a counter dump that held buttons, $50 for a large store window banner, and $100 for an elaborate die-cut cardboard floor display.

Second Season Star Trek Publicity Folder

PROPS AND PROP REPRODUCTIONS

The dream of almost every collector is to own an original prop from the set of one of the TV shows or movies. For ordinary collectors this is not a realistic goal. Paramount is extremely vigilant in regard to release of these items and anyone who offers a prop as original should be suspect. If suitable authentication is provided, a price for a recognizable prop in the thousands is not unreasonable. Even a very minor item or one in very bad condition can cost hundreds of dollars simply because it was actually used on one of the Star Trek productions. For this reason, there was a period of time in which handmade prop reproductions were extremely popular. Though not inexpensive themselves, they were at least obtainable and, surprisingly to many people, almost always of superior quality to the majority of originals, since most original props do not have to hold up to close scrutiny unless they are slated specifically for use in a close-up shot.

This all changed drastically when prop look-alike toys began to be produced (primarily by Playmates). First of all, the customer could now purchase a reasonable facsimile of many of the most popular prop items—a phaser, communicator, or tricorder, for instance—with light and sound functions at a fraction of the cost of a similar handmade prop replica, which was more fragile and neither as finished looking nor had as many functions as the toy. In addition, Paramount now had a good reason, namely the protection of a lucrative license, to use its considerable legal resources to do away with a cottage industry of which it had never approved. The result,

unhappily for all the customers who bought the expensive prop replicas, is that there is now virtually no demand for these items that originally cost hundreds of dollars to purchase. For all practical purposes, they have no collectible value whatsoever and, ironically, as the toy props go out of production, and taking into consideration the strong investment potential for toys in general, the toy "props" are the items likely to be the high priced collectibles of the future.

NOTE: An actual functioning data gathering instrument licensed by Paramount and called a Tricorder exists and can be found in Housewares. For toy prop replicas see Toys section in this book.

INVESTMENT POTENTIAL
Actual authenticated props: excellent. Prop reproductions: poor.

CARE
Both props and prop reproductions are notoriously fragile. Most are made from cast resin, an excellent material for manufacturing a small quantity of like items quickly but brittle and subject to cracking and breaking. For this reason the primary care concern for props is to store and display them in a secure place where they are not likely to be dropped or jarred. Water, heat, and sunlight will not harm the resin itself but may damage paint or decals used in detailing the piece.

PUZZLES

Though puzzles have long been considered fairly minor collectibles they are one of a group of hitherto under-appreciated collectible categories that recently have gained in popularity. Perhaps this is due to the rapid increase in prices of some of the more popular areas of collecting, such as toys or action figures. As these types of items price themselves out of many people's budgets, they begin to look for less expensive categories to collect that are still close to their area of interest.

INVESTMENT POTENTIAL
Good.

CARE
The primary concern about condition with jigsaw puzzles is, of course, that they be complete. Ideally, a puzzle's box should be unopened but few older puzzles can still be found in this condition. If the puzzle is opened it is wise to keep the pieces sealed in a plastic bag. This is a better solution to keeping the puzzle intact than taping down the lid, which may damage the other major consideration, the box. It should be kept in good condition and protected from moisture, fading, and being crushed or torn. Unboxed jigsaws and puzzles mounted on boards are of little value. Most plastic novelty puzzles either come unpackaged or on header cards. As with any blister-carded item, to preserve maximum collectibility the package should be left unopened.

SECTION NOTES
This section is organized alphabetically by manufacturer. For word and pencil puzzles see Books.

Another Pleasure Product

(Michael Stanfield Holdings, British)

Jigsaw Puzzle—1972. "Star Ship Enterprise," 11″ × 9″ 100-piece color photo of ship firing phasers. ....$35–$50

Applause

Cube Puzzle—1995. 2³/4″. Folded displays six square color photos (character portraits and logo). Can be rearranged to show three additional rectangular color photos (two groups and the Enterprise-D). ....$5–$10

Aviva

Star Trek: The Motion Picture—1979. 18″ × 24″ color photo jigsaw puzzles, 551 pieces.
    Mr. Spock. ....$35–$50
    Starship USS Enterprise. ....$35–$50

Braintrust Games

(European)

"Star Puzzle"—1996. 1000-piece puzzles. Box art has picture of puzzle on tan puzzle piece background. Two different.
    Star Trek: Generations (Movie Poster Art). ....$15–$20
    Star Trek: Voyager (Ship in Space). ....$15–$20

Canada Games

Star Trek: The Next Generation—1993. Color photo jigsaw puzzles. 300 pieces.

    Aliens. ....$15–$25
    Alien Ships. ....$15–$25
    Bridge Crew. ....$15–$25
    Crew Photos. ....$15–$25
    Data. ....$15–$25
    Worf. ....$15–$25

Damert Company

Star Trek: The Next Generation Boxed Matching Puzzle—1995. Eight rectangular cardboard pieces with color artwork of ships. Comes in 3″ × 6¾″ box with color ship artwork and logo. ....$5–$10

Star Trek: The Next Generation Triazzle Puzzle—1995. Sixteen-piece triangular frame tray puzzle. Color collage of different ships. ....$6–$10

Star Trek: The Next Generation 3D Slide Puzzles—1995. Eight-piece, 4″ square slide puzzles with raised color designs.

    Command Insignia. ....$3–$5
    Enterprise-D. ....$3–$5

F.X. Schmid

Jigsaw Puzzles—1993. Color artwork.

    Star Trek, 17¾″ square collage of original ship, crew, and aliens, 600 pieces, square box. ....$10–$15
    Star Trek: The Next Generation, 26½″ × 17¼″ collage of Enterprise-D, crew, and aliens, 1000 pieces, rectangular box. ....$10–$15

Golden

(Western Publishing)

Star Trek Poster Puzzle—1993. 3′ × 2′ jigsaw with color artwork of Kirk, Spock, and Enterprise from original TV show superimposed on space scene, 300 pieces. Box has purple border around horizontal artwork. ....$15–$20

Hasbro

Star Trek Maze—1967. Round plastic marble maze approx. 12″ in diameter with color artwork of characters and planetscape on background. Puzzle has sleeve with logo and color artwork of Kirk and Spock. Came blister-packed in shallow tray. ....$350–$500

H.G. Toys

First Series—1974.

Color cartoon-style artwork (not from the animated series). Two different sizes. Puzzles came boxed or more rarely in cardboard cans.

Attempted Hijacking of the USS Enterprise and Its Officers, 300 pieces, 14″ × 18″. ....$35–$50
Battle on the Planet Klingon, 150 pieces, 10″ × 14″. ....$25–$35
Battle on the Planet Romulon, 150 pieces, 10″ × 14″. ....$25–$35
Capt. Kirk and Officers Beaming Down, 150 pieces, 10″ × 14″. ....$25–$35
The Starship USS Enterprise and Its Officers, 300 piece, 14″ × 18″. ....$35–$50

Second Series—1976

Color artwork. More realistic style than first series. Boxes say "Series II." All are 150 pieces, 14″ × 10″.

Alien, The. ....$25–$35
Capt. Kirk, Mr. Spock, Dr. McCoy. ....$25–$35
Force Field Capture. ....$25–$35

King International

Color Photo Jigsaw Puzzle—1993. 1000-piece puzzle. Star Trek: The Motion Picture Poster Art. ....$15–$20
Color Photo Jigsaw Puzzle—1993. 54-piece puzzles.

    Enterprise (Original). ....$8–$15
    Enterprise-D. ....$8–$15
    Klingon Battle Cruiser (Original). ....$8–$15
    Klingon Bird-of-Prey. ....$8–$15
    Romulan Bird-of-Prey. ....$8–$15
    Romulan Warbird. ....$8–$15

Larami

Star Trek: The Motion Picture—1979. Fifteen-piece sliding puzzles. Came blister-packed on header card with color Star Trek: The Motion Picture logo.

    Enterprise. ....$15–$25
    Kirk. ....$15–$25
    Spock. ....$15–$25

Lighttrix

Star Trek: The Next Generation Magnetic Hologram Jigsaw Puzzles—1994. Approx. 6½″ square, 29 pieces. Comes packaged in a sealed window envelope with a hole at the top for hanging. Logo is at top.

    Enterprise-D. ....$5–$10
    Montage of 9 small pictures. ....$5–$10

Merrigold Press

(See Whitman)

Milton Bradley

Star Trek: The Motion Picture—1979. 19⅞″ × 13⅞″, 250-piece color photo puzzles. (Arrow in Britain did these puzzles in 100-piece versions.)

    Crew (Collage). ....$20–$35
    Enterprise, The. ....$20–$35
    Faces of the Future (Aliens Collage). ....$20–$35
    Sickbay. ....$20–$35

Mind's Eye Press

USS Enterprise NCC 1701-A, Star Trek IV: The Voyage Home—1986. 18″ × 24″. 551 pieces. Color cutaway artwork. ....$30–$40

Springbok

(Hallmark)

Jigsaw Puzzle—1993. Star Trek Journey to the Undiscovered Country. 24″ × 30″, 1000-piece jigsaw. Color artwork collage of crew below space scene with ship. Square box. .....
....$15–$20
Jigsaw Puzzle—1994. Three-dimensional optical illusion puzzle of various Hallmark Christmas ornaments, 18″ × 13½″, 500 pieces. ....$15–$20

Whitman

Frame Tray Puzzles—1978. Color cartoon-style artwork. Tray measures 8½″ × 11″. Four different. Puzzles with the Whitman brand name use the original TV Star Trek logo. Exact same artwork was used with Star Trek movie logo under Merrigold brand name.

    Bridge Scene. ....$10–$15
    Kirk in Spacesuit. ....$10–$15
    Kirk, Spock, and Enterprise. ....$10–$15
    Transporter Scene. ....$10–$15
Jigsaw Puzzles—1973. British (Medallion) division only. Color artwork. 125 pieces. 15″ × 11¾″. Box art shows puzzle on star background with logo underneath.

    Bridge Scene. ....$35–$50
    Planet Scene. ....$35–$50
Jigsaw Puzzles—1975. British (Medallion) division only. Color artwork. 224 pieces. 18½ × 13″. Box art shows puzzle on solid color background with logo above.

    Crew on Planet, with black cat creatures. ....$35–$50
    Kirk, Spock, McCoy and Aliens with Eyestalks. ....
....$35–$50
Jigsaw Puzzles—1978. Color cartoon artwork depicts major characters, ships, and alien planetscapes, 200 pieces each. All are 14″ × 18″.

    Collage with Red Box. ....$15–$25
    Collage with Green Box. ....$15–$25
    Collage with Purple Box. ....$15–$25
    Collage with Yellow Box. ....$15–$25

Another Pleasure Product 1972 Star Trek Jigsaw Puzzle

Golden Star Trek Jigsaw Puzzle

HG Toys First Series Jigsaw Puzzle

Arrow Version of Faces of the Future *Star Trek: The Motion Picture* Puzzle

Minds Eye Press Cutaway Jigsaw Puzzle

British Whitman (Medallion) Jigsaw Puzzle

Laramie Sliding Puzzles

RECORDS, AUDIO TAPES, AND COMPACT DISKS

For a long time records have enjoyed their own well-developed collector market outside of the Star Trek field. This market has had to rebound somewhat after the slump suffered by the advent of audio tapes and later compact disks. Recently there has been a noticeable increase in the interest in records by Star Trek collectors as well. Though at this time CD's are too new to have attained any real collectible value, it is quite possible that in the future they will follow a similar path to that of records. Audio tapes, simply because they are so much easier to duplicate than records or CD's, are probably a much poorer candidates for collectibility.

INVESTMENT POTENTIAL
Good.

CARE
Obviously it is important to keep a record, CD, or tape intact, free from scratches, and generally in playable condition. Beyond that, care of the packaging is the major concern. With records, the dust jacket is as important to the collectibility of the item as the record itself and it would be expected that in the future the exterior packaging might be similarly important with CD's. Special plastic collectors' bags are made specifically to protect record albums. The hard plastic cases that CD's and tapes usually come in are generally sufficient for their protection and should not be discarded. It might also be wise to preserve the larger, cardboard display boxes that many CD's come in, though relatively few Star Trek CD's come packaged in this manner.

SECTION NOTES
Section is organized in four main categories; Audio Novels, Songs and Narrations by Star Trek Personalities, Soundtracks and Themes, and Story Records. Categories are organized alphabetically by title.

NOTE: For decorative mounted records see Housewares.

AUDIO NOVELS
(Simon and Schuster)
Star Trek Novel Adaptations

This is a current series of dramatic readings by Star Trek personalities done on tape cassettes. All are based on Pocket Star Trek novels.

All Good things . . .—1994. Jonathan Frakes. Two cassettes. ....$15–$17
Ashes of Eden—1995. Shatner. Two cassettes. ....$16–$18
Caretaker—1995. Picardo. Two cassettes. ....$16–$18
Contamination—1991. Dorn. One cassette. ....$9–$11
Dark Mirror—1993. John De Lancie. Two cassettes. ....
....$15–$17
Devil's Heart—1993. McFadden. Two cassettes. ....
....$15–$17
Emissary—1993. Visitor. Two cassettes. ....$15–$17
Enterprise: The First Adventure—1988. Nimoy and Takei. One cassette. ....$9–$11
Entropy Effect—1988. Nimoy and Takei. One cassette. ......
....$9–$11
Faces of Fire—1992. Bibi Besch. Two cassettes. ....$14–$16
Fallen Heroes—1994. Auberjonois. Two cassettes. $15–$17
Federation—1994. Mark Lenard. Two cassettes. ....$15–$17
Final Frontier—1989. Nimoy and Doohan. One cassette. ....
....$9–$11
Gulliver's Fugitives—1990. Jonathan Frakes. One cassette.
....$9–$11
Imzadi—1992. Jonathan Frakes. Two cassettes. ......$15–$17
Kobayashi Maru—1990. Doohan. One cassette. ......$9–$11
Lost Years—1989. Nimoy and Doohan. Two cassettes. ....
....$14–$16
Prime Directive—1990. Doohan. Two cassettes. ....$14–$16

Probe—1992. Doohan. Two cassettes. ....$15–$17

"Q"-In-Law—1992. Majel Barrett and John De Lancie. One cassette. ....$10–$12

"Q"-Squared—1994. John De Lancie. Two cassettes. ....
....$15–$17

Relics-1993. Burton and Doohan. Two cassettes. ....
....$15–$17

Return—1996. Shatner. Two cassettes. ....$16–$18

Reunion—1991. McFadden. Two cassettes. ....$15–$17

Shadows on the Sun—1993. Doohan. Two cassettes. ....
....$15–$17

Spock's World—1989. Nimoy and Takei. Two cassettes. ....
....$14–$16

Star Trek IV: The Voyage Home—1986. Nimoy and Takei.
....$9–$11

Star Trek V: The Final Frontier—1989. Nimoy and Takei.
....$7–$9

Star Trek VI: The Undiscovered Country—1992. Doohan. One cassette. ....$9–$11

Strangers From the Sky—1987. Nimoy and Takei. One Cassette. ....$9–$11

Time for Yesterday—1989. Nimoy and Doohan. One cassette. ....$9–$11

Warped—1995. Auberjonois. Two cassettes. ....$15–$17

Web of the Romulans—1988. Nimoy and Takei. One cassette. ....$9–$11

Windows on a Lost World—1993. Koenig. Two cassettes.
....$15–$17

Yesterday's Son—1988. Nimoy and Doohan. One cassette.
....$9–$11

NOTE: Enterprise: The First Adventure, Strangers from the Sky, and Final Frontier were re-released as a special 25th anniversary set on four CD's. ....$25–$30

Captain Sulu Adventures

This series differs from the regular Star Trek audio novel series in that the stories exist only in audio format. All are narrated by George Takei.

Cacophony—1994. Written by J.J. Molloy.
Cassette. ....$10–$12
CD. ....$14–$16

Envoy—1995. Written by L.A. Graff.
Cassette. ....$10–$12
CD. ....$14–$16

Transformation—1994. Written by Dave Stern.
Cassette. ....$10–$12
CD. ....$14–$16

Other

Star Trek Conversational Klingon—1992. Michael Dorn. One cassette. ....$10–$12

Star Trek Power Klingon—1993. Michael Dorn. One cassette. ....$10–$12

Tek Audio Novels—Based on the books written by William Shatner. All are read by Shatner.
TekLords, 1991. Two cassettes. ....$14–$16
TekWar, 1989. Two cassettes. ....$14–$16

SONGS AND NARRATIONS BY STAR TREK PERSONALITIES

Beyond Antares and Uhura's Theme—Sung by Nichelle Nichols, 7″ 45 rpm. R-Way Records. ....$8–$10

Captain of the Starship—Canadian pressing of "William Shatner—Live!" Two 12″ LP albums. Imperial Music. ....
....$35–$50

Captain of the Starship—Another Canadian pressing of "William Shatner—Live!" Two 12″ LP albums. K-TEL Record. ....$30–$45

Christmas Carol, A—1991. Narration by Patrick Stewart. Simon and Schuster.
Two cassettes. ....$14–$16
Two CD's. ....$18–$20

Consilium and Here We Go 'Round Again—Sung by Leonard Nimoy from the album "The Way I Feel." 7″ 45 rpm. Dot Records. ....$10–$15

Dark Side of the Moon—Sung by Nichelle Nichols. Two 7″ 45 rpm records, four songs, EP album jacket opens out to a poster. Americana Records. ....$10–$15

Disco Trekin' and Star Child—Sung by Grace Lee Whitney (Yeoman Rand from Star Trek) and Star. 7″ 45 rpm. GLW Star Enterprises. ....$8–$10

Down to Earth—Sung by Nichelle Nichols, eight popular songs. 12″ LP album. Epic Records. ....$15–$25

Golden Throats—Out of character songs sung by an assortment of personalities. Includes "Proud Mary" and "If I Had a Hammer" by Leonard Nimoy, and "Lucy in the Sky with Diamonds" and "Mr. Tambourine Man" by William Shatner. Rhino.
Cassette. ....$10–$12
CD. ....$15–$20

Golden Throats 2—Same format as first Golden Throats album. Includes "Put a Little Love in Your Heart" by Leonard Nimoy and "It Was a Very Good Year" by William Shatner. Rhino.
Cassette. ....$10–$12
CD. ....$15–$20

Green Hills of Earth, The, and Gentleman, Be Seated— By Robert A. Heinlein, read by Leonard Nimoy. 12″ LP album or cassette. Caedmon Records.
Album. ....$20–$25
Cassette. ....$19–$15
Re-release, four-cassette set. ....$20–$25

Halley's Comet: Once in a Lifetime—1986. Narrated by

Leonard Nimoy with artificial space music and sound effects by Geodesium. Notes by Dr. William Gutsch, Chairman of American Museum, Hayden Planetarium. Audio cassette. Caedmon Cassette. ....$10–$15

Illustrated Man, The—By Ray Bradbury, read by Leonard Nimoy. 12″ LP album. Caedmon Records. ....$20–$25

Inside Star Trek—Recorded by Gene Roddenberry and features William Shatner, Isaac Asimov, Mark Lenard, De Forest Kelley. Discussion of the origin of the series, the personalities involved, and other insider information. Selected musical themes. Columbia Records. ....$25–$30

Inside Star Trek: The Real Story—Simon and Schuster. 1996. Based on the book by Herbert F. Solow and Robert H. Justman. Read by the authors. Two cassettes. ....$16–$18

Leonard Nimoy—12″ album from Sears. Re-issues previously recorded Dot records. ....$15–$20

Leonard Nimoy Presents Mr. Spock's Music from Outer Space—Leonard Nimoy sings and recites 11 songs. 12″ LP album. Dot Records. ....$30–$50

Leonard Nimoy—You Are Not Alone. Cassette. Features some of Nimoy's previously released material. MCA. ....$9–$12

Martin Chronicles, The—by Ray Bradbury, read by Leonard Nimoy. 12″ LP album. Caedmon Records. ....
....$20–$25

    Re-release, four-cassette set ....$20–$25

Mimsy Were the Borogoves—by Henry Kuttner, read by William Shatner. 12″ LP album. Caedmon Records. ....
....$20–$25

    Re-release, four-cassette set. ....$20–$25

Mysterious Golem, The—Leonard Nimoy narrates the story of the Mysterious Golem which, in Jewish folklore, is an artificially created human being endowed with life by supernatural means. 12″ LP album. JRT Records. ....$20–$30

New World of Leonard Nimoy, The—Leonard Nimoy sings eight popular songs. 12″ LP album. Dot Records. ....
....$30–$50

Nichelle, Out of This World—Selection of songs and an interview by Nichelle Nichols. Crescendo.

    Cassette. ....$10–$12

    CD. ....$15–$20

Ol' Yellow Eyes Is Back—Fifties pop songs sung by Brent Spiner, some with backups by the "Sunspots" (LeVar Burton, Michael Dorn, Jonathan Frakes, and Patrick Stewart). Infinite Visions.

    Cassette. ....$10–$12

    CD. ....$15–$20

Outer Space/Inner Mind—Two-record album contains all of "Leonard Nimoy Presents Mr. Spock's Music from Outer Space" and cuts from "The Two Sides of Leonard Nimoy," "The Touch of Leonard Nimoy," "The Way I Feel," and "The New World of Leonard Nimoy." Two 12″ LP albums. Paramount Records Famous Twinsets. ....$40–$60

Please Don't Try to Change My Mind and I Love Making Love to You—Sung by Leonard Nimoy from the album "The Way I Feel." 7″ 45 rpm. Dot Records. ....$10–$15

Psychohistorians, The—From "Foundation" by Isaac Asi-

mov, read by William Shatner. 12″ LP album or cassette. Caedmon Records. ....$20–$25

    Re-release, four-cassette set. ....$20–$25

Slaves of Sleep and The Masters of Sleep—By L. Ron Hubbard, read by René Auberjonois. Four cassettes. Bridge Audio. ....$18–$20

Space Odyssey—Nine cuts from Leonard Nimoy's five Dot Records albums. Pickwick/33 Records. ....$20–$30

Starfleet Beat—Phasers on Stun, Special Star Trek 20th anniversary record. 12″ LP album. Penguin Records. ....
....$15–$20

Star Trek Comedy: The Unofficial Album—Collection of comedy skits and songs about Star Trek. Vince Emery Productions. 12″ album or cassette.

    Album. ....$15–$20

    Cassette. ....$9–$12

Star Trekkin' by "The Firm"—12″ 45 rpm record featuring "Star Trekkin' " and "Dub Trek." Precision Records and Tapes.
....$10–$15

Star Trekkin' by "The Firm"—7″ 45 rpm. ....$8–$10

Star Trek Philosophy, The, and Star Trek Theme—Performed by Gene Roddenberry and The Inside Star Trek Orchestra. From the "Inside Star Trek" album. 7″ 45 rpm. Columbia Records. ....$10–$15

Star Trek Memories—Harper Audio. 1993. Based on the book by William Shatner. Read by the author. Four cassettes.
....$20–$25

Star Trek Movie Memories—Harper Audio. 1994. Based on the book by William Shatner. Read by the author. Four cassettes. ....$20–$25

Star Trek Tapes—A compilation of official press recordings featuring the cast of Star Trek television show. Jack M. Sell, Producer. ....$15–$20

Sun Will Rise, The, and Time to Get It Together—Sung by Leonard Nimoy from the album "The New World of Leonard Nimoy." 7″ 45 rpm. Dot Records. ....$10–$15

Take a Star Trip—45 rpm by Grace Lee Whitney. ......$8–$10

To the Stars—Simon and Schuster. 1994. Based on George Takei's autobiographical book. Read by the author. Two cassettes. ....$16–$18

Touch of Leonard Nimoy, The—Leonard Nimoy sings 11 songs. Dot Records. ....$25–$40

Transformed Man, The—Performed by William Shatner. Six selections with chorus and instrumental background. 12″ LP album. Decca Records. ....$50–$70

Transformed Man, The, and How Insensitive—From the album "The Transformed Man," read by William Shatner. 7″ 45 rpm. Decca Records. ....$10–$15

Trek Bloopers—Compiled from unedited sound tapes of six third-season episodes of the original Star Trek series. Features audio bloopers made by original casts. 12″ LP album and cassette. Blue Pear Records. ....$10–$15

Two Sides of Leonard Nimoy—Leonard Nimoy sings and recites 13 songs. 12″ LP album. Dot Records. ....$40–$60

Uhura Sings—1986. Nine songs by Nichelle Nichols. Cassette. AR-WAY Productions. ....$12–$15

Visit to a Sad Planet and Star Trek Theme—1967. Sung by Leonard Nimoy from the album "Leonard Nimoy Presents Mr. Spock's Music From Outer Space." 7″ 45 rpm. Dot Records. ....$10–$15

Voice Tracks, U.S. Marine Corps Toys for Tots—Readings by Leonard Nimoy, Clarence Williams III, Charlton Heston, Phyllis Diller, John Wayne, Jimmy Stewart, Jack Webb, Jimmy Durante. Introduction by Efrem Zimbalist, Jr. Music played by U.S. Marine Band. Edward Mulhare, Natalie Wood, Col. Frank Borman. 7″ 33⅓ rpm. Warner Bros.—Seven Arts Records. ....$15–$20

Voyage of Star Trek, The—Coming Attractions—1982. 60-minute radio special, from The Source, NBC Radio's Young Adult Network. Promotional copy, not originally for sale to public. Discusses Star Trek from television years to Star Trek: The Wrath of Khan. 12″ LP album. ....$20–$30

War of the Worlds, The—By H.G. Wells, read by Leonard Nimoy. 12″ LP album. Caedmon Records. ....$20–$25

Way I Feel, The—Twelve songs sung and narrated by Leonard Nimoy. 12″ LP album and reel to reel. Dot Records. ....$25–$35

Whales Alive—By Paul Winter and Paul Halley with narration by Leonard Nimoy and voices of the humpback whales. 12″ album. Living Music. ....$25–$35

William Shatner—Live!—Two-record LP album. Dramatic narratives recited with musical background. William Shatner's college tour. Lemli Records. ....$30–$45

SOUNDTRACKS AND THEMES

Children's TV Themes—By Cy Payne and His Orchestra. Contains theme from Star Trek original TV series. 12″ LP album. Contour Records (English). ....$15–$20

Classic Space Themes—By the Birchwood Pops Orchestra. Includes the main theme from Star Trek: The Motion Picture. 12″ LP album. Pickwick Records. ....$10–$15

Close Encounters—Performed by Gene Page and His Orchestra. Contains theme from Star Trek. 12″ LP album. Arista Records. ....$10–$15

Conquistador—Performed by Maynard Ferguson and His Orchestra, 1977. Contains theme from original Star Trek TV. 12″ LP album. Columbia Records. ....$10–$15

Dementia Royale—Compiled by Dr. Demento. Contains Star Trek, a parody of Star Trek by Bobby Pickett and Peter Ferrara. 12″ LP album. Rhino Record. ....$10–$15

Dyn-O-Mite Guitar—Performed by Billy Strange. Contains theme from Star Trek. 12″ LP album. Crescendo Record. ....$10–$15

Fifty Popular TV Themes—Performed by The Bruce Baxter Orchestra. Contains main theme from original Star Trek TV. Two 12″ LP albums. Pick-Wick Records. ....$15–$20

Genesis Project—Two-record album containing new expanded versions not in the original soundtracks of Star Trek II: The Wrath of Khan and Star Trek III: The Search for Spock.

Composed and performed by Craig Huxley. Sonic Atom Spheres.

    Album. ....$20–$30
    Cassette. ....$15–$20

Hustle, The—1976. Performed by Van McCoy and His Orchestra. Contains theme from original Star Trek TV. 12″ LP album. H & L Records. ....$10–$15

Love Theme from Star Trek: The Motion Picture (A Star Beyond Time)—Sung by Shaun Cassidy. 7″ 45 rpm. Warner Bros. Records (promotional record). ....$10–$15

Main Theme from Star Trek: The Motion Picture—Arranged and conducted by Bob James. 7″ 45 rpm. Tappan Zee (Columbia) Records. ....$5–$10

Main Theme from Star Trek: The Motion Picture—Music from the original soundtrack of Star Trek: The Motion Picture. Composed and conducted by Jerry Goldsmith. 7″ 45 rpm. Columbia Records. ....$5–$10

Masterpiece—Performed by Charles Randolph Grean Sounde. Contains theme from Star Trek (original TV). 12″ LP album. Ranwood Records. ....$10–$15

Music from Return of the Jedi and Other Space Hits—Performed by the Odyssey Orchestra. Includes main theme from original Star Trek TV by Alexander Courage. 12″ LP album. Sine Qua Non Records. ....$10–$15

Music from Star Trek and the Black Hole—Disco music performed by Meco Monardo. Casablanca Record. ....$10–$15

Music from the Original Soundtrack, Star Trek: The Motion Picture—Music by Jerry Goldsmith. 12″ LP album. CBS/SONY Record. Japanese Pressing. ....$15–$20

Nadia's Theme—Performed by Lawrence Welk and His Orchestra. Contains theme from original Star Trek TV. Ranwood Records. ....$10–$15

1984—A Space Odyssey—Performed by John Williams and The Boston Pops Orchestra. Includes main theme from original Star Trek TV and main theme from Star Trek: The Motion Picture. 12″ LP album. J & B Records. ....$10–$15

Out of This World—Performed by John Williams and The Boston Pops Orchestra. Includes the main theme from original Star Trek TV and main title from Star Trek: The Motion Picture. Phillips Digital Recording. ....$10–$15

Spaced Out Disco Fever—Contains main theme from original Star Trek TV. 12″ LP album. Wonderland Records. ....$10–$15

Spectacular Space Hits—Performed by The Odyssey Orchestra. Contains theme from original Star Trek TV. 12″ LP album. Sine Qua Non Records. ....$10–$15

Starship—Frank Argus. 1984. 45 rpm. Fan-produced. ....$5–$10

Star Tracks—Performed by The Cincinnati Pops Orchestra, conducted by Erich Kunzel. Contains main theme from original Star Trek TV. Telarc Digital Records. ....$15–$20

Star Trek: Deep Space Nine—Original music from "The Emissary." Crescendo.

    Cassette. ....$10–$12
    CD. ....$20–$25

Star Trek: Generations—Original soundtrack from the movie. Crescendo.

    Cassette. ....$10–$12

    CD. ....$20–$25

Star Trek: The Astral Symphony—Medley of songs from the original soundtracks of movies I–V. Paramount.

    Cassette. ....$10–$12

    CD. ....$20–$25

Star Trek: The Motion Picture—1981. 7″ 45 rpm. Capital Expositions Record. ....$5–$10

Star Trek: The Motion Picture—Music from the original soundtrack. Composed and conducted by Jerry Goldsmith. Digital recording. 12″ LP, CD, or cassette. Columbia Records.

    Album. ....$20–$30

    Cassette. ....$15–$25

    CD. ....$25–$35

Star Trek, Main Theme from the Motion Picture—Contains "A Star Beyond Time" (Love Theme from Star Trek: The Motion Picture) and Star Trek original TV theme. Performed by The Now Sound Orchestra. 12″ LP album. Synthetic Plastics Record. ....$10–$15

Star Trek Volume I: The Cage, and Where No Man Has Gone Before—Original television soundtrack. Music composed and conducted by Alexander Courage. Crescendo Records.

    Album. ....$10–$15

    Cassette. ....$8–$11

    CD. ....$20–$25

NOTE: A picture disk of this album (Kirk and Spock from "Where No Man Has Gone Before" front, transporter scene back) was produced in England by Precision Records & Tapes Ltd. ....$20–$25

Star Trek Volume II: The Doomsday Machine and Amok Time—Original television soundtrack. Music composed and conducted by Sol Kaplan and Gerald Fried. Crescendo Records.

    Album. ....$10–$15

    Cassette. ....$8–$11

    CD. ....$20–$25

Star Trek Volume III: Shore Leave and The Naked Time—Original television soundtrack. Music composed and conducted by Gerald Fried and Alexander Courage. Crescendo Records.

    Cassette. ....$10–$12

    CD. ....$20–$25

Star Trek Volume I: Is There in Truth No Beauty? and Paradise Syndrome—Symphonic suites arranged from original television scores, recorded by the Royal Philharmonic Orchestra. Conducted by Tony Bremner. Label X Record.

    Album. ....$10–$15

    Cassette. ....$10–$12

    CD. ....$20–$25

Star Trek Volume II: I, Mudd, The Enemy Within, Specter of the Gun, and Conscience of the King—Symphonic suites arranged from the original television scores. Recorded by the Royal Philharmonic Orchestra, conducted by Tony Bremner. Label X Record.

    Album. ....$10–$15

    Cassette. ....$10–$12

    CD. ....$20–$25

Star Trek Volume I: Charlie X, The Corbomite Maneuver, Mudd's Women, and The Doomsday Machine—Selected episodes of the Paramount Pictures Corporation Television series by the Royal Philharmonic Orchestra, conducted by Fred Steiner. Varese Sarabande Records.

    Album. ....$10–$15

    Cassette. ....$10–$12

    CD. ....$20–$25

Star Trek Volume II: Mirror, Mirror, By Any Other Name, The Trouble with Tribbles, The Empath—Symphonic suites from the original TV scores. 1986. Varise Sarabande.

    Album. ....$10–$15

    Cassette. ....$10–$12

    CD. ....$20–$25

Star Trek: Voyager Main Title—Three different versions of the theme to the TV series. Crescendo.

    Cassette. ....$8–$10

    CD. ....$10–$15

Star Trek: Voyager—Original music from "Caretaker." Crescendo.

    Cassette. ....$10–$12

    CD. ....$20–$25

Star Trek: 21 Space Hits—Contains theme from original Star Trek TV. 12″ LP album. Music World (Music World, Ltd. New Zealand). ....$15–$20

Star Trek II: The Wrath of Khan—Original motion picture soundtrack. Composed and conducted by James Horner. 12″ LP album. Atlantic records. ....$40–$60

Star Trek II: The Wrath of Khan—Original motion picture soundtrack. Crescendo.

    Cassette. ....$10–$12

    CD. ....$20–$25

Star Trek III: The Search for Spock, The Audio Movie Kit—Kit contains transcripts of "The Movie for Radio" and "Behind the Scenes" narrative regarding the story of the movie. Two audio cassette tapes cover the same material. Two audio cassette tapes and a script in folder. Riches/Rubinstein and Radio, Inc. ....$35–$60

Star Trek III: The Search for Spock—Original motion picture soundtrack. 1984. Music composed and conducted by James Horner. Two 12″ LP albums, CD, or cassette. Capital-EMI.

    Album. ....$25–$45

    Cassette. ....$10–$12

    CD. ....$20–$25

Star Trek III: The Search for Spock—Original motion picture soundtrack. Crescendo.

    Cassette. ....$10–$12

    CD. ....$20–$25

Star Trek IV, The Voyage Home—Soundtrack from the movie. 12″ LP, CD, or cassette. MCA.

Album. ....$15–$20
Cassette. ....$10–$15
CD. ....$20–$25

Star Trek V: The Final Frontier—Movie soundtrack. 12″ LP, CD, or cassette. Epic.

Album. ....$11–$15
Cassette. ....$11–$15
CD. ....$20–$25

Star Trek VI: The Undiscovered Country—Original motion picture soundtrack. MCA.

Cassette. ....$10–$12
CD. ....$18–$20

Star Trek Sound Effects—From the original TV soundtrack. 12″ LP, CD, or cassette. GNP Crescendo.

Album. ....$10–$15
Cassette. ....$10–$12
CD. ....$20–$25

Star Trek: The Next Generation Volume I—Music from the original TV soundtrack. 12″ LP, cassette, or CD. GNP Crescendo.

Album. ....$10–$15
Cassette. ....$10–$12
CD. ....$20–$25

Star Trek: The Next Generation Volume II—Music from "Best of Both Worlds Parts I and II." Crescendo.

Cassette. ....$10–$12
CD. ....$20–$25

Star Trek: The Next Generation Volume III—Music from "Yesterday's Enterprise," "Unification Parts I and II," and "Hollow Pursuits." Crescendo.

Cassette. ....$10–$12
CD. ....$20–$25

Star Wars—Performed by Ferrante and Teicher. 1978. Contains theme from Star Trek TV. 12″ LP album. United Artists Record. ....$15–$20

Themes from E.T. and More—Arranged and conducted by Walter Murphy. Contains main theme from original Star Trek TV. 12″ LP album. MCA Records. ....$10–$15

Theme from Star Trek TV—From the album "Masterpiece," by The Charles Randolph Green Sounde. 7″ 45 rpm. Ranwood Records. ....$5–$10

Theme from Star Trek (Original TV) Greatest Science Fiction Hits—Performed by Neil Norman and His Cosmic Orchestra. 12″ LP album or cassette.

Album. ....$10–$15
Cassette. ....$10–$15

Theme from Star Trek—performed by Tristar Orchestra and Chorus. Produced by John Townsley. 7″ 45 rpm. Tristar Records. ....$5–$10

Theme from Star Trek—Performed by The Jeff Wayne Space Shuttle. Wonderland Records. ....$10–$15

Theme from Star Trek—By Warp Nine. Fan-produced electronically synthesized space music. Record was sold to make money to get Star Trek back on television. 7″ 45 rpm. Privilege Records. ....$5–$10

Theme from Star Trek—Performed by Ferrante and

Teicher. 7″ 45 rpm. From the album "Star Wars." United Artists. 1978. ....$5–$10

Theme from Star Trek—Performed by Meco Monardo from the album "Music From Star Trek and the Black Hole." 7″ 45 rpm. Casablanca Records. ....$5–$10

Theme from Star Trek—Performed by Gene Page and His Orchestra. From the album "Close Encounters." 7″ 45 rpm. Arista Records. ....$5–$10

Theme from Star Trek—Performed by Billy Strange. From the album "Dyn-O-Mite Guitar." 7″ 45 rpm. Crescendo Records. ....$5–$10

Theme from Star Trek: The Motion Picture—Greatest Science Fiction Hits II. Performed by Neil Norman and His Cosmic Orchestra. 12″ LP album. Also available on cassette. Crescendo Records. ....$10–$15

Theme from Star Trek II: The Wrath of Khan—Performed by James Horner and Orchestra. 1982. From the original soundtrack, Star Trek II: The Wrath of Khan. 7″ 45 rpm. Atlantic Records. ....$10–$15

Theme from Star Trek III—By James Horner. From the original soundtrack "Star Trek III: The Search for Spock." 7″ 45 rpm. Capitol Records. ....$8–$12

Theme Scene, The—Performed by Henri Mancini and His Orchestra. Contains theme from original Star Trek TV. 12″ LP album. Victor Records. ....$10–$15

Time Warp—Erich Kunzel and The Cincinnati Pops Orchestra. Includes music from Star Trek: The Motion Picture and the original TV show. CD. 1984. Telarc. ....$18–$20

TV Themes—Performed by the Ventures. Contains theme from Star Trek TV. 12″ LP album. United Artists Records. ... .$10–$15

Very Together—Performed by Deodata. Contains main theme from Star Trek TV. 12″ LP album. 1976. MCA Records. ....$10–$15

STORY RECORDS

Star Trek: The Motion Picture—A read-along adventure record with 24-page color illustrated book. 7″ 33⅓ rpm. Also available on cassette. Buena Vista Records.

Album. ....$10–$15
Cassette. ....$8–$10

Star Trek—Book and record set. Contains adventure story Passage to Moauv. 7″ 45 rpm record and 20-page illustrated book. Two different covers—color photo of Spock, Kirk, and the Enterprise (Peter Pan, 1979), and (earlier edition) drawing of Kirk and Spock and alien animal (Power Records, 1975). ....$5–$10

Star Trek—Book and record set. Contains adventure story The Crier in Emptiness. 7″ 45 rpm record and 20-page full-color illustrated book. Two different covers—color photo of Kirk, Spock, and McCoy (Peter Pan, 1979, #26), and (earlier edition) a drawing of Kirk, Spock, and Uhura (Power Records, 1975). ....$5–$10

Star Trek—Book and records set. Contains adventure story Dinosaur Planet. 7″ 45 rpm record and 20-page full-color illustrated book. Peter Pan Records. ....$5–$10

Star Trek—Book and record set. Contains adventure story The Robot Masters. 7″ 45 rpm record and 20-page full-color illustrated book. Peter Pan Records. ....$5–$10

Star Trek—Book and record set. Contains two adventure stories, A Mirror for Futility and The Time Stealer. 12″ LP album and 16-page full-color comic book. Power Records. (These two adventure stories are also recorded on Peter Pan Records.). ....
....$5–$10

Star Trek—Book and record set. Contains two adventure stories, The Crier in Emptiness and Passage to Moauv. 12″ LP album and 16-page full-color comic book. Peter Pan Records. (These two adventure stories are also recorded on Power Records.). ....$5–$10

Star Trek—"Five incredible all-new action adventures." The Time Stealer, In Vino Veritas, To Starve a Fleaver, Dinosaur Planet, and Passage to Moauv. 12″ LP album. Peter Pan Records. ....$5–$10

Star Trek—"Original stories for children." Inspired by Star Trek, In Vino Veritas. 7″ 45 rpm. Power Records. ....$3–$5

Star Trek—"Original stories for children." Inspired by Star Trek, The Human Factor. 7″ 45 rpm. Peter Pan Records. ....
....$3–$5

Star Trek—"Original stories for children." Inspired by Star Trek, The Time Stealer. 7″ 45 rpm. Power Records. ....
....$3–$5

Star Trek—"Original stories for children." Inspired by Star Trek, To Starve a Fleaver. 7″ 45 rpm. Power Records. ....
....$3–$5

Star Trek—"Three exciting new complete stories." Passage to Moauv, In Vito Veritas, and The Crier in Emptiness. 12″ LP album. Power Records. (These stories are also recorded on Peter Pan Records.). ....$5–$10

Star Trek—"Four exciting all-new action adventure stories." The Time Stealer, To Starve a Fleaver, The Logistics of Stampede, and a Mirror of Futility. 12″ LP album. Power Records. (This album appears in two different jackets.). ....
....$5–$10

Star Trek—"Four exciting all-new action adventure stories." The Man Who Trained Meteors, The Robot Masters, Dinosaur Planet, and The Human Factor. 12″ LP album. Peter Pan Records. ....$5–$10

Star Trek and Other Movies Songs—1978. Contains original Star Trek television theme along with other TV (not movie as the title implies) themes. Cover shows generic spaceship with planet in background. Kid Stuff Records. ......
....$5–$10

Star Trek II: The Wrath of Khan—A read-along adventure record with 25-page full-color illustrated book. 7″ 33⅓ rpm. Buena Vista Records. ....$10–$15

Star Trek III: The Search for Spock—A read-along adventure record with 24-page full-color illustrated book. 7″ 33⅓ rpm. Also available on cassette. Buena Vista Records.
    Album. ....$10–$15
    Cassette. ....$8–$10

Star Trek IV: The Voyage Home—A read-along adventure record with 24-page full-color illustrated book. 7″ 33⅓ rpm. Also available on cassette. Buena Vista Records.
    Album. ....$10–$15
    Cassette. ....$8–$10

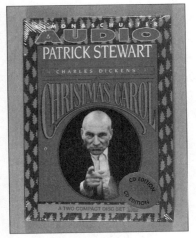

Patrick Stewart narrates "A Christmas Carol"

Golden Throats CD

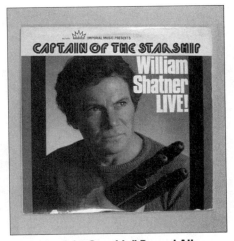

"Captain of the Starship" Record Album

Star Trek: The Motion Picture Soundtrack

Crescendo Star Trek: Volume I Music CD

Star Trek Book and Record LP Album Set

SCHOOL AND OFFICE SUPPLIES

Though in the past items in this section have not gotten much serious attention from collectors, the recent trend toward manufacturing products aimed specifically at the collector market has generated some potentially good future collectibles that fit into this category. It only requires a little thought on the part of the individual to determine which items are likely to appreciate in value. As in many categories, more complex, harder to reproduce items are generally the most promising investments for the future.

INVESTMENT POTENTIAL
Fair.

CARE
Paper items requiring protection from moisture and wear are best kept stored in plastic collector bags. Protection from sunlight is also recommended to keep paper items from fading or yellowing. Most other items are fairly durable, but in the few cases where decorative packaging is provided, it should be preserved. Do not throw away boxes or open blister-carded items.

SECTION NOTES
Because they are extremely easy to produce (and therefore virtually worthless as collectibles), the large volume of unlicensed and fan-made products will be omitted from this section. Types of items in this category include writing paper, note cards, book covers, business cards, portfolios, stickers, bookmarks, etc.—almost any one- or two-color printed paper or plastic product that can be made quickly and inexpensively. Section is organized alphabetically by item.

Address Book—Antioch. 1994. 6½″ × 4¾″ hardbound book with color photos of Star Trek: The Next Generation crew and ship, plus logo and "Addresses" on cover. Interior pages alphabetically indexed. ....$5–$7
Address/Telephone Books—Reed Productions. Small booklets with photo covers.

Original TV Series, 1983 Printing.
    Bridge Crew. ....$5–$8
    Kirk and Spock in Transporter. ....$5–$8
Original TV Series, 1989 Printing.
    Kirk. ....$5–$8
    Kirk and Spock in Transporter. ....$5–$8
    Kirk, Spock, and Enterprise Modes. ....$5–$8
Star Trek V: The Final Frontier, 1989.
    Bridge Crew. ....$5–$8
    Enterprise. ....$5–$8
    Kirk and Spock. ....$5–$8
    Kirk, Spock, McCoy, and Sybok. ....$5–$8
Album—Antioch. 1993. Expandable post-bound notebook approx. 12″ × 15″ with color photo cover of McCoy, Kirk, and Spock on transporter with smaller inset photo of original Enterprise. ....$20–$25
Attache Case—QVC. 1995. Soft-sided black leather case approx. 12″ × 15″. Detachable shoulder strap. Two-section side pocket with "Star Trek: Deep Space Nine" embroidered in gold and silver thread. ....$100–$150
Bookend—Willits. 1993. Cast resin approx. 8¾″ high. Three-dimensional hand-painted replica of original Enterprise on a space backdrop with swirling galaxy motif. Box has photo of product with "Star Trek" above in gold. ....
....$60–$70
Bookend—Willits. 1993. Three-dimensional, gold-plated original Enterprise replica on black marble backing with gold command insignia above and "Star Trek" below on base. Box has photo of product and "Star Trek" above in gold. $40–$50
Bookmarks—A.H. Prismatic (British). 1992/93. Silver diffraction hologram bookmarks approx. 6¼″ long with slightly pointed tops. Each has three different scenes in a vertical format. Three variations in scenes for each series.
    Star Trek (Original Series). ....$2–$4
    Star Trek: The Next Generation. ....$2–$4
    Star Trek: Deep Space Nine. ....$2–$4
Bookmark—Antioch. 1991. Gift Enclosure Bookmark.

Horizontal color photo of Enterprise NCC 1701-D with "To boldly go where no one has gone before" in upper corner and logo in lower corner. "To" and "From" spaces on back. Came with small envelope. ....$2–$4

Bookmark—One Stop Posters. 1987. Color photo of Next Generation Enterprise and logo at top. "Explore new worlds with books!" at bottom. 7″ long. ....$1–$3

Bookmarks—Antioch. 1993/96. Thin plastic, approx. 6″ long. Vertical format (except where noted), color photos from various Star Trek productions. Hole at top for hanging on display. All have tassels in assorted colors.

Early Original Series, full figure with logo below.
    Kirk. ....$1–$3
    Spock. ....$1–$3
Later Original Series, short saying and logo below photo.
    Enterprise. ....$1–$3
    McCoy. ....$1–$3
    Scotty. ....$1–$3
    Uhura. ....$1–$3
Early Star Trek: The Next Generation, small inset photo of Enterprise and logo below photo.
    Data. ....$1–$3
    Dr. Crusher. ....$1–$3
    Enterprise (Horizontal format, no inset photo). ...$1–$3
    Geordi. ....$1–$3
    Picard. ....$1–$3
    Riker. ....$1–$3
    Troi. ....$1–$3
    Worf. ....$1–$3
Later Star Trek: The Next Generation, short quote and logo below photo.
    Data as Sherlock Holmes. ....$1–$3
    Guinan. ....$1–$3
    Picard as Locutus. ....$1–$3
    "Q." ....$1–$3
    Wesley Crusher. ....$1–$3
Star Trek: Deep Space Nine, small inset photo of space station and logo below photo.
    Bashir. ....$1–$3
    Dax. ....$1–$3
    Group. ....$1–$3
    Jake Sisko. ....$1–$3
    Kira. ....$1–$3
    O'Brien. ....$1–$3
    Quark. ....$1–$3
    Sisko. ....$1–$3
Star Trek: Generations, character above movie logo.
    Kirk. ....$1–$3
    Picard. ....$1–$3
Star Trek: Generations, die-cut bookmarks.
    Kirk. ....$1–$3
    Lursa. ....$1–$3
    Picard. ....$1–$3
    Soran. ....$1–$3
Star Trek: Voyager, small inset photo of ship and logo below photo

    Capt. Janeway. ....$1–$3
    Chakotay. ....$1–$3
    Kes. ....$1–$3
    Kim. ....$1–$3
    Neelix. ....$1–$3
    Paris. ....$1–$3
    Torres. ....$1–$3
    Tuvok. ....$1–$3
Voyager Ship, horizontal artwork with logo in lower corner.
........................$1–$3

Bookplates—Antioch. 1991. Color photo of original Enterprise in space with logo above and space for name below. Box of 30 3″ × 4″ self-sticking bookplates. Packaged in black and gold box with box parts nested and shrink-wrapped to display product. ....$5–$6

Bookplates—Antioch. 1991. Color photo of Next Generation crew on bridge with logo above and space for name below. Box of 30 3″ × 4″ self-sticking bookplates. Packaged in black and gold box with box parts nested and shrink-wrapped to display product. ....$5–$6

Bookplates—Antioch. 1994. Blue, white, and gold command insignia/USS Enterprise NCC-1701 emblem on black background with "Star Trek" in upper corner and space for name below. Box of 30 3″ × 4″ self-sticking bookplates. Packaged in black and gold box with box parts nested and shrink-wrapped to display product. ....$5–$6

Checkbook Cover—Anthony Grandio Co. 1995. Regular pocket-size checkbook cover with swirl pattern and foil-stamped Star Trek: The Next Generation logo and generalized Star Trek command logo on cover. ....$7–$10

Checkbook Cover—Anthony Grandio Co. 1996. Regular pocket-size checkbook cover with color photo of Enterprise-D. ....$5–$10

Checkbook Cover—Lincoln Enterprises. Plush maroon vinyl checkbook/calculator. Small gold-plated original TV command symbol on outside lower left corner. ....$20–$25

Checkbook (Notebook/Address Book) Cover—Reed Production. 1990. Black and white photo of original cast inserted into standard-size clear plastic checkbook cover. ....$3–$4

Checkbook (Notebook/Address Book) Covers—Reed Productions. 1993. Standard-size clear plastic checkbook cover with color photo inserts on cover.
    Enterprise (Original), orbiting planet. ....$5–$8
    Enterprise (Original), and introductory monologue. ....
    ....$5–$8
    Kirk, McCoy, and Spock (Original Series). ....$5–$8
    Spock from "Amok Time" (Vulcan Salute). ....$5–$8

Checks—Anthony Grandio Co. 1993. Classic Star Trek checks. Regular-size bank checks with color photos from the original Star Trek series on face of checks. Four different photos alternate in check pad: Enterprise; Spock; Kirk and Spock; Kirk, McCoy, and Scotty. Price for box of 200 checks. ....$15–$20

Checks—Anthony Grandio Co. 1996. Star Trek: The Next Generation checks. Regular-size bank checks with eight rotating color photo scenes from show per check pad. Price for box of 200 checks. ....$15–$20

Checks—Anthony Grandio Co. 1995. Star Trek: The Next Generation checks. Regular-size bank checks with one-color photo of Enterprise on face. Price for box of 200 checks. ....$15–$20

Checks—Anthony Grandio Co. 1993. United Federation of Planet checks. Regular-size band checks with one-color movie-style UFP emblem on face. Price for box of 200 checks. ....$15–$20

Computer Disk Holder—Brainworks. 1995. Star Trek: The Next Generation. Blue shuttlecraft replica with pink accents. Shuttle is hollowed out to hold disks. ....$12–$15

Computer Keyboard—Brainworks. 1995. Star Trek: The Next Generation. Blue with pink accents and Next Generation–style command insignia below keys. Rounded top and bottom. PC or Mac. ....$80–$90

Computer Mask—Brainworks. 1995. Star Trek: The Next Generation. Decorative frame for computer screen. Blue with pink accents. Next Generation Enterprise above and Next Generation–style command insignia below in relief. ....$20–$30

Computer Mouse and Mousepad—Brainworks. 1995. Star Trek: The Next Generation. Rounded blue dual button IBM mouse with pink buttons. Next Generation–style command symbol at base. Mousepad is pink and silver insignia-shaped. ....$30–$40

Credit Cards—In use since 1989. Various banks. Standard Visa or MasterCards with color photos of the Enterprise on front. Price is for defunct card (sans value of card holder's account).

    Enterprise NCC 1701 (Original TV Series). ....$10–$15
    Enterprise NCC 1701-D. ....$10–$15

Desk Set—Tel Rad. 1975. Gray plastic pen decorated with original TV Enterprise. Stand/memo holder has nameplate. ....$15–$20

Desk Set—Rarities Mint. 1990. Marble base with gold-plated silver Enterprise (original TV) clock coin. Includes gold-plated pen. Numbered limited edition. ....$100–$125

Erasers—Diener Industries. 1983. Six different character heads and ships from Star Trek III. Assorted colors. Came blister-packed on color header card with Star Trek III logo.

    Enterprise. ....$2–$4
    Excelsior. ....$2–$4
    Kirk. ....$2–$4
    Kruge. ....$2–$4
    McCoy. ....$2–$4
    Spock. ....$2–$4

Journals—Antioch. 1994/95. Hardbound notebooks approx. 5½″ × 8½″ with 160 lined pages for entries. All have either color photos or artwork from their respective Star Trek productions. Were often sold shrink-wrapped with a complimentary Star Trek bookmark.

    Star Trek (Original), Spock (photo). ....$8–$10
    Star Trek: The Next Generation, Enterprise (photo). ....$8–$10
    Star Trek: Deep Space Nine, space station (photo). ....$8–$10

Star Trek: Voyager, ship (artwork). ....$8–$10
Star Trek: Voyager, Ship's Log, PADD design displaying artwork of ship. ....$8–$10

Journals—Antioch. 1995. Star Trek: Voyager mini-journals. Similar to Antioch's larger journals, with color photos and artwork, but in a smaller (approx. 4½″ × 6″), 64-page format.

    Personnel Log, PADD design with photos of crew. ....$4–$6
    Ship (artwork). ....$5–$6

Journals—Longmeadow Press. 1992. Black hardbound notebooks approx. 8½″ × 5½″ with gold or silver embossed designs on binder. Inside front and back covers have black and white photos of appropriate crew. Interiors have lined pages with small ship silhouettes in corners.

    Star Trek Captain's Log Book, original Enterprise. ....$4–$8
    Star Trek Quote Journal, original Enterprise, and interior black and white photos and quote every other page. ....$4–$8
    Star Trek Ship's Log Book, gold original Enterprise. ....$4–$8
    Star Trek: The Next Generation Data's Log Book, gold Next Generation Enterprise. ....$4–$8

Laser Pointer—Mek-Tek. 1996. Shaped like handle version Next Generation phaser. Sound effects with on/off option. Packaged in velvet case with Certificate of Authenticity. ....$135–$150

Letter Holder—Applause. 1994. Rectangular 4″ × 4¾″ black plastic base with starfield design and "USS Enterprise" on one side and Star Trek: The Next Generation logo on other. Attached black wire spiral to hold letters has extension to support silver plastic Next Generation Enterprise, approx. 4½″ long. Limited to 9000 pieces. ....$12–$15

Memo Boards—Antioch. 1994/95. Wipe-off rectangular thin plastic memo boards approx. 7½″ × 11¼″. Each is decorated with a color photo/photos and has a hole at top for hanging. Pens and clip on pen holders, designed to be attached to slot in side of board, are included.

    Star Trek: The Next Generation, Enterprise. ....$4–$6
    Star Trek: Deep Space Nine, space station and crew. ....$4–$6
    Star Trek: Voyager, overall design resembles PADD. ....$4–$6
    Star Trek: Generations, Enterprise and logo at top. ....$4–$6

Mousepads—Moustrak. 1992–1995. Color photos or artwork on regular computer mousepads. All but one are 8½″ × 11″ in size. The exception (Enterprise-A and Exploding Planet) is 10½″ square to accommodate artwork.

    Balok's Puppet (Photo). ....$15–$20
    Deep Space Nine Space Station (Photo). ....$15–$20
    Enterprise 1701-A and Excelsior (Photo). ....$15–$20
    Enterprise 1701-A and Exploding Planet (Artwork). ....$15–$20
    Enterprise 1701-D (Artwork). ....$15–$20
    Kirk with Tribbles (Photo). ....$15–$20

Klingon Bird-of-Prey (Photo). ....$15–$20
Star Trek: Generations Movie Poster Artwork. ....
....$15–$20
Star Trek: The Next Generation Crew (Artwork). ....
....$15–$20
Three Enterprises (Artwork). ....$15–$20

Nameplates—One Stop Posters. 1988. Color photo of Next Generation Enterprise with words "Star Trek" below. Packaged in plastic bag of 24 with blue and yellow header. ....
....$3–$5

Notebook—Reed. 1989. 4″ × 6″ spiral-bound with photo cover of bridge crew from original TV series. ....$4–$6

Notebooks—Reed. 1983. 4″ × 6″ spiral-bound with photo covers from original TV series.

Kirk and Spock. ....$4–$8
Kirk, Spock, and Enterprise Model. ....$4–$8

Notecards—Portico. 1994. Star Trek: The Next Generation. Color photo covers. Cards open up with UFP logo on left. Right side is blank. Assorted characters and ships. Price each.
....$3–$5

Notepad Holder—Applause. 1994. 4″ × 5″ rectangular black plastic tray with overall starfield design. Circular tab at top has command insignia and "Captain's Log." Stem to left of tab holds silver plastic Next Generation Enterprise approx. 4¹⁄₂″ long. Hole at right of tab holds pen. Plain white note paper sheets and plain black ballpoint pen included. Limited to 9000 pieces. ....$12–$15

Notepads—Applause. 1994. Die-cut, approx. 4″ × 5¹⁄₂″, with color logos in corner, half-tone color background photos, and magnetic strips on back.

Deep Space Nine (Space Station Photo). ....$4–$6
Star Trek (Original Enterprise). ....$4–$6
Star Trek: The Next Generation (Enterprise 1701-D). ....
....$4–$6

Notepads—Creation. 1994. Rectangular 5¹⁄₂″ × 8¹⁄₂″ gummed white paper notepads with black line art or (in the case of photo designs) black titles and logo with sepia half-tone character photos. Appropriate logo at bottom of each design.

Captain's Log, Next Generation command insignia. ....
....$2–4
From the Bridge of the Enterprise, Next Generation ship.
....$2–4
From the Desk of Capt. James T. Kirk, photo. $2–4
From the Desk of Capt. Jean-Luc Picard, photo. ....
....$2–4
From the Desk of Science Officer Spock, photo. ....
....$2–4
Hailing Frequencies Open, Uhura (art). $2–4
Live Long and Prosper, Vulcan salute. $2–4
PADD, overall design simulating device (no logo). ....
....$2–4
Some Advice From Counselor Troi, photo. $2–4
Starfleet Academy, Starfleet emblem. $2–4
Starfleet Command, small command insignia. $2–4
United Federation of Planets, Next Generation UFP insignia.
....$2–4

Vulcan Science Academy, overall IDIC design. $2–4

Pen—Fisher. 1992. Star Trek Space Pen. Ordinary looking click ballpoint pen with lid with clip. Designed to write under extreme conditions, including underwater and weightlessness. "Star Trek" on barrel. Comes in assorted colors with gold or silver lid and trim. Comes blister-packed on hanging card with photo of original Enterprise with logo above and product information below. ....$5–$8

Pen—Fisher. 1992. Star Trek 25th anniversary pen. Silver ballpoint with red enameled original-style insignia with "Star Trek" on clip and original Enterprise, Earth, and stars engraved in gold on barrel. Came packaged embedded in velveteen base covered with clear plastic cover with logo in gold at top. ....$40–$50

Pen—Fisher. 1993. Star Trek: The Next Generation Black Bullet Pen. Two-piece ballpoint (bottom and lid). Flat black barrel 4″ long when closed with gold and silver insignia emblem on lid. Comes packaged in black plastic case with "Fisher Space Pen" on lid and blue and white cardboard slipcase printed with Star Trek: The Next Generation logo and ship. .....
....$30–$40

Pen—Fisher. 1993. Star Trek: The Next Generation Chrome Bullet Pen. Two-piece ballpoint (bottom and lid). Silver barrel 4″ long when closed with "Star Trek: The Next Generation" etched on lid. Packaging is the same as black bullet pen above. ....$30–$40

Pen—Fisher. 1994. Star Trek: The Next Generation Official Crew Pen. Flat, black, click ballpoint with "For Official Use Only" and "USS Enterprise NCC-1701-D" on barrel. Small insignia emblems on clip and button. Comes packaged in clear plastic tube with label and instructions inserted around pen. ....
....$15–$20

Pen—Fisher. 1996. Star Trek: 30 Years Commemorative Anniversary Pen. Chrome two-piece bullet pen with official 30th anniversary logo embossed in gold on the barrel. Comes packaged in black plastic box inside of cardboard slipcase with 30th anniversary logo in gold and color photo of Enterprise below. ....$30–$40

Pen—Rainbow Symphony. 1993. Standard nonretractable ballpoint with black plastic clip cap. "Star Trek: The Next Generation" on silver, gold, or copper-colored holographic foil with "Star Trek" background pattern. ....$3–$4

Pen—Rainbow Symphony. 1993. Two-piece ballpoint with both bottom and clip on lid covered in gold, silver, or copper-colored holographic foil with "Star Trek" background pattern.
....$4–$6

Pen—Smithsonian. 1979. Floater pen containing Enterprise. From Air and Space Museum gift shop. ....$5–$10

Pens—Creation. 1992/94. Floater pens. Ballpoint pens approx. 5″ long. Barrel is half opaque white or black plastic and half clear plastic containing insert with appropriate logo on one side and space scene on other side, liquid and "floating" ship. Pen lid has key ring attachment.

Deep Space Nine Space Station. ....$5–$7
Enterprise 1701. ....$5–$7
Enterprise 1701-A. ....$5–$7

Enterprise 1701-D. ....$5–$7
Klingon Bird-of-Prey. ....$5–$7
Romulan Warbird. ....$5–$7

Pen Set—Fisher. 1994. Plastic stand approx. 7½″ tall designed to resemble a transporter platform. Black and white circular base with "Star Trek: The Next Generation" in silver on front and button which produced transporter sound. Clear plastic back holds up circular black plastic canopy with gold and silver command insignia inset in top. Magnet in canopy allows pen placed on stand to "float." Accompanying black ballpoint pen has "For Official Use Only" and "USS Enterprise NCC-1701-D" on barrel, and small command insignias on clip and top of button. White cardboard box with black line drawing of product on front. ....$50–$60

Pencil—Lincoln Enterprises. Blue with star design and "Star Trek Lives" in gold. ....$1–$2

Pencil Cup—Applause. 1994. Circular black plastic cup approx. 4½″ high. Overall starfield design with command insignia and "Star Trek: The Next Generation" on front. Silver plastic Next Generation Enterprise approx. 2″ long attached to base at side of cup. Limited to 9000 pieces. ....$12–$15

Pencils—Applause. 1994. Black pencil topped with a color plastic ship approx. 2″ long attached with a stationary horizontal arm. Two different.

Enterprise NCC 1701-D. ....$3–$4
Romulan Warbird. ....$3–$4

Pencils—Hamilton. 1992. Blue pencil with star design and logo topped with red plastic ringed planet. Color plastic ship approx. 1½″ long "orbits" planet on thin wire. Two different.

Enterprise (Original). ....$4–$5
Enterprise 1701-D. ....$4–$5

Pencils—Rainbow Symphony. 1993. Standard eraser-tipped lead pencils wrapped in holographic foil with black printing. Variations include stars or "Star Trek" background design. Silver, gold, or copper-colored foil and regular or thick pencils.

"Engineering," with original engineering emblem. ....
....$1–$3
"Star Trek: The Next Generation." ....$1–$3
"Star Trek," with universal log. ....$1–$3
"Star Trek VI," logo. ....$1–$3
"USS Enterprise NCC-1701-D," with emblem. ....$1–$3

Photo Album—Antioch. 1996. 6″ × 6½″ hardback two-ring looseleaf binder decorated with sepia photo collage of characters from all forms of Star Trek and 30th anniversary logo. Pages for 60 regular-size photos. ....$6–$10

Pocket Address Books (Locator Logs)—Antioch. 1991/93. 3½″ × 6¼″ staple-bound booklets with color photo covers and alphabetized interiors designed for addresses.

Deep Space Nine Space Station. ....$1–$3
Next Generation Enterprise. ....$1–$3
Spock on Transporter Pad (Original Series). ....$1–$3

Pocket Notebooks (Personal Logs)—Antioch. 1991/93. Same size and format as address books above but with interiors designed for notes.

Deep Space Nine Space Station. ....$1–$3
Kirk on Transporter Pad (Original Series). ....$1–$3

Next Generation Enterprise. ....$1–$3

Post-It-Pad—Shoebox Greetings (Hallmark). 1992. Forty-sheet pad of 3″ × 4″ white post-its with color photo of McCoy from original TV series at side. "Dammit, Jim! I'm a doctor, not an answering service!" ....$2–$4

Rubber Stamps—Aviva. 1979. White or blue plastic two-piece cylinders. Top is stamp, bottom is ink pad. Paper decal shows design. Came blister-packed on header card with Star Trek: The Motion Picture logo and small inset picture of Spock. Four different.

Enterprise. ....$10–$15
Kirk. ....$10–$15
Spock. ....$10–$15
Vulcan Salute. ....$10–$15

Rubber Stamps—Stamp Oasis. 1991/93. Stamps are affixed to bottom of a block of wood covered with a decal that has a color representation of the stamp.

Crew (Star Trek Original TV Series).

Chekov. ....$7–$10
Kirk. ....$7–$10
McCoy. ....$7–$10
Scotty. ....$7–$10
Spock. ....$7–$10
Sulu. ....$7–$10
Uhura. ....$7–$10

Enterprise (Original). ....$7–$10
Enterprise NCC-1701-D. ....$8–$12
"To Boldly Go . . . ," with NG Enterprise and command emblem. ....$8–$12
"Starfleet Communique Stardate," with Starfleet Academy emblem. ....$8–$12
Twenty-Fifth Anniversary Logo. ....$7–$10

Rubber Stamp Sets—Stamp Oasis. 1991/93. Several stamps to each set. Shrink-wrapped into square or rectangular plastic boxes with insert sheet depicting color representations of the stamps in the set.

Klingons, warrior, Bird-of-Prey, symbol, Klingon script, and "It is Better to Die on Your Feet Than Live on Your Knees." ....$9–$12
Star Trek (Original) Crew, Kirk, Spock, McCoy, Enterprise, command insignia, stars, and planets. ....
....$15–$20
Star Trek: The Next Generation Crew (Large Set), Riker, Picard, Data, Worf, Stars, Enterprise, and UFP seal. ....
....$15–$20
Star Trek: The Next Generation Crew (Small Set), Dr. Crusher, Geordi, Guinan, and Enterprise (top view). ....
....$9–$12
Trek Talk, movie Enterprise, "Red Alert! Shields at Maximum," "Warp Factor 9!," and "From the Bridge of the USS Enterprise." ....$9–$12

Sketchbooks—Antioch. 1993/94. Hardback books with 144 quadrille ruled pages approx. 8½″ × 11″. Color photos on cover.

Star Trek: The Next Generation (Enterprise). ....
....$10–$15
Star Trek: Deep Space Nine (Space Station). ....$10–$15

Stationery—Lincoln Enterprises.

Original Star Trek TV Stationery, top has black Enterprise and Star Trek logo on lined blue background.

    Envelopes (15). ....$5–$10
    Letter Size (15). ....$5–$10
    Memo Pad. ....$2–$4

Star Trek: The Motion Picture, blue movie Enterprise on light blue star background.

    Envelopes (15). ....$5–$10
    Letter Size (15). ....$5–$10
    Memo Pad. ....$2–$4

Star Trek III: The Search for Spock, standard logo with small silhouette of Enterprise above words.

    Envelopes (15). ....$5–$10
    Letter Size (15). ....$5–$10
    Memo Pad. ....$2–$4

Star Trek: The Next Generation, publicity memo, logo on light blue background.

    Envelopes (15). ....$5–$10
    Letter Size (15). ....$5–$10
    Memo Pad. ....$2–$4

Star Trek: The Next Generation, logo over spiral galaxy design on dark blue.

    Envelopes (15). ....$5–$10
    Letter Size (15). ....$5–$10
    Memo Pad. ....$2–$4

Telephone Cards—Mercurycard (British). 1995. Rectangular, horizontal format plastic cards with color photo on face and either original Star Trek or Next Generation logo in upper corner.

Original TV Series.

    Chekov. ....$15–$30
    Enterprise. ....$15–$30
    Kirk. ....$15–$30
    Klingon Ship. ....$15–$30
    McCoy. ....$15–$30
    Rand. ....$15–$30
    Scotty. ....$15–$30
    Spock. ....$15–$30
    Sulu. ....$15–$30
    Uhura. ....$15–$30

Star Trek: The Next Generation.

    Borg. ....$15–$30
    Borg Ship. ....$15–$30
    Cardassians. ....$15–$30
    Data. ....$15–$30
    Dr. Crusher. ....$15–$30
    Enterprise. ....$15–$30
    Ferengi. ....$15–$30
    Ferengi Ship. ....$15–$30
    Geordi. ....$15–$30
    Guinan. ....$15–$30
    Klingon. ....$15–$30
    Klingon Ship. ....$15–$30
    Picard. ....$15–$30
    "Q." ....$15–$30
    Riker. ....$15–$30

    Romulan. ....$15–$30
    Romulan Ship. ....$15–$30
    Shuttlepod. ....$15–$30
    Troi. ....$15–$30
    Worf. ....$15–$30

Telephone Cards—TEC Card (Future Call). 1994. Rectangular plastic cards approx. 2¼″ × 3½″ in size with color photos from various Star Trek productions on face. Cards are issued in 10 "unit" increments which entitle the card holder to five units of long distance telephone service and five units of pre-recorded talk time with Star Trek personalities. Though prices are for individual cards, originally only sets could be purchased from the manufacturer. Four different sets.

Star Trek Classic (Original TV Series).

    Enterprise. ....$15–$20
    Kirk. ....$15–$20
    McCoy. ....$15–$20
    Spock. ....$15–$20

Star Trek: Generations, movie logo borders each card.

    Data. ....$15–$20
    Chekov, Kirk, and Scott. ....$15–$20
    Enterprise. ....$15–$20
    Enterprise, firing phasers. ....$15–$20
    Excelsior. ....$15–$20
    Kirk, dying. ....$15–$20
    Kirk and Picard. ....$15–$20
    Kirk and Picard, on horseback. ....$15–$20
    Klingon Bird-of-Prey. ....$15–$20
    Lursa and B'Etor. ....$15–$20
    Nexus Effect, Soran in foreground. ....$15–$20
    Soran. ....$15–$20
    Worf. ....$15–$20

Star Trek: The Next Generation.

    Data. ....$15–$20
    Enterprise. ....$15–$20
    Picard. ....$15–$20
    Riker. ....$15–$20

Star Trek: Voyager.

    Chakotay. ....$15–$20
    Janeway. ....$15–$20
    Tuvok. ....$15–$20
    Voyager. ....$15–$20

Telephone Cards—TEC Card. 1995. Collector's Edition Entertainment Calling Cards. Unlike this company's earlier series, cards are good only for the info talk features. Cards are issued in 10 "unit" increments and come blister-carded on color cardboard header. All include bonus card good for three units. Cards picture ship applicable to series. Bonus cards have small pictures of all four ships.

Star Trek (Original). ....$10–$15
Star Trek: Deep Space Nine (Space Station). ....$10–$15
Star Trek: The Next Generation. ....$10–$15
Star Trek: Voyager. ....$10–$15

Wallet Cards—Antioch. 1994–1996. Plastic-coated cards designed to fit into standard-size wallet compartments. Cards have color photo or artwork on front and text on reverse.

Star Trek (Original).
    Command Insignia. ....$1–$2
    Engineering Insignia. ....$1–$2
    Klingon Symbol. ....$1–$2
    Sciences Insignia. ....$1–$2
    Vulcan IDIC. ....$1–$2
Star Trek: The Next Generation.
    Bridge Pass (Crew). ....$1–$2
    Crew Pass (Enterprise). ....$1–$2
    Enterprise. ....$1–$2
    Romulan Symbol. ....$1–$2
Star Trek: Deep Space Nine.
    Ops Pass (Crew). ....$1–$2
    Quark's Bar Gold Card. ....$1–$2
    Runabout Access. ....$1–$2
    Space Station Visa. ....$1–$2
Star Trek: Generations.
    Enterprise-D. ....$1–$2
    Klingon Bird-of-Prey. ....$1–$2
    Logo. ....$1–$2
    Picard. ....$1–$2

Star Trek: Voyager.
    Starfleet Officer (Command Insignia). ....$1–$2
    Voyager (Ship). ....$1–$2
Wallet Cards—Portico (British). 1994. Standard-size plasticized wallet cards with color photos of Star Trek: The Next Generation and Star Trek: Generations subjects.
    Data. ....$2–$3
    Deanna Troi. ....$2–$3
    Dr. Crusher. ....$2–$3
    Enterprise-D. ....$2–$3
    Ferengi. ....$2–$3
    Ferengi Ship. ....$2–$3
    Geordi La Forge. ....$2–$3
    Guinan. ....$2–$3
    Hugh Borg. ....$2–$3
    Locutus. ....$2–$3
    Picard. ....$2–$3
    Picard, 18th-century outfit. ....$2–$3
    Riker. ....$2–$3
    Romulan Warbird. ....$2–$3
    Worf. ....$2–$3

Antioch Book Marks

Antioch Memo Boards

Fischer 30th Anniversary Bullet Pen

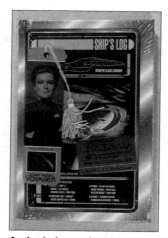

Antioch 30th Anniversary Photo Album

Antioch Journal with Bookmark

Aviva *Star Trek: The Motion Picture* Rubber Stamp

Antioch Wallet Cards

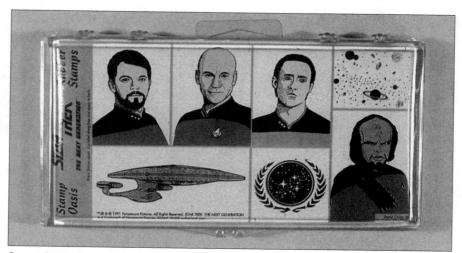

Stamp Oasis Rubber Stamp Set

SCRIPTS

Scripts are one of the most popular items among collectors and one of the hardest to authenticate. Unless you have positive proof to the contrary, you should assume the script is a copy, not an original. All scripts these days, including the ones the actors use, are photocopies. Different color pages, sometimes used for revisions, can be a clue, though by no means a conclusive one to authenticity. People using scripts on the set often write notes in the margin and, of course, an autograph adds to the value even if the script is a copy. If you are sure the script is original, $200–$500 would be reasonable depending on the episode or movie. One Stop Publishing has produced licensed, bound issues of the six classic movie scripts for $20 each and Lincoln Enterprises has an agreement with Paramount which allows them to sell episode scripts as well (about $10 each). All other scripts that are often seen in specialty shops and at conventions are unlicensed and highly disapproved of by Paramount.

INVESTMENT POTENTIAL
Authentic Script: Good. Reproduction: Poor.

CARE
Like all paper collectibles, scripts require protection from moisture and the fading caused by sunlight. Plastic collector bags are best suited for this purpose. In addition, since they are not actual bound books, they are rather flimsy and hold up better if a cardboard backing board is inserted in the bag along with the script, especially if it is to be stored vertically.

STANDEES

Standees are simply photos or drawings affixed to cardboard with a fold-out support leaf. In the case of Star Trek standees, color photos of characters or ships are depicted. Promotional movie standees (see Promotional Material) and, to a lesser degree, commercial standees promoting various products have long been in demand as collectibles. The idea of offering standees for sale to the general public is fairly new. To date, all are still being manufactured and it is probably still too soon to ascertain whether or not these items will eventually become collectible. However, the fact that they are very popular novelty items speaks well for possible future collectibility, especially if they were to go out of production.

INVESTMENT POTENTIAL
Good.

CARE
Because of their more convenient size, smaller tabletop standees pose few care problems. They are made of sturdy cardboard and are small enough to fit in a plastic collector's bag to protect them from moisture. The larger standees present a much more difficult situation. Fortunately they fold in half, which makes it a little easier to store them in a manner that prevents creasing. A large plastic bag is provided by the manufacturer for each standee, which provides the best protection from moisture possible for such an awkward item.

SECTION NOTES
Section is organized alphabetically by manufacturer.

Advanced Graphics

1992/95

Full-size color photo standees of various Star Trek characters and ships. Standees come folded in large plastic bag. No other individual packaging.

Original TV Series.
    Kirk. ....$15–$20
    McCoy. ....$15–$20
    Spock. ....$15–$20
Star Trek: Deep Space Nine.
    Bashir. ....$15–$20
    Comdr. Sisko. ....$15–$20
    Dax. ....$15–$20
    Kira. ....$15–$20
    O'Brien. ....$15–$20
    Odo. ....$15–$20
    Quark. ....$15–$20
Star Trek: Generations.
    Dr. Soran. ....$15–$20
    Kirk. ....$15–$20
    Lursa and B'Etor. ....$15–$20
    Picard. ....$15–$20
    Troi. ....$15–$20
    Worf. ....$15–$20
Star Trek: The Next Generation.
    Data. ....$15–$20
    Dr. Crusher. ....$15–$20
    Enterprise-D. ....$15–$20
    Hugh Borg. ....$15–$20
    La Forge. ....$15–$20
    Picard. ....$15–$20
    Riker. ....$15–$20

Troi. ....$15–$20
Worf. ....$15–$20
Star Trek: Voyager.
B'Elanna Torres. ....$15–$20
Chakotay. ....$15–$20
Doctor. ....$15–$20
Janeway. ....$15–$20
Kes. ....$15–$20
Kim. ....$15–$20
Neelix. ....$15–$20
Paris. ....$15–$20
Tuvok. ....$15–$20
Voyager (Ship). ....$15–$20

Portico

1994

Color photo standees of Next Generation characters approx. 1' high. Come with mailing envelopes.

Dr. Crusher. ....$5–$10
Geordi. ....$5–$10
Picard. ....$5–$10
Worf. ....$5–$10

Triangle Enterprises

1992

Stand-Me-Up. Tabletop-sized color photo standees. Each comes with plain white envelope. Packaged in clear plastic bag with header for hanging.

Enterprise NCC-1701-D. ....$5–$10
Star Trek (Original) Crew. ....$5–$10
Star Trek: The Next Generation Crew. ....$5–$10

STILLS, SLIDES, FILM CLIPS, AND PHOTOGRAPHS

There is a great deal of confusion about these items among collectors. To start with, many collectors do not realize the difference between lithographs and photographs. A photograph is a film process. A lithograph is a printing process. Lithographs are much cheaper to produce than photographs and are practical only in large quantities. Where it concerns films, all one needs to do to make slides is have a print of the film and a pair of scissors. Another slide or a photograph can be made easily from any frame of the film. For this reason there are as many possible photographs and slides from a film as there are frames in that film. All of the "stills" in this section and others (including posters and lobby cards) are therefore lithographs. Fair prices for slides range from about $.50–$2 for mounted slides, less for unmounted film clips. Photographs should sell for $2–$4 for black and white photographs, and $5–$10 for color.

INVESTMENT POTENTIAL
Poor.

CARE
As with all paper items, stills should be protected from moisture, creasing, and fading caused by direct sunlight. The protective plastic and Mylar bags made for comics, magazines, and books can be used to protect stills as well. Slides are more tolerant of moisture but more sensitive to heat, which can cause them to warp and may alter the color of the image.

SECTION NOTES
Section is organized alphabetically by manufacturer (when known).

Disney/MGM Studios

Black and White Cards—Pictures of characters for autographing when actor is present at the attraction. ....$1–$3

Fantasy House

Mini-Posters—Set of six 4″ × 6″, Kirk, Sulu, Kirk and Chekov, McCoy, Spock, and Spock close-up (each). ....
....$2–$5

Kelly Freas

Portfolio—1976. Set of seven color artwork stills of characters, 8½″ × 11″. (This set was also incorporated into a one-shot magazine "Officers of the Bridge.")...................$10–$15

Langley and Associates

1976

All are 8″ × 10″ color on light card stock, licensed.
Chekov, portrait. ....$1–$2
Crew, The, on a barren planet. ....$1–$2
Crew, The, in mid-beam. ....$1–$2
Crew, The, portrait on bridge. ....$1–$2
Dr. McCoy, close-up portrait. ....$1–$2
Enterprise, firing phasers. ....$1–$2
Enterprise, following another Federation ship. ....$1–$2
Enterprise, in starburst. ....$1–$2
Enterprise, The, captioned "Star Trek."......................$1–$2
Enterprise, surrounded by alien ships. ....$1–$2
Kirk, cocked head, looking flirtatious. ....$1–$2
Kirk, head shot of the captain. ....$1–$2
Kirk, looking seductive. ....$1–$2
Kirk, surrounded by Tribbles. ....$1–$2
Kirk, three-quarter shot in dress uniform. ....$1–$2

Kirk, using communicators. ....$1–$2
Kirk, Spock, McCoy, and Scotty, at conference table. ....
....$1–$2
Lt. Uhura, color portrait. ....$1–$2
Mr. Scott, in dress uniform, looking tense. ....$1–$2
Spock, close-up with beard. ....$1–$2
Spock, color portrait. ....$1–$2
Spock, giving Vulcan hand signal. ....$1–$2
Spock, rare smile. ....$1–$2
Spock and Kirk, seen through hole in cavern. ....$1–$2
Sulu, on the bridge. ....$1–$2

Lincoln Enterprises

Artwork Prints—By Doug Little, color. Star Trek: The Motion Picture, 11″ × 14″.
    Chapel. ....$1–$3
    Chekov. ....$1–$3
    Decker. ....$1–$3
    Ilia. ....$1–$3
    Klingon. ....$1–$3
    McCoy. ....$1–$3
    Saavik. ....$1–$3
    Scotty. ....$1–$3
    Spock. ....$1–$3
    Sulu. ....$1–$3
    Uhura. ....$1–$3

Artwork Prints—By Probert, color. Original Star Trek television show, 8½″ × 11″
    Chapel. ....$1–$2
    Chekov. ....$1–$2
    Enterprise. ....$1–$2
    Kirk. ....$1–$2
    McCoy. ....$1–$2
    Scotty. ....$1–$2
    Spock. ....$1–$2
    Sulu. ....$1–$2
    Uhura. ....$1–$2

Evolution of the Enterprise—Original ship in different phases of conception, 12 different pictures per set. ....
....$4–$6

Star Trek: The Next Generation—8½″ × 11″, color.
    Data. ....$1–$3
    Dr. Crusher. ....$1–$3
    Enterprise. ....$1–$3
    Geordi. ....$1–$3
    Picard. ....$1–$3
    Riker. ....$1–$3
    Tasha Yar. ....$1–$3
    Troi. ....$1–$3
    Wesley. ....$1–$3
    Worf. ....$1–$3

Wallet pictures—Color, 2″ × 3″, 15 per set.
    Costumes, #1, per set. ....$1–$3
    Costumes, #2, per set. ....$1–$3
    Kirk, per set. ....$1–$3
    Makeup and Aliens, per set. ....$1–$3
    Scenes from Star Trek: The Motion Picture, per set. ....
....$1–$3
    Scenes from Star Trek: The Motion Picture, action, per set.
....$1–$3
    Spock, per set. ....$1–$3
    Stars and Groups (Star Trek: The Motion Picture), per set.
....$1–$3
    Star Trek: The Wrath of Khan #1, per set. ....$1–$3
    Star Trek: The Wrath of Khan #2, per set. ....$1–$3
    Star Trek: The Wrath of Khan #3, per set. ....$1–$3
    Star Trek: The Wrath of Khan #4, per set. ....$1–$3
    Star Trek Television Series #1, per set. ....$1–$3
    Star Trek Television Series #2, per set. ....$1–$3
    Star Trek Television Series #3, per set. ....$1–$3
    Star Trek III #1, per set. ....$1–$3
    Star Trek III #2, per set. ....$1–$3
    Star Trek III #3, per set. ....$1–$3
    Star Trek III #4, per set. ....$1–$3

Weapons and Field Equipment—Color, 12 different pictures per set. ....$3–$5

NOTE: Lincoln also did several series of postcards. (See Postcards section.)

LMH

Film Cels—1995. Three frames of ordinary film specially mounted in backlit vertical glass displays with appropriate photo above film clip. Numbered. Includes Certificate of Authenticity.
    Original Star Trek Series
        Amok Time. ....$150–$175
        City on the Edge of Forever. ....$150–$175
        Mirror, Mirror. ....$150–$175
    Star Trek: The Next Generation
        Encounter at Farpoint. ....$150–$175
        Relics. ....$150–$175

Film Cels—1996. One frame of 70mm film encased in Lucite with appropriate accompanying pictures on front and back. Numbered. Comes packaged in window box with logo above window. Star Trek: The Motion Picture.
    Enterprise. ....$20–$25
    Adm. Kirk. ....$20–$25
    Spock. ....$20–$25
    Voyager. ....$20–$25

NOTE: These cels were also presented in a boxed set.

Lobby Cards and Stills

(See Promotional Material Section)

Space Shuttle Enterprise Print

Print—Shows the starship Enterprise in background, "To Go Places and Do Things That Have Never Been Done Before . . ." ....$3–$5

Star Trek Episode Cards

1978

Fan produced, large picture with three smaller insets on each card, color.

All Our Yesterdays. ....$2–$4
Amok Time. ....$2–$4
Bloopers. ....$2–$4
Cage, The. ....$2–$4
City on the Edge of Forever. ....$2–$4
Doomsday Machine. ....$2–$4
Journey to Babel. ....$2–$4
Mirror, Mirror. ....$2–$4
Paradise Syndrome. ....$2–$4
Patterns of Force. ....$2–$4
Star Trek. ....$2–$4
Tholian Web. ....$2–$4
Trouble with Tribbles. ....$2–$4
What Are Little Girls Made Of? ....$2–$4
Where No Man Has Gone Before. ....$2–$4

Star Trek Galore

1976

Unlicensed, color, 8″ × 10″ or 8½″ × 11″.

Alien Ship, firing lasers. ....$1–$2
Bridge, The, Chekov and Sulu, in forefront. ....$1–$2
Bridge, The, Kirk, Spock, Uhura, and Mr. Chekov. ....$1–$2
Capt. Pike, early episode with Jeffrey Hunter. ....$1–$2
Chekov, portrait. ....$1–$2
Crew, The, minus Capt. Kirk. ....$1–$2
Crew, The, on the bridge of the Enterprise. ....$1–$2
Crew, The, portrait on bridge. ....$1–$2
Crew, The, suspense on the bridge. ....$1–$2
Dr. McCoy, Capt. Kirk, and Mr. Spock. ....$1–$2
Enterprise, The, firing phasers. ....$1–$2
Enterprise, The, looming overhead. ....$1–$2
Enterprise, The, surrounded by alien ships. ....$1–$2
Galileo, The, zooming through space. ....$1–$2
Kirk, drowning in Tribbles. ....$1–$2
Kirk and Spock, shooting phasers at the Horta. ....$1–$2
Kirk, looking debonair. ....$1–$2
Kirk, with Federation flag. ....$1–$2
Mr. Scott, looking worried. ....$1–$2
Scott, on the bridge of the Enterprise. ....$1–$2
Spock, aiming phaser. ....$1–$2
Spock, giving Vulcan hand gesture. ....$1–$2
Spock, making a point. ....$1–$2
Spock, a rare display of emotion. ....$1–$2
Spock, with beard. ....$1–$2
Spock, with child Vulcan. ....$1–$2
Spock, with harp. ....$1–$2
Spock, with three-dimensional chess board. ....$1–$2
Sulu, portrait. ....$1–$2
Transporter Room, The, Kirk, McCoy, Uhura, Scotty, beaming. ....$1–$2
Tribbles, The, Capt. Kirk looking dismayed. ....$1–$2
Uhura and Chekov, smiling on the bridge. ....$1–$2

TOYS AND CRAFTS

Though the demand for older Star Trek toys has leveled off somewhat in recent years due to the influx of an enormous amount of new, high-quality Star Trek items, toys in general are still one of the major Star Trek collectible fields. If anything, this abundance of product has led to stricter criteria when judging the collectibility of the older toys. The newer items, many designed specifically for the collectibles market, make collectors more aware of condition, quality, availability, and other factors determining collectibility in the older items. It should also be recognized that toys encompass a wide range of different products. As a general rule, the larger, more complex toys tend to accrue more value than simple novelties. Complete toys with their original packages intact and in good condition are by far the most desirable. Larger and harder to find toys may retain up to 50% of their value unpackaged if complete, but the percentage is 25% or less for smaller and newer items.

INVESTMENT POTENTIAL
Excellent.

CARE
As with many collectible items, the package is just as important (and often much less durable) than the toy itself. For boxed items, never discard the box, any interior packaging (cardboard, Styrofoam, etc.), or instructions. Take special care that any small parts stay with the toy. For maximum collectibility, do not apply decals to toy. Leave them intact on the decal sheet. Do not work craft kits. To do so destroys almost 100% of the item's collectible potential. Store boxes so that they are protected from scuffing, fading, and being crushed. For blister-carded items, do not remove the item from the package. Store the toy so that the card cannot be creased or scuffed and so that the plastic bubble does not become crushed, scuffed, or yellow from exposure to light and heat. Store unpackaged toys in a box or bag so that all small parts remain with the toy. Incomplete or damaged toys are unacceptable to the serious collector.

NOTE: It has been a trend in recent years for toy manufacturers to advertise products they later decide not to produce due to poor advance sales to large retailers. In particular, Galoob advertised several toys in its 1988 Star Trek: The Next Generation line which, though pictured on many of their products, were never actually made.

SECTION NOTES
Section is first organized alphabetically by type of item, then chronologically by date of manufacture and alphabetically by manufacturer within specific subcategories. Prices are for packaged toys in excellent condition.

COMMUNICATORS

"Personal Communicator"—Playmates. 1992. Oversized 2½" plastic replica of the original oval uniform communicator pin. Clip on back. Light and chirping sound function. Color box art displays toy and picture of Picard with window to test toy's function and header card with Star Trek: The Next Generation logo for hanging. ....$6–$10

Communicator—Kohn. 1993. Authentic-size gold and silvertone plastic Star Trek: The Next Generation replica. Beeps when pressed. Affixed to cardboard back inside container designed to stand up or hang. Color photo of cast and Earth in space with logo. ....$10–$15

NOTE: There were several unlicensed electronic devices designed to beep or speak that could be used in conjunction with the jewelry version of the communicator pin. None have appreciable collector value.

"Starfleet Communicator"—Playmates. 1994. Oversized plastic replica of the uniform communicator pin used in Star Trek: Generations (movie). Light and chirping sound function.

Box art has small window for viewing and testing toy, and header with Star Trek: Generations logo for hanging. Bonus movie mini-poster included. ....$6–$10

"Classic Star Trek Communicator"—Playmates. 1994. Three sound functions and lights. Color box art shows toy with original Enterprise and logo above. Opening in front of box to test toy's functions. Blueprint and Certificate of Authenticity included. ....$50–$60

"Personal Communicator Mini-Playset"—Playmates. 1995. Fold-out playset approx. 3″ long × 2″ wide in the shape of the Star Trek: The Next Generation TV series communicator insignia. Opens to form transporter playset. Comes with two 1″-high figures (Comdr. Riker and Lt. Comdr. Data). Color box art shows open playset with two small insert photos in upper left (shows toy in closed and open position). Small window at right displays figures. Low header has product logo. ....$15–$20

"Star Trek Talk-Back Classic Communicator"—Playmates. 1996. Original TV series–style toy with built-in record/playback and light functions. Box art shows toy on star background with logo above and inset photo of child with toy. ....$25–$35

"Starfleet Wrist Communicator"—Playmates. 1996. Star Trek: The Motion Picture style. White plastic toy straps to wrist. Light and sound functions. Color box art shows toy strapped to wrist wearing blue, original TV series–style uniform. Small opening in front to test sound functions. Logo at top corner and small inset photo of toy. ....$30–$40

"Star Trek Astro Walkie-Talkies"—Remco. 1967. Blue plastic cups with handgrip connected by string. Blister-packed on cardboard header with line art of Kirk, Spock, and Enterprise. ....$40–$50

"Star Trek Inter-Space Communicator"—Lone Star (British). 1974. Black and yellow plastic cups with handgrip connected by string. Came in blue 6″ × 9½″ box with line art of Kirk, Spock, and Enterprise. ....$25–$35

Communicators—Mego. 1976. Blue plastic with flip-up grid and retractable antennae. Working toy walkie-talkies. Sold in pairs. Early models were boxed. Later packaging was 9″ × 14″ cardboard header. Both package styles utilized color art of characters and toy. ....$150–$225

"Star Trek: The Motion Picture Wrist Communicators"—Mego. 1980. Plastic wristband walkie-talkies attached by wire to battery belt pack. Sold in pairs. 6½″ × 4½″ box. Color art shows toys. Low header shows logo and Enterprise. ....
....$200–$350

Communicators—P.J. McNerney & Assoc., Inc. 1989. Black plastic with flip-up grid and retractable antennae. Working toy walkie-talkies. Proctor and Gamble Star Trek V promotion. Plain white box (mail order only item). Sold in pairs. ....
....$50–$75

Communicator Walkie-Talkie—Playmates. 1993. Set of two clip-on belt units with wires attaching them to oversized oval uniform insignias that act as microphones. Belt box has antennae and decal with insignia design and logo. Window box has logo at top and photos of children with toy. ....
....$35–$45

FIGURINES

(See also Action Figures and Pewter for other figural representations)

Applause

NOTE: Though the 9″ series of Applause figures are referred to as "dolls" by the manufacturer, they are jointed only at the waist and where the arms meet the body.

Star Trek: Deep Space Nine Vinyl Figures—1994. 9″ tall, molded from colored vinyl. Dressed in costume from the show appropriate to character. No accessories, stand, or packaging except a plastic bag to protect against scuffing during shipping. Folded tag with show logo and short character biography.

Comdr. Benjamin Sisko	$10–$15
Maj. Kira Nerys	$10–$15
Proprietor Quark	$10–$15
Security Chief Odo	$10–$15

Star Trek: Deep Space Nine Collectible Figurine Set—1994. Six colored PVC plastic figurines approx. 3″ tall set in action poses. Dressed in costumes appropriate to the character. Set includes Odo, Dax, Kira, O'Brien, Quark, and Comdr. Sisko. Packaged in window box with star motif and show logo at bottom of package. Figurines were not originally sold individually. ....$20–$25

Star Trek: Generations Vinyl Figures—1994. 9″ tall, molded from colored vinyl. Dressed in movie uniforms appropriate to the character. No accessories, stand, or packaging except a plastic bag to protect against scuffing during shipping. Folded tag with movie logo and short character biography.

Capt. James T. Kirk	$10–$15
Capt. Jean-Luc Picard	$10–$15
Comdr. William T. Riker	$10–$15
Lt. Comdr. Data	$10–$15
Lt. Comdr. Deanna Troi (released slightly later than the others and included a base).	$10–$15
Lt. Comdr. Geordi La Forge	$10–$15
Lt. Comdr. Worf	$10–$15

Star Trek: Generations PVC Figurines—1994. 3″ tall, molded from colored PVC plastic. Each is wearing a costume appropriate to the character and is permanently attached to an oval, black base with the Star Trek: Generations movie logo.

B'Etor	$3–$4
Capt. Kirk	$3–$4
Capt. Picard	$3–$4
Comdr. Riker	$3–$4
Counselor Troi	$3–$4
Data	$3–$4
Dr. Crusher	$3–$4
Dr. Soren	$3–$4
Guinan	$3–$4

Lt. Comdr. La Forge. ....$3–$4
Lt. Comdr. Worf. ....$3–$4
Lursa. ....$3–$4
Scotty. ....$3–$4

Star Trek: Generations Collectible Figurine Set #1— 1994. Included Kirk, Picard, Data, Worf, La Forge, and Lursa 3″ PVC figures. Came packaged in a window box with "Nexus Effect" background and movie logo at bottom. ....
....$20–$25

Star Trek: Generations Collectible Figurine Set #2— 1994. Included B'Etor, Dr. Crusher, Guinan, Riker, Dr. Soran, and Counselor Troi 3″ PVC figures. Came packaged in a window box with "Nexus Effect" background and movie logo at bottom. ....$20–$25

Enesco (Previously Hamilton Gifts)

Star Trek: The Next Generation Figurines— 1992/93. 10½″ tall. Made of colored plastic with arms jointed only at the body. Each comes with a doll stand, the base of which is shaped like the TV show communicator insignia, and a small folded "To/From" card with the logo on the front. Packaged only for shipping in plastic bag and open cardboard sleeve.

Data. ....$10–$15
Ferengi. ....$10–$15
La Forge. ....$10–$15
Picard. ....$10–$15
Riker. ....$10–$15
Troi. ....$10–$15
Worf. ....$10–$15

Galoob

Star Trek V Collector Figures— 1989. Unjointed, permanently posed statuettes. Approx. 7″ tall. Came packaged in window boxes with color photos of character on side and color artwork backdrop for figure.

Capt. James T. Kirk. ....$40–$60
Dr. Leonard McCoy. ....$40–$60
Klaa. ....$40–$60
Mr. Spock. ....$40–$60
Sybok. ....$40–$60

Hamilton Gifts

(See also Enesco)

Star Trek Figurines— (Original TV Series)—1991. 10½″ high. Made of colored plastic, joints at waist and where arms join body. Each came with a doll stand, the base of which was shaped like the original TV uniform insignia for Enterprise crew members or round for aliens, and a small folded "To/

From" card with logo on the front. Packaged only for shipping in plastic bag and open cardboard sleeve.

Andorian. ....$10–$15
Chekov. ....$10–$15
Kirk. ....$10–$15
McCoy. ....$10–$15
Scotty. ....$10–$15
Spock. ....$10–$15
Sulu. ....$10–$15
Talosian. ....$10–$15
Uhura. ....$10–$15

Star Trek PVC Figurines (Original TV Show)—1991. Approx. 4″ tall. Colored PVC plastic. Permanently affixed to a stand either in the shape of the original TV insignia (with symbol appropriate to character) for Enterprise crew or plain for aliens.

Andorian. ....$3–$4
Chekov. ....$3–$4
Gorn. ....$3–$4
Kirk. ....$3–$4
McCoy. ....$3–$4
Mugato. ....$3–$4
Scotty. ....$3–$4
Spock. ....$3–$4
Sulu. ....$3–$4
Talosian. ....$3–$4
Tellerite. ....$3–$4
Uhura. ....$3–$4

Star Trek: The Next Generation PVC Figurines— 1992. Approx. 4″ tall. Colored PVC plastic. Permanently affixed to a stand either in the shape of a communicator insignia from the show for Enterprise crew or plain for aliens.

Borg. ....$3–$4
Data. ....$3–$4
Ferengi. ....$3–$4
Klingon. ....$3–$4
Picard. ....$3–$4
Q. ....$3–$4
Riker. ....$3–$4
Troi. ....$3–$4
Worf. ....$3–$4

KITES

Hi-Flyer— 1975. Delta wing. Bagged with header showing logo and kite.

Original TV Enterprise. ....$15–$25
Original Enterprise and Klingon. ....$15–$25
Spock. ....$15–$25

Aviva— 1979. Star Trek: The Motion Picture. Octopus style. Assorted colors. Logoon bag.

Enterprise..$15–$25
Spock ....$15–$25

Lever Bros. (Promotional)—1984. Star Trek III. Pictures movie Enterprise. ....$20–$30

Hi-Flyer—1992. 50″ Delta wing. Original TV Enterprise with logo on red and yellow background. Bagged with header showing kite and logo. ....$10–$15

Hi-Flyer—1992. 4′ long, coffin-shaped, includes string. Color artwork of original TV Enterprise, Klingon ship, and logo on colorful background. Bagged with full-length paper insert showing artwork. ....$20–$30

Spectra Star—1993. Star Trek: Deep Space Nine. Delta wing. Color artwork of Comdr. Sisko, Odo, space station, and ships. Bagged with header showing kite and logo. ....$5–$10

Spectra Star—1993. Star Trek: The Next Generation. Delta wing. Color artwork of Picard and Data with small Enterprise. Bagged with header showing kite and logo. ......$5–$10

Spectra Star—1993. Star Trek: The Next Generation. Dual control delta wing. Includes string. Color artwork of Enterprise and Romulan Warbird. Bagged with header showing kite and logo. ....$8–$15

Spectra Star—1993. 6½′ octopus kite. Includes string. Topside artwork of Enterprise-D. Packaged in carry bag with snap-off handle that becomes kite control handle. Bag shows kite and logo. ....$8–$15

NEEDLEPOINT

Kit—Arista Designs. 1980. Star Trek: The Motion Picture. Design imprinted on #10 mesh canvas. Black and white yarn portrait of Spock captioned "Live Long and Prosper." Approx. 14″ × 18″. ....$75–$95

Kit—Arista Designs. 1980. Star Trek: The Motion Picture. Design imprinted on #10 mesh canvas. Capt. Kirk on white background. Approx. 14″ × 18″. ....$75–$95

Pattern—Booth-Hill. Kirk and Spock design from the original TV series. ....$25–$50

Patterns—Star Stitches. 1992. Three different designs.
Enterprise-A, "Heavy Cruiser"....................................$20–$35
Enterprise Firing on Reliant, "The Cripple"..........$20–$35
Romulan Bird-of-Prey....................................$20–$35

PEN AND POSTER SETS

Kit—Open Door. 1976. Four different line posters and felt-tipped pens. 14″ × 22″. Came boxed or bagged with header. Box art shows Enterprise, logo, and crew members.
Enemies of the Federation. ....$25–$40
Journeys of the Enterprise. ....$25–$40
Star Trek Lives. ....$25–$40
Tour of the Enterprise. ....$25–$40

Kit—Open Door. "How Do You Doodle." Two original TV posters and pens. ....$30–$40

Kit—Aviva. 1979. Star Trek: The Motion Picture. One 14″ × 20″ poster and five pens. ....$30–$40

Kit—Placo. 1984. Star Trek III: The Search for Spock. 3-D poster set. Comes with poster, 3-D plastic overlay, 3-D glasses, and four felt-tip pens. Cover photo of Enterprise with small insets of characters. ....$25–$35

Set—Craft House. 1993. Star Trek: The Next Generation. Set of four 11″ × 17″ line art posters and seven felt-tip pens. Packaged in box with low header. Box shows completed posters, logo, and photo of Enterprise-D. ....$10–$15

Set—Craft House. 1993. Star Trek: The Next Generation. Two 16″ × 22″ posters and seven felt-tip pens. Shrink-wrapped with cover sheet showing Enterprise-D, logo, and completed posters. ....$15–$20

PHASERS

Remco—1967. "Star Trek Astro Buzz-Ray Gun." Early ray gun–type toy had three-color flash beam. Came packaged in box with color Star Trek TV artwork. ....$300–$500

Larami—1968. Ray gun. White plastic flashlight toy with "Star Trek" logo. Blister-packed. Color header art. ....$40–$60

Remco—1975. "Star Trek Phaser Gun." Flashlight toy projects target. Electronic sound. Black plastic shaped like pistol phaser. 8″ × 11″ box. Color art shows toy, Kirk, and Spock. . ...$75–$150

Azrak-Hamway—1976. Plastic with "Star Trek" logo. Blister-packed. Header art shows Enterprise. ....$25–$35

Mego—1976. "Star Trek Super Phaser II Target Game." Target reflector game. Black plastic phaser-shaped toy and reflector with picture of Klingon ship. 8″ × 10″ box. Color art shows Kirk and Spock. Reverse pictures toy. ....$35–$50

South Bend—1979. Star Trek: The Motion Picture. Set included two gray plastic phasers. Electronic dueling game. Box art depicts toys. ....$100–$175

Daisy—1984. Star Trek III. White and blue plastic gun has light and sound effects. "Star Trek" logo on handgrip. 6½″ × 10½″ window box. Color art shows Kirk, Spock, and Klingon from movies and toy. ....$50–$85

Galoob—1988. Star Trek: The Next Generation. Gray plastic light and sound hand phaser toy. Blister-packed. Color photo on header shows Yar, Riker, and Enterprise. ....$25–$40

Playmates—1992. Star Trek: The Next Generation. Two sound functions and lights. Color box art shows toy with planetscape in background and Next Generation logo. Opening in front of box to test toy's function. ....$20–$30

Playmates—1994. Star Trek: The Next Generation. Type I (smaller, no-handle version seen on show). Two sounds, light, belt clip. Box art shows toy firing at door. Opening in front to test toy's functions. Blueprint included. ....$15–$25

Playmates—1994. "Classic Star Trek Phaser." Pistol style from original TV series. Two sound functions and lights. Color box art shows toy with original Enterprise and logo above. Opening in front of box to test toy's functions. Blueprint included. ....$30–$40

Playmates—1995. Bajoran. Squarish black and gold toy with enclosed hand grip and red Bajoran emblem on side. Light and sound functions. Box art shows close-up of toy firing on background of Bajoran planetscape. Star Trek: The Next Generation logo in upper corner. Hole near center of box allows testing of toy's sound function. ....$20–$30

Playmates—1996. "Classic Star Trek Movie Series." Light gray plastic replica of phasers used in the first two Star Trek movies. Two sound functions and lights. Color box art show toy on space backdrop. Logo in upper corner and opening in front of box to test sound functions. ....$20–$30

SPACESHIPS

NOTE: Arranged by manufacturer. For other ship representations also see Games, Housewares, Model Kits, and Pewter Ships and Figures.

Applause

Enterprise-D—1995. Approx. 5″ long. White plastic with color details. Removable saucer section and removable stand with Generations logo. Comes blister-carded. Header card has movie logo and color background of "Nexus" effect.

Ship Figurines—1995. All approx. 3½″ long. Colored plastic with painted details. Each comes with black, plastic, pyramid-shaped stand.

    Borg Ship. ....$3–$4
    Enterprise-NCC-1701-D. ....$3–$4
    Fenrengi Marauder. ....$3–$4
    Klingon Bird-of-Prey. ....$3–$4
    Magellan Shuttlecraft. ....$3–$4
    Romulan Warbird. ....$3–$4

Corgi

(Mettoy), British

Enterprise—1981. Star Trek II. Die-cast metal. Approx. 3″ long. Came blister-packed on color header with photo of Kirk and Spock. ....$15–$20

Klingon Cruiser—1981. Star Trek II. Blue die-cast metal with black and yellow decals. Approx. 3″ long. Came blister-packed on color header with photo of Kirk and Spock. ....
....$15–$20

Double Pack—1981. Star Trek II. Both 3″ die-cast ships blister-packed together on color header with photo of Kirk and Spock. ....$30–$40

Dinky

(Meccano), British

Enterprise—1977. Original TV. Die-cast metal. Approx. 9″. Fires plastic disks from saucer section. Includes disks and plastic shuttlecraft. Packaged in window box with low header with color photo of Kirk and Spock. ....$75–$100

Klingon Cruiser—1977. Blue die-cast metal. Approx. 9″ long. Fires plastic disks from front section. Comes with disks. Window boxed with low header. Color photo of Kirk and Spock on front of box. ....$75–$100

Enterprise and Klingon Gift Set—1978. Both 9″ die-cast ships come packaged together in window box with color header showing Kirk, Spock, and ships. ....$250–$300

Enterprise—1979. Star Trek: The Motion Picture. Die-cast metal. Movie Enterprise. Approx. 4″. Blister-packed on color header with photo of Kirk, Spock, and Klingon ship. ....
....$15–$20

Klingon Cruiser—1979. Star Trek: The Motion Picture. Blue die-cast metal. Approx. 4″ long. Blister-packed on color header with photo of Kirk, Spock, and Enterprise. ....
....$15–$20

Ertl

Enterprise—1984. Star Trek III. Movie Enterprise. Die-cast metal. Approx. 4″ long. Blister-packed on color header with artwork of Kirk, Spock, and Klingon. Included black plastic stand. ....$10–$20

Excelsior—1984. Star Trek III. Die-cast metal. Approx. 4″ long. Blister-packed on color header with artwork of Kirk, Spock, and Klingon. Included black plastic stand. ....
....$10–$20

Klingon Bird-of-Prey—1984. Star Trek III. Die-cast metal. Approx. 3½″ across. Blue with "Star Trek" logo on each wing. Blister-packed on color header with artwork of Kirk, Spock, and Klingon. Included black plastic stand. ....
....$10–$20

Enterprise—1989. Star Trek V. Re-issue of Star Trek III. 4″ die-cast with "A" added to NCC-1701 decal. Blister-packed on color header with Star Trek V logo. Includes black plastic stand. ....$5–$10

Klingon Bird-of-Prey—1989. Star Trek V. Re-issue of Star Trek III. 4″ die-cast, mottled green. Blister-packed on color header with Star Trek V logo. Includes black plastic stand.
....$5–$10

Galoob

Enterprise NCC-1701-D—1987. Blue plastic with detachable saucer section. Approx. 4″ long. General Mills cereal mail-in promotion. Originally came packaged in plain white mailing box with two small decal sheets and flyer with decal instructions on one side and Galoob ad on other. Later used in an ERTL promotion for the first-run issue of the Star Trek VI Enterprise model kit. ....$25–$50

Enterprise NCC-1701-D—1988. Star Trek: The Next Generation. Die-cast metal Next Generation Enterprise. Approx. 6″ long. Detachable saucer section. Blister-packed on color header with photo of ship. ....$15–$25

Ferengi Fighter—1989. Star Trek: The Next Generation. Orange plastic. Designed for use with 3³/₄″ action figures. Movable canopy and guns. Decals included. 8¹/₂″ × 12″ box. Color photo of toy and figures. ....$30–$60

Shuttlecraft Galileo—1989. Star Trek: The Next Generation. White plastic. Designed for use with 3³/₄″ action figures. Movable doors and sensor unit. Decals included. 8¹/₂″ × 12″ box. Color photo of toy and figures. ....$25–$50

Micro Machines

Two different series of numbered "collections." Each collection consists of three different ships, 2″–3″ in size, molded from colored plastic with painted details and a stand for each ship. Ships are blister-packed on header cards with Micro Machines logo, color ship photo (either Romulan Warbird or Ferengi Marauder for Next Generation, Reliant for Classic movies, Original Enterprise for first TV show, Space Station for Deep Space Nine, or Enterprise-D for Generations movie), and logo of show appropriate to the ships in the collection.

SERIES ONE, 1993
Initially had pink, orange, and yellow lines behind Micro Machines logo. Later changed to grid pattern over starfield.

Collection #1—USS Enterprise NCC-1701, Klingon Battlecruiser (original), and Romulan Bird-of-Prey. ....$10–$15
Collection #2—USS Excelsior, Klingon Bird-of-Prey, and USS Reliant. ....$10–$15
Collection #3 (Initial Issue)—Klingon Vor'Cha Attack Cruiser, Borg Ship, and Romulan Warbird. ....$25–$35
Collection #3 (Later Issue)—Klingon Vor'Cha Attack Cruiser, USS Enterprise NCC-1701-D, Romulan Warbird. ....$10–$15
Collection #4 (Later Issue Only)—Ferengi Marauder, Borg Ship, and shuttlecraft (Next Generation version). ....$10–$15
Collection #5 (Later Issue Only)—Cardassian Galor Warship, Space Station Deep Space Nine, and Runabout. ....$10–$15
Collector's Set (9-Piece)—A K-mart exclusive. Ships were displayed in window box with pink, orange, yellow Micro Machine logo at top. Ships included Enterprise NCC-1701, Klingon Battlecruiser (original), Romulan Bird-of-Prey, Excelsior, Klingon Bird-of-Prey, Reliant, Klingon Vor'Cha Battlecruiser, Borg Ship, and Romulan Warbird. ....$25–$35
Collector's Set (16-Piece)—Ships were displayed in window box with grid over starfield Micro Machines logo at top. Ships

included Enterprise NCC-1701, Klingon Cruiser (original), Romulan Bird-of-Prey, Excelsior, Klingon Bird-of-Prey, Reliant, Klingon Vor'Cha Battlecruiser, Shuttlecraft (Next Generation version), Romulan Warbird, Enterprise NCC-1701-D, Borg Ship, Ferengi Marauder, Runabout, Space Station Deep Space Nine, Cardassian Galor Warship, and Enterprise NCC-1701-A. The Enterprise A was exclusive to this set and is displayed in its own window at the top of the box. ....$50–$75

EARLY SERIES TWO, 1994
Same packaging as later Series One.

Collection #1—The Original Star Trek. Botany Bay, Klingon Battlecruiser, and Romulan Bird-of-Prey. ....$8–$12
Collection #2—The Original Star Trek. Galileo II, Space Station K-7, and USS Enterprise NCC-1701. ....$8–$12
Collection #3—The Movies. Federation Space Dock, Klingon Bird-of-Prey, and USS Reliant. ....$8–$12
Collection #4—The Movies. Vulcan Shuttle Surak, USS Grissom, and USS Excelsior. ....$8–$12
Collection #5—Star Trek: The Next Generation. Klingon Vor'Cha Attack Cruiser, USS Enterprise NCC-1701-D, and Romulan Scout Ship. ....$8–$12
Collection #6—Star Trek: The Next Generation. Borg Ship, Ferengi Marauder, and USS Enterprise NCC-1701-C. ....$8–$12
Collection #7—Star Trek: The Next Generation. Romulan Warbird, Shuttlecraft, and USS Stargazer. ....$8–$12
Collection #8—Star Trek: Deep Space Nine. Space Station Deep Space Nine, Cardassian Galor Warship, and Runabout. ....$8–$12
Collection #9—Star Trek: Generations. USS Enterprise NCC-1701-B, Klingon Bird-of-Prey, and USS Enterprise NCC-1701-D. These ships are different castings than similar ships found in other assortments. ....$15–$25

NOTE: Packages of this collection are not numbered but they are referred to as #9 on later assortments.

LATER SERIES TWO, 1996
Only backs of packages are different.

Collection #10—Star Trek: Deep Space Nine. Bajoran Fighter, Klaestron Ship, and Miradorn Ship. ....$10–$12
Collection #11—Star Trek: The Movies. Space Dock Shuttle, HMS Bounty, Klingon Bird-of-Prey, and USS Farragut. ....$10–$12
Collection #12—Star Trek: Deep Space Nine. USS Defiant, Jem'Hadar Ship, and USS Saratoga. ....$10–$12
Collection #13—Star Trek: Voyager. USS Voyager, Kazon Fighter, and Maquis Ship. ....$10–$12
Collection #14—Star Trek: Voyager. Kazon Fighter (different ship from Collection #13), Numiri Ship, and Kazon Mother Ship. ....$10–$12
Collector's Set II (16-Piece)—Ships are displayed in win-

dow box with light purple frame and Micro Machines logo at top. Limited edition. Galileo II, Space Station K-7, Botany Bay, Enterprise-C, Stargazer, Romulan Scout, Defiant, Enterprise-B, Enterprise-D (with detachable saucer), Farragut, Vulcan Shuttle Surak, Federation Space Dock, Grissom. Three ships from "All Good Things . . ." Three-nacelled Enterprise-D, Pasteur, and Future Klingon Battlecruiser are exclusive to this set and are displayed separately in upper corner. ....$50–$75

Television Series I Collector's Edition Set—Predominantly gray window box with Micro Machines logo at top and color photo of Enterprise NCC-1701-D at bottom. Eight pewter colored plastic Micro Machine ships—Romulan Bird-of-Prey (original TV show), Enterprise 1701 (original TV show), Stargazer, Cardassian Galor Class Ship, Runabout, Botany Bay, Klingon Vor'Cha Class Ship, Borg Ship. ....$25–$30

Television Series II Collector's Edition Set—Predominantly gray window box with Micro Machines logo at top and color photo of Enterprise NCC-1701-D at bottom. Eight pewter-colored plastic Micro Machine Ships—Deep Space Nine Space Station, Enterprise NCC-1701-C, Space Station K-7, Romulan Warbird, Ferengi Marauder, Romulan Scout, Galileo Shuttlecraft (original TV), Klingon Battlecruiser. .....
....................$25–$30

Star Trek: The Movies Collector's Edition Set—Predominantly gray window box with Micro Machines logo at top and color photo of Enterprise NCC-1701-D at bottom. Eight pewter-colored plastic Micro Machine ships—Enterprise-A, Reliant, Enterprise-D, Grissom, Klingon Bird-of-Prey, Space Dock, Vulcan Shuttle Surak, and Enterprise-B. ....$30–$40

Bronze Collector's Sets—1995. Suncoast Exclusive. Two different seven-ship sets. Regular Star Trek Micro Machine ships in bronze-toned plastic.

　　Aliens. ....$10–$15
　　Federation. ....$10–$15

Hamilton

Enterprise (Original TV)—1992. Approx. 2½″ long. Semiflexible plastic. Permanently affixed to original insignia-shaped stand. No individual packaging. ....$3–$4

Enterprise-D—1992. Approx. 3″ long. Semiflexible, light blue plastic. Permanently affixed to Next Generation insignia-shaped stand. No individual packaging. ....$3–$4

Klingon Bird-of-Prey—1993. Approx. 2″ long. Semiflexible, light green plastic. Permanently affixed to Klingon symbol–shaped stand. No individual packaging. ....$3–$4

Mego

Enterprise—1980. Star Trek: The Motion Picture. White plastic movie Enterprise. Detachable saucer section. Includes decals. Approx. 12″ long. Box shows photo of toy. Made primarily for Pacific market. ....$125–$200

Klingon Cruiser—1980. Star Trek: The Motion Picture. Green plastic, with decals. Approx. 8″ long. Box shows photo of toy. Made primarily for Pacific market. ....$125–$200

Vulcan Shuttle—1980. Star Trek: The Motion Picture. Yellow plastic. Approx. 8″ long with detachable sled and decals. Box shows photo of toy. Made primarily for Pacific market. .
....................$125–$200

Paramount

(Promotional)

Enterprise—1988. Color die-cut cardboard movie Enterprise. Came in five pieces. Approx. 4½′ long when assembled. "The Star Trek Video Collection" is printed on sides of primary hull. ....$50–$75

Playmates

Enterprise NCC-1701-D—1992. White plastic, 15″ long. Light-up engines and four different sound functions. Color box art of ship over planet with Next Generation logo in upper corner and small opening in front of box to test toy's functions. Bonus blueprint included. ....$40–$50

Enterprise NCC-1701-D—1992. "7th Season Anniversary Edition" Gold version of the above ship. A Toys-R-Us exclusive. Came packaged in a window box instead of normal Playmates toy packaging. Included stand and insignia-shaped limited edition plaque for stand. ....$100–$150

Shuttlecraft Goddard—1992. White plastic, 11″ long. Two sound features, light-up engines. Designed for use with action figures. Color box art shows toy and Next Generation logo in upper corner and has opening to test toy's functions. Blueprint and cargo pallet included. ....$40–$50

Enterprise Glider—1993. White Styrofoam, 18″ long with weighted hand-hold on lower front of saucer section. Color box art shows toy flying through air. ....$15–$25

Klingon Attack Cruiser—1993. Green plastic, 15″ long. Four sound functions, light-up engines. Color box art shows toy in front of planet with Next Generation logo in corner. Opening in front of box to test toy's functions. Blueprint included. ....$40–$50

Romulan Warbird—1993. Green plastic, 14″ long. Four sounds, light-up engines. Color box art shows toy over planet with Next Generation logo in corner. Opening in front to test toy's functions. Blueprint included. ....$40–$50

Borg—1994. Black and gray plastic, 7″ square. Three sound features, light-up interior. Color box art shows ship in battle and Next Generation logo above. Opening in front to test toy's features. Certificate of Authenticity and stand included.
....................$40–$50

Borg Ship Mini-Playset—1994. "Star Trek: The Next Generation Innerspace Series." Black plastic approx. 2½″ square.

Opens up to accommodate 1″ mini-action figures. Borg and Picard action figures included. Blister-packed on predominantly red card with meteors and logo above toy. ....
....$8–$10

Enterprise NCC-1701-B—1994. White plastic with gray, red, and blue detail, approx. 15″ long. Three sound functions, light-up engines, and navigational deflector. New-style communicator stand. Includes technical blueprint. Color box art shows toy with Nexus effect in background. Generations movie logo in upper left corner. small window to test sound effects near middle. This toy was released rather late for a Generations toy and therefore did not spend much time in this format on the shelves. It soon re-emerged as the much more common Excelsior toy. Except for box style and decals, the toys are identical. ....$100–$150

Enterprise NCC-1701-D—1994. White plastic, 15″ long. Three regular sound effects. Light-up engines. Light and sound blow-apart battle damage panels. Color box art shows ship blowing apart with Nexus effect in background and Star Trek: Generations (movie) logo in upper corner. Blueprint and stand included. ....$50–$60

Klingon Bird-of-Prey Mini-Playset—1994. "Star Trek: The Next Generation Innerspace Series." Green and red plastic, approx. 3½″ long with fold-down display stand. Opens up to accommodate 1″ mini-figures. Worf and Gowron mini-figures included. Blister-carded on predominantly red card with meteors and logo above toy. ....$8–$10

Romulan Warbird Mini-Playset—1994. "Star Trek: The Next Generation Innerspace Series." Green plastic, approx. 4½″ long. Opens up to accommodate 1″ mini-figures. Sela and Picard as a Romulan mini-figures included. Blister-carded on predominantly red card with meteors and logo above toy. ....$8–$10

Runabout Orinoco—1994. White plastic, 14″ long. Two sound features, light-up nacelles. Designed for use with action figures. Color box art shows toy and Deep Space Nine logo in upper corner. Opening in front of box to test toy's functions. Blueprint and Certificate of Authenticity included. ....$40–$50

Shuttlecraft Goddard Mini-Playset—1994. "Star Trek: The Next Generation Innerspace Series." Beige plastic, approx. 4″ long. Opens up to accommodate 1″ mini-action figures. Cargo pallet and La Forge and Troi mini-figures included. Blister-packed on predominantly red card with meteors and logo above toy. ....$8–$10

Space Station Deep Space Nine—1994. Green plastic, 13″ across. Four sound functions, light-up sail towers. Color box art shows station with ship and Deep Space Nine logo above. Blueprint, Certificate of Authenticity, miniature Enterprise replica, and stand included. ....$50–$60

Cardassian Galor-Class Warship Mini-Playset—1995. "Star Trek Innerspace Series." Tan plastic approx. 5″ long. Opens up to accommodate 1″ mini-action figures. Gul Dukat and Odo figures included. Comes blister-packed on predominantly red card with logo above toy. ....$8–$10

Enterprise 1701—1995. Classic Star Trek toy series. White

plastic approx. 15″ long. Four sounds and light-up engine nacelles. Includes display stand. Color box art shows toy in space with original Klingon Cruiser in background and logo in upper left corner. Small opening near center of box to test sound functions. ....$40–$50

Enterprise NCC-1701-D Space Talk Series—1995. White plastic, 15″ long. Has over 100 different sayings and sound effects. Comes with stand and blueprint. Color box art shows toy in space with logo in upper left corner. Small opening near center to test sounds. ....$40–$50

Enterprise NCC-1701-D Mini-Playset—1995. "Star Trek: The Next Generation Innerspace Series." White plastic. Opens up to accommodate 1″ mini-figures. Picard, Riker, and Data mini-figures included. ....$25–$30

Excelsior NCC-2000—1995. Color box art shows toy with rainbow effect background. "Star Trek The Movie Collection" logo is in upper left corner, and small opening is near center to test sound effects. Except for box art and decals this toy is identical and earlier Enterprise NCC-1701-B. Excelsior version is much more common. ....$50–$60

Excelsior-Class Starship Mini-Playset (USS Hood)—1995. "Star Trek Innerspace Series." Blue plastic approx. 5″ long. Opens up to accommodate 1″ mini-figures. Riker and Geordi figures included. Comes blister-carded with logo above toy on predominantly red background. ....$8–$10

Ferengi Marauder Mini-Playset—1995. "Star Trek Innerspace Series." Orange plastic approx. 3½″ long. Opens up to accommodate 1″ mini-action figures. Picard and Ferengi figures included. Comes blister-packed on card with predominantly red background and logo above toy. ....$8–$10

Klingon Bird-of-Prey—1995. Green plastic, 12″ long. Three sound functions, light-up engines, and torpedo launcher. Color box art shows ship in foreground and Next Generation (or Generations) logo above. Opening in front to test toy's functions. Blueprint and stand included. ....$75–$100

Stargazer Starship Mini-Playset—1995. "Star Trek Innerspace Series." Light gray plastic, approx. 5″ long. Opens up to accommodate mini-action figures. Picard and "Q" figure included. Comes blister-carded on predominantly red card with logo above toy. ....$8–$10

Voyager—1995. Light blue plastic, approx. 15″ long. Two sounds, light-up navigational deflector, pivoting warp nacelles. Color box art shows ship in space, with logo in upper corner. Opening near center of box to test toy's functions. Stand included. ....$40–$50

Shuttlecraft Galileo—1996. From original TV series. Spring firing "phaser canon." Toy included action figure of Capt. Kirk in early original TV series uniform that was only available with this toy. ....$40–$50

Enterprise NCC-1701-D (Transwarping)—Ship converts from regular Enterprise-D to three-nacelled version from "All Good Things . . ." Color box art shows ship transforming while flying thru space with inset photos of ship displayed in each mode. "Star Trek" is at top of box. Includes stand in shape of "All Good Things . . ." future insignia. ....
....$25–$35

Shreddies

(Canadian), 1992

The following four ships were cereal premiums. Each is approx. 2½″ long, made of gray plastic and comes with a small sheet of color decals. Packaged in clear plastic bags for inclusion in cereal boxes.

Enterprise NCC-1701. ....$5–$10
Ferengi Marauder. ....$5–$10
Klingon Bird-of-Prey. ....$5–$10
Romulan Warbird. ....$5–$10

South Bend

Enterprise—"Star Trek Electronic USS Enterprise." 1979. Star Trek: The Motion Picture. White plastic. Battery-powered lights and sound. Approx. 20″ long. Included stand and decals. Modular design for conversion to other ships. Box shows picture of toy. ....$150–$200

Sterling

Enterprise—1986. Star Trek IV. Inflatable silver plastic. Approx. 24″ when inflated. Star Trek IV and Paramount 75th anniversary logos on top and bottom of saucer section. Promotional item. ....$20–$35

Sun

Enterprise—1986. Star Trek IV. Inflatable blue plastic. Approx. 24″ when inflated. Star Trek IV logo on top, Star Trek and Paramount 75th anniversary logos on bottom of saucer section. Promotional item. ....$20–$35

TRICORDERS

Mego—1976. Blue plastic battery-operated working toy tape recorder. Flip-open top and plastic shoulder strap. Includes tape with excerpts from "The Menagerie" TV episode. 8″ × 11″ box displays color artwork of Kirk, Spock, and toy. ....
....$125–$200
Playmates—1993. Star Trek: The Next Generation. Three sound and two light functions. Flip-open design, belt clip. Color box art shows toy with planetscape in background and logo above. Opening in front of box to test toy's functions. Blueprint included. ....$50–$60
Playmates—1995. Classic Star Trek tricorder. From original TV show. Authentic looking, slightly undersized. Three sound effects. Light-up view screen and indicators. Color box art shows toy with logo at top right and small opening near center to test toy's functions. Comes with technical blueprint. ....
....$20–$25
Tricorder—Playmates. 1995. Bajoran. Irregular-shaped, copper-colored toy approx. 9″ long. Light and sound functions. Box art shows close-up of toy on background of Bajoran planetscape. Star Trek: The Next Generation logo in top corner. Hole near center of box to test toy's electronic functions. ....
....$20–$30

VIEW-MASTERS

GAF—1968. Three viewer reels with scenes from "Omega Glory" TV episode. Includes 16-page story booklet. Color envelope shows photo of Enterprise and other starship. ....
....$10–$15
GAF—1974. "Mr. Spock's Time Trek." Three viewer reels with scenes from "Yesteryear" animated episode. Includes 16-page story booklet. Color envelope art shows scenes from episode. ....$10–$15
GAF—1974. Talking View-Master. "Mr. Spock's Time Trek." Three reels for talking viewer. Packed in 8″ × 8″ box with color scenes from "Yesteryear" episode. ....$10–$20
GAF—1979. Star Trek: The Motion Picture. Three reels with scenes from movie. Includes story booklet. Color envelope shows movie logo. ....$10–$15
GAF—1979. "View-Master Gift Pak." Star Trek: The Motion Picture. Set includes viewer, three reels, 3-D poster, and glasses. Packaged in cylindrical cardboard can with plastic lid. Container depicts child with toy and photos of characters in background. ....$75–$125
GAF—1981. "View-Master Double-Vue." Star Trek: The Motion Picture. Double plastic cassette with two film strips. Blister-packed on color header with movie logo. .....$10–$20

YO-YOS

Aviva—1979. Star Trek: The Motion Picture. Blue sparkle plastic with Enterprise and logo on side. Blister-packed on monotone header with artwork of Spock. ....$15–$25
Spectra Star—1993. Star Trek: Deep Space Nine. Plastic. Character Yo-Yos come in two styles: gold with color photo sticker in center, and communicator and Bajoran insignias in raised design around edge, or photo sticker to edge of less rounded yo-yo. Neither style character yo-yo seems to be more prevalent. Space station is blue with silver raised design. Blister-packed on round-bottomed header card with logo and space station.

Kira. ....$5–$10

Quark. ....$5–$10
Sisko. ....$5–$10
Space Station. ....$8–$12

Spectra Star—1993. Star Trek: The Next Generation. Plastic. Character and logo yo-yos come in two styles: silver with color photo sticker in center and raised logo around edge, or photo sticker to edge of less rounded yo-yo. Neither style seems more prevalent. Ship is blue with raised silver design. Blister-packed on round-bottomed header card with logo and Enterprise-D.

Data. ....$5–$10
Enterprise-D. ....$8–$12
Logo. ....$5–$10
Picard. ....$5–$10
Riker. ....$5–$10
Worf. ....$5–$10

MISCELLANEOUS

Action Fleet—Star Trek: The Motion Picture. 1979. Color cardboard mobile of various ships. Came in white envelope with logo on cover. Candy promotion. ....$20–$30

Astro-Helmet—Remco. 1967. Yellow plastic helmet with large blue plastic eyepieces and Star Trek decals. Box has color photo of toy and two small color inset photos from original TV show. ....$3000–$8000

Astrotank—Remco. 1967. Small yellow toy tank with Star Trek decals. Includes four shells and three red plastic toy soldiers. Box has color photo of toy and three small color inset photos from original TV show. ....$3000–$8000

Astrotrain—Remco. 1967. Three cars and track. Box has color photos of toy and three small color inset photos from original TV show. ....$3000–$8000

NOTE: The Remco Astro toys, which are actually Star Trek re-packaging of other Remco toys, are extremely rare, possibly prototypes. There are probably no more than 10 Astro toys total *still in existence.*

Belt, Buckle, and Insignia—South Bend. 1979. Star Trek: The Motion Picture. Thermal strip and storage compartment in buckle. Box has color photos on front top and header. ....
....$25–$35

Binoculars—Larami. 1968. White and orange with Star Trek logo. Blister-packed on color cardboard header depicting Spock. ....$45–$65

Balloon—Anagram International (British). 1994. USS Enterprise 1701. Stylized white starship-shaped helium balloon with color accents. Approx. 4′ long. Comes packaged sealed in 8½″ × 12″ plastic bag with color photos of product and hole at top for hanging. ....$20–$25

Bop Bag—Azrak-Hamway. 1975. Inflatable plastic Spock. Came packaged in 6″ × 5″ box. Color box art shows toy and Enterprise. ....$100–$150

Bridge—Mego. 1975. "Star Trek USS Enterprise Action Playset." Designed to be used with 8″ dolls. Blue plastic fold-out with picture of Enterprise on front. Accessories included two stools, console, Captain's chair, and three screens. Box art showed toy with figures. ....$250–$400

Bridge—Mego. 1980. Star Trek: The Motion Picture. "USS Enterprise Bridge." Designed to be used with 3¾″ action figures. White molded plastic. Box art shows toy and figures.
....$175–$250

Bridge—Playmates. 1993. Eight sound functions, light-up screen, fold-down access panels. Designed to be used with Playmate action figures. Color box art shows playset with action figures and Next Generation logo in corner. ..$200–$300

Cartoon Capers—Wiggins Teape. 1978. Made in France for British market. Battery-powered light box, overlays, and colored pins. ....$75–$100

Collector's Case—Tara Toys. 1993. Plastic case containing two divided plastic trays designed to hold 12 action figures. Lid latches at side and has color artwork of Enterprise-D, logo, and insert photo of crew in lower corner. ....$10–$15

Colorforms Star Trek Adventure Set—Colorforms. 1975. Plastic stick-ons and color cardboard bridge scene. Color box art shows Kirk, Spock, McCoy, and Enterprise. ....$25–$35

Color N' Recolor Game Cloth, Star Trek—Avalon. 1979. 40″ × 36″ reusable plastic game cloth, eight crayons, and sponge. Color box art shows children coloring cloth. ....
....$25–$35

Command Communications Console—Mego. 1976. Approx. 13″ long. Blue plastic with light-up screen. Working toy base station to be used with walkie-talkies. Box art shows Spock and toy. ....$100–$150

Controlled Space Flight—Remco (Burbank in Britain). 1976. Plastic Enterprise counterbalanced on hub connected by wire to control lever. Battery powered. Includes color printed background board with "Star Trek" logo and pictures of ships and three objects to be retrieved, 23½″ × 6″ box shows photo of toy. ....$150–$175

Crystal Growing Kit—Kristal Corp. 1995. "Star Trek: The Next Generation Space Age Crystal Growing Kit." Kit contains molds, stirrers, instructions, and powder for making 14 different artificial crystals. Color box art shows crystals and photo of Next Generation crew below Enterprise-D on starfield. ....$30–$35

Engineering Playset—Playmates. 1994. Three sound features, two fold-down features, light-up reactor. Designed to be used with action figures. Color box art shows toy and action figures with Star Trek: Generations (movie) logo above. Stool and movie mini-poster included. Can be attached to Playmates Bridge Playset. ....$60–$70

Figurine Painting—Crafts by Whiting (division of Milton Bradley). 1979. Star Trek: The Motion Picture. Blister-packed. Includes plastic figurine, brush, and five paints. Color header art.

Kirk. ....$30–$40
Spock. ....$30–$40

Flying Disc (Frisbee)—Spectra Star. 1993. Star Trek: Deep Space Nine. Purple with color photo sticker of space station and crew. Bagged with header showing logo and space station. ....$4–$8

Flying Disc (Frisbee)—Spectra Star. 1993. Star Trek: The Next Generation. Red with color photo sticker of ship and crew. Bagged with header showing logo and ship. ....$4–$8

Frisbee—Remco. 1967. Flying USS Enterprise. "Star Trek" and Spock decal. ....$25–$50

Frisbees—Star Trek Official Fan Club. 1993. Schematic of saucer section of Enterprise. Three different.

NCC-1701, on white. ....$10–$15

NCC-1701-A, on white. ....$10–$15

NCC-1701-D, on blue. ....$10–$15

Happy Meals—McDonald's Premium. 1979. Star Trek: The Motion Picture. Colorful cardboard boxes with games. Included small prize. Six different box styles. Price each. ....$10–$15

NOTE: The prizes—a picture bracelet, a game card, a set of two iron-on mini-decals, a toy communicator (five different), or a box ring (four different)—are in demand among McDonald's collectors but are considered relatively minor by most Star Trek collectors.

Helmet—Enco (Remco). 1976. Plastic with flashing red light on top. Included decals for characters. Electronic sound. Color box art of child wearing toy. ....$150–$200

I.D. Set—Larami. 1979. Star Trek: The Motion Picture. Red plastic folder. Blister-packed on header with color photo art. ....$5–$15

Kite String—Aviva. 1979. Wrap-around string shows movie Enterprise and logo. Plastic or cardboard spool. ....$10–$15

Kite String—Spectra Star. 1993. Star Trek: The Next Generation. Plastic spool with logo on ends. Affixed to color header with logo and photo of Enterprise-D. ....$5–$10

Klingon Disrupter—Playmates. 1995. Light and two sound functions. 11″ long. Brown and silver barrel. Black handle with Klingon emblem. Box shows toy and either New Generation or Generations logo. Opening in box to test toy's function. Technical blueprint included. ....$15–$25

Magic Putty—Larami. 1979. Star Trek: The Motion Picture. Putty comes in blue plastic egg, blister-packed with tube of transfer solution on cardboard header with photo of Kirk and Spock. ....$5–$10

Magic Slates—Whitman. 1979. Four different designs.

Enterprise (Original TV). ....$10–$15

Kirk. ....$10–$15

Kirk and Spock. ....$10–$15

Spock. ....$10–$15

Marbles—Spectra Star. 1993. Star Trek: Deep Space Nine. Packaged in set of five different characters. Color photos of Comdr. Sisko, Odo, O'Brien, Kira, and Quark. Packaged on color header card with logo at top and rounded bottom. ....$5–$10

Marbles—Spectra Star. 1993. Star Trek: The Next Generation. Packaged in set of five different characters. Color photos of Picard, Riker, Data, Troi, and Geordi. Packaged on color header card with logo at top and rounded bottom. ......$5–$10

Medical Kit—Playmates. 1996. "Dr. McCoy's Medical Kit." Contains two original TV series medical instrument toys— Medical Scanner and Anabolic Protoplaser. Scanner has sound function. Protoplaser has light function. Kit includes Starfleet Medical School diploma. ....$20–$30

Metal Detector—Jetco. 1976. Working toy metal detector. White with "Property USS Enterprise" decal. Red and white 24″ × 10″ box. ....$200–$350

Mission to Gamma VI—Mego. 1976. 18″ high. Plastic "Cave Creature." Movable jaws, and trap door and cardboard base. Glove manipulator. Comes with four small colored plastic "Gamma People." Comes in large dark blue box with photo of toy. ....$600–$1000

Mix 'n Mold—Catalog Shoppe. 1975. Plaster casting set. Mold, molding compound, paint, and brush to make character. Box shows color artwork of character from original TV show.

Kirk. ....$50–$75

McCoy. ....$50–$75

Spock. ....$50–$75

Mobile Kit—DeMert. 1995. Punch-out color cardboard photos of planets and various ships from Star Trek: The Next Generation. Includes string, supports, and logo hanger. Approx. 30″ across. Comes shrink-wrapped with instruction booklet. ....$10–$15

Movie Viewer—Chemtoy. 1967. 3″ red and black plastic viewer toy. Includes two film strips. Blister-packed. Color header shows color photo of characters. ....$15–$25

Outdoor Fun Pack—Spectra Star. 1993. Star Trek: Deep Space Nine. Packaged assortment of various Spectra Star toys. Includes Frisbee, Delta Wing Kite and String, and Yo-Yo (various styles). Shrink-wrapped on 30″ × 10″ cardboard header with logo at top. ....$10–$15

Outdoor Fun Pack—Spectra Star. 1993. Star Trek: The Next Generation. Packaged assortment of various Spectra Star toys. Includes Frisbee, Delta Wing Kite and String, and Yo-Yo (various styles). Shrink-wrapped on 30″ × 10″ cardboard header with logo at top. ....$10–$15

Paint by Numbers—Hasbro. 1972. Canvas paint and instructions. Came boxed. Two sizes:

Large, 12″ × 19″, photo of Kirk, Spock, and Enterprise. ....$60–$80

Small, 11″ × 11″, photo of Kirk, Spock, and Enterprise. ....$40–$60

Paint By Number Plaque—Craft House. 1993. "Easy Painting." Two-piece plastic ship scenes with raised outlines of picture. Includes brush and nine different paints. Blister-packed on header card with logo and partially completed plaque pictured at top.

Enterprise (Main Ship). ....$10–$15

Romulan Warbird (Main Ship). ....$10–$15

Phaser Mini Playset—Playmates. 1995. Star Trek: The Next

Generation Innerspace Series. Type II (handle version) phaser that opens into a playset for mini-figures. Includes Worf, "Q," and Data mini-figures. Color box art shows toy in folded and unfolded positions with small window in lower corner to display figures and low header with logo. ....$15–$20

Phaser Battle Game—Mego. 1976. Battery-powered electronic target game. Black plastic. Approx. 13″ high. LED scoring lights, sound effects, and adjustable speed controls. Large red box with color artwork of Spock and toy. ....$500–$800

Phaser Rocket Gun—Lone Star (British). 1974. Black and yellow plastic. Fires projectile. Orange window box with logo and artwork of Spock. ....$50–$75

Planetarium—Mego. 1977. "Star Trek Intergalactic Planetarium." Large plastic toy planetarium, Enterprise light pointer, 14 constellation cards, and 20-minute information audio tape. Color box art shows toy, logo, and adult and two children. Extremely rare toy; possibly prototype. ....$1500–$2000

Pocket Flix—Ideal. 1978. Hand-held movie viewer with film cartridge with scenes from original TV episode "By Any Other Name." Battery operated. Came packaged in window box. ....$30–$50

Pool Lounge—Creata. 1995. "USS Enterprise Pool Lounge." Blow-up pool float resembles Enterprise-D. Approx. 80″ × 52″. Box art shows ship with insert photo of girl in pool on float. ....$40–$50

Rocket Pistol—Remco. 1967. Projectile firing cap pistol. Star Trek decals on side. Box has photo of Spock and inset photos from show and of toy. Vary rare, possibly prototype. *(NOTE: See also Astro toys from Remco in Miscellaneous section).* ....$3000–$8000

Saucer Gun—Azrak-Hamway. 1976. Plastic, phaser-shaped. Shoots 2″ plastic spinners. Three spinners included. Blister-packed on color header picturing Kirk and Spock. ...$20–$30

Space Design Center—Avalon. 1979. Star Trek: The Motion Picture. Craft kit consists of blue plastic tray, crew member cut-outs, paints, pens, crayons, etc. and project book. 14½″ × 18½″ box shows photo of child and kit. ....$125–$175

Space Viewer—Larami. 1979. Star Trek: The Motion Picture. Dome-shaped viewer toy with two film strips. Blister-packed on color header with photos of Kirk, Spock, and aliens. ....$15–$25

Spinning Disc—A.H. Prismatic (British). 1992. 4″ metal disc surfaced with silver diffractive foil in different patterns and printed with various Star Trek or Star Trek: The Next Generation motifs. Shrink-wrapped on header card with appropriate logo at top. Four different.

    Original Enterprise, with logo. ....$5–$7
    Star Trek: The Next Generation Logo. ....$5–$7
    25th Anniversary Logo (Original Star Trek). ....$5–$7
    USS Enterprise 1701-D. ....$5–$7

Spinning Disc (Orbiters)—Lightrix. 1994. Set of three 2″ discs surfaced with silver diffractive foil and printed with

Generations motifs (Kirk, Picard, and logo). Blister-packed on header card with logo at top. ....$5–$7

Sky Diving Parachutist—Azrak-Hamway. 1975. 4½″ painted, weighted figure attached to plastic parachute with Star Trek logo. Blister-packed on color header with artwork of Enterprise.

    Kirk. ....$35–$40
    Spock. ....$35–$40

Starpooler—Starpool, Inc. 1982. Color photo cardboard busts of characters in Star Trek II uniforms which attach to car window. Hinged hand "waves" when car is in motion. Packaged in plastic bags with hanging header that displays company logo.

    Kirk. ....$65–$95
    Spock (Vulcan Salute). ....$65–$95

Star Trekulator—Mego. 1976. Blue plastic battery-powered desk top calculator. L.E.D. and sound effects. Console shows bridge scene from original TV show, 6″ × 10″ box shows color artwork of Spock and toy. ....$100–$150

String Art Kit—Open Door. 1976. Craft kit with pins and colored string to create picture on 18″ × 24″ background. Color box art shows completed work. ....$75–$150

Telescreen—Mego. 1977. Battery-operated target game. Light and sound effects. Seat for action figure in front of screen. Plastic. Approx. 14″ × 10″. Box shows toy. ....$175–$250

Tracer Gun—Rayline (Ray Plastic, Grand Toys in Canada). 1966. Plastic pistol-shot-colored plastic discs. Discs included. Blister-packed. Color header showed Kirk, Spock, and Enterprise. ....$30–$40

Tracer Gun Discs (Jet Discs)—Rayline. 1966. 100 replacement discs for Tracer Gun. Blister-packed on color header showing toy. ....$5–$10

Tracer Scope—Rayline. 1968. Rifle version of Tracer Gun. Included discs. Blister-packed on color header showing Kirk, Spock, and Enterprise. Rare toy. ....$500–$750

Transporter—Palitoy (British). 1976. Spinning cylinder allows figure to "disappear." This is actually the transporter part of the Mego 1976 Bridge for the 8″ action figures. Comes in box with color artwork. ....$100–$125

Transporter—Playmates. 1993. Lights and sound. Designed to be used with Playmates action figures. Color box art shows figure beaming in toy and Next Generation logo. Blueprint included. ....$60–$70

Tribbles (Nonpurring)—JAM-G (for Starstruck). 1991. Ball of hair approx. 6″ across. Three colors: dark brown, light brown, and white. Packaged loosely on header card with product label, original TV logo, and color inset pictures from original TV episode "The Trouble with Tribbles." ....$10–$15

Tribbles (Purring)—JAM-G (for Starstruck). 1991. Ball of hair approx. 6″ across. Two battery-operated sound functions: purr and squeal. Three colors: dark brown, light brown, and white. Comes packaged in open tray box with header with product label, original TV logo, and color inset pictures from the original episode "The Trouble with Tribbles." ....$20–$25

NOTE: Fan-made Tribbles in a great variety of sizes and colors, many with other features such as squeakers, exist. Though these have been popular convention and mail order items for years, none have any collectible value.

Tricorder Mini-Playset—Playmates. 1995. "Medical Tricorder Mini-Playset." Star Trek: The Next Generation Innerspace Series." Toy opens into playset for mini-figures. Includes Dr. Crusher, La Forge, and Picard as Locutus mini-figures. Color box art shows toy in open and closed positions with small window in upper corner to display figures and low header with logo. ....$15–$20

Utility Belt—Remco. 1975–1978. Miniature black plastic phaser, tricorder, communicator, and belt with Star Trek buckle. Packaged in 8″ × 14½″ window box. At least two styles of box art are known. Both depict Kirk, Spock, and the Enterprise. Earlier style has light blue background, later style background is dark purple. Phaser in later toys shoots discs. ....$150–$250

Water Pistol—Azrak-Hamway. 1975. Plastic. Phaser-shaped. Blister-packed on color header with characters. ....$30–$50

Water Pistol—Azrak-Hamway. 1976. "USS Enterprise" Water Gun. White plastic shaped like Enterprise. Blister-packed on color header with artwork of Enterprise and photos of Kirk and Spock. ....$50–$75

Water Pistol—Aviva. 1979. Star Trek: The Motion Picture. Gray plastic replica of early movie phaser. Blister-packed on monotone header with artwork of Enterprise and Kirk. ....
....$30–$50

Window Scenes—Craft House. 1993. Reusable cling-on window decals designed to be painted and arrange by user. Includes brush, nine paints, and assorted ship, people, planet, and logo decals. Packaged in box with low header showing color photo of painted decals and child with logo and Enterprise-D above. ....$10–$15

NOTE: For other window decals see Decals, Stamps, and Stickers.

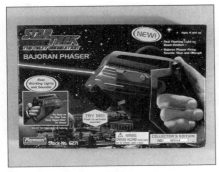

Playmates Bajoran Phaser

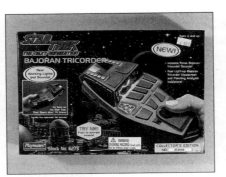

Playmates Bajoran Tricorder

Playmates *Next Generation* Bridge Playset

Azrak Hamway Star Trek Bop Bag

Colorforms Star Trek Adventure Set

Avalon Color 'n Recolor Gamecloth

Playmates Classic Star Trek Communicator (bottom) and Talk Back Communicator

Lone Star Star Trek Interspace Communicators

Whiting Spock and Kirk Figurine Painting Sets

Spectra Star *Next Generation* Flying Disk

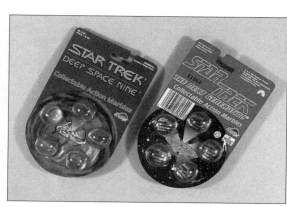

Spectra Star *Next Generation* and *Deep Space Nine* Marble Sets

Aviva *Star Trek: The Motion Picture* Pen and Poster Kit

Craft House Easy Painting Paint-by-number Placque

Mego Star Trek Super Phaser II Target Game

Playmates Classic Star Trek Phaser

ERTL *Star Trek III* Die Cast Ships

Galoob *Next Generation* Ferengi Fighter

Galoob Micro Machine Collection #3, initial issue (left) and later issue (without Borg Ship)

Galoob Star Trek: Micro Machine Collection #2

Galoob *Next Generation* Die Cast Metal Enterprise

Galoob Star Trek: Micro Machine Collection #13: *Voyager*

Galoob *Star Trek: The Movies* Collector's set

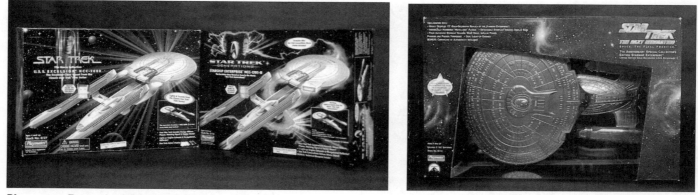

Playmates: *Enterprise* NCC 1701-B (right) and *Excelsior*

Playmates: *Enterprise* NCC 1701-D Limited Gold Edition

Playmates: *Enterprise* Glider

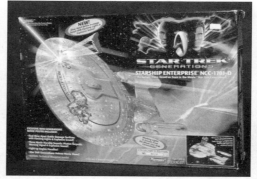

Playmates: *Enterprise* NCC 1701-D with blow-apart feature

Playmates: *Enterprise* NCC 1701-D Innerspace Series

JAM-G Non-purring Tribble

Playmates: Klingon Bird-of-Prey (*Generations* and *Next Generation* box styles)

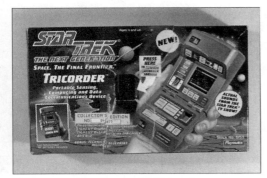

Playmates *Next Generation* Tricorder

Mego Star Trekulator

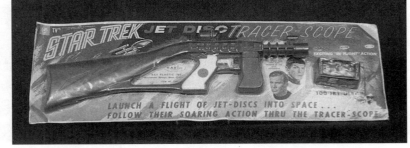

Rayline Tracer Scope

Playmates: Klingon Attack Cruiser

Larami Space Viewer

Mego Bridge

South Bend Belt Buckle and Insignia Playmates

Remco Utility Belts (both box styles)

Galoob (right) and Playmates Hand Phasers

TRADING CARDS

There has been an incredible resurgence of interest in non-sports trading cards over the past four to five years and Star Trek cards have led the way. Star Trek trading cards (we can no longer call them "gum cards") have always been highly collectible and continue to be so. The values for many of the older Star Trek sets of cards have increased by 100% to 400% since the last edition of this price guide. The scarcity of many of the "chase" cards makes them a very good potential investment. This added interest has been spurred by Impel/Skybox. This card company first started producing Star Trek cards for the 25th anniversary of Star Trek in 1991 and continues today. They introduced the first "chase" cards to the field of Star Trek. These are called "chase" cards because the collector has to chase them down. They are inserted "randomly" into individual packs of cards and they vary in rarity from fairly easy to obtain to virtually impossible. In this section "chase" cards will be listed along with their ratios (1:12) of insertion into individual packs.

INVESTMENT POTENTIAL
Excellent.

CARE
The main enemies of trading cards are moisture, sunlight, and rubber bands. Before 1970 there were very few items available to help protect trading cards. Early cards often show edge damage from rubber bands. This is often more prevalent with the first and last cards in a numbered set as they were usually on the top and bottom of the stack. There are vinyl pages available to hold cards in loose-leaf albums, hard plastic holders for single cards, and plastic boxes to hold complete sets. Any of these will effectively protect your collection. These quality supplies should be available at your local card or comic shops. Store your collection in a climate-controlled area, i.e., air-conditioned and away from sunlight. A bookcase inside your house will do fine.

SECTION NOTES
This trading card section will be divided into three sections: American Trading Cards, Customizable Card Games, and Foreign Trading Cards. Listings will be first by date of issue with continuing series grouped together. Some items may be listed in other sections, i.e., sticker albums and sticker sets in the Decals, Stamps, and Stickers section.

AMERICAN TRADING CARDS
The Early Years

This period extends from 1967 until the first Topps set in 1976. The price ranges for cards in this group vary widely as cards are often found in lesser conditions. The lower end of the price listings would be for cards in good or very good condition and the higher end for cards in near mint condition.

Star Trek

LEAF, 1967
Set includes 72 black and white cards. Limited distribution, very difficult to obtain in excellent condition! There is a lot of controversy about this set. Issued in the very early days of Star Trek by Desilu Studios, before Paramount, there is no one left with any records or information about this set. The set was removed from the marketplace after limited distribution for reasons undetermined. Conjecture has it that reasons may have been due to licensing problems or the poor quality (almost humorous) of the text on the cards.

Complete Set. ....$1000–$2500
Display Box. ....$600–$1000
Single Cards. ....$10–$35

Unopened Box.	SUPER RARE
Unopened Pack.	$300–$500
Wrapper.	$200–$400
#1, 72.	$20–$50

Star Trek (European)

LEAF, 1967

Set of 72, reprinted in Europe sometime between 1967 and 1993. Cards are a little blurrier on fronts and on back picture of Kirk and Spock than original 1967 Leafs. Uncut sheets exist.

Complete Set.	$25–$75
Single Cards.	$1
Uncut Sheet.	$50–$100

The Topps Years

This period extends from 1976 through 1979 and represents the period that most Star Trek fans use as their starting point for collecting. Values here are for cards in excellent to near mint condition. Lesser grades are generally not collectible.

Star Trek

TOPPS, 1976

First major U.S. Star Trek set, 88 color cards and 22 stickers.

Complete Set.	$200–$400
Display Box.	$20–$30
Single Cards.	$4–$6
#1, 88.	$5–$10
Single Stickers.	$5–$8
Sticker Set (22).	$100–$175
Unopened Box.	$500–$1000
Wrapper.	$3–$6

Star Trek: The Motion Picture

TOPPS, 1979

Set of 88 cards and 22 stickers based on the first movie. This was the last set of Star Trek cards issued with gum.

Complete Set.	$50–$75
Display Box.	$10–$20
Single Cards.	$1
Single Stickers.	$1
Sticker Set (22).	$15–$20
Unopened Box.	$100–$175
Wrapper.	$1–$2

Star Trek: The Motion Picture

BREAD, 1979

Issued by several different bread companies. Each set included 33 cards with identical fronts to Topps set but different backs. Cases of these have surfaced.

Colonial Bread Set.	$20–$30
Kilpatrick Bread Set.	$20–$30
Manor Bread Set.	$30–$40
Rainbo Bread Set.	$15–$20
Single Cards.	$.50–$1

The Fan Period

This period extends from 1982, with the release of cards by Fantasy Trading Card Company, through 1991, when Impel/Skybox first started issuing Star Trek cards. It also marks a period of cards being issued by smaller companies due to the indifference of major manufacturers.

Star Trek II: Wrath of Khan

FANTASY TRADING CARD COMPANY, 1982

Larger sized (5″ × 7″) set of 30 cards. Full-color fronts, text on backs.

Complete Set.	$60–$90
Display Box.	$10–$20
Single Card.	$2–$3
Unopened Box.	$75–$100
Unopened Pack.	$5–$6
Wrapper.	$2–$3

Star Trek III: Search for Spock

FANTASY TRADING CARD COMPANY, 1984

This set included 60 regular cards and 20 "space ship" cards.

Complete Set.	$60–$90
Display Box.	$10–$15
Promo cards (12″ × 12″), two different.	$10–$15
Single Cards.	$1–$2
Unopened Box.	$75–$100
Unopened Pack.	$3–$4
Wrapper.	$2–$3

Star Trek IV: Voyage Home

FANTASY TRADING CARD COMPANY, 1987

Set of 60 cards.

Complete Set.	$35–$50
Display Box.	$8–$12
Single Cards.	$.50–$1

Unopened Box.	$50–$75
Unopened Pack.	$2–$3
Wrapper.	$1–$2

Star Trek: Next Generation

PANINI, 1987

See Decals, Stamps, and Stickers section for Panini listings.

Personality Comics Star Trek Cards

Issued by Personality Comics in conjunction with their "biography" series of comics. Artwork is in full color with descriptions on back. The artwork is pretty amateurish on these sets of 36–37 cards.

Original Crew, set of 36.	$15–$25
Original Crew, signed and numbered by artist, limited to 750 signed sets.	$35–$50
Original Crew Series II.	$25–$35
New Crew, set of 36.	$12–$20
New Crew, signed and numbered as above.	$35–$50
New Crew, Series II, set of 37.	$15–$25

The Skybox Years

This recent period extends from 1991 to present and is dominated by the issues of Impel/Skybox. Impel/Skybox has issued loose-leaf binder albums in which to house many of their card sets. The values of these albums range from $15 to $25 each.

Star Trek 25th Anniversary

IMPEL, 1991

In 1991 Impel (later renamed Skybox) picked up the Star Trek license and started a still continuing series of Star Trek cards. This first set alternated classic and Next Generation cards for an interesting effect. Randomly inserted "chase" cards were first inserted in this series.

Display Box.	$3–$5
Holograms	
H1 Classic Ship.	$20–$35
H2 Next Generation Ship.	$20–$35
H3 Capt. Kirk.	$20–$35
H4 Capt. Picard.	$20–$35
Limited Edition Tin Set, includes both series (310 cards) and all four holograms along with a special card only in the tin.	$100–$125
Series I Set (160).	$15–$25
Series II Set (150).	$15–$25
Sealed Packs, two different per series.	$.50–$1
Single Cards.	$.25–$.50
Unopened Box.	$15–$25

Star Trek: Next Generation

IMPEL, 1992

The first set based exclusively on the new Star Trek series. This 120-card full-color set included two different subsets of "chase" cards. These were holograms and "foreign language" cards. The holograms were issued in two versions. The first version had incorrect numbering on the reverse and the second version fixed the mistake. The first version (error version) is more difficult to obtain.

Complete Set.	$15–$25
Display Box.	$3–$5
Foreign Language Cards, set of 5.	$8–$10
01A Japanese.	$2–$3
01B Spanish.	$2–$3
01C German.	$2–$3
01D French.	$2–$3
01E Russian.	$2–$3
Holograms.	
01H Bird-of-Prey.	$10–$15
02H Klingon Vorcha.	$10–$15
03H Romulan Warbird.	$10–$15
04H Ferengi Marauder.	$10–$15
05H Gold Enterprise (mail-in offer).	$15–$20
Holograms, Error.	
031 Bird-of-Prey.	$15–$25
033 Klingon Vorcha.	$15–$25
034 Romulan Warbird.	$15–$25
035 Ferengi Marauder.	$15–$25
Sealed Box.	$25–$50
Single Cards.	$.25–$.50
Unopened Pack.	$1–$2

Star Trek: Next Generation, Behind the Scenes

SKYBOX, 1993

This set features cards of all the major behind-the-scenes people: directors, producers, prop makers, security guards, etc. Sold as a complete set of 39 cards in a sealed plastic box.

Complete Set.	$10–$15

Star Trek: Deep Space Nine Boxed Set

SKYBOX, 1993

This set of 48 regular and 2 chrome cards was sold only as a boxed set and featured mostly publicity shots as an introduction to the new series.

Complete boxed set.	$10–$15

Star Trek: Deep Space Nine

SKYBOX, 1993

This set consists of 100 cards along with 5 different spectra "chase" cards and a mail-in "redemption" card good for a raised printing mini-set of 10 character cards.

Complete Set.	$15–$20
Display Box.	$3–$5
Redemption Card (Expired).	$35–$45
Redemption Set (10).	$100–$150
Single Card.	$.25–$.50
Spectra Cards.	
SP1 Planet Bajor.	$10–$12
SP2 Emissary.	$10–$12
SP3 Energy Creature.	$10–$12
SP4 The Mission.	$10–$12
SPG Wormhole Gold.	$15–$20
Unopened Box.	$40–$60
Unopened Pack.	$1–$2

Star Trek Master Series

SKYBOX, 1993

This set features 90 cards by various artists. All versions of Star Trek are included in these paintings. A five-card subset of spectra cards is featured as "chase" cards.

Complete Set.	$20–$25
Display Box.	$3–$5
Single Cards.	$.25–$.50
Spectra Cards:	
S1 Docking at DS9.	$12–$15
S2 Romulan Warbird.	$12–$15
S3 Asteroid Field.	$12–$15
S4 Enterprise vs. Bird-of-Prey.	$12–$15
S5 Doomsday Machine.	$12–$15
Unopened Box.	$20–$40
Unopened Pack.	$1–$2

Star Trek Master Series II

SKYBOX, 1994

This 100-card set features artwork like Series I but has a nine-card subset featuring artwork by Boris Vallejo, Julie Bell, and Joe Jusko. These "chase" cards form a triptych, three panels by each artist.

Complete Set.	$20–$25
Display Box.	$3–$5
Single Cards.	$.25–$.50
Triptych Cards.	
F1 Scotty/Chekov.	$10–$12
F2 Kirk/Spock/McCoy.	$10–$12
F3 Sulu/Uhura.	$10–$12
F4 Picard/Worf.	$10–$12
F5 Riker/Troi.	$10–$12
F6 Bev/Data/Geordi.	$10–$12
F7 Sisko/Dax.	$10–$12

F8 Quark/O'Brien/Kira.	$10–$12
F9 Julian/Odo.	$10–$12
Unopened Box.	$35–$50
Unopened Pack.	$1–$2

Star Trek: The Next Generation, Making of

SKYBOX, 1994

This set of 100 cards was sold exclusively through the mail by Skybox directly to the public. It was available in three versions, each with a different premium enclosed with the set. Nowhere near the number of "limited edition" sets made were ever sold, so values are still near the original issue price.

Collector's Set.	$25–$40
Gold Set.	$40–$50
Platinum Set.	$60–$80

Star Trek: Generations

SKYBOX, 1995

This was Skybox's first set devoted to the series of Star Trek movies. It consisted of 72 wide-vision/cinemascope cards.

Complete Set.	$20–$25
Display Box.	$3–$5
"F" Cards, three different.	$8–$10
F1 Escaping Reality.	
F2 Renegades.	
F3 Fragile Alliance.	
"Large" Skymotion Card, $4'' \times 5\frac{1}{2}''$.	$75–$125
"S" Cards.	$20–$30
S1 One Last Time.	
S2 The Greatest Legacy.	
S3 Legends Meet.	
Single Cards.	$.50–$.75
Skymotion Card.	$75–$100
Skymotion Redemption, expired.	$40–$60
Unopened Box.	$50–$65
Unopened Pack.	$2–$3

Star Trek, Cinema Collection

SKYBOX, 1994

Skybox tried to capitalize on their ever-growing Star Trek series of cards by offering a direct mail only set in the same format as their set based upon the seventh Star Trek movie. Each set was based on one of the movies and consisted of 72 wide-vision cards and came in a colorful cardboard box. Supplies far outreached demand and these were still available from the manufacturer in early 1996.

All Six Sets, plus promo cards.	$125–$175
Complete Set for Each Movie.	$20–$25

Star Trek: Next Generation Episode Collection

SKYBOX, 1994/95

Following the popularity of Star Trek: Next Generation, Skybox decided to issue a set based on each season. Each set had a continuing set of six "chase" cards (three characters and three Klingon) and super-rare holograms, issued only one per 180 packs.

SEASON I

Complete Set (108).	$25–$35
Display Box.	$3–$5
Foil Cards (1:12).	$12–$15

SP1 Klingon Empire Symbol.
SP2 Klingon Blade of the Warrior.
SP3 Klingon Tactical Display.
SP4 Lt. Natasha Yar.
SP5 "Q."
SP6 The Traveler.

Holograms (1:180).

HG1 Picard.	$150–$200
HG2 Data.	$150–$200
Sealed Box.	$80–$100
Sealed Pack.	$2–$4
Single Cards.	$.25–$.50

SEASON II

Complete Set (96).	$18–$25
Display Box.	$2–$4
Foil Cards (1:12).	$10–$12

SP7 H'Vort Class Pagh.
SP8 Klingon Sword of Honor.
SP9 Age of Ascension.
SP10 Guinan.
SP11 Dr. Katherine Pulaski.
SP12 Prof. Moriarity.

Holograms (1:180).

HG3 Riker.	$125–$150
HG4 Troi.	$125–$150
Single Cards.	$.25–$.50
Unopened Box.	$60–$80
Unopened Pack.	$2–$3

SEASON III

Complete Set (108).	$18–$25
Display Box.	$2–$4
Foil Cards (1:12).	$10–$12

SP13 Klingon Family Values.
SP14 Klingon Disrupter Rifle.
SP15 Klingon Battle Cruiser.
SP16 Locutus.
SP17 Lal.
SP18 K'Ehler.

Holograms (1:180)

HG5 Dr. Crusher.	$125–$150
HG6 Worf.	$125–$150
Single Cards.	$.25–$.50

Unopened Box.	$45–$60
Unopened Pack.	$2–$3

SEASON IV

Complete Set (108).	$18–$25
Display Box.	$2–$4
Foil Cards (1:12).	$8–$12

SP19 Klingon Communicator.
SP20 Klingon Sash.
SP21 Klingon Food.
SP22 Soong.
SP23 Keiko O'Brien.
SP24 Shelby.

Holograms (1:180).

HG7 Geordi.	$80–$100
HG8 Wesley.	$80–$100
Single Cards.	$.25–$.50
Unopened Box.	$45–$60
Unopened Pack.	$1.50–$2

SEASON V

Complete Set (108).	$18–$25
Display Box.	$2–$4
Foil Cards (1:12).	$8–$12

S25 Klingon Great Hall.
S26 Lursa and B'Etor.
S27 Klingon Homeworld.
S28 Dathon.
S29 Spock.
S30 Sela.

Holograms (1:90).

HG9 Guinan.	$50–$60
HG10 Ens. Ro.	$50–$60
Single Cards.	$.25–$.50
Unopened Box (48).	$65–$80
Unopened Pack.	$1.50–$2

Star Trek Voyager

SKYBOX, 1995

Skybox started their series of Voyager cards with Series I, based on the pilot episode, and Series II, based on the rest of Season I. Each set had a nine-card set of foil "chase" cards of crew members and other characters, as well as a Skymotion card (1:180) and other "chase" cards.

SERIES I, PILOT EPISODE

Complete Set (108).	$20–$25
Display Box.	$2–$4
Doctor Hologram (1:180).	$60–$100
Expand-A-Cards (1:18).	$8–$10

X1 USS Voyager.
X2 The Bridge.
X3 Engineering.

Single Card.	$.25–$.50
Skymotion Card.	$75–$100

Skymotion Exchange Card (1:180), expired. ....$40–$60
Spectra Character Cards (1:12).
    F1 Janeway. ....$15–$20
    F2 Chakotay. ....$12–$15
    F3 Tuvok. ....$12–$15
    F4 Tom Paris. ....$12–$15
    F5 B'Elanna Torres. ....$12–$15
    F6 Harry Kim. ....$12–$15
    F7 The Doctor. ....$12–$15
    F8 Neelix. ....$12–$15
    F9 Kes. ....$12–$15
Unopened Box. ....$50–$75
Unopened Pack. ....$2–$3

SERIES II, SEASON I

Complete Set (98). ....$18–$24
Display Box. ....$2–$4
Neelix's Recipe Cards (1:18). ....$10–$12
    R1 Vulcan Plomeek Soup.
    R2 Laurelian Blue Pudding.
    R3 Taker Loggerhead Eggs.
    R4 Proteinaceous Coffee Cocktail.
    R5 Macaroni and Brill Cheese.
    R6 Spinach Shake With Pear.
Single Card. ....$.25–$.50
Skymotion Card. ....$75–$100
Skymotion Exchange Card, expired. ....$40–$60
Spectra Cards (1:12). ....$10–$12
    S1 Seska.
    S2 T'elek.
    S3 Gathoerel Labin.
    S4 Dr Neria.
    S5 Sulan.
    S6 Jetrel.
    S7 Jabin.
    S8 Lidell.
    S9 Toscat.
Unopened Box. ....$45–$60
Unopened Pack. ....$2–$3

Star Trek 30th Anniversary

SKYBOX, 1996

These 30th anniversary cards come in three phases or series. The first series covers equipment, technology, and a preview of character cards. A series of nine gold foil equipment cards (1:12), three die-cut cards (1:36), nine gold foil ship registry cards (1:72), and a Skymotion card (1:180) fill out the "chase" cards in this set. An attractive display box comes with these cards.

PHASE I

Complete Set (98). ....$20–$25
Die-Cut Technology Cards (1:18). ....$12–$20
    D-1 Klingon Knife.
    D-2 Starfleet Phaser.
    D-3 Romulan/Klingon Disrupter.

Display Box. ....$8–$10
Gold Foil Cards (1:12). ....$8–$12
    E1 Mid 23rd-Century Phaser.
    E2 Late 23rd-Century Phaser.
    E3 24th-Century Phaser.
    E4 Mid 23rd-Century Communicator.
    E5 Late 23rd-Century Communicator.
    E6 24th-Century Communicator.
    E7 Mid 23rd-Century Tricorder.
    E8 Late 23rd-Century Tricorder.
    E9 24th-Century Tricorder.
Ship Registry Plaque, gold foil embossed cards, rare (1:180).
....$60–$80
    R-1 USS Enterprise.
    R-2 NCC 1701-A.
    R-3 NCC 1701-B.
    R-4 NCC 1701-D.
    R-5 USS Excelsior.
    R-6 USS Stargazer.
    R-7 USS Brittain.
    R-8 USS Sutherland.
    R-9 USS Voyager.
Single Cards. ....$.25–$.50
Skymotion Card. ....$75–$100
Skymotion Exchange Card. ....$40–$60
Unopened Box. ....$60–$75
Unopened Pack. ....$2–$3

Star Trek 30th Anniversary: Phase II

SKYBOX, 1996

The second series of Star Trek 30th anniversary cards consists of 100 cards (numbered 101–200) and continues where Phase One left off. Phase Two consists of Alien, Personnel, and Cosmic Phenomena cards. Subsets include a nine-card spectra "Dopplegangers" set and a nine-card lenticular "Undercover Personnel" set. The Skymotion Exchange card can be exchanged for an Odo Skymotion card. There is an attractive display box.

PHASE II

Complete Set of 100 Cards (#101–200). ....$18–$25
Display Box (Empty). ....$5–$8
Exchange Card. ....$40–$60
Lenticular "Undercover Personnel" Cards (1:18). ....
....$15–$25
    L1 Capt. Kirk as Romulan.
    L2 Comdr. Spock as Iotian.
    L3 Capt. Picard as Romulan.
    L4 Comdr. Riker as Malcorian.
    L5 Comdr. Chakotay as Vidian.
    L6 Lt. Worf as Borralan.
    L7 Lt. Comdr La Forge as Tarchannen.
    L8 Lt. Troi as Romulan.
    L9 Maj. Kira as Cardassian.
Odo Skymotion Card. ....$60–$100

Sealed Box. ....$65–$95
Sealed Pack. ....$1.50–$2.50
Single Cards. ....$.25–$.50
Spectra "Dopplegangers" Cards (1:12). ....$8–$12
    F1 Capt. Kirk in "The Enemy Within."
    F2 Spock in "Mirror, Mirror."
    F3 Sulu in "Mirror, Mirror."
    F4 Capt. Picard in "All Good Things."
    F5 Riker in "Second Chances."
    F6 Data in "Descent."
    F7 Kira in "Looking Glass."
    F8 Tuvok in "Looking Glass."
    F9 Torres in "Faces."

CUSTOMIZABLE CARD GAMES

Based on the popular customizable card game Magic: The Gathering, these games have become incredibly popular. The sheer size of the sets (over 300 cards) and the scarcity of many of the cards makes these sets difficult, if not addictive, to complete. The basic game can be played by two people, each with a "Starter deck." But here is where the interest is piqued. Player can purchase "booster packs" which include additional cards, some of which are "rare" and very powerful cards for playing the game. The player who purchases the most cards, or trades with his friends, will usually have a more powerful "deck" when playing the game and will usually win more often.

Star Trek: The Next Generation Customizable Card Game

This was the first of the Star Trek Customizable card games. This 360-card set contains 120 "rare" cards, making sets extremely difficult to obtain. These cards were issued in three editions by Decipher. The Black Border Limited Edition was a complete sell out within two weeks of release and values escalated quickly but have now settled down. The White Border Unlimited Edition followed a few months later and was issued in an Alpha and Beta edition. There are minor differences and most collectors do not distinguish between them. A Limited Edition Silver Border complete set was issued in a collector's tin. It was not well received by collectors.

Complete Sets

Complete Black Border Limited Edition Set (360 Cards). ....$800–$1500
Complete White Border Unlimited Edition Set (360 Cards). ....$400–$800
Complete Limited Edition Silver Border Set (360)—This set comes in an attractive tin along with a Certificate of Au-

thenticity listing this as one of 10,000 sets issued worldwide. ....$100–$250

Single Cards (Divided by Type)

The "rare" cards in this set are truly hard to find. There is only one "rare" card for every three "uncommon" cards and only one "rare" card for every 11 "common" cards. In order to have even a chance for a complete set, one would have to purchase over 120 Booster packs (at a cost of well over $350). The Limited Edition Black Border cards were sold out virtually before they were issued and prices vary widely. Rarity is in parentheses: (C) Common, (UC) Uncommon, or (R) Rare.

Single Common Cards
    Black Border Limited Edition. ....$.50–$1
    White Border Unlimited Edition. ....$.25–$.50
Single Uncommon Cards
    Black Border Limited Edition. ....$2–$4
    White Border Unlimited Edition. ....$1–$2
Single Rare Cards—The first value listed is for the Unlimited White Border cards and the second value is for the Limited Edition Black Border cards.

ARTIFACT CARDS
Betazoid Gift Box (R).	$10	$30
Horga'hn (R).	$12	$25
Interphase Generator (R).	$8	$25
Kurlan Naiskos (R).	$10	$25
Thought Maker (R).	$10	$25
Time Travel Pod (R).	$8	$25
Tox Uthat (R).	$10	$25
Varon-T Disrupter (R).	$10	$25
Vulcan Stone of Gol (R).	$12	$25

DILEMMA CARDS
Anaphasic Organism (C).
Archer (C).
Female's Love Interest (C).
Iconian Computer Weapon (C).
Impassable Door (C).
Male's Love Interest (C).
Menthar Booby Trap (C).
Microbiotic Colony (C).
Microvirus (C).
Phased Matter (C).

Alien Abduction (UC).
Alien Parasites (UC).
Birth of "Junior" (UC).
Chalnoth (UC).
Cosmic String Fragment (UC).
El-Adel Creature (UC).
Firestorm (UC).
Gravitic Mine (UC).
Hologram Ruse (UC).

Hyper-Ageing (UC).
Matriarchal Society (UC).
Nanites (UC).
Nausicaans (UC).
Nitrium Metal Parasites (UC).
Null Space (UC).
Portal Guard (UC).
Radioactive Garbage Scow (UC).
Rebel Encounter (UC).
REM Fatigue Hallucinations (UC).
Shaka, When the Walls Fell (UC).
Tarellian Plague Ship (UC).
Two-Dimensional Creatures (UC).

Ancient Computer (R). ....$5–$10
Armus-Skin of Evil (R). ....$5–$10
Barclay's Protomorphosis Disease (R). ....$5–$10
Borg Ship (R). ....$15–$25
Crystalline Entity (R). ....$6–$12
Cytherians (R). ....$5–$10
Ktarian Game (R). ....$5–$10
Nagilum (R). ....$5–$10
"Q" (R). ....$15–$25
Sarjenka (R). ....$7–$12
Temporal Causality Loop (R). ....$5–$10
Tsiolkovsky Infection (R). ....$5–$10
Wind Dancer (R). ....$6–$12

EQUIPMENT CARDS
Engineering Kit (C).
Engineering PADD (C).
Federation PADD (C).
Klingon Disrupter (C).
Klingon PADD (C).
Medical Kit (C).
Medical Tricorder (C).
Romulan Disrupter (C).
Romulan PADD (C).
Starfleet Type II Phaser (C).
Tricorder (C).

EVENT CARDS
Atmospheric Ionization (C).
Espionage: Federation on Klingon (C).
Espionage: Klingon on Federation (C).
Espionage: Romulan on Federation (C).
Espionage: Romulan on Klingon (C).
Pattern Enhancers (C).
Plasma Fire (C).
"Q"-Net (C).
Red Alert (C).
Res-"Q" (C).
Spacedock (C).
Static Warp Bubble (C).
Subspace Warp Rift (C).
Tetryon Field (C).

Treaty: Federation/Klingon (C).
Treaty: Federation/Romulan (C).
Treaty: Romulan/Klingon (C).
Where No One Has Gone Before (C).

Alien Probe (UC).
Distortion Field (UC).
Gaps in Normal Space (UC).
Genetronic Replicator (UC).
Holo-Projectors (UC).
Kivas Fajo, Collector (UC).
Masaka Transformations (UC).
Metaphasic Shields (UC).
Neural Servo Device (UC).
Nutational Shields (UC).
Raise the Stakes (UC).
Telepathic Alien Kidnappers (UC).
The Traveler: Transcendence (UC).

Anti-Time Anomaly (R). ....$6–$10
Bynars Weapon Enhancement (R). ....$6–$10
Goddess of Empathy (R). ....$8–$15
Lore Returns (R). ....$10–$25
Lore's Fingernail (R). ....$8–$20
Supernova (R). ....$8–$20
Warp Core Breach (R). ....$6–$10

FEDERATION PERSONNEL CARDS
Calloway (C).
Christopher Hobson (C).
Darian Wallace (C).
Giusti (C).
Linda Larson (C).
McKnight (C).
Mendon (C).
Simon Tarses (C).
Sito Jaxa (C).
Taitt (C).
Taurik (C).

Alexander Rozhenko (UC).
Alyssa Ogawa (UC).
Benjamin Maxwell (UC).
Dr. Selar (UC).
Eric Pressman (UC).
Exocomp (UC).
Fleet Adm. Shanthi (UC).
Hannah Bates (UC).
Jenna D'Soru (UC).
Kareel Odan (UC).
Mot the Barber (UC).
Nikolai Rozhenko (UC).
Norah Satie (UC).
Riva (UC).
Sirna Kolrami (UC).
Soren (UC).

T'Pan (UC).
Toby Russell (UC).

Albert Einstein (R). ....$10–$25
Alynna Nechayev (R). ....$10–$15
Beverly Crusher (R). ....$25–$45
Data (R). ....$45–$80
Deanna Troi (R). ....$35–$50
Dr. La Forge (R). ....$8–$12
Dr. Leah Brahms (R). ....$8–$16
Geordi La Forge (R). ....$35–$50
Jean-Luc Picard (R). ....$60–$95
K'ehleyr (R). ....$10–$20
Leah Brahms (R). ....$10–$20
Lwaxanna Troi (R). ....$20–$35
Morgan Bateson (R). ....$8–$16
Neela Daren (R). ....$10–$16
Reginald Barclay (R). ....$10–$16
Richard Galen (R). ....$8–$16
Ro Laren (R). ....$16–$30
Sarek (R). ....$15–$30
Satelk (R). ....$8–$15
Shelby (R). ....$10–$20
Sir Isaac Newton (R). ....$10–$20
Tam Elbrun (R). ....$10–$16
Tasha Yar (R). ....$20–$40
Thomas Riker (R). ....$25–$40
Vash (R). ....$12–$20
Wesley Crusher (R). ....$25–$45
William T. Riker (R). ....$35–$60
Worf (R). ....$40–$60

FEDERATION SHIP CARDS
Runabout (C).
Type VI Shuttlecraft (C).
USS Excelsior (C).
USS Galaxy (C).
USS Miranda (C).
USS Nebula (C).
USS Oberth (C).

USS Sutherland (UC).

USS Brittain (R). ....$20–$35
USS Enterprise (R). ....$60–$95
USS Hood (R). ....$12–$25
USS Phoenix (R). ....$12–$25
USS Yamato (R). ....$20–$35

INTERRUPT CARDS
Asteroid Sanctuary (C).
Disrupter Overload (C).
Emergency Transporter Armbands (C).
Escape Pod (C).
Klingon Right of Vengence (C).
Long-Range Scan (C).

Loss of Orbital Stability (C).
Palor Toff, Alien Trader (C).
Particle Fountain (C).
Rogue Borg Mercenaries (C).
Scan (C).
Ship Seizure (C).
Subspace Interference (C).
Tachyon Detection Grid (C).
Wormhole (C).

Amanda Rogers (UC).
Auto-Destruct Sequence (UC).
Distortion of Space/Time Continuum (UC).
Energy Vortex (UC).
Full Planet Scan (UC).
Incoming Message—Federation (UC).
Incoming Message—Klingon (UC).
Incoming Message—Romulan (UC).
Kevin Uxbridge (UC).
Life-Form Scan (UC).
Near Warp Transport (UC).
Q2 (UC).
Subspace Schism (UC).
Temporal Rift (UC).
The Juggler (UC).
Transwarp Conduit (UC).
Vulcan Mindmeld (UC).

Alien Groupie (R). ....$5–$10
Crosis (R). ....$10–$20
Honor Challenge (R). ....$5–$10
Hugh (R). ....$10–$16
Jaglom Shrek-Info Broker (R). ....$5–$10
Klingon Death Yell (R). ....$5–$10
The Devil (R). ....$5–$12

KLINGON PERSONNEL CARDS
B'iJik (C).
Batrell (C).
Divok (C).
Dukath (C).
Gorath (C).
J'Ddan (C).
K'Tesh (C).
Klag (C).
Kle'eg (C).
Kromm (C).
Torin (C).
Vekma (C).

Ba'el (UC).
Fek'lhr (UC).
K'mpec (UC).
K'Tal (UC).
K'Vada (UC).
Kell (UC).

Konmel (UC).
Koral (UC).
Koroth (UC).
Korris (UC).
L'Kor (UC).
Morag (UC).
Nu'Daq (UC).
Toq (UC).
Torak (UC).
Toral (UC).
Vagh (UC).

B'Etor (R). ....$20–$40
Duras (R). ....$12–$25
Gowron (R). ....$25–$40
Kahless (R). ....$10–$20
Kargan (R). ....$10–$20
Kurak (R). ....$10–$20
Kurn (R). ....$12–$24
Lursa (R). ....$15–$30

KLINGON SHIP CARDS
I.K.C. K'Vort (C).
I.K.C. Vor'Cha (C).
I.K.C. Vorn (UC).
I.K.C. Bortas (R). ....$10–$24
I.K.C. Buruk (R). ....$10–$20
I.K.C. Hegh'ta (R). ....$8–$16
I.K.C. Pagh (R). ....$10–$20
I.K.C. Qu'Vat (R). ....$10–$20

MISSION CARDS
Covert Installation (C).
Excavation (C).
Fever Emergency (C).
Investigate Anomaly (C).
Relief Mission (C).
Repair Mission (C).
Study Plasma Streamer (C).
Study Stellar Collision (C).
Test Mission (C).

Cloaked Mission (UC).
Covert Rescue (UC).
Diplomacy Mission (UC).
Evacuation (UC).
Expose Covert Supply (UC).
First Contact (UC).
Krios Suppression (UC).
Plunder Site (UC).
Restore Errant Moon (UC).
Secret Salvage (UC).
Strategic Diversion (UC).

Avert Disaster (R). ....$4–$8
Cultural Observation (R). ....$4–$8

Evaluate Terraforming (R). ....$4–$8
Explore Black Cluster (R). ....$4–$8
Explore Dyson Sphere (R). ....$4–$8
Explore Typhone Expanse (R). ....$4–$8
Extraction (R). ....$4–$8
Hunt for DNA Program (R). ....$4–$8
Iconia Investigation (R). ....$4–$8
Investigate "Shattered Space" (R). ....$4–$8
Investigate Alien Probe (R). ....$4–$8
Investigate Disappearance (R). ....$4–$8
Investigate Disturbance (R). ....$4–$8
Investigate Massacre (R). ....$4–$8
Investigate Raid (R). ....$4–$8
Investigate Rogue Comet (R). ....$4–$8
Investigate Sighting (R). ....$4–$8
Investigate Time Continuum (R). ....$4–$8
Khitomer Research (R). ....$4–$8
Medical Relief (R). ....$4–$8
New Contact (R). ....$4–$8
Pegasus Search (R). ....$8–$12
Sarthong Plunder (R). ....$4–$8
Seek Life-form (R). ....$4–$8
Study "Hole in Space" (R). ....$4–$8
Study Ionka Pulsar (R). ....$4–$8
Study Nebula (R). ....$8–$12
Survey Mission (R). ....$4–$8
Wormhole Negotiations (R). ....$4–$8

OUTPOST CARDS;
Federation (C).
Klingon (C).
Romulan (C).

ROMULAN PERSONNEL CARDS
Galathon (C).
Jaron (C).
Jera (C).
Palteth (C).
Selok (C).
Takket (C).
Tallus (C).
Tarus (C).
Taul (C).
Thei (C).
Tomek (C).
Varel (C).

Bochra (UC).
Mirok (UC).
Movar (UC).
N'Vek (UC).
Neral (UC).
Pardek (UC).
Parem (UC).
Taibak (UC).

Tebok (UC).
Tokath (UC).

Alidar Jarok (R). ....$8–$16
Mendak (R). ....$8–$16
Sela (R). ....$15–$30
Tomalak (R). ....$10–$16
Toreth (R). ....$8–$14

ROMULAN SHIP CARDS
D'deridex (C).
Science Vessel (C).
Scout Vessel (C).

Devoras (R). ....$12–$24
Haakona (R). ....$12–$24
Khazara (R). ....$12–$20
Pi (R). ....$6–$15

UNALIGNED PERSONNEL CARDS
Dr. Farek (C).
Gorta (C).
Narik (C).
Vekor (C).

Amarie (UC).
Baran (UC).
Bok (UC).
Devinoni Ral (UC).
Dr. Reyga (UC).
Etana Jol (UC).
Evek (UC).
Ishara Yar (UC).
Jo'Bril (UC).
Ocett (UC).

Roga Danar (R). ....$15–$25

UNALIGNED SHIP CARDS
Zibalian Transport (C).
Yridian Shuttle (C).
Mercenary Ship (C).
Combat Vessel (C).

Husnock Ship (UC).

Alternate Universe Supplemental Set

The first supplemental card set to the Star Trek Customizable Card Game, the "Alternate Universe," is similar to the previous set but is one-third the size (122 cards). It consists of cards in all of the regular categories previously used and includes "common," "uncommon," and "rare" cards. These cards were only issued in the Limited Edition Black Border version.

Complete Sets

Complete Set (121), without ultra-rare. ....$50–$75
Complete Set (122), with ultra-rare. ....$125–$200
Booster Packs. ....$3–$4
Common Cards. ....$.25–$.50
Uncommon cards. ....$.50–$1
Rare cards (or as marked in list below). ....$4–$5
Ultra-Rare Card: Future Enterprise. ....$75–$125

Single Cards (Divided by Type):

Rarity in parentheses: (C) Common, (UC) Uncommon, or (R) Rare.

ARTIFACT CARDS
Cryosatellite (R).
Data's Head (R).
Iconian Gateway (R).
Ophidian Cane (R).
Receptacle Stones (R).
Ressikan Flute (R).
Samuel Clemen's Pocketwatch (R).

DILEMMA CARDS
Alien Labyrinth (C).
Conundrum (C).
Empathic Echo (C).
Ferengi Attack (C).
Hidden Entrance (C).
Hunter Gangs (C).
Interphasic Plasma Creatures (C).
Malfunctioning Door (C).
Outpost Raid (C).
Punishment Zone (C).
The Gatherers (C).
Thought Fire (C).
Worshiper (C).

Cardassian Trap (UC).
Edo Probe (UC).
Frame of Mind (UC).
Maman Picard (UC).
Parallel Romance (UC).
Quantum Singularity Life forms (UC).
Rascals (UC).
Royale Casino Blackjack (UC).
The Higher . . . The Fewer (UC).
Zaldan (UC).

Coalescent Organism (R).

DOORWAY CARDS
Alternate Universe Door (C).

Devidian Door (R).

EQUIPMENT CARDS
I.P. Scanner (C).

Echo Papa 607 Killer Drone (R).

EVENT CARDS:
Baryon Buildup (C).
Particle Scattering Field (C).
Rishen Uxbridge (C).
The Mask of Korgano (C).
Yellow Alert (C).

Captain's Log (UC).
Engage Shuttle Operations (UC).
Intruder Force Field (UC).
Klim Dokachin (UC).
Lower Decks (UC).
Mot's Advice (UC).
The Charybdis (UC).
Thermal Deflectors (UC).

Interrogation (R).
Revolving Door (R).
Wartime Conditions (R).

INTERRUPT CARDS
Anti-Matter Spread (C).
Countermanda (C).
Destroy Radioactive Garbage Scow (C).
Devidian Foragers (C).
Eyes in the Dark (C).
Fire Sculptor (C).
Hail (C).
Howard Heirloom Candie (C).
Humuhumunukunukuapua's (C).
Jamaharon (C).
Kevin Uxbridge: Convergence (C).
Latinum Payoff (C).
Phaser Burns (C).
Security Sacrifice (C).
Thine Own Self (C).
Vulcan Nerve Pinch (C).

Barclay Transporter Phobia (UC).
Brain Drain (UC).
Dead in Bed (UC).
Incoming Message: Attack Authoriz. (UC).
Isabella (UC).
La Forge Maneuver (UC).
Rescue Captives (UC).
Romulan Ambush (UC).
Senior Staff Meeting (UC).
Temporal Narcosis (UC).
Wolf (UC).

Seize Wesley (R).
Vorgon Raiders (R).

MISSION, FEDERATION CARDS
Reunion (R).
Risa Shore Leave (R).

MISSION, KLINGON CARDS
Brute Force (R).
Warped Space (R).

MISSION, ROMULAN CARDS
Quash Conspiracy (R).

MISSION, ROMULAN/KLINGON CARDS
Compromised Mission (R).

MISSION, ROMULAN/KLINGON/FEDERATION CARDS
Diplomatic Conference (R).
FGC-47 Research (R).
Fissure Research (R).

MISSION, NONALIGNED CARDS
Qualor Li Rendezvous (R).

OUTPOST CARDS
Neutral Outpost (C).

PERSONNEL, FEDERATION CARDS
Montgomery Scott (C).

Lt. (J.G.) Picard (UC).
Paul Rice, Holo Re-Creation (UC).
Richard Castillo (UC).

Beverly Picard (R). ....$8–$10
Ian Andrew Troi (R). ....$6–$8
Jack Crusher (R). ....$6–$8
Rachel Garrett (R). ....$5–$8
Tasha Yar-Alt (R). ....$8–$10

PERSONNEL, KLINGON CARDS
Targ (C).

Governor Worf (R). ....$10–$15
K'mtar (R). ....$4–$6

PERSONNEL, NONALIGNED CARDS
Ajur (UC).
Boratus (UC.)
Lakanta (UC).
Maques (UC).
Micky D. (UC).

Berlingoff Rastmussen (R).
Dathon (R).

PERSONNEL, ROMULAN CARDS
D'Tan (C).

Comdr. Tomalak (R). ....$4–$6
Maj. Rakal (R). ....$8–$10
Stefan DeSeve (R). ....$4–$6

SHIP, FEDERATION CARDS
USS Enterprise-C (R). ....$10–$12

SHIP, KLINGON CARDS
I.K.C. K'Ratak (C).

I.K.C. Fek'lhr (R). ....$6–$8

SHIP, NONALIGNED CARDS
Edo Vessel (R). ....$4–$6
Gomtuu (R). ....$4–$6

SHIP, ROMULAN CARDS
Decius (R). ....$6–$8

SHIPS, NONALIGNED CARDS
Tama (UC).

Star Trek Classic Customizable Card Game

Fleer/Skybox, 1996

This game consists of 307 cards of differing "rarity." The basic game can be played by two players, each with a "Starter Deck" of 65 cards. Additional cards were available through the purchase of "Booster Packs" consisting of 15 cards each. The more cards one obtains, the better one's chances to create a winning "deck." The need for more powerful cards as well as the differing rarities of the cards creates a high demand for the rarer cards. Complete sets are quite expensive to complete due to the large number of cards and the rarity of many cards.

Complete Sets

Starter Deck. ....$9–$10
Booster Pack. ....$2–$3
Sealed Box of Booster Packs (36). ....$80–$110
Single Cards:
    Super Common (8). ....$.25–$.50
    Common (120). ....$.25–$.50
    Uncommon (90). ....$.50–$1
    Rare (59). ....$2–$3
    Very Rare (30). ....$10–$25
Complete Set (307). ....$300–$500

Single Cards (Divided by Type)

Rarity is in parentheses: (SC) Super Common, (C) Common, (UC) Uncommon, (R) Rare, (VR) Very Rare.

CORE CARDS (ONLY AVAILABLE IN STARTER DECKS)
Capt. James T. Kirk (SC).
Comdr. Spock (SC).
Default Discovery (SC).
Default Mission (SC).
Default Plot (SC).
Dr. Leonard "Bones" McCoy (SC).
Info Card (SC).
USS Enterprise (SC).

CHALLENGE CARDS
Alice in Wonderland (C).
Alien Savages (C).
Andorian (Head Shot) (C).
Capellans (C).
Col. Green (C).
Don Juan (C).
Dr. Brown (C).
Dr. Simon Van Gelder (C).
Gorn Captain (C).
Hostile Miners (C).
Insane Colonists (C).
Kaylar, The (C).
Klingon Landing Party (C).
Lawgivers (C).
Lazarus (C).
Magda Kovacs (C).
Onlies (C).
Planetary Guards (C).
Romulan Bird-of-Prey Commander (C).
Ruk (C).
Ruth Bonaventure (C).
Samurai Warrior (C).
Tellarites (C).
Trelane (C).
White Rabbit (C).

Ben Childress (U).
Bilar (U).
Black Knight (U).
Dr. Tristan Adams (U).
Elias Sandoval (U).
Eve McHuron (U).
Genghis Khan (U).
Horta (U).
Kang (U).
Klingon Warrior (U).
Kor (U).
Leila Kalomi (U).
Mara (U).
Melkotians (U).
Military Officers, 20th Century (U).
Miri (U).
Mudd's Women (U).
Otto (U).
Plasus (U).

Romulan Battlecruiser Commander (U).
Romulan Centurion (U).
Talosians (U).
Trefayne (U).
Vina (U).
Witch (U).

Ayelborne (R).
Balok (R).
Bele (R).
Cladius Marcus (R).
Denevan Neural Parasites (R).
Dr. Roger Korby (R).
Hacom (R).
Jahn (R).
Kahless (R).
Kahn Noonien Singh (R).
Landru (R).
Lenore Karidian (R).
Lethe (R).
Cladius Marcus (R).
Metron (R).
Mugato (R).
Rojan (R).
Vina, the Orion Dancer (R).
Yamek (R).

Android Duplicate! (VR).
Com. Jose Mendez (VR).
Dikironium Cloud Creature (VR).
Dr. Elizabeth Dehner (VR).
Former Love (VR).
Former Rival Finnegan (VR).
Galactic High Commissioner Ferris (VR).
Keeper, The (VR).
Klingon Sniper (VR).
Lt. Comdr. Gary Mitchell (VR).
M-113 Monster (Natural Form) (VR).
M-113 Monster (Crewman Green Form) (VR).
Nomad (VR).
Organian Council of Elders (VR).
Transporter Duplicate (VR).

CREW CARDS
Ens. Angela Martine (C).
Ens. Matthews (C).
Ens. Rayburn (C).
Lt. D'Amato (C).
Lt. Gaetano (C).
Lt. Comdr. Giotto (C).
Lt. Comdr. Kelowitz (C).
Lt. Lang (C).
Lt. Charlene Masters (C).
Lt. O'Neil (C).
Lt. Esteban Rodriquez (C).
Lt. Spinelli (C).

Lt. Robert Tomlinson (C).
Yoeman Karen Greene (C).
Yeoman Mears (C).
Yeoman Smith (C).
Yeoman Teresa Ross (C).

Dr. Elizabeth Dehner (U).
Ens. Pavel Chekov (U).
Lt. Comdr. Montgomery Scott (U).
Lt. DePaul (U).
Lt. Hikaru Sulu (U).
Lt. Joe Tormolen (U).
Lt. Latimer (U).
Lt. Lee Kelso (U).
Lt. Leslie (U).
Lt. Lindstrom (U).
Lt. Mira Romaine (U).
Lt. Painter (U).
Lt. Uhura (U).
Nurse Christine Chapel (U).
Yeoman Janice Rand (U).
Yeoman Tina Lawton (U).

Dr. Mark Piper (R).
Geological Tech Fisher (R).
Lt. Alden (R).
Lt. Comdr. Benjamin Finney (R).
Lt. Comdr. Gary Mitchell (R).
Lt. DeSalle (R).
Lt. Karl Jaeger (R).
Transporter Tech Wilson (R).
Yoeman Martha Langdon (R).

Lt. Kyle (VR).
Lt. Marla McGivers (VR).
Lt. Thom Parham (VR).

DISCOVERY CARDS
"A Devil in the Dark" (C).
"Alternative Factor, The" (C).
"Balance of Terror" (C).
"Cage, The" (C).
"Charlie X" (C).
"City on the Edge of Forever, The" (C).
"Corbomite Maneuver, The" (C).
"GALILEO Seven, The" (C).
"Man Trap, The" (C).
"Menagerie, The" (C).
"Mudd's Women" (C).
"Operation: Annihilate!" (C).
"Shore Leave" (C).
"Space Seed" (C).
"Squire of Gothos, The" (C).
"This Side of Paradise" (C).

"Arena" (U).
"Dagger of the Mind" (U).

"Enemy Within, The" (U).
"Errand of Mercy" (U).
"Miri" (U).
"Return of the Archons" (U).
"What Are Little Girls Made Of?" (U).
"Where No Man Has Gone Before" (U).

"A Taste of Armageddon" (R).
"Conscience of the King, The" (R).
"Court-Martial" (R).
"Naked Time, The" (R).

EFFECT CARDS
Medikit (C).
Medikit (C).
Phaser Blast (C).
Phaser Blast (C).
Slug of Saurian Brandy (C).
Tricorder Reading (C).

Disrupter Blast (U).
Have Some Tranya (U).
Makeshift Weapons (U).

Dose of the Venus Drug (R).
IDIC (R).
Medical Readout (R).
Mind-Sifter (R).
Phaser on Overload (R).
Phaser Rifle Fire (R).
Song of a Vulcan Harp (R).

MISSION CARDS
"A Devil in the Dark" (C).
"Alternative Factor, The" (C).
"Arena" (C).
"Balance of Terror" (C).
"Cage, The" (C).
"Corbomite Maneuver, The" (C).
"Errand of Mercy" (C).
"Man Trap, The" (C).
"Menagerie, The" (C).
"Miri" (C).
"Mudd's Women" (C).
"Operation: Annihilate!" (C).
"Shore Leave" (C).
"Space Seed" (C).
"Squire of Gothos, The" (C).
"Tomorrow Is Yesterday" (C).
"What Are Little Girls Made Of?" (C).
"Where No Man Has Gone Before" (C).

"A Taste of Armageddon" (U).
"Charlie X" (U).
"City on the Edge of Forever, The" (U).
"Conscience of the King, The" (U).

"Court-Martial" (U).
"GALILEO Seven, The" (U).
"Naked Time, The" (U).
"Return of the Archons" (U).
"This Side of Paradise" (U).

"Dagger of the Mind" (R).
"Enemy Within, The" (R).

PERMANENT WILD CARDS
Ion Storm (U).
New Life and New Civilizations (C).
Romulan Bird-of-Prey (U).
Shuttlecraft Galileo (C).

Starbase 11 (R).

SS Fesarius (VR).
Talos IV (VR).

PLOT CARDS
"A Devil in the Dark" (C).
"Arena" (C).
"Balance of Terror" (C).
"Cage, The" (C).
"Charlie X" (C).
"City on the Edge of Forever, The" (C).
"Corbomite Maneuver, The" (C).
"Errand of Money" (C).
"GALILEO Seven, The" (C).
"Man Trap, The" (C).
"Menagerie, The" (C).
"Miri" (C).
"Squire of Gothos, The" (C).
"This Side of Paradise" (C).
"What Are Little Girls Made Of?" (C).
"Where No Man Has Gone Before" (C).

"A Taste of Armageddon" (U).
"Alternative Factor, The" (U).
"Conscience of the King, The" (U).
"Court-Martial" (U).
"Dagger of the Mind" (U).
"Enemy Within, The" (U).
"Mudd's Women" (U).
"Naked Time, The" (U).
"Operation: Annihilate!" (U).
"Shore Leave" (U).
"Space Seed" (U).
"Tomorrow Is Yesterday" (U).

"Return of the Archons" (R).

WILD CARDS
Are You of the Body? (C).
Communications Jammed (C).

Corbomite Maneuver (C).
Court-Martial (C).
Deflector Shields at Maximum (C).
Distraction (C).
Great Bird of the Galaxy (C).
Heroic Sacrifice (C).
HypoSpray (C).
Lay in New Course (C).
Logical Argument (C).
Long-Winded Speech (C).
Personal Challenge (C).
Phasers from Space (C).
Tinkering with the Engines (C).
Transporters Operational (C).

Beam Me Up, Scotty! (U).
Capt. John Christopher (U).
Direct Hit! (U).
Guardian of Forever (U).
"Jim—This Man's a Klingon!" (U).
Omicron Ceti III Spores (U).
Photon Torpedoes (U).
Red Alert! (U).
Romulan Disguise (U).
Standard Procedures (U).
Starfleet Commendation (U).
The Play's the Thing (U).
Unknown Virus (U).
Vulcan Mind-Melds (U).

Boot Scene (R).
Caretaker (R).
Decisive Action (R).
Klingon Arms Suppliers (R).
Miraculous Recovery (R).
Oddly Familiar Culture (R).
Orders from Starfleet (R).
Psi 2000 Virus (R).
Red Hour (R).
Report to the Bridge! (R).
Romulan Cloaking Device (R).
Shuttlecraft Crew Revolt (R).
Talosian Illusion (R).
Time Travel (R).
Transporter, Fully Energized (R).

Amb. Robert Fox (VR).
Cultural Envoy (VR).
Edge of the Galaxy (VR).
Edith Keeler, 20th-Century Reformer (VR).
"I'm a Doctor, Not a . . ." (VR).
Samuel T. Cogley, Attorney (VR).
Slingshot Effect (VR).
Tantalus Chamber (VR).
Thasians (VR).
Turnabout Intruder (VR).

FOREIGN TRADING CARDS

Perhaps one of the most neglected aspects of card collecting has been foreign sets. Often the cards are more pleasing to the eye and the foreign language aspect is often not significant. Obviously with British or Australian card sets the language problem is nonexistent. There have been quite a few extremely interesting and significant Star Trek trading card sets from foreign countries.

Probably the most significant and most sought after is the British AB&C set from 1969. Actually a little controversy exists here. A few cards have been found with a 1968 copyright by Desilu Studios instead of the 1969 Paramount Pictures copyright on most cards. This is by far the first full-color Star Trek trading card set, predating the American Topps set by seven years. The British cards are slightly smaller in size than their American counterparts and all 55 cards in this set are from the episode "What Are Little Girls Made Of?"

Gordon Currie Caricature Set

(1968)

Black and white caricatures of Star Trek crew on 1″ × 4″ white cards.

Complete Set. ....$15–$25

Star Trek, AB&C

(British, 1969)

This color set of 55 cards from England was the first set of Star Trek cards with wide distribution. Sets are extremely hard to come by and may be as rare as the 1967 Leaf cards.

Complete set. ....$500–$1250
Display Box. ....$200–$500
Single Cards. ....$5–$20
  #1, 55. ....$15–$35
Unopened Box. ....RARE
Unopened Pack. ....RARE
Wrapper. ....$200–$400

Primrose Confectionary Stamp Set

(British, Early 1970s)

See listing in Decals, Stamps, and Stickers section.

Morris Sales Star Trek Sticker and Album Set

(Canadian, 1975)

This series of stickers with album was issued in 1975 and pre-dates the Topps American cards. Originally sold as a packet of 3–4 stickers designed to be affixed to a full-color album with a story inside. Sticker packets consisted of a sheet of stickers (1–4 stickers) and a harder cardboard "cover" that has a put-together puzzle on the back. The album is 12 pages in full color. Thirty-two stickers fill the album and there are 30 pieces to the puzzle (approx. 24″ × 14″). Also included in the album is a full-color centerfold of one of the cards (four different known to exist) and a small blueprint of the ship and the bridge on the back cover. These sets are very difficult to assemble as each packet has 3–4 stickers that vary, making obtaining all 33 stickers very difficult.

Completed puzzle (30). ....$100–$150
Complete set in album. ....$400–$500
Display Box (empty). ....$50–$100
Single album (4 diff.). ....$25–$50
Single packet of stickers..$5–$10
Unopened box. ....$200–$400

"O Caminho Das Estrelas" Sticker Album Set

(Portuguese, 1978)

Believed by many to be the "rarest" Star Trek set, this set was issued in 1978 and comes with an album and 460 stickers! This makes it the biggest set ever produced. These stickers are not the peel-off kind. They must be glued into the 36-page album!

Complete set of 480 stickers with album. ....$600–$1000

Star Trek: The Motion Picture O-Pee-Chee Cards

(Canadian, 1979)

Canadian version of Topps Set with 88 cards. Virtually the same set with a few changes in cards/numbers on much nicer card stock.

Complete set. ....$200–$300
Single Cards. ....$3–$4

Star Trek: The Motion Picture Wheatabix Set

(British, 1979)

Full-color two-sided cards featuring full body artwork on one side and photograph and very brief description on back. Approx. 1″ × 4″ each.

Complete set (18). ....$75–$150

Starship Enterprise Panini Sticker Album Set

(European, 1979)

Panini has been issuing sticker sets in Europe for decades. They are printed in Italy and distributed in many different languages (usually only the albums need to be in different languages) in several countries. The German editions were sold in Germany, Switzerland, and Austria.

Complete sets with album. ....$400–$500

Star Trek II: Wrath of Khan Monty

(Dutch, 1982)

100-card set issued in Holland. Smaller in size, color fronts, blank backs. Uncut sheets exist. Hoard found in Europe in 1993.

Complete Set. ....$15–$35
Display Box. ....$10–$15
Single Cards. ....$.25–$.50
Uncut Sheet. ....$25–$50
Unopened Box. ....$35–$50
Wrapper. ....$2–$4

Star Trek: Next Generation and Deep Space Nine Mini-Cards Hostess

(Canadian, 1993)

These smaller cards were issued inside Hostess products in Canada. Each one was sealed in its own plastic bag. A complete set consists of 50 cards and 10 fold-out episode cards. The fold-out cards are much harder to obtain than the regular cards.

Complete set (50 cards). ....$100–$175
Complete Set of Fold-Out Cards (10). ....$100–$150
Single Cards. ....$2–$4
Single Fold-Out Cards. ....$10–$15

Gold pair of pogs, #58 and #59. ....$20–$30
Sealed Box. ....$20–$35
Single Pairs of Pogs. ....$.50–$1
Unopened Pack. ....$1–$2

Star Trek: Next Generation Pogs, Stardisk Enterprises

(Canadian, 1994)

This set of 60 pogs (or milkcaps or disks) was released in Canada and in Europe. Each pack included two strips that each had two pogs. Most people collect these in their un-punched form. Two of the pogs, #59 and #60, were issued as "chase" pogs and are not normally considered part of the basic set.

Complete Set (58). ....$15–$25

Star Trek Generations and Next Generation Weetabix Cards

(British, 1994)

This combination Next Generation and Generations movie set of 194 cards featuring characters and ships consists of 10 separate cards that are designed to be punched out with two characters on each card. Also issued was the 18″ × 24″ poster designed to have the ship pictures on the reverse of each card attached.

Poster. ....$20–$30
Set of 10 Cards. ....$25–$40

Trading Cards

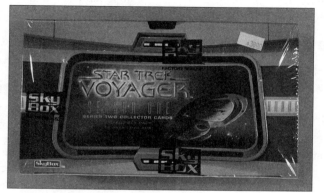

Skybox Voyager Box of Cards

Impel 25th Anniversary Limited Edition Tin Set

Trading Cards

WATCHES

Watch collecting has enjoyed a recent boost in popularity encouraged by companies, such as Fossil, which manufacture a variety of quality products. In addition to being interesting conversation pieces with good investment potential, collector watches have the added advantage of being functional accessories virtually everyone can use.

INVESTMENT POTENTIAL
Excellent.

CARE
Most people prefer to display their watches by wearing them. Only the pickiest of collectors would object to a collectible watch that had been worn, as long as the wearer was careful to keep the piece from being damaged or scuffed. Be sure to preserve all original packaging and instructions even if it's just a plastic sleeve. Though batteries for modern watches are usually readily available at most drugstores and supermarkets, it is best to have them replaced by a qualified jeweler to avoid nicking the watch casing, especially in the case of the more expensive watches.

SECTION NOTES
Section is organized alphabetically by manufacturer and then chronologically by date. Unlicensed watches, primarily watches with faces made by using color photocopiers, have been omitted. (One very common watch showing Kirk, Spock, and McCoy from the original series on a red and blue background was most likely done in this manner.)

ASA

Enterprise Watch—1974. Analog watch with original ship and "Star Trek" above on blue face. Black band. ....
....$175–$200

Bradley

Star Trek: The Motion Picture—1979. Analog. Artwork of Spock in movie uniform and "Star Trek" on light blue face. Enterprise and Shuttlecraft on second hand. Black band. Packaged in cylindrical plastic box with clear lid. ....$100–$150
Star Trek: The Motion Picture—1980. Analog. Front view of movie Enterprise with "Star Trek" below. Space background surrounded by metal ring with numbers. Black band with brushed steel insets. ....$75–$125
Star Trek: The Motion Picture—1980. Digital. Light blue face with "Star Trek" above time display and artwork of Kirk and Spock below. Metal case with black band. Men's and women's. ....$75–$125

CMI

Star Trek "Message Reveal" Watch—1993. Promotional watch included with boxed set of first six Star Trek movie video cassettes. Analog. Black face with gold original command emblem at top and "Star Trek" and "To Boldly Go Where No Man Has Gone Before" around edge which is slowly "revealed" by a moving disk that acts as second hand. Gold case. Black band. Limited to 5000 pieces. ....
....$175–$200

Collins

Star Trek II: The Wrath of Khan Game Watch—1982. Square black plastic case with black band. Large display area has movie logo above and Enterprise below and at side. Came in window box with photos of Kirk, Spock, Dr. Marcus around window, and Khan, and watch, Enterprise, and logo on side leaf. ....$25–$50

Star Trek II: Radio Watch—1982. Watch has date and alarm functions and has earphone jack for built-in radio. Movie logo is on case. ....$100–$150

Fossil

Federation Watch
USS Enterprise Watch—1995. Analog. Original Enterprise in center of pewter finish face with "USS Enterprise" above and "Star Trek" below. Gold rim around face. Black band with original command symbol inset below watch. Packaged in insignia-shaped box with "Star Trek" superimposed over command insignia. Includes numbered, pewter-finish collector coin. Limited to 15,000 pieces. ....$100–$150
Klingon Watch—1996. Analog. Klingon emblem and Star Trek: The Next Generation logo on red and gray patterned face. Brushed metal rim and black leather band. Packaged in lozenge-shaped display tin with Klingon symbol and Star Trek: The Next Generation logo on top. Includes pewter finish Klingon pin. Numbered. Limited to 15,000 pieces. Certificate of Authenticity included. ....$85–$100
Gold Klingon Watch—1996. Same as regular Klingon version but with antique gold finish and light-up face. Limited to 1000 pieces. ....$150–$200
30-Year Commemorative Watch—1996. Analog pocket watch. Watch shaped like original TV series insignia. Command star is indented with "Star Trek" in black letters on lower left. Packaged in black plastic insignia-shaped box with 30th Anniversary logo in silver. Limited to 15,000 pieces. Includes Certificate of Authenticity. ....$95–$125
Gold 30-Year Commemorative Watch—1996. Same as regular version but with antique gold finish. Limited to 1000 pieces. ....$150–$175

Franklin Mint

25th Anniversary Watch—1991. Analog. Stainless steel casing with original Enterprise and command emblem on black background. Red hands. Black band. 25th Anniversary logo is engraved on back of watch casing. ....$175–$200

Hope Industries

Star Trek: Deep Space Nine Watch—1993. Digital. Black face with line drawing of space station. Gold and silver tone plastric rim. Black band with star pattern and logo. Blister-packed on blue background with DS9 logo at top. ....$10–$15
Star Trek: Deep Space Nine Space Station Watch—1994. Digital. Starfield face with time displayed at bottom. Plastic space station floats above face in bubble. Blue plastic rim. Black band with DS9 logo. Blister-packed on blue background with DS9 logo and photo of space station at top. ....
....$10–$15

Star Trek: Deep Space Nine Special Edition Collector's Watch—1994. Digital. Two-tone gold and silver metal lid with original communicator insignia design opens to reveal face designed to resemble UFP seal. Brushed steel band with gold detailing. Packaged in octagonal blue metal tin with DS9 logo and space station on lid and eight different color character photos and synopsis on sides. ....$50–$75

Lewco

Spock Character Watch—1986. Color plastic relief of Spock and Enterprise on predominantly gray band. Digital watch face offset to side. Packaged in shallow yellow plastic tray with hanging tab at top and 20th Anniversary sticker. ....
....$50–$75

Lincoln Enterprises

Enterprise Watch—1982. Analog watch with black face. Artwork of movie Enterprise in light burst and Vulcan salute in middle, "Star Trek" and "Gateway to the New Beginning" below. Gold rim. Black band. Men's and women's. ......$50–$75

Malibu

Enterprise Painted Face Watches—1989. Analog watches have color artwork of ship with space background. Gold rim and "Star Trek" at bottom of each design. Black rims. Packaged in clear sleeve with Paramount logo. Four different.
    Movie ship and Klingon Bird-of-Prey. ....$100–$150
    Original Ship, side view. ....$100–$150
    Original Ship, front view. ....$100–$150
    Original Ship, orbiting planet. ....$100–$150

Rarities Mint

Coin Watch—1989. Analog. Original Enterprise design from reverse of this company's Star Trek collector's coin series minted in silver and gold plated. Gold rim. Black band. Limited edition. Numbered. Included Certificate of Authenticity. Packaged in brown plastic case with padded top. Men's and women's. ....$175–$250
Coin Watch—1989. Variation prototype. Approx. 30 of these watches were made in which the background is silver and the Enterprise is detailed in gold. This version also had a metal rather than a leather band. Men's only. .....$900–$1200

Timex

Next Generation Insignia Watch—Analog. 1993. Black face with glitter "stars" and small Next Generation–style insignia in lower potion. Face encircled by gray plastic ring with dots instead of numbers and "Star Trek" at top. Black band. ....$25–$40

Next Generation Insignia Watch—Analog. 1993. Silver case. Black face with blue semicircular detailing lines and small Next Generation–style command insignia in lower portion. "Star Trek" at top of case. Black band. ....$30–$45

Next Generation Insignia Watch—Analog. 1993. Silver case. White face with regular numbers. Small Next Generation–style command insignia on lower portion. "Star Trek" at top of case. Black band. ....$30–$45

Next Generation Insignia Watch—Digital. 1993. Rectangular L.E.D. window is surrounded by black background with dash design running top to bottom on right and small Next Generation–style insignia in upper left corner. Gray plastic watch casing. Black band with "Star Trek" and "NCC-1701." ....$50–$75

Chronoscanner—Digital. 1994. Multifunction watch has Next Generation Enterprise in center with time display below and red and blue liquid crystal second indicator above. Rim of case has "Star Trek: The Next Generation," "Chronoscanner," Next Generation–style command emblem, and labels for four function buttons in gold. Black band. ....$35–$50

Disappearing Warbird Watch—Analog. 1994. Face shows colorful planets with Enterprise-D in lower left portion. Movement of disk that serves as second hand causes image of Romulan Warbird to repeatedly appear and disappear. Chrome watch casing. Black band. ....$75–$100

Enterprise Indiglow Watch—Analog. 1994. Face shows Enterprise-D on starfield. Chrome watch casing. Black band. ....$175–$200

Klingon Chronometer—Digital. 1994. Multifunction watch has black face with time display at bottom and function indicator displayed above in six circles. "Klingon," Klingon emblem, and Klingon symbols in red appear on the rim. Black band. ....$35–$50

Rotating Enterprise Watch—1994. Analog. Face shows colorful planets on star background. Second hand is clear disk with Enterprise-D printed on edge which disappears behind planet as disk rotates. Chrome watch casing. Black band. ....$75–$100

Wesco

(British)

Voyager Electronic Light Watch—1995. Analog. Color photo of Voyager on space background. Gold-tone metal case. Black band embossed with Voyager logo. Packaged in flat, rectangular metal tin with black lid depicting white artwork of Voyager and blue logo. ....$75–$95

Star Trek II Game Watch

Hope Industries *Deep Space Nine* Watch

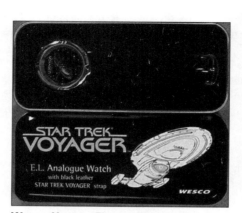

Wesco *Voyager* Electronic Light Watch

Lewco Spock Watch

INDEX

About the Authors

SUE CORNWELL graduated from Hood College with a BA. She attended the first Star Trek convention in New York in 1972 while still in college. In 1974 she was a dealer at a convention for the first time, and she has attended hundreds of conventions since that time.

MIKE KOTT graduated from Rensselaer Polytechnic Institute with degrees in physics and geology. After a short time as an engineering geologist, he entered the collectibles field as a comic book dealer.

In 1976 the authors formed Intergalactic Trading Corp., Inc., specializing in Star Trek and Star Wars collectibles. Intergalactic is currently the most active company in the United States dealing with these collectibles.

BEAM UP A WHOLE UNIVERSE OF STAR TREK COLLECTIBLES!

Explore this phenomenal multi-billion-dollar marketplace for fun and profit—the largest array of collectibles in the history of entertainment!

With the 30th anniversary of Star Trek upon us, Star Trek is hotter than ever. This new CD-ROM guide boldly goes where none has gone before – to the far reaches of Star Trek collecting. Essential for any Trekker, it takes you on an enterprising voyage with leading-edge technology through the vast universe of Star Trek collectibles, including official items that have boosted Star Trek into a $2 billion phenomenon!

Now discover electronically "what's out there" as well as current prices ... from Star Trek action figures to watches and everything in-between. Passionate Trekkers can plan ahead for the next convention ... and starters can energize their interest. "Make it so" – order the House of Collectibles CD-ROM Guide to Star Trek Collectibles today! (see next page for details)

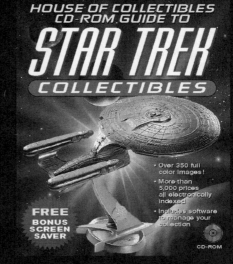

HOUSE OF COLLECTIBLES CD-ROM GUIDE TO

STAR TREK COLLECTIBLES

- Over 350 full color images!
- More than 5,000 prices all electronically indexed
- Includes software to manage your collection

FREE BONUS SCREEN SAVER

CD-ROM

INSTANT CURRENT PRICE
Track any of over 5,000 prices in a flash on the electronic index.

Introducing the 21st century's way to look at Star Trek collectibles!

SPECTACULAR VIEWS
Beam up over 350 high-resolution full-color photos of important collectibles, including seldom-seen rarities.

COLLECTION COMMAND
Manage your Star Trek collection from your PC screen and keyboard ... fast and easily.

OVER, PLEASE ☞

HOUSE OF COLLECTIBLES CD-ROM GUIDE TO STAR TREK COLLECTIBLES

PRODUCT FEATURES

THE PHOTO GALLERY

View over 350 large, full-color pictures covering the entire universe of Star Trek collectibles.

- The high-resolution photos show all the intricate details of each collectible – an invaluable identification reference.

- All your favorite Star Trek characters are included: Captain Kirk, Mr. Spock, Captain Picard, Doctor McCoy, Mr. Scott, Tasha Yar, Klingons, Cardassians, Vulcans, Romulans and many more ... plus the Starship Enterprise and a full array of insignias, uniforms and symbols.

- In addition to familiar items, see many rarities from private collections. Discover items you never dreamed existed!

- Each photo comes with essential information: full description, date of manufacture, manufacturer, identification markings and current market value.

- Easily search through detailed descriptions for each collectible – it's like an electronic catalog.

- Listen to narrative descriptions and the sounds that some collectibles make!

- Search through the photos by series, movie or type of collectible.

- Get full introductions to Star Trek collecting and each category of collectibles.

- **FREE BONUS:** show off your passion for Star Trek by customizing your PC with screensavers!

COLLECTORWARE

- Instantly check any of over 5,000 current market prices in the huge database – virtually every type of Star Trek treasure is covered.

- Use these prices to spot bargains and get full value for your collectibles.

- Systematically track and plan your collection with interactive access to electronic Star Trek data that no other source provides.

- **BROWSE** from item to item or **SEARCH** by series/movie, character, manufacturer, category of collectible or key word.

- Quickly **FIND** any Star Trek collectible from the most comprehensive and authoritative database.

- **COPY** and **STORE** information under "MY COLLECTION" – your customized inventory of the collectibles you own and their current trading value. It's ideal for insurance purposes – and you can automatically total up your collection's value anytime.

- Print out **WANT LISTS** of collectibles you're looking for – keep them handy when shopping for new items.

- Create **PROFIT AND LOSS STATEMENTS** – your complete record of purchases and sales really organizes your collecting hobby.

- Automatically **SORT** your collection by series, character or price – cross-referencing items shows your collection's strengths and weaknesses.

- **EDIT** as changes occur or add non-listed items – there's also room for your personal comments on any item in your collection.

- -

Order Form

❑ **YES, Please send me the House of Collectibles CD-ROM Guide to Star Trek Collectibles. My price direct from the publisher is just $39.95 plus $3.95 shipping and handling. If not satisfied, I may return this software at the end of 30 days for a full refund.**

Name _____

Address _____

City _____ State _____ Zip Code _____

❑ **Check enclosed for $ _____** *(payable to House of Collectibles)
❑ **Charge my**
  ❑ **VISA**   ❑ **MasterCard**   ❑ **American Express**   ❑ **Discover**

_____ _____ _____
Credit Card Number   Expiration Date   Signature(required)

FOR IMMEDIATE DELIVERY, CALL TOLL-FREE • 1-800-800-1462

* Please add applicable sales tax. All orders subject to acceptance.

HOUSE OF COLLECTIBLES
P.O. Box 3580 • Wallingford, CT 06494

Dept. E13-001